Programming in Turbo Prolog™

With an Introduction to Knowledge-based Systems

LEE TEFT
University of Bridgeport

PRENTICE HALL, Engelwood Cliffs, New Jersey 07632

Library of Congress Cataloging-in-Publication Data

TEFT, LEE

Programming in Turbo Prolog.

On t.p. the registered trade mark symbol "TM" is superscript following "Prolog" in the title.

Includes index.

1. Prolog (Computer program language) 2. Turbo Prolog (Computer program) 3. Expert systems (Computer science) I. Title.

QA76.73.P76T43 1989 006.3'3 88-9814

ISBN 0-13-729054-3

Editorial/production supervision and
interior design: Joan McCulley and Debbie Young
Cover design: Wanda Lubelska Design
Manufacturing buyer: Mary Noonan

Printed in the United States of America
10 9 8 7 6 5 4 3 2 1

ISBN 0-13-729054-3

PRENTICE-HALL INTERNATIONAL (UK) LIMITED, *London*
PRENTICE-HALL OF AUSTRALIA PTY. LIMITED, *Sydney*
PRENTICE-HALL CANADA INC., *Toronto*
PRENTICE-HALL HISPANOAMERICANA, S.A., *Mexico*
PRENTICE-HALL OF INDIA PRIVATE LIMITED, *New Delhi*
PRENTICE-HALL OF JAPAN, INC., *Tokyo*
SIMON & SCHUSTER ASIA PTE. LTD., *Singapore*
EDITORA PRENTICE-HALL DO BRASIL, LTDA., *Rio de Janeiro*

Contents

TRADEMARKS

Preface

The purpose of this book is to provide an accessible primer for programming knowledge-based software in Turbo Prolog™. The basic pedagogical strategy is teaching by example, and complete source code for several miniature knowledge-based systems is provided for the reader to study and enhance.

This book presumes no special technical background and is intended for readers with an interest in artificial intelligence, natural-language processing, fifth-generation programming, logic and logic programming, computer science, and database or knowledge-based computer applications to business or the social sciences. The book can be used equally well for self-instruction or as a text in conjunction with introductory courses in Prolog, artificial intelligence, or knowledge-based (e.g., expert) systems.

My goal has been to produce a text that provides a more supportive and informal approach to teaching the use of Prolog for implementing knowledge-based systems than is currently available for beginning students. In explaining major concepts I have opted for detailed explanations using relatively large example programs rather than the terse and highly formalized presentations more characteristic of computer science texts.

My hope is that this book will fill the niche I perceive between the increasing numbers of excellent technical books on Prolog and knowledge-based systems written for the advanced student or AI specialist and the plethora of elementary primers on these topics directed at the trade and novice audiences. After completion of this introductory book, the reader should be well prepared to tackle more rigorous and scholarly texts covering advanced topics in Prolog, logic programming, artificial intelligence, and knowledge-based systems. References to these works will be given at appropriate points throughout this book.

The reader with programming experience will discover that Turbo Prolog is quite different from conventional computer languages such as COBOL, BASIC, Pascal, or C. Conventional programming languages are imperative. Using these languages, the programmer's task is to code step-by-step instructions for the computer to follow in processing data to arrive at a solution. In conventional programs, knowledge is represented throughout the program in the form of procedures. Given a set of data inputs, a conventional program will, if properly coded, deterministically produce the single correct output. Prolog programs, by contrast, are able to solve problems nondeterministically. This means that a Prolog program can deduce a set of all possible solutions that can satisfy a user's query.

To use the Turbo Prolog language, the programmer focuses attention on the logical structure of knowledge in some domain of interest. Turbo Prolog, therefore, represents a descriptive style of programming where the programming task is to declare what is known about a knowledge domain as Prolog sentences (a subset of predicate logic clauses called Horn clauses). This knowledge comprises facts about domain entities (their attributes and the relations that hold among them) and rules that permit inferencing about them. The programmer adds to this knowledge definitions required by the Turbo Prolog compiler for efficient processing, thus producing an executable program that can be used to answer queries pertaining to the knowledge domain.

Prolog's answers to user queries can be either direct or indirect. Turbo Prolog exploits its pattern-matching and intrinsic database functionality in searches for facts to support direct answers to user queries. Indirect answers are deduced from facts and rules in the database. Many examples of Turbo Prolog's pattern-matching and inferencing behavior are provided in this book to assure that essential principles are understood and mastered.

It is my belief that learning to program using Turbo Prolog will produce a transfer of training effect that will enhance the reader's general analytic and problem solving skills. Another plus is that because Turbo Prolog is such a high level declarative language, the novice can write useful programs much earlier on the learning curve than is possible using conventional programming languages.

Although Turbo Prolog is primarily known as a declarative language, the reader will learn that it has powerful procedural capabilities. Several of the programs included in this book document procedural uses of Prolog. However, the reader with experience in the procedural style of programming may find Turbo Prolog's deemphasis on program control structures temporarily disconcerting. Turbo Prolog does not, for example, provide IF-THEN-ELSE, WHILE-DO, GOTO, or CASE structures. However, these and other procedural constructs can be readily implemented by the Turbo Prolog programmer to accomplish specific procedural tasks (Covington, 1986).

Although this book is not intended to replace the Turbo Prolog Manual, it does explain and illustrate the use of the implementation-specific features of this version of Prolog that will be of most use to the beginning student. The book does assume that the reader is familiar with the basic features of the Turbo Prolog environment (this book is compatible with Versions 1.xx and 2.0) and the use of the integrated editor. For readers who are brand-new to computers and programming, I suggest a preliminary review of the introductory chapters in the Borland Manual.

The first chapter of this book introduces the reader to the general issues and features of knowledge-based systems. This chapter considers such topics as knowledge acquisition and representation, approaches to the design of inference engines, the use of uncertain knowledge in programs, and natural-language processing. Implementing these features of knowledge-based systems using Turbo Prolog will comprise the programming goals for the remainder of the book.

Part 2—Chapters 2 through 6—provides an introduction to the Prolog problem-solving mechanism and its origins in logic and builds the basic programming skills necessary to begin using Turbo Prolog. This section also covers use of the editor to enter facts and rules into programs; making program declarations; the use of the tracing facility, helpful in debugging programs; data structures; list processing; recursion; input/output and file handling procedures; doing math; software design using windows, graphics, and sound; and the use of the many built-in predicates (primitives) provided with the Turbo Prolog language.

Part 3—Chapters 7 through 10—treats more advanced programming topics. The reader will learn fundamentals of knowledge engineering and methods for designing larger programs. Also covered are techniques for implementing programs that query the user for missing or incomplete information, make decisions using certainty estimates, offer explanations for program behavior, and process natural language.

Readers who are eager to try their hand at Turbo Prolog programming may be tempted to skip over the two introductory chapters and go directly to Chapter 3. Those who succumb to this temptation are urged to return and read the first chapters before proceeding too far in the book, for thorough understanding and mastery of Turbo Prolog depend on several fundamental concepts that are introduced in the two introductory chapters.

Turbo Prolog provides users with a well-designed and efficient programming environment. This environment includes an incremental compiler for developing fast and efficient stand-alone programs; a Wordstar-like integrated editor with debugging assistance and tracing facilities; a rich set of primitives for both random and sequential file I/O and implementing graphics (BGI in version 2.0), sound, and windows in programs; methods for linking Prolog and other languages; easy access to the DOS operating system and its functions; and predicates for bit-level machine control.

Some readers will note that the Turbo Prolog dialect is a departure from what has become the standard in the Prolog world. This standard, called Edinburgh or core Prolog is outlined by Clocksin and Mellish in their authoritative book entitled *Programming in Prolog* (1984). The differences between the Turbo and

Edinburgh versions, though important, are significant only for the advanced Prolog programmer; to avoid any possible confusion for the novice, a discussion of these differences is deferred to Appendix B.

Readers who wish to avoid the tedium of typing may obtain, from the publisher, a diskette containing all program source code.

Acknowledgments

This book is dedicated to my wife Kim, without whose love, support, and infinite patience it could not have been written!

Thanks go also to the students, colleagues, and readers who contributed thoughtful and productive corrections and criticism. They helped me to write a better book. Any remaining errors are, of course, my responsibility.

Part 1
Introduction to Knowledge-based Systems

Chapter 1
Overview of Knowledge-based Systems

CHAPTER OBJECTIVES

Study of this chapter should enable you to do the following:

1. List the major functions of knowledge-based systems and some of the ways in which these systems differ from conventional programs.
2. List attributes of human expertise and problem solving that are simulated in knowledge-based systems.
3. Discuss methods used in computational systems for representing knowledge including semantic nets, frames, and production rules.
4. Compare and contrast forward and backward chaining, two inferencing schemes often used in knowledge-based systems.
5. State the difference between the depth-first and breadth-first searching strategies.
6. Discuss some criteria for evaluating knowledge-based systems.
7. Discuss some future applications for knowledge-based systems.

IMPORTANT TERMS AND PHRASES

Algorithm
Artificial intelligence
Backward chaining
Breadth-first search
Declarative programming
Depth-first search
Deterministic programming
Expert systems and shells
Forward chaining
Frame
Graphs
Heuristics
Human expertise
Inference engine
Inheritance
Knowledge acquisition
Knowledge-based system
Knowledge engineering
Knowledge representation
Knowledge transfer
Productions and rules
Semantic net

> Artificial Intelligence research has sought to find ways to embody knowledge in machines. But this problem itself has several parts: we must discover how to acquire the knowledge we need, we must learn how to represent it, and, finally, we must develop processes that can exploit our knowledge effectively.
>
> [Marvin Minsky *The Society of Minds*, p. 74]

In the summer of 1956, a group of scientists was convened at Hanover, New Hampshire, by Dartmouth mathematics professor John McCarthy, Claude Shannon of Bell Labs, IBM's Nathaniel Rochester, and Marvin Minsky, then at Harvard and later to cofound the artificial intelligence (AI) lab at MIT, to discuss current research in the computer and cognitive sciences and to outline new directions for an emerging discipline that McCarthy dubbed "artificial intelligence." The participants, funded by a Rockefeller grant, were called together "on the basis of the conjecture that every aspect of learning or any other feature of intelligence can in principle be so precisely described that a machine can be made to simulate it" (McCorduck, 1979, p. 93).

The topics considered by the symposiasts that summer included robotics, computational models of the brain and cognition, chess-playing programs, and the simulation of human intelligence in problem-solving computer software. Though no major breakthroughs were achieved, the conference did serve to attract widespread attention to the potential for using computers to perform a wide range of "intelligent" functions. In particular, the Dartmouth symposium sparked interest in the speculative notion of embodying human reasoning and expertise in computational systems.

Currently, interest in the development of knowledge-intensive "expert" programs is high, not only here in the United States but throughout the rest of the world. According to Feigenbaum and McCorduck in their book *The Fifth Generation: Artificial Intelligence and Japan's Computer Challenge to the World* (1984), the Japanese Institute for New Generation Computer Technology (ICOT) project represents the first national commitment to the development of knowledge-intensive computer systems—what the Japanese prefer to call "knowledge information processing systems."

The remarkable worldwide growth of interest in intelligent computer systems since the Dartmouth conference is explained in part by the technological advances made by AI researchers and the success of a few systems in commercial applications. Many experts, however, caution that in the continuing race for AI, anticipation is still running well ahead of realization. Yet expectations for AI continue to grow, based in the hope that AI technology will provide a cost-effective means for storing and widely disseminating knowledge embodied in relatively inexpensive and highly portable computer programs. In this "age of information," knowledge is the most precious of all resources, and increasingly corporations are turning to AI and expert systems for an effective means to manage this resource.

Consider also that recent advances in microcomputer technology have made it possible for small businesses and individuals to have on their desks the computing power available just a decade ago only to large corporations, governments, and prestigious universities. These hardware advances have fueled a rising demand for "intelligent" software able to solve increasingly difficult problems. Entrepreneurs eager to exploit this market are turning to AI and knowledge-based systems research for the means to create software products that will meet this demand. If predictions hold, this burgeoning market will drive significant increases in research and development in AI over the next decade. One estimate has the total AI market valued at $2 to $3 billion by 1990 (Harmon & King, 1985, p. 10).

1.1 WHAT ARE KNOWLEDGE-BASED OR EXPERT SYSTEMS?

> Several traits characterize an expert system, including the symbolic nature of the task it performs, a broad and robust intelligence, an ability to rationalize and justify its behavior, a capacity to expand its range of capabilities and refine its skills, and an ability to solve important problems involving complexity and uncertainty.
>
> [R. J. Brachman, et al., "What Are Expert Systems?" in Hayes-Roth et al., *Building Expert Systems,* p. 31]

In the decade that followed the Dartmouth conference, AI research, led by Allen Newell and Herbert Simon at Carnegie-Mellon University, emphasized the development of generalized problem-solving programs. Using algorithms based on principles of human problem solving, Newell and Simon created remarkable programs designed to simulate human thought processes. One of these programs, the Logic Theorist, was able to prove theorems presented in Whitehead and Russell's *Principia Mathematica* (1910). Another program, the General Problem Solver, was to a degree proficient in solving problems across a range of domains including playing chess, proving theorems, and solving classic puzzles such as the Tower of Hanoi.

However, interest in software crafted to simulate human thought processes waned in the 1970s as prototypes generally proved to be of limited success and many researchers argued persuasively for a different and more pragmatic approach to the design and implementation of AI programs. This new approach stressed programs with knowledge bases containing vast stores of domain-specific expert knowledge and an inferencing module for reasoning about this information. In part due to the early success of Dendral, a knowledge-intensive chemical analysis program built by Edward Feigenbaum and Nobel laureate Joshua Lederberg at Stanford, the focal point of research at many AI labs shifted toward the development of domain-specific expert systems. For example, programs were written to locate mineral deposits, diagnose disease and prescribe treatment, configure and price computer systems, solve equations, predict molecular structures, model the behavior of enemy military forces, control mechanical systems, debug computer code, and even help in the process of developing other expert systems.

The label *expert system* (ES) has attained wide circulation as a designation for this new generation of knowledge-intensive software. The label has evoked some controversy, however. Some critics argue that the label ES conveys a false impression of the efficacy of the state of the AI software art and contend that it encourages people to draw untenable parallels between human and software competence and performance. These critics argue, at times very convincingly, that such human processes as intuitive judgment, commonsense reasoning, creativity, and tolerance for ambiguity have not as yet been even remotely simulated in ES software and for this reason such programs cannot be termed "expert." Stuart and Hubert Dreyfus, two of the best known critics, have suggested use of the more modest appellation *competent systems* (Dreyfus & Dreyfus, 1986).

In part as a response to these criticisms and in part as the result of the evolution of the software itself, there is currently a shift away from use of the label *expert system* toward the more generic term *knowledge-based systems (KBSs)*. Recognizing that there are distinctions that can be made between the terms (e.g., expert systems are considered by many to be a subset of KBS technology) with some exceptions made in the interest of stylistic variety, KBSs will be the label of choice for the remainder of this book.

At best, KBSs can be said to be "intelligent" because they possess massive stores of information and exhibit many of the attributes commonly associated with human experts performing difficult tasks using specialized knowledge and sophisticated problem-solving strategies. A few of these programs perform as well as, or in some cases better than, their human counterparts. At worst, the labels AI, ES, and KBS are little more than marketing gimmicks used by software hucksters to peddle programs of dubious value.

To date, the marketplace has been enthusiastically receptive to advances in AI software technology. Clearly, the existence of computerized expertise promises many commercial benefits. However, the market is maturing and shows signs of becoming much more discriminating regarding the "value added" to computer systems by so-called artificial intelligence. This is probably the best thing that could happen at this stage in the evolution of this technology. Hopefully, overly zealous developers will be discouraged from rushing to market with software that cannot live up to the expectations of an increasingly demanding and sophisticated marketplace, products that will serve only to impede the development and acceptance of good products in the future.

In sum, KBSs are computer programs designed to simulate the problem-solving behavior of human experts in bounded knowledge domains. KBSs are programs that contain large stores of information, most often in the form of facts and rules, together with procedures for manipulating this information to infer solutions to problems normally requiring the attention of a human expert. In addition, KBSs have the capability to conduct a dialogue with the user in order to solicit information pertaining to the problem at hand and to offer explanations of program behavior.

1.2 CONVENTIONAL PROGRAMS, DATABASES, AND KNOWLEDGE-BASED SYSTEMS

Knowledge-based systems differ from conventional software such as database systems in that they are able to reason about data and draw conclusions employing heuristic rules. Heuristics embody human expertise in some knowledge domain and are sometimes characterized as the "rules of thumb" that one acquires through practical experience and uses to solve everyday problems. Any expert New England fisherman, for example, has learned from experience that a late summer flock of swooping and diving seagulls together with the smell of fish oil indicates the strong likelihood that a school of bluefish is feeding just below the surface of the water. Knowledgeable fishermen will quickly abandon random searching for fish as soon as such signs associated with the presence of fish in the past become evident.

With many heuristic rules encoded into its knowledge base (together with a mechanism for inferencing called an *inference engine*, which we will discuss shortly), a KBS can "reason" about problem situations and can generate a range of likely solutions. In some cases a KBS will provide an estimate of the likelihood of success for each hypothesis or conclusion that is generated. Contrast this with conventional computer programs, which lack both built-in domain expertise and inferencing capabilities. Conventional programs employ step-by-step procedures for processing data and for assuring that the single correct solution for any given set of data inputs will invariably be achieved. "Information" in conventional software is thus spread throughout the entire procedure or program. Information in a KBS, however, is concentrated in a separate module called a knowledge base. Other separate components of the KBS direct the knowledge acquisition, inferencing, and explanatory functions of the system.

Over the past three decades, database systems have been developed that efficiently manage information, making them a quintessential tool for conducting business in today's information-driven society. Many software scientists are focusing on ways to endow fourth-generation database systems with fifth-generation symbol processing and heuristic reasoning capabilities (Kerschberg, 1986). Their goal is to blend inferential reasoning into installed databases, thus creating "intelligent" knowledge-based management systems (KBMSs) that can reason about data as well as manage it efficiently.

Adding expert decision-making capability to existing databases containing information valued in the billions of dollars is a major impetus for research and development in KBS technology. For those interested in decision support, there is a growing market for application of KBS technology in the development of executive support systems (ESS) (Rockart & Bullen, 1986), which can provide upper-level managers with direct access to expert decision-making capabilities supported by existing databases of corporate information and assist top-level management in responding more quickly and effectively to complex changes in the marketplace, thereby providing a valuable competitive edge.

1.3 THE STRUCTURE AND FUNCTION OF KNOWLEDGE-BASED SYSTEMS

Knowledge-based systems come in a variety of designs that have evolved over the past two decades in response to both advances in technology and the widening scope of application domains. KBS design will continue to evolve as (1) cognitive and AI scientists learn more about human cognition and use this knowledge to develop more effective means for obtaining and representing knowledge and develop better problem-solving strategies for computational systems, (2) computer technology makes available more powerful and efficient microprocessors, parallel computer architectures, networking systems, and optical storage devices, and (3) the marketplace defines new areas for application, thus stimulating the development of commercial versions of research prototypes.

Table 1.1 lists a small sample of current KBSs and the problem domains that they serve. Descriptions of many current systems can be found in texts such as *A Guide to Expert Systems* (Waterman, 1986) and *Artificial Intelligence and Expert Systems Sourcebook* (Hunt, 1986) as well as a variety of newsletters servicing the information needs of the growing number of people interested in KBSs. Note that some KBSs perform two or more of the functions specified. For example, a system may perform planning as well as monitoring tasks or carry out both diagnostic and debugging functions.

TABLE 1.1 CATEGORIES OF FUNCTIONS SUPPORTED BY THE CURRENT GENERATION OF KNOWLEDGE-BASED SYSTEMS

Function	Description	Examples
Control	Diagnose, predict, repair, and monitor systems	PTRANS
Debugging	Identify and plan remedies	DRILLING ADVISOR
Design	Configure and design systems within constraints	XCON
Diagnosis	Infer malfunctions from symptoms	MYCIN
Instruction	Interpret and remediate student behaviors	SOPHIE GUIDON
Interpretation	Interpret observables and infer descriptions	DIPMETER DENDRAL
Monitoring	Compare current states with desired states	REACTOR
Planning	Assist in the planning and design of systems	MOLGEN
Prediction	Infer likely consequences from current conditions	I&W

1.3.1 The Nature of Human Expertise

Examining some of the attributes of the human expert may help in clarifying the key issues surrounding KBS structure and function. Consider the obvious fact that one develops expertise only after long years of experience and study. Becoming a domain expert is an extended process of acquisition of first principles (deep theoretical knowledge), facts and heuristics (practical surface knowledge), and general problem-solving experience. Collectively, these are the tools used by the expert in recognizing, understanding, and solving problems.

One estimate has it taking a minimum of 10 years to become expert in any field and that a world-class expert possesses somewhere between 50,000 to 100,000 "chunks" of heuristic information related to his or her field (Harmon & King, 1985). Training experts is, of course, an inordinately time-consuming and costly process and a major reason for corporate interest in KBSs.

Experts are efficient and effective problem solvers; they do easily and quickly what most of us cannot do very well, if at all. Experts are also quick to distinguish between what is important to a problem situation and what is not. Experts are credible because of their relatively high success rates and their ability to justify, though not necessarily explain, their decisions.

Experts are adaptive and can handle the unusual or unexpected as well as routine kinds of tasks, typically without apparent thought or effort. Novel situations for which the expert may have little or no experience can be handled by returning to first principles. The expert can then generate hypotheses regarding likely solutions and test them for validity. Since experts are efficient learners, new solutions acquired in this fashion are added to their existing repertoire of heuristics. The task then is to design programs which are not only knowledgeable but which are efficient, adaptive, trainable, reliable, credible, and robust as well.

1.3.2 A Design for Computer Expertise

Figure 1.1 illustrates a generic design for KBSs. The reader is cautioned to keep in mind that KBS development is a rapidly evolving science and that the best of current designs represent only the present state of the art. Better and perhaps even radically different designs will evolve as more is learned about the nature of knowledge and its application in computational systems.

The KBS, much like its human counterpart, must be trainable. In AI jargon, this process is termed "knowledge acquisition." The KBS must be provided with large stores of information, sometimes employing a special program called a knowledge acquisition module. The facts and heuristics that are taught to the system must be represented in the knowledge base in a form that is both efficient and meaningful; that is, the knowledge must be encoded in a manner that is both compatible with the system's problem-solving procedures and a faithful representation of the significant objects and relations of the domain. In fact, the complex processes of knowledge acquisition, knowledge representation, and design for an

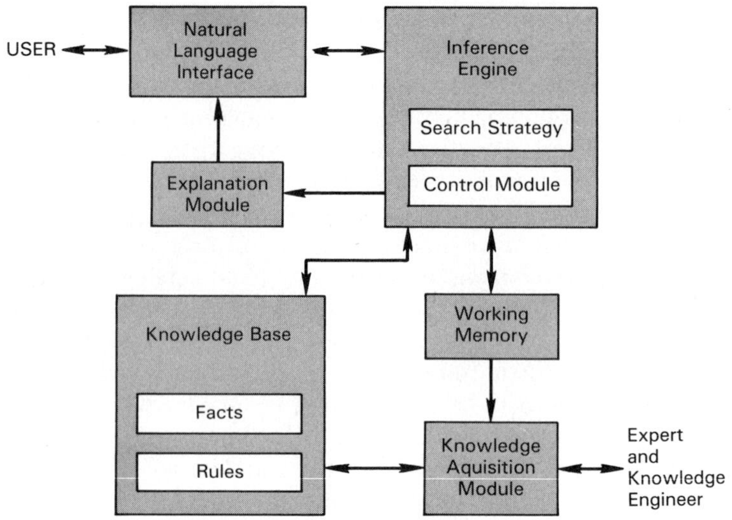

Figure 1.1 Components of an expert system.

inferencing strategy are the most critical ones in the development of a KBS. For this reason, we will examine each of these steps in some detail.

KBSs, again much like their human counterparts, must be able to supplement their knowledge bases with information regarding current conditions. For this reason, KBSs are highly interactive and have the ability to interrupt a consultation midstream to query the user for clarification or for additional information needed by the system in searching for a solution to a problem. To accomplish this, KBSs often have a natural-language interface that allows the system to ask for and receive information from the user in convenient and easily understood English sentence form.

If a KBS is to be regarded as credible, it must meet or exceed levels of human performance. It is unlikely that users will trust a computer system to make important decisions, or even recommendations, if the system's performance is inferior to that of the human expert. To demonstrate the validity of its performance, the KBS must have mechanisms for explaining conclusions and the reasoning that supports them.

1.4 KNOWLEDGE ACQUISITION AND REPRESENTATION

> Intelligence is largely the ability to create and manipulate descriptions. We are thus concerned with the nature of descriptions, what they are, their characteristics, and what their relation is to the things they describe.
>
> [M. A. Fischler & O. Firschein, *Intelligence: The Eye, the Brain, and the Computer*, p. 63]

An important early step in the development of a KBS involves transferring information from one or more human experts to the machine. The difficulties inherent in knowledge transfer have prompted one AI expert to characterize the knowledge acquisition process as the primary bottleneck in the successful development of expert systems (Feigenbaum & McCorduck, 1983). Attempts to devise techniques for automating this process are still in the early stages of research and development. Because of the inherent complexity of the problems associated with knowledge acquisition, it is unlikely that completely automated knowledge transfer will be possible in the near future.

However, expert programs have been designed that can assist in knowledge transfer. TEIRESIAS, an adjunct to MYCIN, is one well-known example. Also, expert shells are making an appearance in the AI marketplace. Shells are programs that assist the user in building KBS applications. These programs vary in their features, but most have built-in inference engines and simplified methods for soliciting domain-specific expertise from the user. Most shells, however, use a predetermined representation formalism to encode information into the system automatically, and although these shells can simplify KBS development, it is often at the cost of imposing constraints on the methods for organizing knowledge and solving problems. For this reason, use of these development tools is often a tradeoff of savings from simplified development measured against losses from forcing the problem to fit the requirements of the shell.

For applications where maximal flexibility during design is required, shells may not be useful at all. In these cases, the system may need to be built from scratch. This means using an AI language to write all components of the program including the knowledge base and inference engine. However, the system developer must first extract the expertise from the domain expert and then encode it into a KBS that can utilize the knowledge in inferring solutions to problems. This is an exceedingly complex process, and the job of one of the world's newest class of domain experts, the knowledge engineer (KE).

To succeed, the KE must gain the confidence and cooperation of a very busy and important person—the resident domain expert. Experience has shown that experts are often not at all convinced that a machine will be able to simulate their years of hard-earned knowledge and problem-solving abilities. As a result, the KE must frequently cope with psychological and social resistance as part of the process of debriefing an expert.

Once the KE has managed to extract from the expert (and other sources of expertise, such as books and manuals) a significant measure of expertise, he or she must analyze the structure of this information and make important decisions about the overall design of the system. At this point, a critical decision must be made regarding the most effective data structure with which to represent the knowledge to the system. As AI researchers have not settled on a single adequate formalism for the representation of knowledge, several approaches are currently in use. These include semantic nets, frames, production rules, first-order predicate logic clauses, scripts, neural nets, and schemata (see Cercone & McCalla, 1987).

1.4.1 Semantic Networks

The *semantic network* is the oldest scheme used in AI for representing knowledge and the one with the clearest ties to psychological research into human language, learning, and memory (Quillian, 1968). The semantic network (often shortened to *semantic net*) is a directed graph used for representing objects and the relations among them. The objects, shown as labeled circles, are referred to as *nodes*. The properties and relations of objects are expressed as directed arrows (*arcs*) connecting nodes. Figure 1.2 depicts an example of knowledge encoded in a semantic net.

The meaning or semantics of an object represented as a node in a semantic net derives from the values of the nodes to which it is directly and indirectly connected and not simply from the content of the node that designates the object itself. Since each individual in the net is represented by a single node, all related information about that individual is accessible from that node via directed arcs to superordinate nodes. In this way, nodes lower in a network may inherit attributes

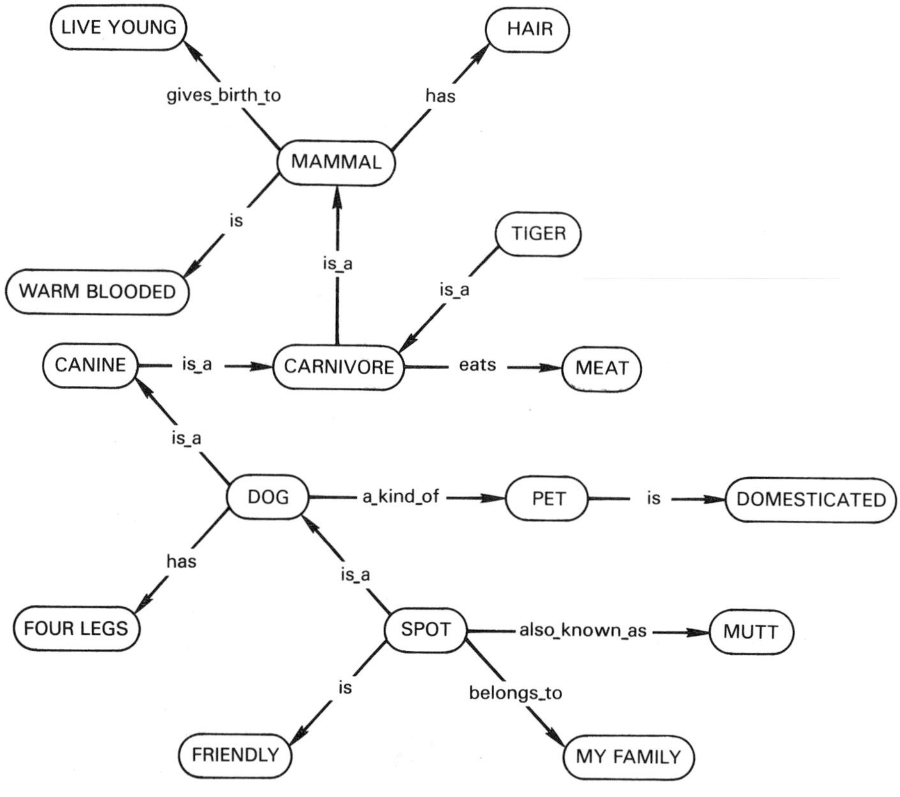

Figure 1.2 A semantic network of related information. Objects are circled. Relations are shown as labeled arrows (arcs).

from nodes represented higher in the network. For example, Spot in Figure 1.2 is known from inspection of the network to belong to my family. However, as Spot is a dog, which is a category of carnivore, which in turn is a mammal, it is also known that Spot possesses the attributes of these nodes, such as having four legs, eating meat, and belonging to a species that gives birth to live young.

The is a arc is a special relation that is used in AI programs to provide a linking mechanism for the transmission of information down the hierarchy of superordinate and subordinate nodes. This is called an *inheritance hierarchy*, and it represents one of the important economies made possible by representing knowledge in semantic nets. This means that information once represented at higher levels need not be redundantly stored at lower levels. In representing complex relationships among large numbers of objects in KBSs, the inheritance hierarchy represents a considerable savings in storage and computational overhead.

From any semantic net, a collection of directed graphs may be drawn. Such a collection of graphs can represent all the information contained in the equivalent semantic net. A partial set of digraphs for Figure 1.2 is shown here to illustrate this point. Once again, objects are represented as labeled nodes with properties or relations shown as labeled arrows linking pairs of nodes.

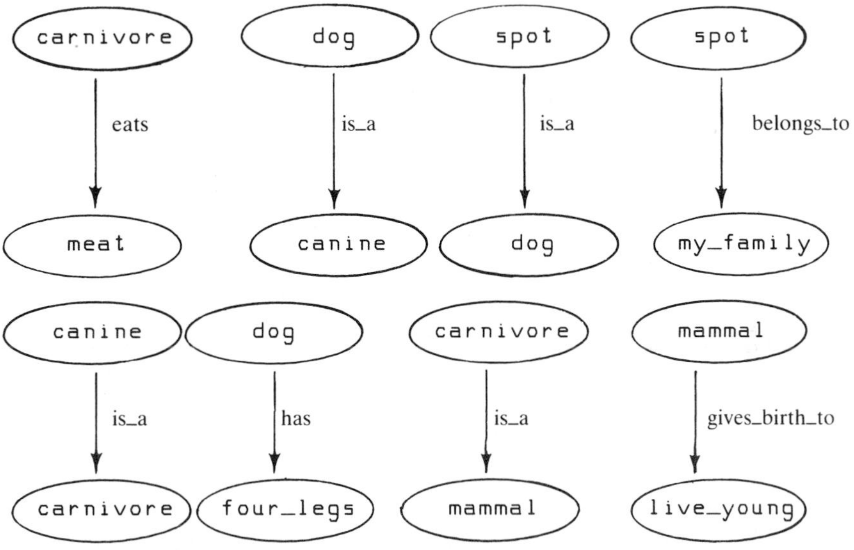

Kowalski (1979) has demonstrated the semantic equivalency of semantic nets and clausal representation in the language of first-order predicate logic. This means that what we can represent in a semantic net we can also represent as logic clauses. Soon we will see that Prolog is based in principles of first-order predicate logic and that we can represent knowledge as Prolog statements. This subject will be covered in Chapter 2, where the relationship between logic, logic programming, and Prolog will be detailed. However, by way of a preview of coming attractions, consider the following collection of Prolog unit clauses or facts. Each fact is made up of a predicate name followed by two arguments enclosed within parentheses and separated by a comma. Each predicate in Prolog expresses an attribute of a single object or, as in this case, a relation that holds between two objects. The knowledge shown before as a set of digraphs is here represented as eight Prolog facts.

```
        predicate(arg_1,arg_2,...arg_n)
1.        is_a(canine,carnivore).
2.        gives_birth_to(mammal,live_young).
3.        is_a(carnivore,mammal).
4.        eats(carnivore,meat).
5.        is_a(dog,canine).
6.        has(dog,four_legs).
7.        is_a(spot,dog).
8.        belongs_to(spot,my_family).
```

1.4.2 Frames

Another formalism often used in AI research to represent knowledge is a data structure related to the semantic net and known as the *frame* (Minsky, 1975, 1987). Frames perform many of the same functions as networks; however, they provide some additional features as well. A frame is an efficient data structure for representing contextual information about objects, concepts, or events. The frame is related to other important representational formalisms such as scripts (Schank & Abelson, 1977) and the objects in Smalltalk, Simula, and Loops.

A frame is labeled, typically with the name of the object it represents, and is made up of a series of slots. Each slot can contain a variable number of facets. Each facet in a slot can in turn hold information pertaining to the object or procedures for generating information relating to the object that may be needed by the program at run time. Facet entries may be values, rules, demons (a colorful name for mechanisms used to invoke procedures needed to produce, change, or delete information for a facet), pointers to other structures, or default information. Like semantic nets, facets in a frame may share information with other frames through an inheritance mechanism.

A simplified frame for our canine friend Spot is presented in Figure 1.3. The frame identifier is `Spot`. The first slot in the frame has the label `is_a`, which indicates that `Spot` is a member of the superordinate class `dog`. Here the `is_a` slot serves as a link between the frames for `Spot` and another for `dog`. Information contained in the `dog` frame (or in frames to which it is linked) need not be repeated in the `Spot` frame as it may be inherited via the `is_a` linking mechanism.

The next slot is labeled `ako`, which is an acronym for *a kind of*. This indicates that Spot is also a member of a class of functionally related animals called `pet`

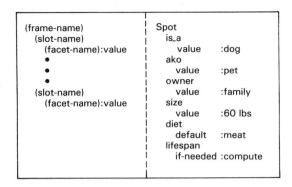

```
(frame-name)
  (slot-name)
    (facet-name):value
    •
    •
    •
  (slot-name)
    (facet-name):value
```

```
Spot
  is_a
    value      :dog
  ako
    value      :pet
  owner
    value      :family
  size
    value      :60 lbs
  diet
    default    :meat
  lifespan
    if-needed  :compute
```

Figure 1.3 Frame-based representation of knowledge. A template for a frame is shown on the left. An example frame for `Spot` is on the right.

and may share attributes and relations defining that class of objects. The `ako` facet name is `value`, which means that it holds the actual value of the facet, namely, the symbol `pet`. This informs the system that the frame for `Spot` can inherit default information contained in the `pet` frame.

The `default` and `if_needed` facets are also included in our example frame. The `default` facet contains the value `meat`, indicating that in the absence of information to the contrary, this particular dog will eat meat. Also, other frames linked to the `Spot` frame will not have to represent diet information. The `if_needed` facet contains as a value a demon that, when invoked, performs the function of computing a run-time value needed by the program.

Like semantic nets, frames can also be represented using Prolog facts (see Cuadrado & Cuadrado, 1986; Floyd, 1988).

1.4.3 Production Rules

The so-called production rule grew out of Alan Newell and Herbert Simon's research in the 1950s and 1960s into human cognitive systems. Working from an information processing model of human memory, Newell and Simon conceived of long-term memory as made up of "situation-action" rules called *productions* with the current situation represented in short-term memory. According to this view, a person recognizes a situation in short-term memory and, matching this situation to the left side of a production rule held in long-term memory, is led to an action represented in the right side of the production rule. The result of the action may produce a change in the situation stored in short-term memory, thus triggering off a search for another production. This entire process was termed a production system and was used by Newell and Simon and their associates in modeling human memory and problem-solving processes.

Production rules are expressed as conditional sentences in the form:

```
IF <condition(s)> THEN <action(s)>
```

Underlying the production rule is the principle of logical inference known as *modus ponens*, which states, "If A is true and B is known to follow A, and we observe

A, then we may conclude *B*." Here is an example of an elementary production rule with two conditions and two conclusions:

If: (1) A dog has a proper diet, and
(2) A dog does not play on a busy street,
Then: (1) Compute life-span as average, and
(2) Compute total vet fees as below average.

Production rules differ from frames in that the emphasis is placed on inferring relations between facts; that is, "If *A* exists, then we have evidence for *B*." Production rules coded in languages such as OPS5 or LISP are used in many successful expert systems. Frames and scripts, on the other hand, are more useful in representing descriptive or stereotypical conceptualizations of objects and events and are frequently used in natural-language story understanding systems (Schank & Abelson, 1977; Schank & Riesbeck, 1981; Lehnert & Ringle, 1982).

MYCIN is one of the better-known examples of a production rule based system. MYCIN, a medical diagnosis and prescription program, uses many hundreds of production rules to draw inferences about the likely presence in the blood of infectious bacterial organisms and the appropriate modes of treatment. An example of a MYCIN production rule (Buchanan & Shortliffe, 1984) is shown here.

If: (1) The morphology of the organism is coccus, and
(2) The stain of the organism is not known,
Then: There is suggestive evidence (0.6) that the stain of the organism is Grampos.

1.4.4 Logic

The final representational formalism we will discuss in this book and the one most important to our study of Prolog is logic. There are several extant logics, including the classical Aristotelian syllogistic logic that dominated Western thought for centuries, propositional logic, predicate logic, and several nontraditional logics (e.g., fuzzy logic, modal logic, multivalued logics).

The relationship of Prolog to logic programming in which a subset of clauses of the first-order predicate logic known as Horn clauses are used as a programming language will require substantially more than a cursory introduction. For this reason, I will reserve further discussion on the relation of Prolog to logic until Chapter 2, where this topic can be covered in some detail.

1.5 REPRESENTING UNCERTAINTY

In most applications, KBSs must work with knowledge that is in varying degrees imprecise, incomplete, and uncertain. If you refer back to the sample MYCIN production rule, you will note that the diagnostic conclusion was stated as suggestive with a certainty factor of 0.6. The presence of this certainty factor in the rule reflects the fact that conclusions drawn from evidence are often to some degree uncertain. Accordingly, conclusions must somehow indicate the degree of expert and user confidence in the facts, rules, and user input employed by the system in arriving at solutions to problems.

Estimating confidence in conclusions is handled in a variety of ways in KBSs. In some applications, probability theory is employed to assess the likelihood or odds associated with evidence and conclusions. More often than not, the formal prerequisite conditions of probability theory cannot be met, and other means for estimating confidence in evidence and conclusions must be employed. Some of the more commonly used techniques for programming with uncertain and qualitative knowledge will be introduced in Chapter 9.

1.6 INFERENCING ISSUES AND SCHEMES

We will now consider the major strategies used by rule-based KBSs for drawing inferences from information contained in a knowledge base. The graphic term *inference engine* is often encountered in this context. The inference engine defines the inferencing strategy and directs all searches for information needed in support of inferencing. The two inferencing strategies commonly used in KBS inference engines are *forward chaining* and *backward chaining*. Within each of these two inferencing strategies, searches for information may proceed in a depth-first or a breadth-first fashion (see Figure 1.4).

1.6.1 Forward and Backward Chaining

The forward-chaining inferencing strategy proceeds from what is known about current conditions. Using a set of rules, it attempts to infer inductively what is unknown, namely some goal state. In a production rule system, the control segment of the inference engine directs searches of the knowledge base to find matches for current conditions with the `IF <CONDITIONS>`, or left side, of rules. All rules found to match are selected and then executed.

The order in which selected rules are executed is controlled by a process called *conflict resolution*. One elementary scheme for conflict resolution is to fire the rules in an order determined by the recency of their past use; that is, rules that have been used recently by the program have priority over those used less recently.

If the right side of the executed rule produces new information, it is "asserted" to working memory. This, of course, alters working memory so that once again the inference engine cycles through remaining rules looking for those that match the new set of conditions. This process concludes when the right side of a rule produces an acceptable goal state or no new rules can be found that add new information to working memory and thus support further searching and inferencing by the system.

Forward-chaining systems are said to be data-driven and reason in a bottom-

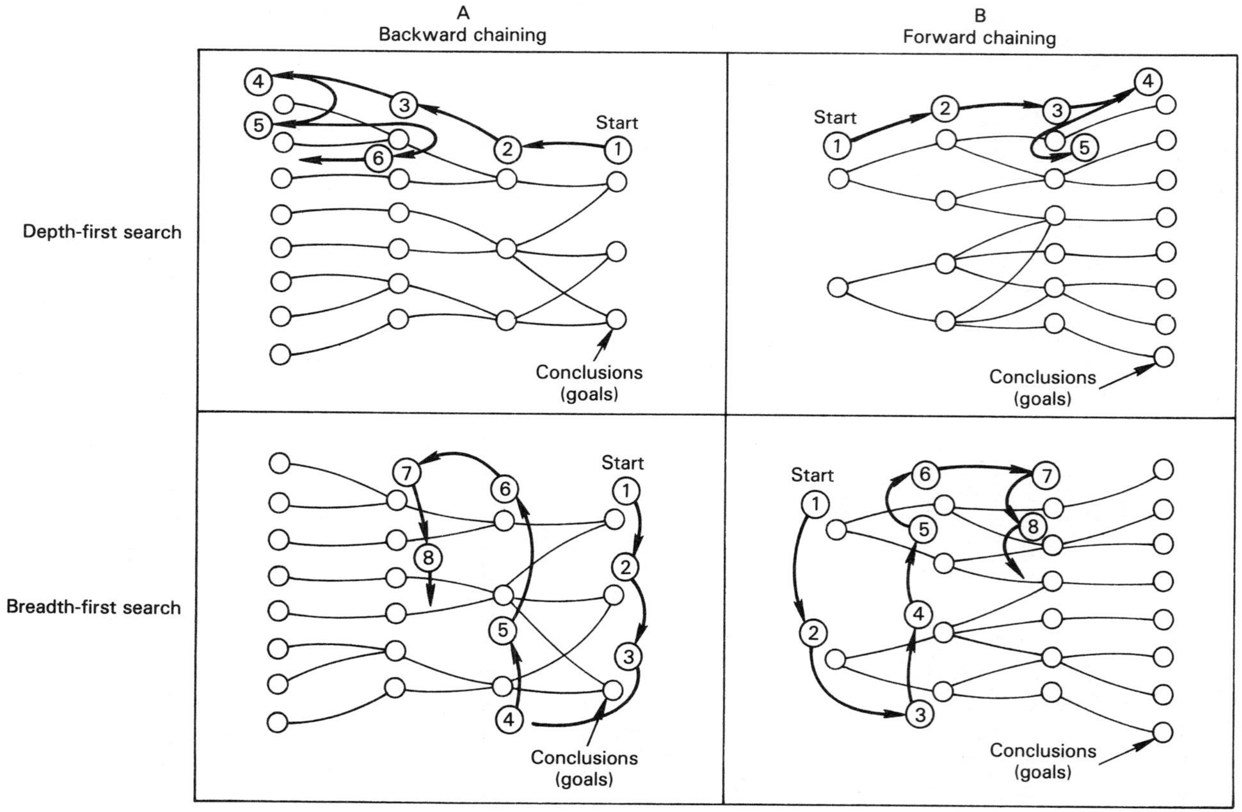

Figure 1.4 Forward- and backward-chaining inference strategies with depth-first and breadth-first searching. Reprinted with permission from P. Harmon and D. King, *Expert Systems: Artificial Intelligence in Business* (New York: John Wiley & Sons, Inc., 1985), p. 57. © 1985 John Wiley & Sons, Inc.

up or inductive fashion. This kind of system is most useful in problem domains where there are many possible goal states and all that is presently known to the program are details of current conditions.

Backward-chaining systems operate in the opposite fashion. These inference engines start by looking at a specifiable set of goals. The inference engine then seeks to find evidence to prove one or more of these goals. This type of inference engine works top-down and is hypothesis-driven. These systems are most useful when a relatively small number of goals are considered to be strong candidates as solutions to the problem. The backward-chaining system attempts to prove these goals by finding evidence for their conditions.

To help concretize these two types of inference engines, consider the following problems. Imagine a patient in consultation with a general practitioner. The patient reports vague symptoms of not feeling well. The doctor does not observe any overt symptoms and does not have any immediate basis for a diagnosis. In this case, the physician will likely chain forward by asking a series of questions pertaining to a wide variety of possible illnesses and will perform several tests. The physician then inductively constructs a diagnosis out of what initially appear to be disparate pieces of evidence.

Now imagine a patient who presents the physician with a complaint of intense sharp pain in the lower right quadrant of the abdomen. The physician observes that the patient does not have any surgical scars in this region. The physician in this instance may elect to chain backward and select a diagnosis of appendicitis. The physician will then proceed to ask questions and conduct tests calculated to prove this specific diagnosis (checking for fever, swelling, elevated white blood-cell count, etc.). If the evidence does not support this initial hypothesis, the physician will select the next most likely diagnosis where pain of this type is a major symptom.

1.6.2 Depth-first and Breadth-first Searching

In depth-first searching, the strategy is to explore in the greatest possible detail each path to a possible goal before another path is selected. For example, the physician will exhaustively test all the conditions that are known to be causally related to appendicitis before abandoning this diagnosis. Study Figure 1.4 and you will observe that for both forward-chaining and backward-chaining inference engines, the depth-first search strategy selects one path and explores it completely. If a goal is found, the search is over. If a goal is not found on this path, the system backs up (backtracks) to try another path. All paths may be systematically and exhaustively explored using this technique. We will see that Prolog employs the backward- chaining depth-first search as its basic strategy in solving problems.

The breadth-first search strategy does not commit initially to one path in searching for a goal. It looks at all nodes at a given level in the network of paths (search space) when searching for a goal. If the goal is not found at this level, the system will try the next level of nodes deeper in the search space.

In some very difficult problems, the search space of possible goals is so large that the time associated with exhaustive depth-first or breadth-first searches for solutions rises exponentially. To shorten the time required to search for solutions, smart (heuristic) search strategies are implemented so that all possible paths in the search space need not be exhaustively explored. Some of these techniques for intelligent nonexhaustive searches will be illustrated in a later chapter.

1.7 NATURAL-LANGUAGE PROCESSING AND COMPUTERS

One of the long-standing goals of artificial intelligence research has been the development of computer systems that can communicate with users in natural human languages rather than in artificial-language commands that are difficult to remember and to understand. Computers with natural-language understanding and generation capabilities will perform a myriad of useful functions including reading the enormous volumes of information that threaten to overwhelm today's scientists, businessmen, and politicians and writing abstracts of essential information; and making quick and accurate translations into various languages to disseminate needed information among nations.

Developing natural-language understanding and generation systems has proved to be far more difficult than at first believed. At the time of this writing, natural-language front ends for popular applications programs are available in the marketplace. However, these programs permit the user to interact with computer applications using only a small subset of English words and sentence structures. Nonetheless, these programs simplify use of complex applications packages and are certain to be a major area for software development in the coming decade. In Chapter 10, we will cover some of the programming techniques more commonly used in natural-language processing.

1.8 EVALUATING KNOWLEDGE-BASED SYSTEMS

Any objective evaluation must include tests of performance. Students are given exams. Automobiles are put through grueling simulations of road conditions. Computer software is subjected to benchmark tests to assess efficiency and reliability.

The first test of a computer system was proposed by Alan Turing, one of the great names in the early history of computing. The Turing Test stated that a computer system could be said to be intelligent only if an observer could not distinguish between responses to a set of queries transmitted to the observer via teletype to eliminate visual cues made by the computer and those made by a human. In this test, no restrictions were placed on the means by which the computer generated answers (lying was possible), only that the answers be indistinguishable from those made by a human.

The Turing test is a stringent one, but some observers suggest that such an evaluation should indeed be considered a prerequisite to a program's being termed intelligent. According to such a test, a KBS should perform its functions and communicate in a manner close to, if not indistinguishable from, that of a human expert. Passing such a test may be justified in instances where a KBS is called on to make important judgments regarding people's health or valuable resources. The following are three criteria by which KBSs of the future may be evaluated.

> 1. A FUNCTIONAL CRITERION
>
> Given a well-defined and bounded knowledge domain of expertise, a KBS should be as competent in its performance as the human expert. Not unlike its human colleague, the system should perform reliably and justify it decisions. Furthermore, it should be readily maintainable and extensible as the knowledge domain it serves evolves.

Increasing numbers of expert programs will qualify according to this first criterion. Some existing programs exceed levels of human achievement in narrowly bounded domains (e.g., XCON, DENDRAL, MACSYMA). The reason some systems are such outstanding performers is not necessarily that they know more but rather that they can be more systematic and reliable in drawing inferences from the extensive knowledge that they do have.

In addition to assessing the merits of program performance in terms of technical capabilities, evaluating the chances of a KBS's success in an actual setting involves serious consideration of additional social, psychological, and economic factors.

> 2. AN ECONOMIC CRITERION
>
> A KBS should have a clearly defined purpose and a bottom-line impact sufficient to justify long-term investment of corporate resources needed to develop and maintain the system.

Knowledge-based system development is highly labor- and knowledge-intensive, and development is therefore a costly process. Apart from university research labs where a primary goal is pursuit of knowledge with a bottom line of academic reputation earned through teaching students state-of-the-art knowledge, many potential consumers of KBS technology cannot justify current development costs of a KBS unless it effectively performs valued services for which there is a limited supply of human expertise. No commercial corporation is likely to sustain the long-term costs of implementation unless a reasonable return on investment is anticipated. This is likely to occur only when the project is managed in a businesslike manner with well-defined goals and realistic projections of problems, costs, and expected returns.

> 3. A SOCIAL CRITERION
>
> Successful development and implementation of a KBS requires a willingness to innovate on the part of the management sponsor, the expert, and the end user.

In addition to the purely economic impact of KBS development, there are social costs that must be evaluated. Any KBS project will require a climate of enthusiasm, or at the very least, tolerance for innovation. KBS technology is new, and for some clients and end users it must be perceived as quite radical. For others, machines doing the work of human experts may well be threatening. We have gotten used to machines doing menial or perhaps dangerous work, but doing the thinking and problem-solving work of humans may be too much for some people to accept.

Very similar problems exist for the implementation of computers as teaching and learning tools in educational institutions. Technology may be physically present but may remain largely unused if teachers and learners are unwilling or afraid to innovate. Changing habits, emotions, and attitudes will take time and planning. The corporation interested in KBS technology must be willing to bear the full social and economic burden of this process.

1.9 THE FUTURE FOR KNOWLEDGE-BASED SYSTEMS

The key problems over the short term for the advancement of KBS technology are development, delivery, and determination.

The development problem is defined by the need to overcome both the knowledge acquisition bottleneck and the inability of current systems to perform robustly when confronted with problems unanticipated by the builders or with information that is changing, tentative, and uncertain. As these and other problems are overcome, the feasibility of the technology will increase by an order of magnitude.

The delivery problem reflects the need for powerful, portable, and inexpensive microprocessors to deliver the technology in widely dispersed locations. Some experts believe that this problem will be solved by the appearance of large, inexpensive RAM chips, powerful 32-bit high-speed microprocessors such as the Intel 80386 and Motorola 68030, and large-capacity optical storage devices.

Over the long term, however, development of KBSs with large knowledge bases able to perform robustly and capable of communication using natural language will depend on many further technical and social breakthroughs. These breakthroughs will require innovative approaches to knowledge acquisition, representation, searching, and inferencing as well as more efficient approaches to computing.

The determination problem centers on the social and psychological inertia associated with general acceptance of any new technology by the people who must write the checks and use the products. Judging from the high level of interest on the part of *Fortune* 500 companies cited in many computer publications, significant vertical markets for this technology exist now. The problem seems to be that many companies lacking in-house expertise do not know how to get started. AI expertise is scarce, and with just a few universities producing AI specialists, many companies must contemplate training staff to handle KBS development. This is a costly venture for those not sure of the bottom-line impact the technology will have on their businesses.

The marketplace for KBSs must mature to the point where there are more working systems in the field to serve as models of success. Also needed is a richer diversity of support services and entry-level products such as shells with which users can experiment for a relatively small investment in time and money. Markets for KBS technology will undoubtedly expand as it becomes more evident that the technology does, in fact, help business meet the challenges of current economic conditions by providing an authentic competitive edge.

Important future applications of KBSs will be in the home, school, and office, serving the personal needs of individuals and families. At the personal level, future KBSs may help people to resolve the increasing complexity of contemporary life. Using KBSs, personalized solutions to problems can be readily achieved. Programs that can know a lot about us as individuals as well as important knowledge domains can achieve a high degree of personal usefulness. These programs can help people to make qualitatively better decisions based on the increased information, logical inferencing, and thoroughness possible with KBS technology.

1.10 SUMMARY

Concepts covered

Artificial intelligence
Graphs
Heuristics

- Inferencing schemes
  - Backward chaining
  - Forward chaining
  - Depth-first search
  - Breadth-first search
- Knowledge acquisition
- Knowledge representation
  - Semantic nets
  - Frames
  - Production rules
  - Logic
- Knowledge-based and expert systems
  - Evaluation criteria
  - Structure
  - Functions
- Natural-language processing

KBSs are knowledge-intensive programs that use a variety of representational schemes and inference strategies to emulate the problem-solving behavior of human experts working in well-bounded domains. Expert systems have been designed to perform a variety of functions, including diagnosis and interpretation, control and debugging, instruction, prediction, planning, and design. The economic advantage made possible by these knowledge-intensive programs promises to create a multibillion-dollar industry in a matter of years.

The representation schemes used in KBSs include semantic networks, frames, production rules, and logic. The logical formalism is used in Prolog-based systems. The inference control strategies used by current systems are backward and forward chaining.

In rule-based systems, backward chaining is an inference strategy that begins with a goal statement and searches backward for facts or conditions to support that goal. Forward chaining starts with facts and looks for rules with a goal statement that is satisfied by those facts. The Prolog language provides a built-in backward-chaining inference mechanism.

The development of a KBS is a costly and time-consuming process fraught with economic, conceptual, and social pitfalls. Successful systems require a clearly defined and relevant problem domain, a financial return to the developer, skilled developers with requisite tools, and a commitment to innovate on the part of all involved in the project.

1.11 EXERCISES

1. Define knowledge-based or expert systems. How do they differ from a word processor, spreadsheet, or database program?
2. In what important ways do contemporary KBSs differ from early AI problem-solving programs?

3. Discuss the major components of a KBS. What is the function of each?
4. Compare and contrast the major formalisms used for knowledge representation in computer systems.
5. Why do some critics of AI eschew the term *expert system*?
6. Give an example from everyday life of the inferencing and search strategies discussed in this chapter:
   a. Forward chaining
   b. Backward chaining
   c. Depth-first search
   d. Breadth-first search
7. What is a heuristic? Why are heuristics employed in KBS?
8. Why are businesses so interested in KBS?
9. What do you think is the future for AI and KBS? Can you think of any applications for AI or KBS that have not been mentioned in this chapter?

Part 2

Introduction to Turbo Prolog and Basic Programming Concepts

Chapter 2

Introduction to Logic, Logic Programming, and Turbo Prolog

CHAPTER OBJECTIVES

Study of this chapter should enable you to do the following:

1. Understand the origins of Prolog in logic and logic programming.
2. Discuss the resolution inference rule.
3. Define and give examples of Turbo Prolog facts and rules.
4. Discuss the components of a Turbo Prolog program.
5. Explain the principle of unification and how it is used by Turbo Prolog in solving for goals entered by the user.
6. Explain what is meant by instantiation of variables and the scope of variable instantiation.
7. Define a problem domain using Prolog objects and relations.
8. List the strengths and weaknesses of Turbo Prolog.

IMPORTANT TERMS AND PHRASES

Argument
Atom
Backtracking
Boolean algebra
Bound variables
Clause
Closed-world assumption
Compound objects
Conjunction
Constant
Deduction
Disjunction
First-order Logic
Free variables
Implication
Induction
Inference
Instantiation
Logic
Negation
Pattern matching
Predicate logic
Propositional logic
Resolution
Rules
Scope of variables
Sentence
Stack
String
Subgoal
Syllogism
Symbolic logic
Term
Truth value
Unification
Variable
Well-formed formula

The Prolog language constitutes a new approach to computer programming. This is because Prolog programs are both a logical description of a knowledge domain and an executable theorem prover that can be used for solving problems in that domain. To write a Prolog program, the programmer declares knowledge about objects and relations in a selected domain in logic clause form. The Prolog system then uses its built-in searching, pattern-matching, and inferencing mechanisms to deductively infer answers to queries posed by the user.

To appreciate fully the Prolog approach to programming, you must first understand the relation of Prolog to both logic and logic programming. Key elements in understanding this relation are (1) how a subset of clauses of the first-order logic called Horn clauses are used for knowledge representation, (2) how principles of logical inference are applied to these clauses to generate deductive conclusions, and (3) the mechanism by which the first two elements are efficiently implemented in the Prolog programming language.

To provide some conceptual background for our study of Prolog, we begin with a cursory review of principles of classical and symbolic logic. This review will introduce the reader to some of the more important issues and terminology. In no way is this discussion offered as a comprehensive treatment of the logical foundations of Prolog. It is intended only as a sketch in broad strokes of the relation of Prolog to logic and logic programming.

Furthermore, in the interests of maintaining simplicity for the nontechnical reader, I have opted to avoid discussion of what I consider to be advanced technical points (that is, concepts that are not essential for a general understanding of the logical foundations of Prolog), such as treatment of proofs of completeness of logical systems and methods for conversion of predicate calculus well-formed formula into Horn clausal form (Skolem function). If you feel the need for a more comprehensive coverage of logic, refer to Hogger, 1984; Maier and Warren, 1988; Clocksin and Mellish, 1984; and Kowalski, 1979.

The chapter concludes with an introduction to the Turbo Prolog programming language. This introduction is intended to build on the elementary principles of logic introduced earlier in the chapter but can be approached directly by those readers who wish to pursue the less rigorous route.

2.1 LOGIC

> It is not . . . the object of logic to determine whether conclusions be true or false; but whether what are asserted to be conclusions are conclusions.
>
> [Attributed to the logician Augustus de Morgan (1806–1871)]

The study of logic reveals principles by which one can distinguish between correct and incorrect reasoning. As pointed out in the quote, it is not the truth of the conclusion that is the focus of study but rather the correctness of the inferential relations that obtain between initial statements called premises, which are assumed to be true, and consequent statements called conclusions. Logic is a formal system in the sense that the form of the argument is independent of the meaning or interpretation given to the specific assertions that constitute the content of the argument.

2.1.1 Classical Logic

Classical or traditional logic began with the work of Plato and in the writings of the great observer and philosopher, Aristotle (384–322 B.C.). To minimize the imprecision of natural-language interpretations and thus to maximize the correctness of conclusions drawn during argument, Aristotle launched the formal study of terms and formulated the first laws of logic embodied in the theory of the syllogism.

Terms. For Aristotle a *term* was a word or collection of words representing classes of objects and events. Every term has a *complement*, which is a more general term that encompasses everything other than what is covered by the term itself. More generally, if we allow *T* to represent a term, *non-T* is the complement of *T*. If *T* represents the term *man*, then *non-T* represents all things that are *not man*. A *non-non-T* is the complement of *non-T*, or just *T*. A *non-non-man* is, therefore, a *man*.

Two terms are *contradictory* if one term is identical in meaning to the complement of the other. The terms *organic* and *inorganic* are contradictory because *inorganic* is consistent in meaning with the complement of *organic*, namely *nonorganic*. Furthermore, the two terms *organic* and *nonorganic* are complementary because they are dichotomous and exhaust all possible values that objects of the class can assume.

Terms that are not identical and do not exhaust all the possibilities existing between them are said to be *contrary*. *Brilliant* and *average* are contrary and not complementary terms in that identifiable categories of intelligence may exist between them (genius, dull, retarded, etc.), categories that collectively do exhaust all possible values on an intelligence dimension.

The *extension* of a singular term applies to a specific object of a class, while the extension of a general term applies to the entire class denoted by the term. The *intension* of a term covers all properties and attributes that an object must possess for the term to apply to that object.

Sentences, statements, and propositions. Logicians distinguish between sentences, statements, and propositions. To illustrate this distinction, consider the following sentences:

1. What word processor do you use?
2. Please write an essay on the future of AI technology.
3. All people who perform experiments are smart.
4. All scientists are intelligent.

All four statements are legitimate English sentences; however, they differ both in the terms used to convey individual meanings and in their communicative functions. The first sentence asks a question. The second sentence is a command. The third and fourth sentences are assertions called *statements*. It is this last type of sentence that has been of most interest to logicians.

It should be evident that differently formed sentences can have an identical meaning. In logic, the term *proposition* is used to refer to the meaning of an assertion without regard for the terms used in expressing the meaning. In other words, the proposition is a statement which, however phrased, conveys a meaning to which a value of *true* or *false* can be attached.

To avoid the inherent ambiguity of words and thus to facilitate analysis of the logical relations obtaining between premises and conclusions, Aristotle restricted argument to four simple forms:

Quantifier	Subject	Copula	Predicate
All	scientists	are	intelligent.
No	scientist	is	intelligent.
Some	scientists	are	intelligent.
Some	scientists	are not	intelligent.

If in each statement S is allowed to represent the subject term and P the predicate term, the four forms can be generalized as follows:

Form	Quantification	Identifier
1. All S is P.	Universal affirmative	(A)
2. No S is P.	Universal negative	(E)
3. Some S is P.	Particular affirmative	(I)
4. Some S is not P.	Particular negative	(O)

The words *all* and *no* in statements are universal quantifiers. Their function is to modify a statement to denote all members of the subject class. The word *some* is an existential quantifier and indicates that the statement applies to a subset of members of the subject class. The modifier *not* indicates the complement of a term it modifies.

Arguments. In logical arguments, reasoning often involves the linking of statements with words such as *if*, *then*, *and*, and *therefore*. Such reasoning falls into two categories, *deductive* and *inductive* argument. An inductive argument produces a synthetic conclusion that follows from one or more initial statements but is not contained in these premises.

If John did not study for the exam *and*
John is a poor student;
Then John will fail the exam today.

The conclusion "John will fail the exam today" is a new idea or *hypothesis* that is not contained in either of the initial statements. Much of modern science operates on inductive reasoning.

Deductive arguments begin with one or more statements or premises and end when an analytic conclusion that is implicit in the premises is inferred. For example:

All scientists are intelligent *and*
Professor Smith is a scientist;
Therefore, Professor Smith is intelligent.

Here, you will note, the conclusion is implicit in the premises.

Syllogism. The *syllogism* spells out rules for drawing valid conclusions and was formulated by Aristotle to protect argument from the frailties of thought and language. Statements appearing in the syllogism must conform to the four statement types outlined. The syllogism takes the form of a deductive argument with two premises and a conclusion.

Premise 1	*All* teachers are garrulous, and
Premise 2	Professor Smith is a teacher;
Therefore,	
Conclusion	Professor Smith is garrulous.

The standard form of the syllogism contains three and only three terms, called *major*, *minor*, and *middle* terms. The subject of the conclusion (*Professor Smith*), which occurs in one of the premise statements, is in this example the minor term. The predicate of the conclusion (*garrulous*) also occurs in one of the premises and is the major term. The term that occurs in both the premises (*teacher*) is the middle term and bridges the two premises.

The concept of distribution of terms is necessary to an understanding of the basic workings of the syllogism. A term is distributed when the statement in which the term occurs refers to the entire class of objects denoted by the term. The term *teacher* in the statement "All teachers are garrulous" is distributed because in this statement the entire class of teachers is referenced. A term is undistributed when only a subset of elements of a class is being referenced or denoted. The predicate *garrulous* is undistributed.

For the conclusion of a syllogism to be formally valid, the following rules must be satisfied (taken from George, 1977, p. 14). Notice that the rules represent a logical analysis of the structure of the premises without regard for the meaning of terms that make up statements.

1. Every term must be distributed once at least in the syllogism.
2. No term is distributed in the conclusion that was not distributed in one of the premises.
3. You can make no inference from two negative premises or two particular premises.
4. If one premise is negative (or particular), the conclusion must be negative (or particular), and vice versa.

The syllogism is made up of three statements with each statement cast in one of the four forms designated A, E, I, and O. It follows then that there are 4 × 4 × 4 or 64 kinds, called *moods* of syllogisms. For example, one mood of syllogism is made up of statements of types AAA. Other moods are AEO, AIA, and EIO. Some of these moods invalidate the syllogism. For example, a syllogism of AIA mood cannot produce a valid conclusion.

All men are mortal. (A)
Some men are wise. (I)

Any conclusion of type A drawn from these premises about "all mortals" or "all wise mortals" will not be valid.

Because of Aristotle's enormous prestige among scholars, the rules of the syllogism were for centuries slavishly memorized and unquestioningly applied. Scholars did, however, eventually come to challenge the syllogism as a complete model of correct inference.

The syllogism is a logic of terms where the relations that hold among terms are explored using four forms for statements. Logicians point out that many interesting propositions cannot be expressed in any of these four elementary subject-predicate forms. Furthermore, the syllogism does not allow for direct reasoning about the complement of a term, nor does it permit inferring the existence of a member of a class. Because of these and other limitations logicians have searched for a more general and expressive approach to logic.

2.1.2 Symbolic Logic

Symbolic or mathematical logic employs symbols in place of terms. Formalized axiomatic systems using symbols have been applied to the study of reasoning, mathematics, and most recently, logic programming. One of the earliest contributions to symbolic logic was made by the students of Aristotle in the formulation of one of the more important inference rules. This rule, called *modus ponens*, formalizes reasoning using the symbols P, Q, and R, to represent propositions. It states:

If P implies Q, and P is true, then Q is true.

Boolean Algebra. In 1854, George Boole, in a book titled *Investigations of the Laws of Thought*, advanced laws that he believed to be fundamental to all rational thought. These laws state that any proposition must be either true or false (the law of the excluded middle); if a proposition is true, it is true, since no proposition can be both true and false. Boole proposed that thought and logic could be quantified and subjected to rigorous analysis using an "algebra of thought."

Boolean algebra has as its basic idea the concept of class membership. One can talk about an individual element a and its relation to a class of all such elements A. For example, a may be an individual person, John Smith, belonging to the class A of human beings. Here we can write

$$a \in A \tag{1}$$

where the Greek letter epsilon signifies the relation "is a member of."

An element may not belong to a given class. For example, if B is a class of females, John Smith is not a member of class B. In this case we write

$$a \notin B \tag{2}$$

Relations among classes encompass class inclusion; that is, all members of class A can be included in class B. For example, the class *male* is included in the superordinate class *human being*. Equation 3 represents the class inclusion relation.

$$A \subset B \tag{3}$$

Relationships between classes can be graphically depicted using Euler-Venn diagrams. Rectangles represent the universe of all entities and circles the classes that are subsets of entities within this universe. Class inclusion is shown diagrammatically like this:

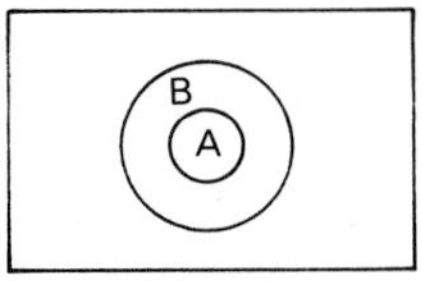

The symbolic statement

$$A \cap B \tag{4}$$

indicates the *conjoining* of classes to represent those elements common to both classes. This statement can be read A and B. If A is the class of all females and

B is the class of all teachers, then the conjunction of A and B includes all female teachers. The relation is shown graphically as follows:

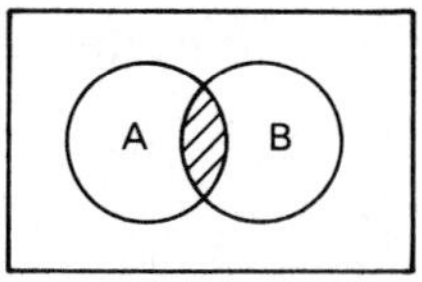

The symbol ∪ as shown in equation 5 expresses the *disjunction* of classes.

$$A \cup B \tag{5}$$

If A is all females and B is all teachers, then $A \cup B$ includes all females regardless of vocation and all teachers regardless of gender. A diagram of this relation is as follows:

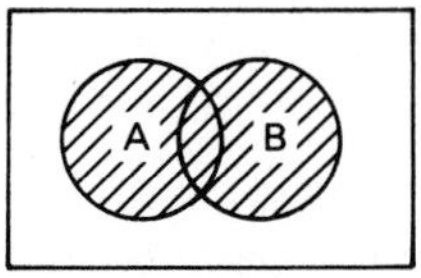

The relation of negation or complementarity is used when the universe is divided into a class A and everything else that does not belong to this class or *not* A. As A' refers to but one class we represent this relation as follows in equation 6. This same relation is graphically displayed below it.

$$A' \tag{6}$$

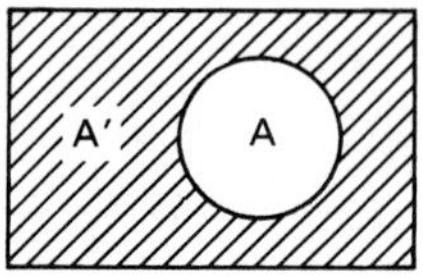

The null class is represented as $\emptyset$ and the entire universe as 1.

We can now apply these concepts to express other possible relations of interest. For example,

$$A' \cap A = 0 \text{ (the null class)} \tag{7}$$

This states that the class of all things common to A and *not* A is an empty class.

$$A \cup A' = 1 \tag{8}$$

This says that the *disjunction* of A and *not* A is equal to the entire universe.

Common arithmetic operations can be applied to Boolean classes. For example, consider the following well-known rules.

$$x = x \qquad \text{(identity)}$$

$$x + y = y + x \qquad \text{(commutativity)}$$

$$x + (y + z) = (x + y) + z \qquad \text{(associativity)}$$

$$x \times (y + z) = (x \times y) + (x \times z) \qquad \text{(distributivity)}$$

For classes, Boole developed equivalent rules. Here, an expression on one side of the equation is logically, rather than arithmetically, equivalent to the expression on the other side.

$$A = A \qquad \text{(identity)}$$

$$A \cup B = B \cup A \qquad \text{(commutativity)}$$

$$A \cap A = A \cup A = A \qquad \text{(commutativity)}$$

$$A \cup 0 = A \cap 1 = A \qquad \text{(commutativity)}$$

$$A \cap (B \cap C) = (A \cap B) \cap C \qquad \text{(associativity)}$$

$$A \cup (B \cup C) = (A \cup B) \cup C \qquad \text{(associativity)}$$

$$A \cap (B \cup C) = (A \cap B) \cup (A \cap C) \qquad \text{(distributivity)}$$

$$(A')' = A \qquad \text{(negation)}$$

Boole's contributions to symbolic logic included the idea that formal procedures that hold in manipulating arithmetic entities also hold for symbolically represented classes of objects and their relations.

2.1.3 The Logic of Propositions

Armed with the concept of a symbol system that could be used in formalizing reasoning, logicians developed the *logic of propositions*. Unlike the Aristotelian statement, which is comprised of smaller units or terms, the *proposition* is an atomic unit and is not further reducible. In the logic of propositions, inferencing proceeds by analysis of the logical relations or syntactical forms that obtain among "truth-valued" propositions. These logical relations include negation (*not*), conjunction (*and*), disjunction (*or*), and antecedence-consequence (*if . . . then*). In propositional logic, a formal system called *propositional calculus* is used to represent both propositions and the inferential relations that hold among them. Note also that the symbols employed in the propositional logic differ somewhat from those used previously in the discussion on classical logic.

Proposition Variables. The lowercase symbols p, q, and r are proposition variables and are used to represent atomic propositions. Variables make it possible to employ a kind of shorthand in logical statements, and when writing logic statements we replace propositions with variables. For example, we can replace the proposition "The student studied last week for the exam" with the lowercase letter p. Now wherever a p occurs in a formula, it carries the informal meaning of the proposition it has replaced.

Negation. The tilde symbol $\sim$ is the negation operator and always precedes a proposition variable called its *argument*. For example, if q stands for the proposition "The student passed the exam," the formula $\sim q$ represents the complement of this proposition ("The student did not pass the exam"). If we carry negation one step further, the formula $\sim\sim q$ stands for the complement of $\sim q$ or the proposition q, which, of course, returns us to the original proposition, "The student passed the exam."

Conjunction Relation. The period . stands for conjunction and links propositions. Again, if p represents "The student studied last week for the exam" and q the proposition "The student passed the exam," the formula $\sim p \, . \sim q$ can be read "The student did not study last week for the exam and the student did not pass the exam."

Disjunction Relation. The symbol $\vee$ represents disjunction in logical statements. It is used to link propositions, as in the formula $p \vee q$. To continue the example, $p \vee \sim q$ would be read "The student studied for the exam last week or the student did not pass the exam."

Implication. The $\supset$ is the symbol for *material implication* and represents the antecedent-consequent relation (*if . . . then*). The formula $p \supset q$ can be read "If the student studied last week for the exam, then the student passed the exam." The formula can also be read p implies q. To say that p implies q is to say that q is deducible from p. This is called *entailment*, a fundamental principle in logic.

Three parallel lines $\equiv$ comprise the symbol for *equivalence*. Equivalence indicates that two formulas are identical if they have identical values in a truth table. For example, if p and q are both true, then $\sim p$ or q and p if q are equivalent.

Table 2.1 displays the symbols and meanings for the logical connectives.

TABLE 2.1

Connectives	
Symbol	Meaning
$\sim$	not
$\cdot$	and
$\vee$	or
$\supset$	implies
$\equiv$	equivalence

Well-formed Formulas (wffs). In addition to representing atomic propositions, the propositional variables p, q, and r can be used to represent compound objects made up of atomic propositions and logical connectives. For example, $\sim p$, $p \, . \, q$, $p \vee q$, $p \supset q$, $p \equiv q$, and $\sim p \, . \, (q \vee r)$ are compound objects called *well-formed formulas*. The propositional variable is also used to represent wffs. For example, if p, q, and s all represent atomic propositions, then the wff $p \vee q$ can be represented by the proposition variable r in the wff $\sim r \vee \sim s$.

Interpretation of a wff. Once propositions and their relations are expressed in wffs, rules of inference can be applied to determine their truth values. That is, once knowledge from some domain is represented by symbols in a set of wffs, the next step is to determine the logical consequences of this knowledge. To illustrate, take the wff $p \,.\, q$ where p and q represent atomic propositions. Of course p and q could represent any number of propositions, some assumed to be true and some false. However, in one possible *interpretation* of this wff, let's say that p and q represent propositions that are both true. For example, we will say that p represents the true proposition that "carnivores eat meat" and q the true proposition that "dogs are carnivores." The question arises whether the wff $p \,.\, q$ is true. To answer this question, we can apply a rule of inference, or we can refer to a truth table as in Table 2.2.

Truth Value of wffs. The first line in this table tells us that the conjunction $p \,.\, q$ is true in any interpretation where p and q are both individually assumed to be true. Under other interpretations with truth values of *false* associated with one, the other, or both propositions, the wff $p \,.\, q$ will not be true. To generalize this relationship, let's call the wff $p \,.\, q$ A and this particular interpretation of A B. Then it can be said that B satisfies A or that B is a model of A.

Table 2.2 also tells us that a wff can be negated, as in $\sim(p \,.\, q)$, thus changing its truth value from true to *false*. Had the conjunction $p \,.\, q$ evaluated to *false* because one or both of the component propositions was false, then the negation operator would have changed the truth value of the wff to *true*.

Let's look at a complete reading of line 1 of the truth table. As we know, if p and q are both known to be individually true, then we can read the conjunction p and q as true, the disjunction p or q as true, the material implication p implies q as true, the material equivalence p is equivalent to q as true, and not p as false. Line 3 is read "if p is false and q is true then 'p and q' is false, 'p or q' is true, 'p implies q' is true, 'p is equivalent to q' is false, and 'not p' is true.

The structure of the wff, that is, how a wff is constructed out of proposition variables linked by logical connectives, is referred to as its *syntax*. The *truth value*

TABLE 2.2

Truth Values		And	Or	Implies	Equivalent	Not
p	q	$p \cdot q$	$p \vee q$	$p \supset q$	$p \equiv q$	$\sim p$
T	T	T	T	T	T	F
T	F	F	T	F	F	F
F	T	F	T	T	F	T
F	F	F	F	T	T	T

of the wff refers to its *semantics*, or logical meaning. Note that linguists and logicians use the term semantics somewhat differently.

Tautologies. Some wffs, called *tautologies*, are always true. The wff $p \vee \sim p$ is an example. Other wffs express contradictions and are always false. Such a contradiction is seen in the wff $p \,.\, \sim p$. Since no proposition can be asserted and denied at the same time, it follows that there can be no interpretation under which this formula can be satisfied.

Rules of Inference. To develop a logic of propositions, logicians have formulated rules to govern the inferencing process. Some of these rules are presented here. One of the first to be developed and one of the more important of these inference rules is *modus ponendo ponens*. This rule states that

If p implies q, and p is true, then q is true.

Another rule of inference is *modus tollendo tollens*, which states

If p implies q, and q is false, then p is false.

The rule *modus ponendo tollens* states that

If p and q are not both true, and p is true, then q is false.

This is also called the "exclusive or."

The rule *Modus tollendo ponens* states

If either p or q is true, and p is not true, then q is true.

This is also called the "inclusive or."

2.1.4 Predicate Logic and Logic Programming

Propositional logic represented a significant advance over traditional logic. In part this was because it offered rules to govern inferencing where the objects of reasoning are expressive wffs. However, in recent years, mathematicians and logicians have pointed to limitations in the logic of propositions. One limitation is that the truth-valued proposition is indivisible. This means that propositions cannot be analyzed into subject and predicate like syllogistic statements. The consequence of this is that reasoning about objects or the quantification of objects is impossible in the propositional logic. However, an evolutionary outgrowth of propositional logic called *predicate logic*, attributable in large measure to the seminal work of Gottlob Frege, addresses these issues and provides the necessary foundation for automated theorem proving using logic programming and Prolog.

The first step in using predicate logic to solve problems is to declare what is known about some knowledge domain of interest. This declaration is made in terms of the *objects* and their *attributes* and the *relations* that hold among these objects for this domain. The next step is to form *sentences* to express the logical properties of the objects and relations of the domain. The final step is to develop a tractable inference procedure to "reason" about the sentences and deductively to provide solutions to problems. Let's start by defining some terms and then move on to examine each of these steps in more detail.

Atomic Formula. The truth-valued object in the predicate logic is the *atomic formula*. An atomic formula is composed of a name called a *predicate* followed by arguments or terms. The arguments are enclosed in parentheses and are separated by commas as illustrated here:

```
p(T1,T2,...,Tn)
```

The lowercase `p` represents the predicate name and `T1,T2,...Tn`, the individual terms. In practice, the predicate name declares a relation that holds among the terms. For example,

```
understand(You,Logic)
```

expresses an instance of an `understand` relation that is assumed to exist between `You` and `Logic`. The predicate `understand` is a binary relation in that it takes the two arguments `You` and `Logic`. Single-argument, or unary predicates, are used to declare the attributes of objects. For example,

```
complex(Logic)
```

and

```
intelligent(You)
```

Terms. The terms `You` and `Logic` used as arguments in the `understand` relation are examples of *constants* in predicate logic. Constants are named atomic entities of a domain. Here are some other examples of constants:

```
John, 3, Three, Side, Angle, Triangle
```

Notice that the selection of names with which to represent atomic objects in a domain is arbitrary, and multiple names, such as 3 and Three, may be used to refer to the same object. Constant names in predicate logic begin with capital letters.

In addition to the constant, a term in an atomic formula may be a variable.

Variables. Variables in predicate logic are the lowercase letters x, y, and z. Variables are used to generalize statements. An example should make this concept clear. Consider the sentence

You can solve problems if you understand logic.

We can transpose this sentence into predicate logic atomic formulas and then link them with the connective $\longleftarrow$ representing the *if*, thus forming a logic sentence:

solve(You,Problems) $\longleftarrow$ understand(You,Logic)

This sentence now refers to relations of `solve`, `implication`, and `understand` obtaining among the objects `You`, `Problems`, and `Logic`. What if we wished to make this logical relation more general so as to denote any person and not a specific individual (i.e., `You`)? We can do so by using a variable in the place of `You`, as in

solve(x,Problems) $\longleftarrow$ understand(x,Logic)

The sentence is now more general in that it applies to any person who understands logic. Here the variable `x` can bind with any individual for whom the relations expressed in the sentence hold.

However, before a sentence containing a variable can be assigned a truth value, each variable in the sentence must be quantified. In predicate logic, there are two kinds of quantification: *universal* and *existential.*

Existential quantification refers to at least one member of a class of objects. The symbol for existential quantification is ∃ and in logic sentences precedes the variable it modifies as in ∃x. It is read "There exists at least one *x*."

Universal quantification refers to the entire membership of a class. The symbol used is ∀ and it also precedes the variable it modifies, as in "∀x." It is read "for all *x*."

The scope of quantification of variables extends to the entire sentence. That is, a variable, once quantified, has the same meaning wherever that variable occurs throughout the entire logic sentence. Unquantified variables are assumed to be universally quantified.

Functions. In addition to predicates, constants, and variables, terms in formulas may also be functions. To illustrate, `twice` may be used to express a function. The function

```
twice(2,4)
```

expresses the relation of the number 2 to a number twice this number, namely, 4. In this case the relation name is referred to as a *functor*.

Well-formed Formulas. As was the case in propositional logic, atomic formulas may be combined with logical connectives to form sentences or well-formed formulas (wffs). Using the capital letters A and B to represent atomic formulas and the comma for conjunction, ∨ for disjunction, ¬ for negation, ← for implication, and the variable quantifiers ∃ and ∀, we can create the following logic sentences:

A	**(1) assertion**
¬ A	**(2) denial**
A , B	**(3) conjunction**
A ∨ B	**(3) disjunction**
A ← B	**(4) implication**
∃ x A	**(5) there exists an *x* such that *A***
∀ x A	**(6) for all *x*, *A***

The set of all such sentences formed by these procedures is called the language of *first-order logic*. This language is highly expressive, and logicians claim that it can be used to represent any domain of knowledge. Not all AI specialists agree, however.

You will recall from the discussion of propositional logic that truth values depend on the particular interpretation given to the propositions represented as symbols in wffs. The same holds true in first-order logic except that proofs are made more complex by the fact that sentences are complex and composed of atomic formulas that may contain variables.

Once again we will now want to ask the question, "Given that premises are represented as a set of wffs, what conclusions are logically implied by this knowledge?" Note that here we will not consider proofs for establishing the completeness and validity of logical inference. This would take us beyond the scope and intention of this introductory chapter. Interested readers are referred to Hogger (1984) and Kowalski (1979).

Logical Inference. Logical inference in first-order predicate logic is the process of deriving a sentence *s* from a set of sentences *S* by application of a set of one or more inference rules. Hogger (1984) illustrates the inferencing process using but one inference rule in a process called *resolution* first described by J. A. Robinson in 1965. Resolution is a fundamental principle underlying logic programming, and for this reason we will examine it more carefully using examples closely following those offered by Hogger.

The examples used employ three types of sentences: denial, assertion, and implication.

denial :	¬(A1 , . . . , An)
assertion :	A
implication :	A ← B1 , . . . Bm

A, A1 , . . . ,An, B1 , . . . Bm in these sentences represent different predicates.

In the implication sentence, the predicate A on the left side of the arrow is called a *consequent*, and the predicates on the right side are termed *antecedents*.

Our example of resolution begins with two parent sentences and the inference rule referred to earlier as *modus tollens*. Each application of this inference rule constitutes an *inference step*. Note that here A represents the same predicate appearing in both S1 and S2.

denial	S1 : $\neg A$
implication	S2 : A $\longleftarrow$ B

In the first inference step, a new sentence called the *resolvent* is inferred.

s : $\neg B$

That is, assuming "not *A*" and "*A* if *B*" we infer "not *B*."

Take another example with these parent sentences:

S1 : $\neg A$
S2 : A

Here the resolvent is a contradiction or the *empty denial*.

s : □

That is, if we assume "not *A*" and "*A*," we infer a contradiction.

Now let's use resolution in a simple example (logic program) to answer a question relating to a specific domain. The parent sentences are

```
S2 : solve(You,Problems) <—— understand(You,Logic)
S3 : understand(You,Logic)
```

The question we wish to ask is

Can you solve problems?

or in predicate logic form

```
solve(You,Problems)
```

To answer this question, we will start by assuming that the theorem we wish to prove is false. We will then attempt to show, using resolution, that this assumption taken together with the premises of the theorem will lead us to a contradiction. We can then conclude that if the negation of the theorem to be proved is inconsistent with the premises, then its complement must be consistent with the premises.

Once again we start with a denial of the question:

```
S1 : ¬solve(You,Problems)
```

What we want to do is refute this denial using S2 and S3 by showing that when we assume S1, we are led to a contradiction. This method of problem solving is called *proof by contradiction.*

In the first inference step, we resolve S1 with S2 and obtain s:

```
s : ¬understand(You,Logic)
```

That is, assuming "not *A*" and "*A* if *B*," we infer "not *B*."

In the second inference step, we resolve S3 with s, which leads to the contradiction

```
S' : □
```

Using but two inference steps, we have shown that S1, S2, and S3 are contradictory. If we can now accept that S2 and S3 are neither retractable nor contradictory, we can conclude that together they contradict S1. This amounts to affirming the negation of S1, which is, of course,

```
solve(You,Problems)
```

or simply

Yes, you can solve problems.

Although our example has been a simple one, we can conclude that wffs may be used to embody knowledge about the objects and relations of domains and to answer questions about this knowledge. Used in this way, wffs are the axioms that can collectively constitute both a theory of the domain and a logic program that, using resolution, can provide answers to questions about the domain.

What remains of our goals for this chapter is to examine the methods that permit us to implement these principles efficiently in a computational system. I will discuss the methods used by Prolog in the next section as I introduce you to the Prolog programming language.

2.2 INTRODUCTION TO PROLOG

The name Prolog was coined in 1972 as an acronym for *PROgramming in LOGic.* Initial development of the language was the result of a collaborative effort by Alain Colmerauer and Philippe Roussel at the Faculty of Sciences at Luminy in Marseilles,

France. Interest in Prolog and the concept of computation based in logic spread rapidly to universities throughout Europe. Implementations of Prolog have flourished at Cambridge, Edinburgh, the Imperial College at London, Warsaw University in Poland, the University of Waterloo in Canada, the University of New Hampshire in the United States, and at the ICOT project in Japan. One of the first serious applications of Prolog was a large-scale natural-language processing system at Marseilles.

The language did not catch on quickly here in the United States. LISP, a symbolic language developed by McCarthy and his students in the late 1950s at MIT, was the language of choice for most AI researchers. At the time of this writing, however, Prolog is gaining rapidly in popularity among researchers and software developers in the United States. The announcement by Japan's Institute for New Generation Computer Technology (ICOT) that Prolog will be the core language for its fifth-generation computer project has prompted considerable interest in the language.

The availability of Prolog for LISP machines and workstations has provided many researchers in the United States with an opportunity to use the language and test its value for AI research and development. An increasing interest among researchers in logic programming and the relative ease of prototyping made possible by Prolog have also led many to add the language to their tool kits for use in the development of knowledge-based systems.

Historically, Prolog and LISP have been interpreted languages, although compiled versions are now common as well. Both are high-level languages that were developed in large system environments and are known for their healthy appetites for memory and instruction cycles. Today, however, relatively low-cost Prolog interpreters are available for 8088- and 68000-based microcomputers. Several vendors currently advertise Prolog compilers for the Apple Macintosh and the IBM PC microcomputers. These affordable microcomputer Prolog implementations will undoubtedly stimulate interest in the development of small-scale knowledge-based systems for educational and commercial uses.

2.2.1 Declarative Programming

As I explain some of the more salient aspects of declarative programming and the operational procedures of Turbo Prolog, I will also introduce you to the details of Edinburgh Prolog syntax, on which the Turbo Prolog version is loosely based. These syntactic details will be covered again, so you are encouraged to assimilate this material where possible without losing track of the more important discussion of major concepts.

The Prolog language is based on the view that knowledge can be represented logically, that computation is but a special case of logical deduction, and that a high level programming language should permit the programmer to focus attention on the logical description of problems rather than on details of how the computer should handle the data in producing a solution to a problem (Kowalski, 1979).

A Prolog program is made up of a knowledge base containing logic clauses representing *facts* and *rules*, to which is added at run time an end user *query*. This is quite unlike conventional procedural computer languages where programs comprise lists of instructions to the central processing unit detailing how to manipulate the data so as to achieve the single correct output (determinism).

In Prolog, when the user enters a query, the program is executed and the inference engine directs a search for all possible solutions that can satisfy the conditions of the query. As each solution is deduced it is reported to the user. Though it is true that Prolog also has conventional procedural capabilities, it continues to be viewed as primarily a declarative and nondeterministic language by many researchers (Kowalski, 1985).

2.2.2 Closed-world Assumption

It is important to understand that Turbo Prolog recognizes as reality only the facts and rules declared in its knowledge base. Prolog, as an implementation of logic programming, is interested in the logical form but not in the content of axiomatic knowledge. What you and I may know to be a true proposition, such as "the United States is in the Western Hemisphere," is not true for Prolog if it is not either explicitly entered as a fact in the knowledge base or deducible from rules processing the facts in the knowledge base. Furthermore, information that you and I may know to be false, if entered into the knowledge base, will be treated as true. If we assert that the United States is in the Eastern Hemisphere, Prolog will treat this as a true fact.

Prolog will fail to solve our queries about objects and their relations if it does not have supporting clauses in its knowledge base. Whenever Prolog concludes program execution with `False`, this means that it has failed to find a satisfactory solution for our query.

2.2.3 Turbo Prolog Facts

Facts, also called *unit clauses*, are declarations of attributes of objects or relations among objects that are by definition true. Here is an example of a declarative fact:

John likes Mary.

This English sentence expresses the "liking" relation of John for Mary. Here is the fact in Prolog form.

```
likes(john,mary)
```

(The correct use of capital letters for the leading character in proper nouns is suppressed here because john and mary are Prolog terms, called *constants*, and as such must begin with a lowercase letter.)

Notice that the `likes` relation declared here is directional or asymmetric. We may not conclude anything from it about Mary's likes. To do this we would require the fact `likes(mary,john)` in our knowledge base. Note that the `likes` relation can also be represented as a directed graph. In such a digraph the arguments are shown as nodes enclosed in circles connected by a directed labeled arc which represents the relation between the objects.

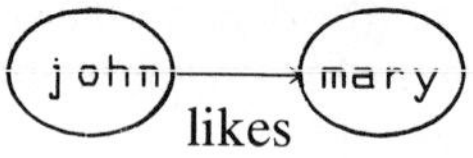

If we were to ask Turbo Prolog to search a knowledge base composed of such facts in order to answer the query

```
likes(john,mary)
```

it would find the matching fact and respond with `True`.

The query can, however, be made more general through the use of another kind of term called a *variable*. Variables in Turbo always begin with a capital letter or the underscore character. Let's use the variable name `Who` in another query.

```
likes(john,Who)
```

Here Turbo would produce the answer

```
Who = mary
```

In actual practice, our knowledge base might contain many facts about things `John` is known to like. Since a variable can stand for any term, this query would nondeterministically produce a listing of all these things.

In Turbo Prolog, the programmer declares the attributes and relations of objects as facts and rules, enters a query, and leaves Turbo Prolog to deduce by the process of matching, unification, and inference the correct answers from the facts and rules in the knowledge base. We will examine this process in great detail shortly.

2.2.4 Turbo Prolog Rules

Rules in Prolog are of two types. A conditional rule is a logic sentence involving a consequent or goal and one or more antecedent conditions to this goal. An unconditional rule is a goal without any antecedent conditions. Rules differ from facts in that variables may be used in rules to make them more general. The Prolog programmer uses rules to draw deductive inferences from the facts in a knowledge base, thereby generating new information.

To illustrate this point, let's consider a problem that will allow us to write our first Prolog program. Keep in mind that Prolog syntax will depart somewhat from what we have seen in the previous section on predicate logic. We will start with a collection of facts expressed in English shown in Table 2.3.

TABLE 2.3 FACTS IN ENGLISH FORM

	Object	Relationship	Object
Fact 1	John	does well in	math.
Fact 2	John	is interested in	accounting.
Fact 3	Math	is important in	accounting.
Fact 4	Accounting	is in demand.	

Remember, we must enter proper nouns into the knowledge base using a lowercase leading letter to signify to Turbo Prolog that the word is the name of a constant object from the domain. Variables, on the other hand, always begin with either a capital letter or an underscore character. By this definition, the following are all variables:

```
X, Y, Z, PERSON, _x1, _Y, _foo, _Foo, _
```

Notice that the names selected to serve as variables in our programs have a meaning that helps us to understand the program and the intent of queries. You should get into the habit of doing this also as it will help you in both reading your programs and in understanding Turbo Prolog's output. Using meaningful names is possible because Turbo Prolog preserves variable names during the compilation procedure. You will see that this is a feature that will simplify writing and debugging programs. Some Prolog implementations convert variable names from words to numbers, making code much more difficult to read during traces of program execution.

Turbo Prolog recognizes several types of objects as data. Some of these objects are simple, such as variables, constants, symbols, and integers. Other objects, such as structures and lists, are complex because they are made up of component objects. Compound objects will be discussed in some depth in Chapter 4.

As you can see from Figure 2.1, a constant in Turbo Prolog can be either an atom or a number. An atom is an indivisible unit: a character, symbol, or string. A number may be either an integer with no decimals or a real number in which decimals are allowed.

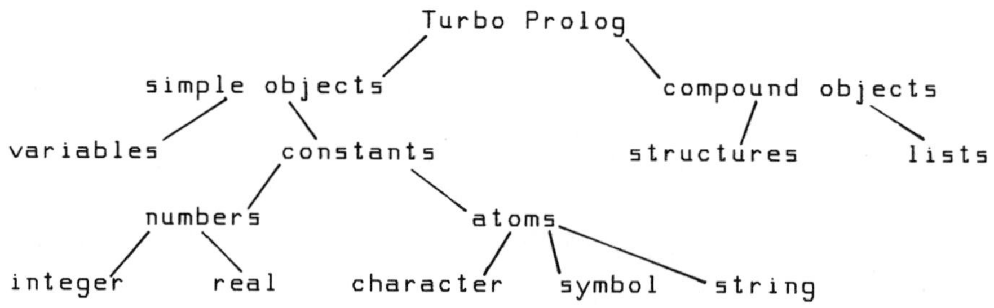

Figure 2.1 Turbo Prolog data objects.

A string is a series of characters, including capitals, underscores, and spaces surrounded by double quotes. Strings are treated as a single unit in Turbo Prolog.

```
"This sentence is 1 example of a Turbo Prolog string."
```

A character is a single ASCII character (the nonprinting space included) surrounded by single quotation marks, as in

```
'a', ' ', 'Z'
```

Constants such as `john` are by definition atoms. More specifically, they belong to the Turbo Prolog data domain called *symbol*. Underscores are commonly used in symbols to make names more meaningful and readable while preserving their status as atoms. For example, `is_in_demand` is highly readable yet remains a Prolog atom.

Now let's return to our example and convert the English statements into Prolog facts. Notice that the first fact in Table 2.3 expresses the relation `does_well_in()` between `john` and `math`. In general, a binary relation exists when the predicate expresses a relation between two arguments. The last fact is a unary predicate; that is, the predicate `is_in_demand()` takes the single argument `accounting`.

It is standard practice in the Edinburgh syntactic form of Prolog for a predicate and its arguments to be expressed in the form

```
predicate(argument-1,argument-2,...,argument-n).
```

This is termed *prefix syntax*. In prefix syntax, a predicate precedes arguments that are enclosed in parentheses and separated by commas. Each fact is terminated by a period. Do not confuse this use of punctuation with the logical connective symbols comma and period. Here the comma is used only to separate conditions and the period merely signals the end of a clause.

In some versions of Prolog, infix and postfix syntactic forms are used. To avoid confusion, further discussion of these forms of syntax will be deferred to Appendix B of this book. It is best for you to start learning Turbo Prolog by

TABLE 2.4 FACTS IN TURBO PROLOG PREFIX FORM

	Predicate Argument(s)	Relation Type
Fact 1	`does_well_in(john,math).`	Binary
Fact 2	`is_interested_in(john,accounting).`	Binary
Fact 3	`is_important_in(math,accounting).`	Binary
Fact 4	`is_in_demand(accounting).`	Unary

considering only prefix syntax. After you have been programming for awhile, the other syntactic forms you may encounter will cause you little difficulty.

Throughout this book you will see facts in the form shown in Table 2.4. The first predicate can be read "John does well in math." It is a useful convention to put the subject of the English reading in the first argument slot and the object in the second. After some experience, you will have little difficulty reading these terms. A similar logic can be used for relations with more than two arguments (n-ary):

```
studies(john,math,accounting).
```

This Prolog fact has the English reading "John studies math and accounting."

Remember that once a scheme for the ordering of arguments in a relation has been selected, it must be maintained throughout the program. If the scheme is not maintained, the program may run anyway, but most likely not according to the planned logic. In Turbo Prolog, it is more likely that the program will not even compile. This is because Turbo Prolog is strongly "typed," and if the terms of a predicate are of different data domains, the compiler will abort execution.

If a college counselor were to advise John regarding the choice of a major course of study, the following heuristic might apply:

> IF a student is interested in a discipline AND the student is demonstrably capable in a subject AND this subject is basic to some discipline AND the professionals practicing this discipline are in demand THEN the student should major in this discipline in college.

Here the heuristic is cast in the form of a production rule. It can be translated into Prolog form as follows:

```
should_major_in(Student,Discipline) :-          Head of the Rule
   is_interested_in(Student,Discipline),  }
   does_well_in(Student,Subject),         }  Body of the Rule
   is_important_in(Subject,Discipline),   }
   is_in_demand(Discipline).              }
```

Spend a few moments comparing the two forms of this rule. Notice that in the Prolog rule, the goal or consequent is stated in the head of the rule. The antecedent conditions of the goal are declared in the body of the rule.

Prolog uses a subset of first-order logic sentences called Horn clauses. Horn clauses have a single unnegated goal stated in the head of the rule with conditions called *literals* declared after the `if` (neck) in the body. Furthermore, the head of the rule must not contain the quantifiers `forall` or `exists`, negation, or multiple goals. The following are illegal clauses in Turbo prolog:

```
not(should_major_in(Student,Discipline)) :-
                     ......................,
                     ......................,
                     ......................

likes_sports(Person), plays_sports(Person) :-
                     ......................,
                     ......................,
                     ......................
```

Turbo Prolog, like the standard Edinburgh version of Prolog, recognizes the symbol `:-` (a colon followed by a dash) as a substitute for `if` and the comma `,` separating literals in a clause as the logical connective `and`. If you find this notation too cryptic, Turbo Prolog will also accept `if` and `and` in rules. It is suggested, however, that you adhere to the original Edinburgh syntactic form as this will maximize the ease with which programs written in Turbo Prolog can be ported over to standard Prolog implementations. Notice the use of descriptive variable names beginning with capital letters.

2.2.5 Querying Turbo Prolog

Let's look at how Turbo Prolog answers queries. Assume that these four facts and one rule are entered into the Turbo editor. After compiling the program, you could present Turbo Prolog with the query

```
should_major_in(john,What).
```

Turbo Prolog would respond with

```
What = accounting
```

You can see from Table 2.4 that the knowledge base does not contain this fact. To solve this query Turbo Prolog had to use the rule to establish by inference the conclusion "John should major in accounting." To do this Turbo Prolog searched the knowledge base and found a match for the query

```
should_major_in(john,What)
```

in the head of the rule that reads

```
should_major_in(Student,Discipline)
```

This is a match because the arguments in the head of the rule are variables and Turbo Prolog may match such a query to either a fact or the head of a rule where the predicates match exactly and the arguments of the query and the clause can be unified.

2.2.6 Unification

Unification is the procedure by which Turbo Prolog matches and makes equal terms in the controlled process of searching for solutions to queries. The conditions for unification are summarized in the following rules.

- A free variable (currently unbound to any term) can be unified (bound) with any term. Thus the variable `Student` in the query can be bound to the constant `john` and the variables `What` and `Discipline` bound to each other.
- A constant can unify with itself or with a free (unbound) variable.
- A compound term can unify with another compound term provided they both have the same functor or predicate and they have the same number of arguments and all paired subterms similarly unify.

Unification makes possible the following essential programming procedures:

- The assignment of values to variables (i.e., parameter passing).
- Accessing information in data structures using variables and pattern matching.
- The performance of tests of equality. An example of this is seen in the user-defined unconditional rule `equals(X,X)`. If this rule is called with `equals(3,3)`, it will succeed directly because of unification (X and X unify).

Let's continue with our example. Through unification, Turbo Prolog was able to match the user query to the head of the rule. Since the rule has conditions, Turbo Prolog must next prove this conjunction of literals in the order in which they appear in the body of the rule.

2.2.7 Instantiation and Scope of Variables

In our example, Turbo Prolog bound the variable `Student` to the constant term `john`. Furthermore, this binding, called *instantiation*, occurred everywhere the variable `Student` appeared in the rule. This is because the scope of variable instantiation in Prolog encompasses an entire rule. Variables of the same name in other rules, however, remain unaffected by this binding.

After this initial instantiation, the clause appeared as follows:

```
should_major_in(john,Discipline) :-
        is_interested_in(john,Discipline),
        does_well_in(john,Subject),
        is_important_in(Subject,Discipline),
        is_in_demand(Discipline).
```

The first condition to the goal states

```
is_interested_in(john,Discipline)
```

Turbo Prolog searched for a match and found it in fact 2:

```
is_interested_in(john,accounting)
```

Through unification, the variable `Discipline` was instantiated to the term `accounting` wherever the variable `Discipline` appeared in the rule. The rule then read

```
should_major_in(john,accounting) :-
        is_interested_in(john,accounting),
        does_well_in(john,Subject),
        is_important_in(Subject,accounting),
        is_in_demand(accounting).
```

As you can see from an inspection of the head of the rule, Turbo Prolog has arrived at an answer to the query by proving the first condition. However, logical inference decrees that Turbo Prolog has to prove all the (top-down) conditions if the goal is to be proved true. Prolog proceeded to prove the next condition,

```
does_well_in(john,Subject)
```

`Subject` now remained as the only free variable in the clause. Turbo Prolog began another search of the knowledge base (top-down) looking for a matching fact and unified `Subject` to `math` using fact 1. `Subject` was now bound to the constant `math` throughout the rule. All the variables in the rule are instantiated; however, Prolog had yet to prove the remaining conditions.

The next condition states

```
is_important_in(math,accounting)
```

Prolog searched and found a match with fact 3.

The final condition,

```
is_in_demand(accounting)
```

was also found and as all conditions had been proved, the entire rule was proved. Keep in mind that the query succeeded because, through unification, matches were found in the knowledge base for all conditions in the body of the rule.

Prolog then printed the value of the variable `Discipline`, (i.e., accounting) to the screen along with a `True` to signal its success in solving for the query. Had any one of the conditions of the rule failed, the entire rule would also have failed and Prolog would have responded with `False`.

To sum up, the user defined the domain by declaring salient facts and a rule. Supplied with a specific query, Prolog used its built-in searching, inferencing, and unification procedures to infer a value for the variable in the query and thereby provide an answer to the query. Had the query not employed a variable, perhaps because the user anticipated the correct answer and simply wanted verification, Turbo Prolog would have responded with a simple `True` or `False`. That is,

```
should_major_in(john,accounting).
```

would elicit from Turbo Prolog the response `True`, and

```
should_major_in(john,psychology).
```

would return `False`.

2.2.8 Backtracking to Solutions

You have seen Turbo Prolog's strategy of backward chaining and depth-first searching in answering queries. It is backward chaining because the process starts with the goal statement in the head of the first rule that matches the query and works backward to proofs of any conditions to that goal in the body of the rule. It is depth-first searching because one rule is exhaustively proved before the next candidate rule is selected and any "child" rules invoked by a condition in a "parent" rule are proved first before Prolog continues to prove any remaining conditions in the parent rule.

In our elementary example, matches were found for all conditions of the goal. Solutions for queries are, however, seldom this simple. More typically, should Prolog fail to find a match for a condition in a child rule, it must back up to the point of last binding in order to continue the search for a match further down in the knowledge base. This procedure is called *backtracking*. Once again, I will use a concrete example to introduce this important concept.

Consider the following simple Prolog program. The line numbers are provided for convenience and are not part of the program.

Line Numbers	Clauses
1	`body_contact(hockey).`
2	`body_contact(basketball).`
3	`fast_paced(ping_pong).`
4	`fast_paced(hockey).`
5	`fast_paced(basketball).`
6	`fast_paced(badminton).`
7	`played_with(hockey,puck).`
8	`played_with(ping_pong,ball).`
9	`played_with(basketball,ball).`
10	`played_with(badminton,birdie).`
11	`likes_sport(john,X) :-`
12	`        has_action(X),`
13	`        played_with(X,ball).`
14	`has_action(X) :-`
15	`        body_contact(X),`
16	`        fast_paced(X).`

As I discuss Prolog's strategy for producing solutions, I will provide a step-by-step program trace of the path to solution. For now, just follow this trace mentally. Later on, when you have mastered the skills necessary to create and run a Turbo Prolog program, you may wish to return to this example and follow the steps to solution using the program trace facility provided by Borland.

1. A query succeeds when Prolog finds a matching fact in the knowledge base, so if we enter the following query, Prolog will return `True`.

```
Goal: fast_paced(hockey).
True
```

Note that the fact at line 4 matches the query, and since there is no variable value to report, Prolog simply answers `True`.

2. In the case of a goal made up of subgoals, the subgoals must be satisfied in the order they appear.

```
Goal : body_contact(X),fast_paced(X).
X = hockey
X = basketball
True
```

The first solution was achieved by finding a match for `body_contact(X)`. This occurred at line 1, and `X` was instantiated to `hockey`. Turbo Prolog then attempted to prove `fast_paced(hockey)`. Remember that the scope of instantiation for variables is a single rule or, in this case, the entire list of subgoals of a query. The second goal found a match at line 4 and

```
X = hockey
```

was then printed to the screen.

Since there are no more ways to prove this conjunction of goals, Turbo Prolog then returned variables to their status prior to the last binding and backtracked in the knowledge base to where the first subgoal was matched (not all the way back to the top). Turbo Prolog can easily return to values of variables prior to bindings because it produces internal copies or variants of variables and works with these while storing the originals for reuse later in the program cycle should backtracking become necessary.

Turbo Prolog then searched for an alternative match for `body_contact(X)` and found it at line 2 and `X` is now instantiated to `basketball`. Prolog next attempted to find a match for `fast_paced(basketball)` by starting at the top of the knowledge base and found the match at line 5. `X = basketball` was next printed to the screen. There are no more clauses with which to match `body_contact(X)` so Turbo Prolog terminated with `True`.

3. Clauses are tested in the order in which they are listed in the knowledge base, that is, from top to bottom. We will see that this means that the order in which you enter clauses into the knowledge base can affect the answers you get to queries!

4. When a query matches the head of a rule, each condition of the rule must be proved in the order first to last.

```
Goal: likes_sport(john,X).
```

This query matches the head of the rule at line 11. The conditions of the rule at lines 12 and 13 must now be proved for the query to succeed. `has_action(X)` is first to be proved.

This subgoal finds a match with the head of another rule at line 14. Now the conditions of this rule at lines 15 and 16 must be proved before returning to the remaining condition of the previous rule. Let's review what has happened. The query began with the single goal

```
likes_sport(john,X).
```

To solve this goal, Prolog invoked a rule and its conditions replaced the original goal. These subgoals then had to be proved. The first of these conditions matched with the head of another rule. As long as Turbo Prolog encounters rules and their conditions, it will build a list of goals with the ones encountered last added to the head of the list. This is, in fact, a functional definition of the term *depth-first searching*.

The condition to prove is now `body_contact(X)`. This matches the fact at line 1 and `X` is instantiated to hockey. The last condition of the `has_action()` rule now reads `fast_paced(hockey)`. Remember that the scope of instantiation covers the entire rule and wherever `X` occurs in `has_action()` it takes on the value `hockey`. A match for `fast_paced(hockey)` is found at line 4.

The rule `has_action(hockey)` has been proved. Control returns to the final condition of the `likes_sport()` rule which is now

```
played_with(hockey,ball).
```

This goal fails as there is no matching fact or head of a rule in the knowledge base.

Here is where Prolog must backtrack to look for alternatives. You will recall that `X` acquired the value `hockey` by matching the first condition [`body_ contact(X)`] of the `has_action(X)` rule with the fact at line 1. Now Prolog uninstantiates `X` and returns to the point just after line 1 and begins another search for a match for `body_contact(X)`. It finds a match at line 2 and `X` is instantiated to `basketball`. Prolog matches the condition `fast_paced (basketball)` at line 5 and in doing so, proves `has_action (basketball)`.

All that is left is to prove the final condition `played_with (basketball,ball)`. This subgoal finds a match at line 9 and `likes_sport(john,basketball)` is proved.

Be sure to note the two crucial events that occurred in this complicated process of searching and matching:

a. When a matching fact for a condition was found in the knowledge base, the constant value in the match was instantiated with the corresponding variable throughout the entire rule or query list. For example, when a match was found for `body_contact(X)` with the fact `body_contact(hockey)`, `X` was instantiated to `hockey` throughout the rule.

b. When Prolog failed to match a condition to a fact in the knowledge base, it backtracked to where the last instantiation had taken place, uninstantiated any variables, and continued on with the original search. Prolog abandoned `likes_sport(john,hockey)` because it could not find a matching fact for `played_with(hockey,ball)`. Prolog then continued on to search for an alternative match lower in the knowledge base.

Prolog maintains, in a memory area called a *pushdown stack*, a record of addresses of where in the knowledge base it has found matches. It can then, if necessary, go back to renew a search at a point in the knowledge base just after the last match.

5. Turbo Prolog carries an instantiated value(s) forward for further matching in subsequent clauses. Failure to find a match causes Turbo Prolog to uninstantiate the variable(s) and backtrack to where it made this instantiation in order to look for alternative matches.

The following is a more formal statement of the unification procedure that underlies all this matching. This algorithm is described in a number of authoritative sources (Bratko, 1986; Hogger, 1984; Kowalski, 1979; Kluzniak & Szpakowicz, 1985; Sterling & Shapiro, 1986; Campbell, 1984; Cohen, 1985), to which you are encouraged to refer. Our discussion of unification follows closely after Bratko.

The process begins with a user query, that is, a goal or a series of goals which we will represent here as `G1 ,G2 , . . . ,Gm`.

When the list of goals in a query is empty, Turbo Prolog will terminate execution and print the values of any variables used in the query to the user, followed by `True`.

If the list of goals is not empty, then Turbo Prolog will invoke a procedure that I will arbitrarily call SOLVE.

Solve.

1. Turbo Prolog will take the first goal `G1` in the list of goals `G1 ,G2 , . . . ,Gm` and search the knowledge base, starting at the top, for a match. This match may be with either a fact or the head of a rule.

If there is no match to be found, then Turbo Prolog will terminate program execution and print `False`. Backtracking in this instance is impossible because, as the first goal has failed, there are no parent clauses to which Prolog can backtrack.

If a matching fact is found, the goal is satisfied and this goal is removed from the list of goals in the query. Remember that finding matching facts and eliminating goals from the query list is what the SOLVE process is all about.

2. If a match for `G1` is made with the head of a rule, we will call this rule `R`:

```
R :-
    A1 ,
    A2,
    . . . ,
    An.
```

Turbo Prolog will rename any variables in this clause `R` to produce `R'` (*R* prime) so that `G1` and `R'` have no variables in common. `R'` is called a variant of `R`.

```
R':-
    A1',
    A2',
    . . . ,
    An'.
```

Turbo Prolog will unify `G1` and `R'` and call the instantiated variables `S`.

3. In the goal list

```
G1,G2,...,Gm
```

G1 is replaced by the preconditions of R′ which are

```
A1′,A2′,...An′
```

The goal list now is

```
A1′,A2′,...,An′,G2,...,Gm
```

4. Turbo Prolog next substitutes for the appropriate variables in this list the values of S. This is now a new list of goals represented as

```
A1″,A2″,...,An″,G2′,...,Gm′
```

Turbo Prolog recursively executes the procedure SOLVE with this new list of goals. (Note that in the event that a recursive call to SOLVE fails, then Turbo Prolog will return to the point of the last binding and try to find an alternative match farther down in the knowledge base.) If this new list of goals is successful, then Turbo will terminate the original list with True. If this new list of goals is not successful, then it will abandon this new list and return and start searching at the point just after the clause R and try again. If all attempts to find a match fail, then Turbo Prolog will terminate with False.

2.3 STRENGTHS AND LIMITATIONS OF TURBO PROLOG

An attractive feature of Prolog is its built-in inference engine. This feature permits the AI program developer to save considerable time and effort that would normally be expended in designing and building an inference engine. The Prolog language is particularly useful in rapid development of KBS prototypes for trying out designs, debugging, and maintaining the participation of the domain expert who might otherwise lose interest during a protracted development cycle.

As you know, Prolog is a declarative language and a software specification can also be a Prolog program. Program development is enhanced through the use of logic for both specification and implementation.

Turbo Prolog's problem-solving strategy is founded in principles of logical inference, yet it must be noted that the language is not an ideal implementation of logic programming principles. Searches are made from the top down and the order in which facts and rules are entered into a program can influence solutions. In the ideal logic system, inferencing would not be affected by the ordering of facts and rules.

The logic programming ideal is a nondeterministic system. In practice the Turbo Prolog programmer often finds it necessary to modify the nondeterministic behavior of Prolog. This is particularly true in cases where the programmer uses procedures for their side-effects or must, in the interests of efficiency, modify Prolog's searching behavior by using the cut. The cut is notoriously deterministic and, used carelessly, it can have unpredictable consequences. We will learn more about the cut and program control in Chapter 3.

One of the strengths of Borland's implementation of Prolog is that programs normally compiled in RAM may also be compiled to disk as native code. This permits conversion of debugged source code into stand-alone `exe` programs. By this method, the programmer can develop programs that run very efficiently, even on a stock PC. It also means that an application program can be executed independently of the Turbo Prolog compiler. You simply execute it from the operating system prompt. Because of this, the Borland Turbo Prolog compiler is needed only for the development of programs. There are no run-time costs associated with use of your programs once they have been fully tested and compiled in `exe` form.

To achieve efficiency, the Borland people have made some trade-offs and compromises with the Prolog "standard" outlined in the authoritative work by Clocksin and Mellish (1984). For example, Turbo Prolog is a strongly typed language. This restricts the programmer's freedom in using terms and expressions as arguments. Also, some of the "tried and true" primitives are missing in this version of the language. Longtime Prolog programmers will miss `functor()`, `arg()`, `univ()`, `call()`, and `clause()` when manipulating clauses and when writing meta-level programs (see the Borland publication "Turbo Technix" as a source for many "workarounds"). And very important, Turbo Prolog does not allow the programmer to `assert()` or `retract()` rules to the dynamic database. More about this in Chapter 8.

Also, Turbo Prolog does not support virtual databases, so working with large knowledge bases requires some additional overhead and programming effort in defining convenience procedures for manipulating files out on disk. However, these omissions are on the whole balanced by many additions to what has come to be accepted as "core" Prolog.

Turbo Prolog provides several predicates for floating-point arithmetic as well as bit-level manipulations of data. There is also easy access to DOS functions from within Turbo Prolog programs. Borland has also added many file- and screen-handling predicates and a "tool box" of procedures that will be most useful in developing professional-looking and effective programs.

On balance, Borland has provided the programming public with a well-designed, efficient, and accessible vehicle for working with this powerful fifth-generation language, a vehicle that can be used to develop a variety of small to medium-sized knowledge-based systems.

This has been a difficult chapter. However, all your efforts here have been well spent, for it is very important that you understand both the logical foundations of Turbo Prolog and the specific procedures by which Prolog solves goals. I recommend that you return to this chapter later to review the examples and explanations. Your understanding of these fundamental concepts will deepen with each reading.

2.4 SUMMARY

Concepts covered

Backtracking
Binary predicates
Closed-world assumption
Conjunction
Disjunction
Edinburgh syntax
Inference
Instantiation
Negation
Prefix syntax
Prolog facts and rules
Prolog objects
- Atoms
- Characters
- Constants
- Integers
- Reals
- Strings
- Symbols
- Variables

Quantification of variables
Querying Prolog
Resolution
Scope of variable instantiation
Searching
Unary predicates
Unification

Prolog is a logic-based approach to programming developed by Colmerauer and Roussel in Marseilles in 1972. The language represents a significant conceptual departure from the procedural languages that have been used up to now in producing software. Prolog solves problems using a knowledge base of facts and rules and a built-in inferencing system. The inferencing system uses the facts and rules to find or deduce new facts needed to solve problems (queries). Although the language is largely nondeterministic, some extralogical features are provided for purposes of program control, interactivity, and user convenience.

A Turbo Prolog fact is a logical assertion with the implicit assumption of truth. Binary facts are stated in prefix form such as `likes(john,mary)`, which has the English meaning John likes Mary. Facts do not use variables as terms.

Prolog rules may be either conditional or unconditional and variables are used as terms in both to make them general in scope. Unconditional rules express a general relationship that lacks conditions of proof. Conditional rules also express a general relationship but they have conditions that must be satisfied for the relation to hold. Conditions in rules are conjunctive or disjunctive and may be negated. The head of a rule must have but one unnegated literal. Here is an example of a conditional rule:

```
likes(X,Y) :-
        enjoys(X,Z),
        enjoys(Y,Z).
```

An English reading of this rule is "Someone likes someone else if they both enjoy the same thing."

Prolog solves queries by searching top-down through its knowledge base for matching terms that will permit unification and instantiation of variables. Failure to produce matches prompts Turbo Prolog to backtrack to find alternatives. The basic inferencing scheme is top-down resolution.

The powerful inference engine built into Prolog permits the rapid development of complex programs such as expert systems.

2.5 EXERCISES

1. Review the following terms to be sure you understand them before moving on to the next chapter:
   - **a.** resolution
   - **b.** classical logic
   - **c.** symbolic logic
   - **d.** syllogism
   - **e.** class
   - **f.** term
   - **g.** proposition
   - **h.** well-formed formula
   - **i.** predicate logic
   - **j.** interpretation
   - **k.** implication
   - **l.** instantiation
   - **m.** conjunction
   - **n.** disjunction
   - **o.** negation
   - **p.** variable
   - **q.** closed-world assumption
   - **r.** Horn clause
   - **s.** backtracking
   - **t.** scope of variables
   - **u.** backward chaining
   - **v.** depth-first searching
2. Do you understand the relationships between propositional logic, predicate logic, the language of first-order logic, and Prolog?
3. What role do the logical connectives play in the Prolog goal resolution mechanism?
4. What is essential to the success or failure of a rule?
5. Do you understand how Prolog concluded that `John` should major in `accounting`? If not, you should review that section before moving on!

6. Can you review the steps in unification and explain them to another student?
7. Trace the steps Turbo Prolog takes in solving for the following queries given the program below. Letters are used and are assumed to have the syntax of clauses. For each query, make an ordered list of the subgoals (conditions of an invoked rule) Turbo Prolog must prove. Indicate where goals fail and backtracking will occur.

	Knowledge Base	
Queries	Rules	Facts
`Goal: a.`	`a :- b, k.`	`d.`
`Goal: b.`	`b :- d, e, f.`	`e.`
`Goal: c.`	`b :- c, d.`	`f.`
`Goal: h.`	`c :- g, j.`	`g.`
`Goal: a, f.`	`c :- h, i.`	`h.`
`Goal: b, i.`		`i.`
		`k.`

Chapter 3
Up and Running

CHAPTER OBJECTIVES

Study of this chapter should enable you to do the following:

1. Discuss the program declarations required in Turbo Prolog.
2. Give examples of the use of comments in programs.
3. Enter facts and rules into a program.
4. Enter CLAUSES, PREDICATES, and GOAL declarations for a program.
5. Form queries using external and internal goals.
6. Trace program execution, using mental traces and the Turbo Prolog trace facility, and discuss program backtracking and unification.
7. Query and trace a program using a conjunction of goals.
8. Define rules as logic clauses.
9. Write a rule that implements disjunction using the ; operator and show how two rules accomplish the same result.
10. Use the `assert()` and `retract()` primitives to add and remove facts in a dynamic database.
11. Define red and green cuts and discuss their benefits and dangers.
12. Discuss negation and its use in logic programs.
13. Explain uses of the `fail` primitive, including the `cut` and `fail` combination.

IMPORTANT TERMS AND PHRASES

Anonymous variables
Binary relations
Compiled code
Data types
Debugging
Dynamic database
External goal
Extralogical primitives
Keywords
Procedure box control flow model
Program declarations
Program tracing
Red and green cuts
Resatisfying goals
Semantic and procedural interpretation
Static database

3.1 GETTING STARTED USING TURBO PROLOG

In Chapter 2 we examined the Turbo Prolog goal resolution mechanism and syntax governing the use of facts and rules. In this chapter we will take a look at the details of implementing programs in the Turbo Prolog programming environment.

I will assume that you have loaded the Turbo Prolog program and you are ready to enter some facts and rules. If you are not familiar with the procedures for using the editor, loading, and running programs, refer to the Turbo Prolog and PC DOS manuals before continuing. The menu-driven Turbo Prolog system is an outstanding example of a well-designed and intuitive program interface, so a little practice should be all that is required for you to continue.

3.1.1 Structure of a Turbo Prolog Program

Before a Turbo Prolog program can be executed, it must be converted by the compiler from Turbo Prolog source code, which the programmer understands, to machine code, which the computer understands. Turbo Prolog programs are divided into sections. Each section, headed by an identifier, contains information declared by the programmer and used by the compiler in generating efficient machine code.

The program identifiers we will use include DOMAINS, DATABASE, PREDICATES, CONSTANTS, CLAUSES, FILE, and GOAL. (Note that the Turbo Prolog compiler recognizes both uppercase and lowercase spelling of keywords; however, I will use identifiers in capital letters to help the reader pick out declarations in source code.)

The GOAL section is used to provide a program with an internal start-up goal. It is common practice to start a program here with a driver rule that performs setup procedures or prompts for the user to provide initializing input. Examples of the use of GOAL declarations will be provided in demonstration programs throughout this book.

The PREDICATES section contains a declaration for each predicate and terms that are to be used in the program. CONSTANTS declarations are one of many new features added in Version 2.0. This declaration allows the programmer to use what amounts to *macros* in programs. The CLAUSES section contains the actual clauses or program code.

Programs that employ dynamic facts store them by default in an internal database. *Dynamic facts* are unit clauses that are added or removed during program execution. Turbo Prolog requires that these predicates and their terms be declared in a DATABASE section. Dynamic changes to the program state can be made in one or more internal databases stored in RAM or in extended memory. These changes last only for the duration of program execution. To make these changes permanent, the programmer must save them in a file on disk. We will learn more about the use of dynamic database facts later in this chapter.

Programs that use compound terms will require a DOMAINS section. Compound terms will be discussed in Chapter 4, with examples and explanation of declarations given at that time. FILE declarations are needed in programs that read and write to files.

The programmer may elect to build a program in pieces or in modules that are linked together at compile time. Modularized programs require that the GLOBAL forms of DOMAINS, PREDICATES, and DATABASE declarations be made in the master module. This is useful technique for the advanced Prolog programmer and is well documented in the Turbo Prolog manual.

This brief discussion of declarations is intended only to draw your attention to this necessary feature of Turbo Prolog programs. In the remainder of this book, detailed explanations for each type of declaration will be provided as we develop programs that actually require them. In this fashion, each explanation can be paired with an immediate application to ensure that you understand the concepts involved.

In this chapter we will develop a toy auto expert system using the most elementary type of Turbo Prolog program structure. This simple example is presented to be sure that you grasp the proper use of syntax and basic programming principles. Larger and much more interesting programs will be developed after you have mastered the basic techniques. Initially our auto program will include only PREDICATES and CLAUSES compiler declarations. As features are added to the program, DATABASE, GOAL, and DOMAINS declarations will be added.

3.1.2 Selecting a Name for Your Program

We will start by entering some facts for a program, which I will name AUTO_1.PRO. You may, of course, select another name for the program, but be forewarned that this name must not violate any of the rules of either the DOS operating system or the Turbo Prolog compiler. If in doubt, consult both DOS and Prolog manuals for details on the syntax of legal file names. Briefly, a legal file name for your Prolog source code program must not contain more than eight alphanumeric characters, and no embedded spaces or slashes are allowed.

Turbo Prolog will add a `.PRO` extension to all your programs as they are saved to disk. When editing, be sure you do not exit Turbo Prolog before saving your program or it will be lost permanently. Turbo Prolog will provide you with a prompt to remind you that you have not as yet saved an edited file. If you want to save the file, just answer `yes` at the prompt. Remember that programs exist only in RAM until they are saved to disk for permanent storage.

3.1.3 Commenting in a Program

You will want to begin by writing your program name as a comment statement.

```
/*     AUTO_1.PRO     */
```

Prolog will ignore anything, including newlines, enclosed within the comment statement characters /* and */. Be careful to get the sequence of the slash and the asterisk in the correct order. If you have version 2.0 of Turbo Prolog, you may also enter comments on lines using %. Anything entered after the % and before a newline will be ignored.

```
my_rule(X,Y) :-          % This comment is ignored.
   condition(Y,Z).       % So is this one.
```

Commenting with the % was added in version 2.0 as part of Borland's effort to bring Turbo Prolog closer to Edinburgh syntax.

It is a good idea to get used to documenting your programs with comment statements. The declarative nature of Prolog makes reading small programs easy; however, large programs are something else. Comments in larger programs will be invaluable as you refresh your memory regarding program functions.

3.1.4 Entering Facts into a Knowledge Base

Enter the editor and type in the following 10 Prolog facts under the keyword CLAUSES. Don't overlook the period at the end of each fact. The CLAUSES keyword in programs tells Turbo Prolog that program rules (conditional and unconditional) and facts (unit clauses) follow.

```
                              Editor

                    /* AUTO_1.PRO */
            /* A simple auto expert system */
CLAUSES   % Keyword for declaration
caused_by(flat_tire,faulty_valve).
caused_by(flat_tire,blowout).
caused_by(knocking_in_engine,low_octane_gas).
caused_by(poor_gas_mileage,dirty_spark_plugs).
caused_by(stalling,vapor_lock).
caused_by(poor_acceleration,timing_adjustment).
caused_by(poor_ride,worn_shocks).
caused_by(worn_tires,wheel_alignment).
caused_by(brake_squeal,hard_linings).
caused_by(brake_squeal,worn_linings).
```

After you have typed in the comments, the keyword, and the 10 facts, check everything carefully for syntax and spelling errors. Constantly checking for accuracy is a good habit to acquire, especially for the inept typist. However, Turbo Prolog is very helpful in these matters. If you commit a syntax error and fail to correct it before running the program, Turbo Prolog will bring it to your attention by aborting program execution and returning the cursor to the editor window at, or very close to, the location of the error. Spelling errors in relations are caught as Prolog matches them to the list of declared predicates in the PREDICATES section of the program. In the event of a misspelled predicate, Turbo Prolog will complain that it has found an undeclared predicate.

Each of the Prolog facts in `AUTO_1.PRO` states a causal relation obtaining between two domain objects. The facts have as a template

```
caused_by(the_effect,the_cause).
```

The first term is a symptom of auto malfunction and the second a cause of the problem. Notice that some symptoms, such as `flat_tire` and `brake_squeal`, may have two causes, in which case there are two facts entered into the program. The order of these arguments for the `caused_by()` relation or predicate is very important to the successful functioning of the program but of no real consequence to Prolog. You might have chosen to represent the knowledge using an alternative template.

```
causes(the_cause,the_effect).
```

Here the order of the arguments is reversed. This is a program design option during the knowledge representation and design stages of program development. Be careful to think through carefully what the program is supposed to do and, after selecting a scheme, adhere to it faithfully throughout the program.

Before you can query this simple program, information about the predicates and their objects must be declared. The reasons for PREDICATES declarations relate to the fact that the compiler expects terms to be one of six domain types. This is called *datatyping*. To function efficiently, Turbo Prolog must know the domain types of terms prior to compilation. The data domains recognized by Turbo Prolog are listed in Table 3.1.

Providing Turbo Prolog with needed information about domain objects is a process that may appear mystifying at first. In fact it is quite simple. In the case of AUTO_1.PRO it is especially simple because the domain objects will always be symbols. All you need do is identify the predicates you will be using in a PREDICATES section. Then specify symbol in each argument slot of each predicate.

Compound terms, where arguments are constructed using simple terms, will require the more complex user-defined DOMAINS declaration. I will show you how to do this in Chapter 6 when we use structures and lists in programs.

TABLE 3.1 TURBO PROLOG STANDARD DOMAIN TYPES

char	An ASCII character enclosed in single quotes (e.g., `'a'`, `'X'`, `'q'`).
integer	Integers in the range −32,768 to 32,767.

real	Numbers following an optional sign, then an optional decimal point and numbers for the fractional component. This may be followed by an optional exponent part; for example:
	`34.9`
	`+56`
	`-745.65`
	`934.61e+14`
	`-11.04e-23`

string	A sequence of characters enclosed by quotation marks. `"This is an example!"`

symbol	(1) A sequence of letters, numbers, and underscores where the first character must be lowercase or (2) a sequence of letters surrounded by quotation marks that permits use of symbols with spaces or leading capital letters; for example:
	`has_action`
	`"likes sport"`
	`"Major_subject"`

file	A file is declared in the DOMAINS section using a symbolic file name. The system then binds the symbolic file name to the DOS name. This will be explained in Chapter 5.

Enter a PREDICATES declaration to the top of AUTO_1 as follows:

```
                          Editor

                 /* AUTO_1.PRO *
            /* A simple auto expert system */
PREDICATES   % A predicates declaration
caused_by(symbol,symbol)

CLAUSES      % Clauses declaration
caused_by(flat_tire,faulty_valve).
caused_by(flat_tire,blowout).
etc.
```

Now Turbo Prolog knows to expect one predicate with an arity of two where both arguments will be of the symbol data domain.

3.1.5 Querying the Program Using Variables

In a conventional computer language such as C, a variable is a symbol selected by the programmer to represent a value that will occupy a specified location in memory. This value may, through assignment and reassignment, change many times during execution of the program. Reassignment of a new value to the variable address in RAM is destructive to any value currently held at that location.

Prolog handles variables differently. In Prolog, the function of the program is to acquire values for variables. Assigning values for variables is handled by the system through unification and backtracking and not through destructive reassignment. The values carried by variables at the successful conclusion of the program are reported to the user automatically if there is no internal goal. If there is an internal goal, the programmer sees to it that relevant instantiations are passed on to the user by using write statements. With this in mind, let's look at the Turbo Prolog variable at work.

Press Alt-R and at the `GOAL :` prompt type the following query.

```
caused_by(Effect,Cause).
```

Notice the use of meaningful variable names instead of `X` and `Y`. During program traces, Turbo Prolog will preserve these names, making program flow much easier to follow during the debugging stage.

A variable in Prolog can be in two states: free or bound. A free variable does not have a value. That is, it is not currently bound to a term. Bound variables are instantiated and carry the value of a term. Using variables, it is easy for the programmer to enter a query and have Prolog return the values of currently unknown terms.

If the screen configuration is causing the solutions in the dialog window to wrap around, making them difficult to read, use the Shift F9 ⟶ key sequence to make the window larger. Try adjusting your windows. Then save the configuration as `BIG_WIND.SYS`. When you want to use this interface, load the configuration with the Setup Load Configuration option naming `BIG_WIND.SYS`.

Now try the query `caused_by(Effect,Cause).`

```
Dialog

GOAL : caused_by(Effect,Cause).
Effect=flat_tire, Cause=faulty_valve
Effect=flat_tire, Cause=blowout
Effect=knocking_in_engine, Cause=low_octane_gas
```

(continued)

```
Effect=poor_gas_mileage, Cause=dirty_spark_plugs
Effect(stalling, Cause=vapor_lock
Effect=poor_acceleration, Cause=timing_adjustment
Effect=poor_ride, Cause=worn_shocks
Effect=worn_tires, Cause=wheel_alignment
Effect=brake_squeal, Cause=hard_linings
Effect=brake_squeal, Cause=worn_linings
10 solutions
GOAL :
```

Examine what has happened in this query. The goal was to find matching facts where the two variables of the relation, `Effect` and `Cause`, could be instantiated to constant terms. These terms were then reported as each match was made.

Put a bit differently, this query directed Prolog to match the goal with one or more facts in its knowledge base. The presence of variables in the query meant that Prolog could instantiate the variables to any arguments in matching predicates. In this case, there were 10 facts, with each having arguments (constants) that could unify with the variables in the query.

Whenever Turbo Prolog is queried in this fashion with what is called an *external goal* (a query or directive entered by the user at the `GOAL :` prompt), the values of instantiated variables in proven goals will be printed on the screen automatically. An *internal goal* is stated as such inside the program as a GOAL declaration. When the program is run, the goal is invoked by Turbo Prolog. In the case of internal goals, the programmer must direct Prolog to write values to the screen or the only response provided will be `True` or `False`, indicating the success or failure to solve for the query.

Remember that Prolog begins a search at the top of the program. In our example, Prolog matched the first fact and then reported the values for the two instantiated variables. Prolog next uninstantiated the variables and began a search for an alternative solution and found a match with fact 2. It then reported the values of the variables once again. This process continued until Prolog reported all 10 facts and ran out of further clauses to match. This is nondeterminism at work.

3.1.6 Finding Solutions Using Conjunctive Goals

Often, one wishes to query Prolog using more than one goal. This means that Prolog must satisfy two or more conditions before reporting any solutions to the user. Let's see how this works using our auto program. First we will add some additional facts to the program. Consider the 10 auto malfunction causes. Some of them can be categorized as more serious than others. Here the cause of the problem can be designated as a safety problem.

```
safety_problem(Cause).
```

A less serious problem is declared as a performance problem:

```
performance_problem(Cause).
```

Add the following facts and predicate declarations to the AUTO_1 program. Again we will be using only symbols, so they can be declared directly in the PREDICATES section. The entire program is included here once again for clarity and for convenience. In later examples, only new material that is to be added to a program will be provided.

```
Editor

                  /* AUTO_1 */
        /* A simple auto expert system */
PREDICATES
caused_by(symbol,symbol)
safety_problem(symbol)
performance_problem(symbol)

CLAUSES
caused_by(flat_tire,faulty_valve).
caused_by(flat_tire,blowout).
caused_by(knocking_in_engine,low_octane_gas).
caused_by(poor_gas_mileage,dirty_spark_plugs).
caused_by(stalling,vapor_lock).
caused_by(poor_acceleration,timing_adjustment).
caused_by(poor_ride,worn_shocks).
caused_by(worn_tires,wheel_alignment).
caused_by(brake_squeal,hard_linings).
caused_by(brake_squeal,worn_linings).
safety_problem(faulty_valve).
safety_problem(blowout).
safety_problem(worn_shocks).
safety_problem(wheel_alignment).
safety_problem(worn_linings).
performance_problem(timing_adjustment).
performance_problem(low_octane_gas).
performance_problem(dirty_spark_plugs).
performance_problem(hard_linings).
performance_problem(vapor_lock).
```

Be sure to keep all like-named predicates grouped together! This is required by all Prologs. Unlike standard Prolog, Turbo Prolog version 1.xx requires that each predicate have a fixed number of arguments (arity). In version 2.0 of Turbo

Prolog, predicates with the same name may have varying arities. However, you must group predicates of the same name/arity family together and, of course, declare them. From now on, whenever I refer to a predicate with multiple arities, I will use the form predicate/arity. For predicates with a single arity I will use the form predicate().

Next, run the program and at the goal prompt enter

```
caused_by(Effect,Cause),safety_problem(Cause).
```

Now you are asking Turbo Prolog to satisfy two conditions before printing any instantiations for `Effect` and `Cause` to the screen. Here you have introduced a constraint on solutions. You are not interested in all causes; rather, you care about only those that are safety problems.

To solve this conjunction of goals, Prolog must find a fact to match the first goal in your query,

```
caused_by(Effect,Cause)
```

Starting at the top of the program, Turbo Prolog matches the first fact

```
caused_by(flat_tire,faulty_valve)
```

`Effect` is instantiated to `flat_tire` and `Cause` to `faulty_valve`. Turbo Prolog marks this location to keep track of where in the knowledge base this binding occurred so that it can return and continue the search forward for alternative goals.

The first goal succeeds, and Prolog moves on to the next, which reads

```
safety_problem(faulty_valve)
```

When `Cause` unified with `faulty_valve` in the first solution, all like-named variables in the query list acquired this same value. Turbo Prolog starts again at the top of the knowledge base and searches down and finds a match at the first safety problem fact. The query succeeds, and Turbo Prolog prints the value to the screen.

3.1.7 Finding Alternative Solutions

When using external goals, Turbo Prolog will try, unless directed otherwise using control procedures discussed later in this chapter, to find all possible solutions to a query. To accomplish this Turbo Prolog will free variables bound at the previous node, return to the first goal in the query list, and backtrack in the knowledge base to the point where the previous binding occurred. It will then attempt to match the goal to clauses farther down in the knowledge base.

In our example, resatisfying the goal will occur four more times, producing a total of five solutions. After the fifth solution, Prolog will terminate because there are no more facts in the knowledge base to test.

Now try the following query:

```
caused_by(Effect,Cause),performance_problem(Cause).
```

This conjunction of goals should also yield five solutions.

3.1.8 Tracing Conjunctive Solutions

By now the emphasis I am placing on understanding Turbo Prolog's backtracking behavior is apparent. Next do a program trace of the queries to see how Prolog found the solutions. This will give you an opportunity to try out Turbo Prolog's trace facility. This facility will be indispensable to you in debugging your own programs.

Before using the trace facility, however, a few definitions are in order. Turbo Prolog's tracing facility is based on the Procedure box control flow model described in Clocksin and Mellish (1984). The Turbo Prolog adaptation of this model traces the execution of a program using the terms CALL, RETURN, REDO, and FAIL.

GOAL :	indicates query entered by user
CALL :	indicates an attempt to satisfy a goal
RETURN :	indicates a goal has been satisfied and the program returned to the calling predicate. An asterisk indicates that the program is at a backtracking point and there are further clauses in the knowledge base that match input parameters.
FAIL :	indicates a failure to satisfy the predicate named.
REDO :	indicates that backtracking has occurred. The name of the predicate and the values of its parameters are listed.

Invoke the editor and enter the word TRACE at the top of the AUTO_1 knowledge base.

```
─────────────────────── Editor ───────────────────────

                        /* AUTO_1 */
            /* A simple auto expert system */
TRACE
PREDICATES
caused_by(symbol,symbol)
```

Now run the program and enter the query

```
caused_by(Effect,Cause),safety_problem(Cause)
```

Use the F10 function key to step through the program. Go slowly and take the time to look at the text and follow the trace in the various windows. The following is a step-by-step account of what you should see for the first three attempts by Turbo Prolog to find solutions. The first two are successes and the third is a failure.

The first step is

```
CALL : caused_by(_,_)
```

Turbo Prolog attempts to satisfy this goal by starting at the top of the knowledge base to find a match where the variables can instantiate to terms. The first fact is a match, indicated by

```
RETURN :*caused_by("flat_tire","faulty_valve")
```

Prolog sets a marker here and moves to the second goal. Note the asterisk, which signals that there are more predicates matching `CALL` in the knowledge base. The symbols are enclosed in quotation marks because Turbo Prolog treats symbols and strings in a similar, although not identical, fashion.

```
CALL : safety_problem("faulty_valve")
```

A match is found as indicated by

```
RETURN : safety_problem("faulty_valve")
```

The query succeeds and the results are printed to the screen.

```
Effect=flat_tire, Cause=faulty_valve
```

Prolog next frees the variables

```
REDO : caused_by(_,_)
```

Turbo Prolog attempts nondeterministically to find another solution, so it goes to the marker and continues searching lower in the knowledge base.

```
RETURN :*caused_by("flat_tire","blowout")
```

A match is found with the second fact in the knowledge base. Prolog sets a marker and moves on to the second clause.

```
CALL : safety_problem("blowout")
```

Prolog tries to match this goal with the first `safety_problem()` fact. No match, so try the next fact.

```
REDO : safety_problem("blowout")
```

This is a match and Prolog prints the values of the variables to the screen.

```
RETURN : safety_problem("blowout")

Effect=flat_tire, Cause=blowout
```

Prolog frees the most recent binding of variables, returns to the first goal in the query, and proceeds to the marker in the knowledge base (on the second `caused_by()` fact).

```
REDO : caused_by(_,_)
```

This time a match is found with the third fact.

```
RETURN :*caused_by("knocking_in_engine","low_octane_gas")
```

Next Turbo Prolog goes to the second clause in the query.

```
CALL : safety_problem("low_octane_gas")
```

Now Prolog returns to the top of the knowledge base and works down searching for a match. Each `safety_problem()` fact is tried, with no match found, as indicated by `FAIL`.

```
REDO : safety_problem("low_octane_gas")

REDO : safety_problem("low_octane_gas")

REDO : safety_problem("low_octane_gas")

REDO : safety_problem("low_octane_gas")

FAIL : safety_problem("low_octane_gas")
```

It failed that time, but there are still facts to try, so it returns to the marker and continues.

```
REDO : caused_by(_,_)

RETURN :*caused_by("poor_gas_mileage","dirty_spark_plugs")
```

Enough of the trace has been shown to document the meaning of the trace terminology and to illustrate Turbo Prolog's searching behavior. Continue the trace as an exercise. Also, you may wish to go back to the last chapter and do a trace of the sports program as an exercise.

3.1.9 Queries Using Anonymous Variables

There are times when the programmer needs to use a variable as a placeholder but has no need to know its value. For example, you might want to produce a list of the effects of auto malfunction but not care at all about the causes. This is where the anonymous variable represented by the underscore character comes in. The anonymous variable does not acquire values and provides a convenient mechanism for discarding information selectively. Note that, when more than one anonymous variable is used in a query or in a clause, the same underscore character represents different variables.

Try the following query:

```
caused_by(Effect,_).
```

Turbo Prolog will respond with a list of 10 effects, that is, a list of the first arguments in the 10 `caused_by()` facts.

```
Effect=flat_tire
Effect=flat_tire
Effect=knocking_in_engine
Effect=poor_gas_mileage
Effect=stalling
Effect=poor_acceleration
Effect=poor_ride
Effect=worn_tires
Effect=brake_squeal
Effect=brake_squeal
10 solutions
```

Now try

```
caused_by(_,Cause),safety_problem(Cause).
```

This compound query will produce a list of five causes of malfunction that are also listed as safety problems.

```
Cause=faulty_valve
Cause=blowout
Cause=worn_shocks
Cause=wheel_alignment
Cause=worn_linings
```

3.2 ENTERING AND USING RULES

After all this preparation, you are now ready to try some rules that will operate on the facts in the knowledge base and provide deductive conclusions. As we will see, rules also make it possible for us to greatly simplify our queries.

Assume that you wish to query the knowledge base giving a symptom you have observed in your car. You want Turbo Prolog to respond with (1) the cause and (2) advice regarding the urgency of repair. Enter the editor and remove the trace directive; then add the following rules to the auto program.

Editor

```
/* add these predicates declarations */
PREDICATES
help
advice(symbol)

CLAUSES



/* add these rules at the bottom of knowledge base    */
help :-
    clearwindow,
    write("What is your problem?"),
    readln(Effect),
    advice(Effect).

advice(out_of_gas):- write("Take a hike!").
advice(Effect) :-
    caused_by(Effect,Cause),
    safety_problem(Cause),
    write(Effect),
    write(" is a safety problem!"),nl,
    write("Advice is to repair immediately!"),nl.
advice(Effect) :-
    caused_by(Effect,Cause),
    performance_problem(Cause),
    write(Effect),
    write(" is a performance problem!"), nl,
    write("Advice is to repair when convenient!").
```

As you appended these rules to the knowledge base, you certainly noticed that I have introduced a few new concepts, specifically, the primitives `clearwindow`, `nl`, `readln()`, and `write()`. These primitives are introduced here because they provide the necessary means for making our program interactive.

All of these built-in commands are extralogical procedures and each is used in programs for its single deterministic side effect. Here, these side effects are clearing the screen, producing a newline, writing a string to the screen, and reading input from the keyboard. You will see much more of them in later programs.

Run the AUTO_1.PRO program and try these external queries.

```
help.
advice(stalling).
advice(brake_squeal).
advice(poor_gas_mileage).
advice(out_of_gas).
```

As each query is entered, try to predict Prolog's response. This is good practice and will help you to master Prolog's goal resolution mechanism.

Typing `help` at the `GOAL :` prompt invokes the help rule, which procedurally clears the screen, prompts the user for a problem, and passes the problem on to the `advice()` rule as an argument. This is a very elementary example of what is called a *front-end* program. Front ends mediate between the computer and the user by simplifying the use of some application program. Often front ends employ natural-language processing to allow the user to establish a dialogue with the computer. This topic will be covered in detail in later chapters.

Trace Prolog's path to solution in one or two of the foregoing queries. This tracing of Turbo Prolog's backtracking to solutions can be tedious; however, it is also important to your mastery of this language, so bear with it.

When you enter a query seeking advice about running out of gas, Prolog starts at the top of the knowledge base and searches down until it encounters a match for the argument `out_of_gas`. The head of the first rule is the match it seeks.

```
advice(out_of_gas):-
    write("Take a hike!").
```

To prove this rule, Prolog has only to prove the single condition, which happens to be the primitive `write()`. `write()` takes as its argument whatever term, or series of terms, is included within its parentheses. Prolog has only to write `Take a hike!` on the screen for the rule to succeed.

Examine the query `advice(stalling)`. Prolog starts at the top of the knowledge base looking for a match for the query. When it reaches the second rule,

```
advice(Effect):-
    caused_by(Effect,Cause),
    safety_problem(Cause),
```

```
        write(Effect),
        write(" is a safety problem!"), nl,
        write(" Advice is to repair immediately!").
```

Prolog finds a match and binds `Effect` to `stalling` throughout the rule. Turbo Prolog places a marker on the head of this rule to keep track of where it is in the knowledge base and moves on to the first condition, which is

```
caused_by(stalling,Cause)
```

Prolog starts a search for a match beginning at the top of the knowledge base. A match is found with the fact

```
caused_by(stalling,vapor_lock)
```

and `Cause` is instantiated to `vapor_lock` throughout the rule. Prolog then proceeds to the next condition, which is

```
safety_problem(vapor_lock)
```

Starting at the top of the knowledge base, Prolog searches for a match and fails. Prolog is not daunted. It uninstantiates this set of binding of variables and *backtracks* up to where it placed the marker at the first rule.

Prolog then tracks down to the head of the next rule, which is also a match for the query. `Effect` is instantiated to `stalling` and Turbo moves on to the first condition, which is

```
caused_by(stalling,Cause)
```

Next, `Cause` is instantiated, just as in the last attempt, to `vapor_lock`.

Turbo Prolog moves on to the clause

```
performance_problem(vapor_lock)
```

and looks for a match. This time the search succeeds. Now all Prolog has to do is print the value of `Cause`, which is `vapor_lock`, followed by the string `is a performance problem`!

The `clearwindow` predicate does just what its name implies: It clears the window by filling it with the background color, thus erasing any text. The innocuous `nl` in the program is simply another extralogical built-in command, which directs Turbo Prolog to start writing on a new line. Next, Turbo Prolog prints the advice string. The rule succeeds, and Prolog retires with `True`.

Consider what Turbo Prolog has done in solving for this query. It first searched and found a match with the head of a rule. It recorded the location of this match in the event that backtracking would become necessary. After Prolog failed to find a match for one of the conditions, it backtracked to this marker and continued its search for a match. This time matches were found for all conditions in the rule and the query succeeded.

Now return to the editor and add the goal declaration. Be sure to include the period after `help`. Run the program. Now Turbo Prolog will invoke the help rule automatically. Experiment with the program and try all possible problems. If you wish to query the program externally, just place comment characters around everything you have just entered. Experiment with some alternative internal goals.

```
                           Editor

/* add this goal declaration below the predicates   */

GOAL   % keyword and list of predicates
help.
```

Describing the World Using Rules. Defining rules is of fundamental importance in Turbo Prolog programming. Rules are defined by first identifying a goal you wish to achieve. Next you decompose the problem into subproblems. These subproblems then become the list of the conditions that are logically prerequisite to achieving your goal. This is what psychologists and logicians call top-down reasoning.

A simple example should help make this point clear. Imagine that you are getting ready to leave your house and deciding whether or not you should take an umbrella. To make this decision you need information. You look out the window and see dark clouds on the distant horizon. Next you go into the den and turn on the TV weather channel. The weather forecaster announces that there is an 80 percent chance of rain today. You go to the closet, get your umbrella, and leave for work.

What you have just done is to apply a simple heuristic for deciding whether or not to prepare for rain. A Prolog rule that declares this heuristic rule of thumb would read as follows:

```
take_to_work(umbrella) :-
      clouds(dark),
      weather_report_is(rain,Probability),
      Probability is > 0.60.
```

Let's do a little backtracking ourselves at this point and enter a small program that will provide us with some practice in developing rule-defining skills.

Remember that Prolog is a language all about objects and their relations. A

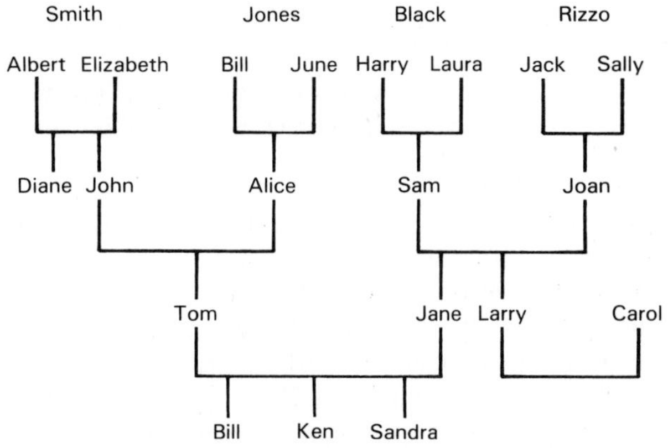

Figure 3.1 A family tree.

good exercise to illustrate this point involves the use of objects and relations that are highly familiar to all of us.

Save any program currently in the editor. Then start a new file and create a family knowledge base using the information in Figure 3.1. A few of these facts are shown here, but you should expand the listing as an exercise.

```
father_of(john,tom).
father_of(tom,bill).
father_of(sam,larry).
father_of(sam,jane).
father_of(harry,sam).
mother_of(laura,sam).
mother_of(alice,tom).
mother_of(june,alice).
mother_of(joan,larry).

sibling_of(larry,carol).

male(larry).
male(john).
male(tom).
male(bill).

female(jane).
female(alice).
female(june).
female(joan).
```

Binary relations are used for relations among people, whereas unary relations are used for declaring attributes of individuals.

Figure 3.2 shows the `mother_of` relation as a directed graph. When using

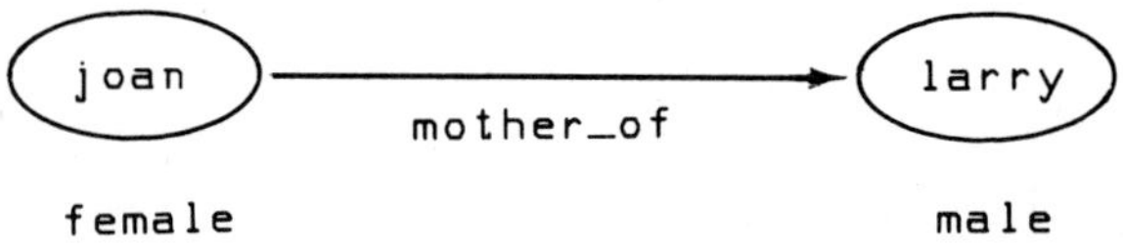

Figure 3.2 The mother_of relation represented as a directed graph.

graphs to illustrate these relations, the object is represented inside a circle (see Figure 3.2). The solid line represents a relation. Attributes of objects are indicated by placing the unary relation name next to the object.

There are some implicit relations in the family knowledge base that are not, as yet, stated. To make these explicit we will have to declare a fact for each relation. Why not save ourselves the trouble and use rules to infer these relations? For example, there is no explicit fact stating that Larry Blake is Bill Smith's uncle. However, we can define a rule that can infer all the uncle relations in our family knowledge base.

Consider the family tree in Figure 3.1. What would a rule defining the `uncle_of()` relation look like? Start by asking yourself, "When is someone an uncle?" One answer is "Person 1 is the uncle of person 2 when person 1 is the brother of person 3 and person 3 is the mother of person 2." Figure 3.3 shows this relation as a set of graphs. In Turbo Prolog, an uncle rule would read

```
uncle_of(Person_1,Person_2) :-
     male(Person_1),
     brother_of(Person_1,Person_3),
     mother_of(Person_3,Person_2).
```

If we were to apply this rule to our family knowledge base, one set of instantiations for the query uncle_of(Uncle,Nephew) would read as follows.

```
uncle_of(larry,bill) :-
     male(larry),
     brother_of(larry,jane),
     mother_of(jane,bill).
```

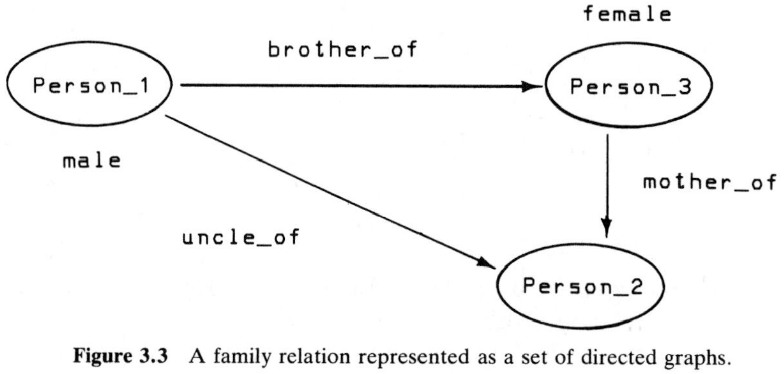

Figure 3.3 A family relation represented as a set of directed graphs.

3.3 BRANCHING WITH THE OR OPERATOR

This uncle_of() rule is somewhat limited in its generality since it does not cover instances where an uncle might be the brother of the father of a child. Stop and think for a moment how you could make our uncle_of() rule more general. Perhaps you could use another rule?

Define a rule parent_of() that includes both fathers and mothers, as follows:

```
parent_of(Person,Child) :-
   mother_of(Person,Child) ;
   father_of(Person,Child).
```

Notice my use of a semicolon instead of the usual comma at the end of the second condition in this rule. The semicolon is the OR operator in Turbo Prolog. Review the logical connectives in Chapter 2 if you do not remember this one. This rule has the English reading "Person is the parent of child if person is either the mother of child OR the father of child." According to the rules of inference, a sentence is true if either of the statements connected by an OR is true. The parent_of() rule will succeed if Turbo Prolog can find a match in the knowledge base for either condition. In actual practice, subsequent conditions in a disjunction of goals are tested when and if an antecedent condition fails.

The ; operator allows the programmer to simulate the IF-THEN-ELSE construct used in procedural languages. The ; also can be used to generate a case statement, which is another way to implement branching in programs.

```
integer_is(X) :-
   X = 1, write("It is 1\n") ;
   X = 2, write("It is 2\n") ;
   X = 3, write("It is 3\n") ;
   X >= 4, write("It is more than 3\n").
```

Note the use of the \n inside the string to be printed to the screen. This is just another way to produce a newline. The backslash tells Turbo that the symbol that follows the backslash is not just another character in a string, but rather that it is a system command.

Some Prolog purists frown on the use of the ; operator and suggest that defining multiple rules is better. The following is a multiple-rule alternative to the case rule.

1.
```
integer_is(1) :-
   write("It is 1\n").
```
2.
```
integer_is(2) :-
   write("It is 2\n").
```

3.
```
integer_is(3) :-
  write("It is 3\n").
```

4.
```
integer_is(_) :-
  write("It is more than 3\n").
```

Next is a two-rule solution for the `parent_of()` rule. Note that it is permissible to use meaningful names in one rule and `X` and `Y` in another. The rules say the same thing in each case.

```
parent_of(Person,Child) :-
  mother_of(Person,Child).
parent_of(X,Y) :-
  father_of(X,Y).
```

With this `parent_of()` rule added to our family knowledge base, you can now redefine the `uncle_of()` rule.

```
uncle_of(Person_1,Person_2) :-
        male(Person_1),
        sibling_of(Person_1,Person_3),
        parent_of(Person_3,Person_2).
```

Now define a `grandfather()` rule.

```
grandfather_of(Person_1,Person_2) :-
      father_of(Person_1,Person_3),
      parent_of(Person_3,Person_2).
```

The `friends()` rule shown here is a bit more complex in that it depends on other relations.

```
friends(Person_1,Person_2) :-
      like_each_other(Person_1,Person_2),
      common_interest(Person_1,Person_2).

like_each_other(Person_1,Person_2) :-
      likes(Person_1,Person_2),
      likes(Person_2,Person_1).

common_interest(Person_1,Person_2) :-
      enjoys(Person_1,Activity),
      enjoys(Person_2,Activity).
```

How about a cousin_of() rule?

```
cousin_of(X,Y) :-
        parent_of(Z,X),
        sibling_of(Z,A),
        parent_of(A,Y).
```

Here is a sibling() rule for our family program.

```
sibling_of(X,Y) :-
        sister_of(X,Y);
        brother_of(X,Y).
```

The use of this sibling() rule would require that we store in our family knowledge base a host of sister_of() and brother_of() facts. Assume that we already have parent-child and gender relations declared in our knowledge base. We can save ourselves the trouble of entering all these facts by defining sister_of() and brother_of() rules in terms of the existing parent-child() and gender() relations.

```
sister_of(X,Y) :-                brother_of(X,Y) :-
  parent_of(Z,X),                  parent_of(Z,X),
  parent_of(Z,Y),                  parent_of(Z,Y),
  female(X).                       male(X).
```

Enter the following Turbo Prolog program.

```
                        Editor

                     /* SIBLING.PRO  */
 /*               A family knowledge base              */
PREDICATES
 sibling_of(symbol,symbol)
 sister_of(symbol,symbol)
 brother_of(symbol,symbol)
 parent_of(symbol,symbol)
 female(symbol)
 male(symbol)
CLAUSES
 sibling_of(X,Y) :-
   sister_of(X,Y) ;
   brother_of(X,Y).
```

(*continued*)

```
sister_of(X,Y) :-
  parent_of(Z,X),
  parent_of(Z,Y),
  female(X).
brother_of(X,Y) :-
  parent_of(Z,X),
  parent_of(Z,Y),
  male(X).
parent_of(tom,sandra).
parent_of(tom,bill).
parent_of(tom,ken).

female(sandra).

male(bill).
male(ken).
```

Run the program with the goal `sibling_of(X,Y)`. Notice what happens. Nine solutions are produced, and not the six that you anticipated. Each child is listed as the sibling of three, not two, children. This is because each child is listed as his or her own brother or sister.

Do a trace of the program to see what has happened. To prove `sibling_of(X,Y)` Turbo Prolog must prove `sister_of(X,Y)`. This matches the head of a rule, so the conditions of the rule must be proved, starting with `parent_of(Z,X)`. `parent_of(Z,X)` is proved with `Z` instantiated to `tom` and `X` to `sandra`. The next condition to prove is `parent_of(tom,Y)`. This is proved by starting at the top of the relevant facts and finding a match where `Y` is instantiated to `sandra`. The variables `X` and `Y` are now both instantiated to `sandra`. Prolog continues in this fashion for the remaining goals. This is an instance where Turbo Prolog's backtracking to resatisfy a goal can produce undesired results. You must keep this point in mind as you define your rules.

A solution to the problem is to add a condition to the `brother_of()` and `sister_of()` rules that states that a person cannot be his own brother or her own sister. For example:

```
sister_of(X,Y) :-
   parent_of(Z,X),
   parent_of(Z,Y),
   not(X = Y),
   female(X).
```

Run the program and it will produce the six solutions you expected, that is, each of the three children has two siblings.

As an exercise, try various queries with and without traces. I will explain the `not()` primitive to you soon. For now, you can intuitively understand that here `not` will succeed only if `X` does not equal `Y`.

3.4 WRITING PROGRAMS THAT LEARN

Zap the family program, load AUTO_1, and run it using an internal goal statement to invoke the `help()` rule. Enter a problem the program knows about, repair advice will be given, and AUTO_1 will then retire. If you wish to query the program once again, it must be compiled and executed again.

Next enter a problem the program doesn't know about. AUTO_1 will terminate without any explanation. No information at all is given regarding reasons for the program's failure to produce a solution. Why not modify the program so that it will run until directed to terminate? Also, it would be desirable to have the program declare the limits of its knowledge, admit its ignorance about certain repair problems, prompt the user for information, and then remember that information for future queries during the current consultation.

To do this we will need to be able to add facts to the program at run time. This requires an internal database and the DATABASE declarations we discussed earlier in this chapter. Turbo Prolog allows you to add and remove facts in either a default internal database called *dbasedom* or (version 2.0) in one or more user-defined internal databases. If you do not name an internal database in your declaration, the default dbasedom is used.

The following is a simple redesign of AUTO_1 to accomplish our objectives. Load AUTO_1 and make the following changes. Then save the revised program as AUTO_2. There are a few new concepts here, which will be discussed in a moment. For now, just run the program a few times to sample its features. This program, you will note, learns new factual information and uses it in answering subsequent queries.

```
                              Editor

                          /* AUTO_2 */
      /* A simple auto expert system that learns */
DATABASE % The default dbasedom will be used.
 caused_by(symbol,symbol)
 safety_problem(symbol)
 performance_problem(symbol)

PREDICATES
 help
 advice(symbol)
```

(*continued*)

```
 remember(symbol,symbol)
 continue
 list_all

GOAL
 help.

CLAUSES

/* 10 caused_by facts here. */
/* 5 safety_problem facts here. */
/* 5 performance_problem facts here. */
/* Add some of your own but be sure to keep */
/* like predicates all grouped together. */

/* help rules */

help :-
 clearwindow,
 write("\nDo you want a list of the problems\n"),
 write("that I know about? yes/no "),
 readln(Request),
 Request = "yes",nl,
 list_all.
help :-
 write("\nTo exit press E.\n"),
 write("\nWhat is your problem? "),
 readln(Problem),nl,
 not(Problem="E"),
 advice(Problem).

/* advice rules */

advice(out_of_gas) :- write("Too bad!\n").
advice(Problem) :-
 caused_by(Problem,Cause),
 safety_problem(Cause),
 write(Problem," is caused by ",Cause,"."),nl,
 write(Problem," is a safety problem!\n"),
 write("Advice is to repair immediately!\n"),
 continue.
advice(Problem) :-
 caused_by(Problem,Cause),
 performance_problem(Cause).
 write(Problem," is caused by ",Cause,"."),nl,
 write(Problem," is a performance problem!\n"),
 write("Advice is to repair when convenient!\n\n"),
 continue.
```

```
advice(Problem) :-
 write("I do not know about ",Problem,"."),nl,
 write("What is the cause? "),
 readln(Cause),nl,
 not(Cause="E"),
 asserta(caused_by(Problem,Cause)),nl,
 write("Is ",Cause),
 write(" a safety_problem or performance_problem?"),
 readln(Response),nl,
 not(Response="E"),
 remember(Response,Cause).

/* remember rules */
remember(safety_problem,Cause) :-
 asserta(safety_problem(Cause)),
 continue.
remember(performance_problem,Cause) :-
 asserta(performance_problem(Cause)),
 continue.

/* continue rules */

continue :-
 write("\nDo you wish to continue? yes/no: "),
 readln(Option),
 Option="yes",
 help.
continue :-
 exit.

/* list_all rule */

list_all :-
 caused_by(Effect,_),
 write(Effect),nl,
 fail.
```

Running the program invokes the internal goal `help`. The conditions of the `help` rule clear the dialog window and prompt for a user request to see a list of the problems AUTO_2 knows about. The user response is checked against the constant `yes` for a match using the relational operator `=`. If there is a match, the `list_all` rule is invoked. The `list_all` rule has four conditions. The last of these conditions is `fail`.

3.5 CAUSING BACKTRACKING WITH `fail`

The first condition `caused_by(Effect,_)` picks up the constant `flat_tire` occupying the `problem` slot in the first `caused_by()` fact. The cause is discarded by the anonymous variable. The second condition writes this value to the screen. The third condition is the primitive `nl`, which causes the cursor to go to the next line on the screen. The fourth condition is the built-in predicate `fail`. This primitive takes no arguments and always fails, causing backtracking to occur where possible.

Prolog backtracks to the second `caused_by()` fact, where it picks up the value of the second problem and prints it on the screen. This continues until Prolog runs out of `caused_by()` facts to match. As you can see, the `fail` predicate is a convenient mechanism for forcing backtracking in order to perform functions such as, in this case, listing a series of values on the screen.

Now, of course, `list_all()` fails, causing the `help` rule that invoked it to fail as well. Turbo Prolog drops down to try to prove the second `help` rule. This rule succeeds by passing the value of the user-entered problem to the `advice()` procedure.

3.6 NEGATION

Notice that the second `help()` rule uses a prompt to get a user problem or request to terminate the program. This has been implemented using the negation standard predicate `not()`. This primitive turns success into failure and failure into success. If the `not()` predicate were not provided by Turbo Prolog, you could define it yourself as follows:

```
not(Clause) :-
        Clause,
        !,
        fail.
not(Clause).
```

Note the exclamation mark as the second condition in the first `not()` rule (the second rule is unconditional). This is another Turbo Prolog primitive called the *cut*. Its role is to modify program-searching behavior. At this point, I will discuss the cut in detail. I will return and explain the operation of the negation rules after explaining this important mechanism for controlling program flow.

3.7 THE CUT

The cut is a primitive that, like `fail`, takes no arguments. Unlike `fail`, however, the cut always succeeds the first time it is called. Should failure cause backtracking and a return to the cut, it will always fail and prevent any further testing of the present rule or alternatives to the present rule.

Specifically, the cut can be used in two ways. First, it can be employed to adapt Turbo Prolog's control strategy to conform to the logical requirements of a problem by inhibiting backtracking. The cut is very useful when the semantics of a program dictate that the one solution first obtained is the only one that is logically possible. This might occur, for example, in a program using a series of rules where each tests the value of a different number. Once the value for the number is established by the success of one rule in a procedure, any more tests must logically fail. Any time Prolog spends exploring these rules is therefore wasted.

```
integer_is(1) :-
  !,
  write("It is 1\n").
integer_is(2) :-
  !,
  write("It is 2\n").
```

The cut assures that Turbo Prolog visits only those rules that are necessary to produce a solution—if the number is 1, only the first rule will be visited, and backtracking over `integer_is()` rules is forbidden.

Used in this fashion, the cut can greatly enhance efficiency in programs where there is a need for preventing Turbo Prolog from attempting to resatisfy goals known in advance by the programmer to have but one solution. In this type of application, where the restriction imposed upon backtracking does not affect solutions or the declarative semantics of the program, the cut is termed "green." Green cuts affect searching and efficiency but not solutions.

Second, the cut can be used to adapt Turbo Prolog's control strategy to conform to the procedural requirements of a particular problem. In such cases, even though the knowledge base may contain additional matching clauses (thus potential solutions) for Turbo Prolog to explore through backtracking, the programmer might wish to prevent that from occurring. This application of the cut affects solutions as well as searching and is called a "red" cut. Cuts of this type are considered to be a somewhat more risky programming venture. This is because red cuts can cloud the declarative meaning of programs, perhaps inducing programmer errors and untoward side effects. This distinction between red and green cuts is attributed to M. van Emden (1982).

Consider an example of the cut at work. Imagine that you had a company knowledge base of employee information. Let's say you would like to list all the employees that work for the company. You write the simple Turbo Prolog program CUT.PRO (without the cut) to accomplish this. The program does its job and produces for you the desired roster of all company employees.

Next you decide that you want a listing of a single representative from each department in order to form a company committee. Committees being what they are, you do not care who these representatives are. Once the first employee in a department is found, you want to discontinue the search in that department and proceed on to the next department to select another employee.

Now, enter the cut as shown below, and the program will list one person (the first) from each department. The cut has modified the normal behavior of the program to produce a single solution.

Enter and run the program. Do a trace of this program with and without the cut in place.

Editor

```
/*                         CUT.PRO
   Illustrates use of the cut to stop backtracking over
   a goal. Remove the cut and the program will produce
   a list of all employees and not just the first one
   listed in each department.
*/
TRACE
PREDICATES
list_employees
get_employees(symbol)
dept(symbol)
employee(symbol,symbol,symbol)
GOAL
  list_employees.
CLAUSES
list_employees  :-
  clearwindow,
  dept(Dept),nl,
  get_employees(Dept).
get_employees(Dept)  :-
  employee(Dept,Firstname,Lastname),
  write(Dept,": ",Lastname," ",Firstname),nl,
  !,
  fail.
dept(accounting).
dept(manufacturing).
dept(maintenance).
dept(shipping).
/* etc. */
employee(accounting,sue,hanes).
employee(accounting,joe,washington).
employee(manufacturing,joan,harris).
employee(manufacturing,don,vitale).
employee(maintenance,sam,duncan).
employee(maintenance,lou,smith).
employee(shipping,bill,isaacs).
/* etc. */
```

With the cut present in the `get_employees()` rule, it serves to freeze the choices made in the conditions that led up to it. The program's first solutions are

```
dept(accounting)
get_employees(accounting)
employee(accounting,sue,hanes).
```

When `fail` causes backtracking to occur rather than finding another alternative solution for `employee()`, in this case

```
employee(accounting,joe,washington)
```

the program must backtrack all the way to the dept condition and then select the next department in the knowledge base. This is

```
dept(manufacturing)
get_employees(manufacturing)
employee(manufacturing,joan,harris)
```

As you can see, Turbo Prolog is committed to the first solution. This process continues until the program runs out of `departments()` to check.

As another example of a red cut in operation, consider the following problem. Let's say you are a graduate assistant and your professor has asked you to make the semester's class assignments and post the results on the bulletin board before tomorrow's classes. You estimate that doing this by hand will take you about four hours.

You need a program that will assign 500 students to different topical discussion sections based on combinations of last semester's grades and performance on a project serving as an indicator of level of interest in the subject. As all student information is on-line, you can write the following Turbo Prolog program, run it, and print the class assignments in less than 30 minutes. You save over three hours that you need to study for your next exam.

```
                              Editor

 /*                       ASSIGN.PRO
          A class assignment program illustrating
                     the use of the cut.
 */
PREDICATES
 make_assignments
 assign_student(integer,integer,char)
 class_list(symbol,symbol,integer,integer)
```

(continued)

```
GOAL
    clearwindow,
    make_assignments.
CLAUSES
 make_assignments :-
        write("\tCLASS ASSIGNMENTS\n"),
        class_list(X,X1,Y,Z),
        assign_student(Y,Z,G),
        write("\n\tGroup ",G,": ",X,", ",X1),
        fail.
 assign_student(Y,Z,G) :-
        Y > 89,
        Z > 86,
        G = 'A',
        !.              /* Try removing cut */
 assign_student(Y,Z,G) :-
        Y > 79,
        Z > 75,
        G = 'B',
        !.              /* Try removing cut */
 assign_student(_,_,G) :-
        G = 'C'.
 class_list(abel,izzie,75,73).
 class_list(smith,john,72,70).
 class_list(williams,kim,94,92).
 class_list(crane,harry,72,70).
 class_list(blake,carol,78,85).
 class_list(levine,sandra,95,92).
 class_list(rizzo,bill,88,89).
 class_list(jones,alice,84,88).
  /* 492 more students */
```

Consider this program with and without the cuts in place. Without the cuts, the program logically assigns the high-scoring students to all three discussion groups. The average students are assigned to both of the two lower groups. Only the below-average students are assigned to a single group. While the declarative meaning of the program has been fulfilled, clearly this will not do, since a procedural requirement is that no student should attend more than one discussion group.

With the cuts in place, however, the program stops making assignments after the first success. Be clear here. Further solutions are logically possible but procedurally undesired. Here the cut is a useful method to prevent resatisfying the `assign_student()` rule, which produces the unwanted additional solutions.

Now put a trace in the program and step through the execution with and without the cuts in place. Notice that the header `CLASS ASSIGNMENT` is printed only once. This is because the deterministic system-defined primitive `write()` can succeed only once.

Let's return to the negation rule and analyze the role of the cut here. The first `not()` uses both the `cut` and `fail` and as we have seen in the CUT.PRO example, the `cut` and `fail` combination can produce a useful effect. The first condition in the first `not()` rule attempts to match the term that is instantiated to `Clause` with a fact in the knowledge base. Let's say that a matching fact does exist. Turbo Prolog then moves on to the next condition, which is the cut we have just discussed. The cut succeeds just this once; `fail` then forces the rule to fail. Backtracking to the second `not()` rule is prevented by the cut, and the goal now fails. The `not()` rule has turned success (remember that a match did exist in the knowledge base) into failure and the parent goal now also fails.

If `not()` fails because a matching fact for its argument does not exist in the knowledge base, program flow never gets to the cut, so Prolog is free to try nondeterministically to prove the second and unconditional `not()` rule. This rule, you will note, is equivalent to a fact. Failure is, in this fashion, turned into success.

As mentioned, the cut is particularly useful in instances where there are multiple solutions but you are interested in only the first success and you do not want the program to backtrack. The cut works by modifying the normal backtracking and is deterministic. It is to be used with caution, as it makes program behavior much more difficult to understand.

3.8 MODIFYING THE INTERNAL DATABASE

Now that our digression into negation and the cut is complete, let's return to the auto example where we will consider procedures for adding or removing facts at run time. Modifying the internal database means that our program can learn new facts and thus enlarge the scope of the advice that it can offer. Modifying the internal database also means that we will change the program state without having to stop the program to edit clauses. We simply direct the program to add new facts or remove old ones as needed. Notice that I did not say that you can add and remove rules.

In Version 2.0 of Turbo Prolog, facts are stored in RAM or EMS memory in an internal or external database. In this chapter we will deal only with changes to the internal database. In later chapters, we will explore extending the internal database to files on disk and methods for modifying an external database. Also, from now on, I will use the terms *internal* or *external* database when referring to the location of facts; however, I will continue to use the term *knowledge base* when referring to a Prolog program or set of both facts and rules. Now let's see how we can make our auto program learn new facts.

Refer back to AUTO_2.PRO. Notice that the function of the `advice()` procedure is quite straightforward until you come to the fourth rule. This rule is invoked only when a new problem, unknown to the program, is entered by the user. This rule has a condition that adds a new `caused_by()` fact to the internal database. This is accomplished by the `asserta/1` primitive that takes a fact as an argument and adds that fact to the beginning of a list of like-named facts in the default internal database called dbasedom.

```
asserta(caused_by(Problem,Cause))
```

Alternatively, the primitive `assertz/1` is used to enter a fact at the end of the listing of `caused_by()` facts in the default internal database. Turbo Prolog also provides a primitive to remove facts from a database. The command `retract/1` removes the first matching fact from the database. (In Version 2.0, `asserta/2`, `assertz/2`, and `retract/2` allow the programmer to name a programmer-declared internal database as the location for assertion and retraction of facts.)

These are dynamic changes to what is otherwise a static database. Turbo Prolog will permit changes only if the relations to be changed have been declared in a DATABASE section at the head of the program. All the relations that are dynamic in the AUTO_2 program are declared as follows:

```
DATABASE    % The default dbasedom will be used.
caused_by(symbol,symbol)
safety_problem(symbol)
performance_problem(symbol)
```

For the duration of program execution, Turbo Prolog can answer queries involving newly asserted `caused_by()` relations. However, these relations will disappear from RAM when the program terminates. It is unlikely, in the absence of some mechanism for truth maintenance in such a changing database of facts, that you would want to save the changes anyway. Should you wish to preserve the changes, use `save()` before the program terminates.

The `remember()` procedure performs in a manner similar to the `advice` procedure. `remember()` prompts for a statement regarding the safety or performance nature of the problem and then asserts the reply to the internal database base.

The `continue()` rules permit the user to exit the program or continue the consultation by recursively invoking the help rule.

Experiment with AUTO_2 by making changes and observing the effects of the changes. Try removing the cut from the `help` rule.

3.9 SEARCH EFFICIENCY

After tracing Prolog's path to solutions in the several examples just given, you can appreciate how much searching and backtracking goes on in achieving solutions to problems. This raises the issue of program efficiency, an issue that is important in all large programs. There are several ways in which the efficiency of programs can be enhanced.

First, heuristic rules can be employed to eliminate costly exhaustive searches in the large solution spaces that are typically associated with difficult problems. Most AI problems are difficult problems. However, it should be noted that only exhaustive searches such as depth-first searching can guarantee to find a solution if one in fact exists. Heuristic searches selectively ignore portions of the search space (to save time) and cannot provide such a guarantee. We will return to the topic of searching in later chapters. Second, we have seen that the cut can be employed to eliminate searching for undesired alternatives by inhibiting backtracking. Third, the order in which rules and conditions within rules are entered into the knowledge base can influence efficiency of searches. Finally, program efficiency is affected by our choice of data structures. We will examine this subject in the next chapter.

3.10 SUMMARY

Concepts covered

Backtracking
Cuts: red and green
Declaring predicates and their arguments
Entering facts and rules into a program
`fail`
Modifying the database
Negation
Querying a program
    Using single and conjunctive goals
    Finding alternative solutions
Search efficiency
; (the OR operator)
Using the trace facility

Prolog, like any language, requires that the programmer master certain fundamental concepts. Among the most important of these concepts is the inference strategy used by Turbo Prolog. Prolog uses backward chaining with depth-first searching in solving goals. A search starts at the top of the knowledge base of facts and rules. When a goal matches with the head of a rule, Prolog attempts to prove all the conditions of that rule. Prolog proves goals by finding matches in the knowledge base. If a match for a goal is not found, Prolog backtracks to the last match and tries to find alternative solutions in the knowledge base. Prolog searches forward carrying instantiated variables, but when backtracking occurs, it frees the most recent bindings and attempts to find alternative values.

Prolog provides built-in standard predicates to permit the programmer to alter the inferencing behavior of Prolog. The cut ! prevents backtracking over previously satisfied goals. Green cuts affect efficiency but not the declarative meaning (solutions) of programs. Red cuts alter solutions, are highly procedural, and must be used with great care. `fail` forces Prolog to backtrack through previously satisfied goals and to search for alternative solutions.

Defining good rules to exploit the inferencing behavior of Prolog is the key to successful programming. Rules are defined by analyzing the goal to be achieved and breaking the goal into subgoals until the present state is reached.

3.11 EXERCISES

1. Create a knowledge base of facts for your own family tree. Write some rules to cover the following relations:
   a. married to
   b. paternal grandfather of
   c. is older than
   d. aunt of
   e. friend of
   f. in-law of
2. a. Declare some facts for a Prolog knowledge base of national holidays, for example, `holiday(independence_day,4th_july).` Add facts to this knowledge base that list the holidays your employer recognizes and gives you off, such as `have_off (independence_day).`
   b. Query this knowledge base to determine the dates of your days off for the year.
3. Declare the predicates domains for the family knowledge base and run the program. Write a rule that prompts the user for a kinship relation and returns the names of all relatives that satisfy the relation.
4. Given the following program, trace the solution to the queries given below. How would you modify the rule using a cut to produce but one answer to the second query?

Queries

```
is_in_demand(What)
should_major_in(john,What)
should_Major_in(Who,What)
```

Knowledge Base

```
should_major_in(Student,Discipline) :-
    is_interested_in(Student,Discipline),
    does_well_in(Student,Subject),
    is_important_in(Subject,Discipline),
    is_in_demand(Discipline).

does_well_in(john,math).
does_well_in(john,psychology).
```

```
is_in_demand(engineering).
is_in_demand(management).
is_important_in(math,engineering).
is_important_in(psychology,management)

is_interested_in(john,engineering).
is_interested_in(john,management).
```

5. Is the cut in the negation rule green or red? Why?
6. Can you redesign CUT.PRO using negation to avoid use of the cut? How?
7. Review the family relation rules. Are there any alternatives to the way I have declared them?

Chapter 4
Working with Compound Objects

CHAPTER OBJECTIVES

Study of this chapter should enable you to do the following:

1. Represent knowledge in Prolog programs using compound objects (structures and lists).
2. Create DOMAINS declarations for compound objects.
3. Describe breadth-first and depth-first searching in a knowledge base.
4. Write procedures to process information represented as structures.
5. Explain how recursion is used in list processing.
6. Write procedures to process information represented as lists.

IMPORTANT TERMS AND PHRASES

Arity
Binary tree
Boundary condition
Breadth-first searching
Child node
Data abstraction
Depth-first searching
Domain declaration
Empty list
Functor
List constructor
List notation
List processing
Parent node
Recursion
Structure
Terminal-node
User-defined data types

4.1 STRUCTURES

Thus far we have covered elementary programming principles using unit clauses (facts) in which the arguments have all been simple terms (symbols, strings, numbers, and variables). Here is an example of a fact in which the two terms are symbols.

```
caused_by(flat_tire,faulty_valve).
```

However, terms in Turbo Prolog may also be compound objects. A compound term, or structure, can be written

```
functor(arg_1,arg_2,...,arg_n)
```

where functor is a descriptive label for the information contained in the data structure and the arguments are terms. Notice the *recursive* nature of the definition of a term; that is, a term is defined in part by referring to itself.

Let's illustrate this concept with a concrete example. Suppose that we are using Turbo Prolog to build a conventional database program. The knowledge we wish to represent in this program is airline schedules. The Prolog fact in Figure 4.1 contains such information including vendor name, connecting flights between cities, and departure and arrival times. Notice that the first term of the principal predicate is simple and the remaining two terms are compound. The advantage to using compound objects as terms is that you can package more related information in each fact. You can then use a single variable to instantiate to each information packet. Using compound objects, your programs can process information very efficiently.

Compound objects are recursive and can be represented as a tree. Examine Figure 4.2. A tree structure is made up of nodes, which are represented as circles in the diagrams. Nodes branch to other nodes with lines representing the branches. A tree begins at a *root node* and each branch of the tree terminates in a *leaf node*. Nodes that connect two other nodes are called *internal nodes*. The empty tree may be used to represent a null set of objects. In Figure 4.2 the root node

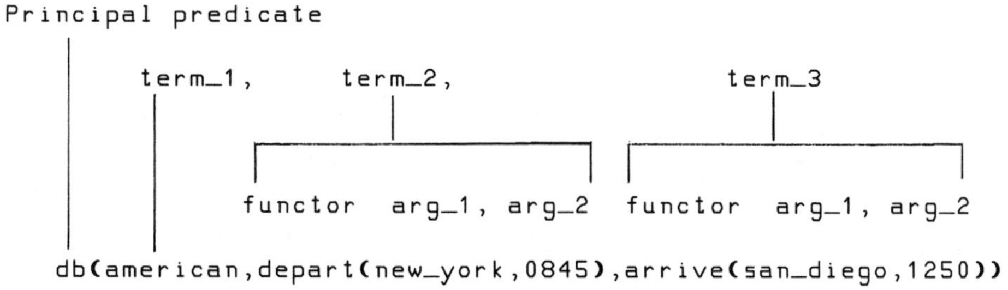

Figure 4.1 A Turbo Prolog fact with simple and compound terms.

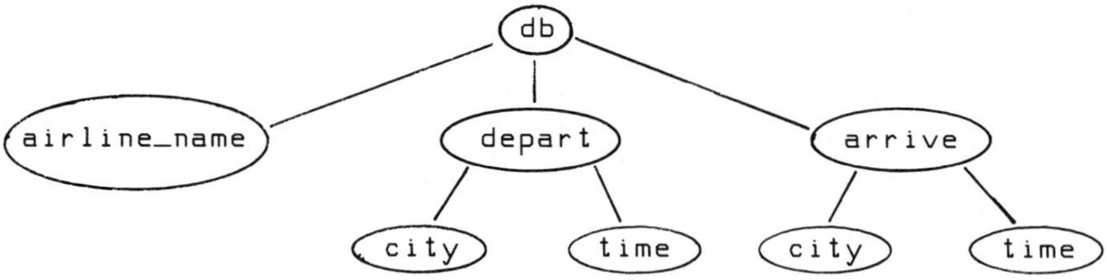

Figure 4.2 Airline information represented in tree form.

represents the principal predicate `db()`. Branches from the root node go to nodes representing the simple and compound terms of the principal predicate (`airline_vendor_name`, `depart_time`, and `arrive_time`). Nodes that represent compound terms branch to terminal nodes denoting city, time, and departure and arrival information.

There are many species of tree structures, but for our purposes in this book, we will limit ourselves to the single variety known as the *binary tree*. A binary tree is defined as a set of hierarchically organized objects which can be represented as a root, a left subtree, and a right subtree. The root can be any object (including the null object, in which case the tree is empty), but subtrees must themselves be binary trees. If you would like more details on other types of tree data structures, refer to Bratko, 1986, Vasta, 1985, and Amsbury, 1985.

A Turbo Prolog program can also be represented as a tree. Consider this simple Turbo Prolog program where rules and facts are represented by lowercase letters.

```
a :-
  b,
  e.
b :-
  c,
  d.
e :-
  f;
  g.
c.
d.
g.
```

Rule `a` is defined by clauses `b` and `e`. `b`, in turn, is defined by the facts `c` and `d`. The clause `e` is defined by facts `f` or `g`. Figure 4.3 displays this program as a tree. The curved arc indicates that subgoals are conjunctive and must both be proved. The broken arc indicates a disjunction of conditions where only a single condition to a goal must succeed. To prove goal `a`, Turbo would have to prove subgoals in the following order: `c` and `d` to prove `b` and `f` or `g` to prove `e`. This

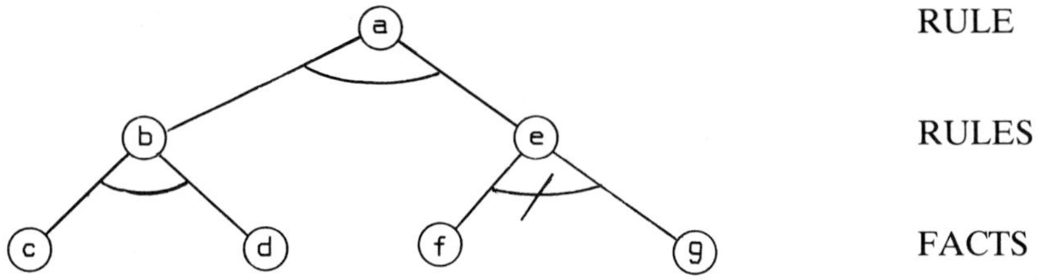

Figure 4.3 An AND/OR tree representation of a Prolog program.

proof, you will notice, traverses the tree from the left side to the right side. Also note that proofs proceed upward from terminal nodes (facts). This is depth-first searching.

Prolog's default depth-first searching is sometimes called a *weak* or *blind search* because it does not use information that might be available at nodes in the tree to guide the search process. Furthermore, searches are exhaustive and always executed in the same manner.

Strong searching methods exploit information made available at each node to implement more efficient searching in tree-structured knowledge bases. For example, heuristics can be used to shorten searches in complex problem spaces where the number of paths to solutions is very large and where blind exhaustive searches are too costly in time and computational overhead. Heuristics embody expert knowledge and are used to evaluate information at each node in order to recommend paths to explore and paths to ignore. By ignoring unlikely paths in the tree, searches are shortened and we can afford to tackle more difficult problems that would be intractable using brute force (exhaustive) searching methods.

Unfortunately, the price of efficiency is voiding the guarantee that a solution that exists will be found. Only exhaustive searches can provide this guarantee. In this chapter we will examine methods of searching. In particular, we will learn how to implement breadth-first searching as an alternative to the depth-first strategy. In Chapter 8 we will explore stronger methods of searching.

4.1.1 Depth-first Searching

Turbo Prolog's depth-first searching strategy has been illustrated in several example programs. We know that Prolog must prove one rule to success or failure before moving on to proving additional rules. If any rules are invoked during this search (a condition of one rule matches the head of another rule), the conditions of the new rule are added to the head of the proof list. This is depth-first searching. This strategy is blind and exhaustive, but it assures that Prolog will find a solution, if one in fact exists.

Consider the following binary tree in Figure 4.4. Note that this tree has a depth of four levels of nodes. Mentally trace a search starting at node `A` and looking for a path to node `M`. What would the solution path look like in a depth-

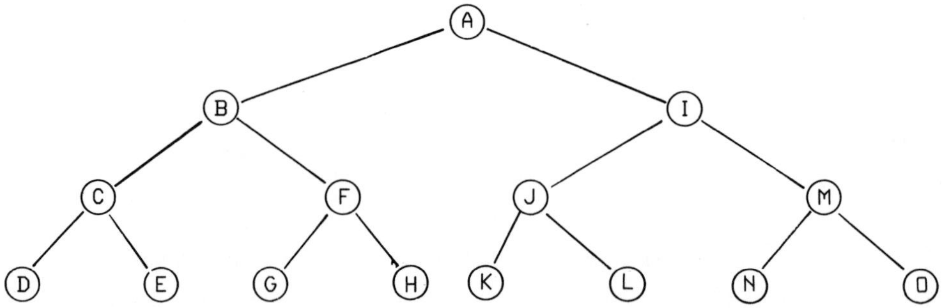

Figure 4.4 A binary tree with a depth of four levels of nodes.

first search? As shown in Figure 4.5, Turbo Prolog would have to visit every node in the left branch of the tree before successfully concluding its search deep into the right branch. The order of nodes visited before finding the goal node in a depth-first search is

```
START ──────────────────────────────→ FINISH
(A: B, C, D, E, F, G, H, I, J, K, L, GOAL: M)
```

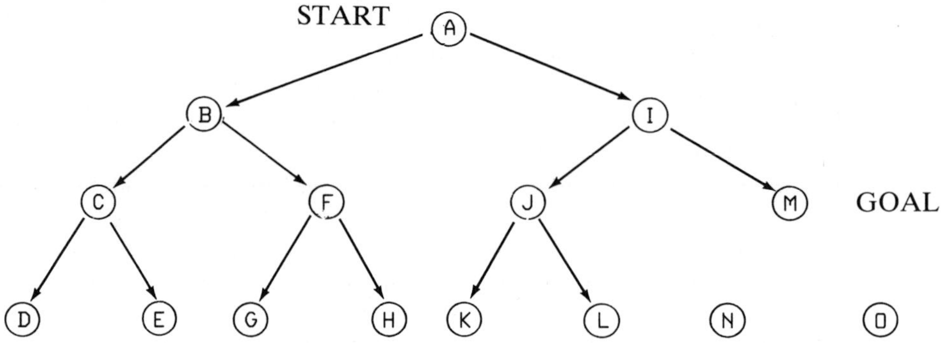

Figure 4.5 A depth-first search for node M starting at node A.

4.1.2 Breadth-first Searching

Breadth-first searching is a viable alternative to the depth-first strategy. Like depth-first searching, the breadth-first search is also exhaustive. This is illustrated in Figure 4.6. A breadth-first search requires that Turbo Prolog visit all nodes at the highest level of nodes before dropping down to visit nodes at the next lower level. Nodes at all levels are visited in the order from left to right. The order of nodes visited on the way to finding the goal node using a breadth-first search for M starting at A is illustrated in Figure 4.6.

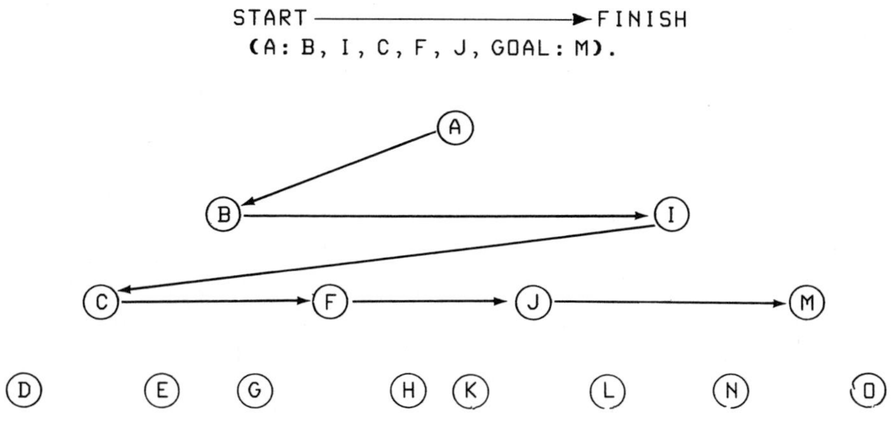

Figure 4.6 A breadth-first search.

If you think about these two exhaustive search strategies for a moment, you will notice that breadth-first searches of binary trees will always be shorter than depth-first ones whenever the goal node is located somewhere near the top of the right subtree. Also, a breadth-first search will find as its first solution the shortest route from the root node to the goal node.

As depth-first searching is Turbo Prolog's default searching strategy, the programmer has some work to do in order to implement the breadth-first strategy. First, rules must be declared to direct the search in breadth-first fashion and second, each node must contain information identifying the nodes to which it is connected. It is this information at each node that organizes the knowledge base hierarchically as a tree.

More specifically, each node must name two *successor nodes*. Each successor node is called a *child* of the *parent* node from which it branches. Furthermore, a child node is designated as a left or right successor node in a binary tree. If the child node is a leaf node, a null value is inserted in the place of each successor, signifying that it has no children. Figure 4.7 displays this information in graphical form.

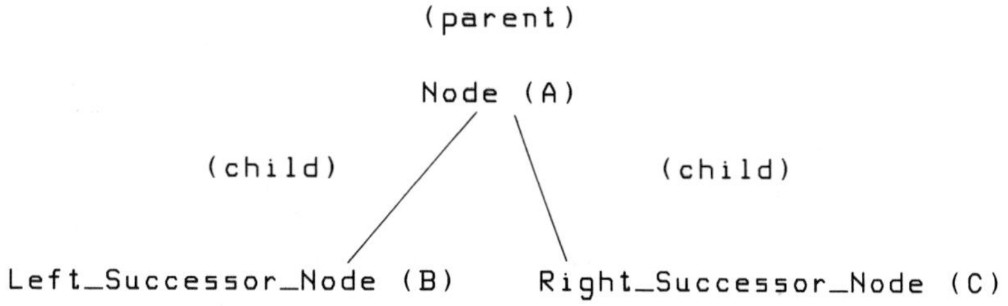

Figure 4.7 A parent node with two children.

The child relation can be stated using two rules:

```
child(X,Y) :-
  node(X,Y,_).
child(X,Y) :-
  node(_,Y,X).
```

In a two-level binary tree, there is no practical difference between depth-first and breadth-first searching. In either case, to find node C, B is checked first, then C is checked. However, in trees where there are children of children, or descendant nodes, significant differences will appear as the depth of the tree (the number of levels of nodes) increases.

A node is a descendant of another node if it is either a child (rule 1) or a descendant of a child of that node (rule 2). Here are the recursive Prolog rules which express these relations.

Rule 1

```
descendant(X,Y) :-
  child(X,Y).
```

Rule 2

```
descendant(X,Y) :-
  descendant(X,Z),          <—— recursion
  child(Z,Y).
```

In Figure 4.8 the relations are shown in graphical form.

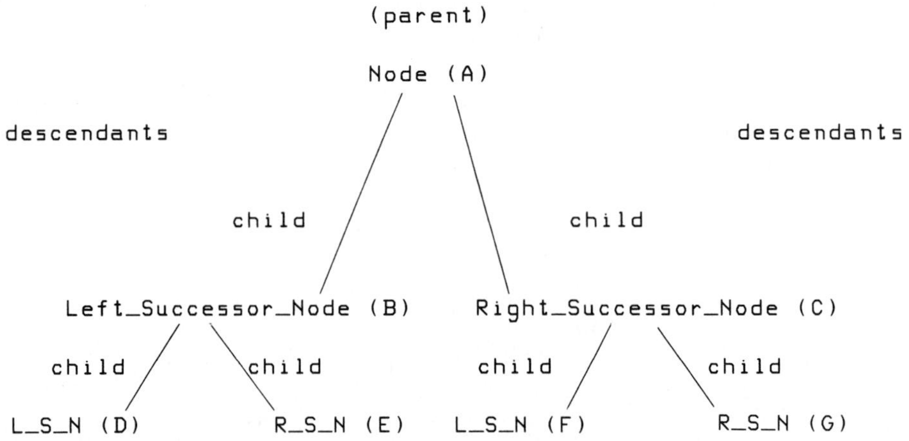

Figure 4.8 A parent node with children and descendant nodes.

The four-level tree in Figure 4.6 can be expressed as a series of Turbo Prolog facts.

```
----------------------------------------

node(left_successor,node,right_successor)

----------------------------------------
```

```
node(B,A,I).
node(C,B,F).
node(J,I,M).
etc.
```

With the child information included at each node the programmer can now instruct Turbo Prolog to visit the nodes in a breadth-first order. The following program illustrates procedures for structuring the knowledge base so that each fact or record has all the information necessary for the programmer to implement a breadth-first search. The simple breadth-first search rules then process this information and visit nodes one level at a time from the top down and from left to right.

I have included a DOMAINS declaration in this program. This declaration provides Turbo Prolog with information about the structures in the program. The specific declaration procedure is recursive. First you declare the structure in the DOMAINS section using a user-defined type. Here I use the word `contents` to represent the structure

```
record(string,char,char,char).

DOMAINS
contents = record(string,char,char,char)
```

Next you enter the user-defined `contents` as the data type of the principal predicate in PREDICATES declarations. Note that if any of these terms were compound rather than simple objects you would have another level of declaration to perform.

```
PREDICATES
 depth_first_search(contents,char)
 descendant(contents,contents)
 child(contents,contents)
 etc.
```

Now let's look at a complete program called TREE.PRO that implements both depth-first and breadth-first searching. While we examine the searching behavior of this program we will also consider some of the elements of what is considered to be good Prolog programming style.

I have written this program in five segments. The first segment contains the program declarations and an internal goal declaration. Turbo Prolog will automatically invoke `run`, which serves to activate or "drive" the program. With internal goals declared in this manner, the user does not have to enter a query to start the program running. However, when internal goals are used in programs, the programmer assumes responsibility for reporting the values of solutions to the user. Turbo Prolog will no longer write the values of instantiated variables to the screen, and the programmer must do so using `write` commands.

The second segment is the top level of the program, which contains the procedures for interacting with the user. This segment prompts the user for input and reports results of program searches. The third and fourth segments incorporate the search engines. The fifth segment contains the structured knowledge base.

4.1.3 Programming Style

Generally speaking, the Prolog programmer should strive to separate programs into declarative and procedural components. The declarative component will include all the logic statements, which represent the entities and organization of the knowledge domain. This component includes the facts and rules that permit the user to actualize the declarative semantics or meaning of the program. The procedural component of a program includes all the deterministic rules. Such rules often make use of primitives such as the `cut !`, `assert/1-2`, `retract/1-2`, `read()`, and `write()`.

Keep in mind that writing programs in which declarative and procedural functions are freely mixed can obscure the meaning of programs and is generally considered to be poor programming style. However, we will see that compromises with the ideal of good style are frequently made, particularly when the programmer must make programs interactive and efficient.

The important point is that the programmer should attempt wherever possible to preserve the semantic clarity of programs. Often the semantic clarity of programs can be enhanced by separating declarative and procedural components. For example, the programmer can declare high-level rules to perform procedural functions, such as communicating with the user, in one module. The high-level rules call the low-level rules which perform nondeterministic searching and inferencing. These rules are then declared in another component of the program.

In TREE.PRO, segments 1 and 2 represent the procedural components and segments 3, 4, and 5 the declarative components of the program. In the declarative components of TREE.PRO, however, you will note that I have included several `write()` and `nl` statements in what are otherwise entirely nondeterministic procedures. I did this for pedagogical reasons to demonstrate the program's searching behavior.

Now enter and run the TREE.PRO program. Do a trace and study the program flow until you understand exactly what is happening as the program conducts a breadth-first or depth-first search for a goal. After you have studied this program thoroughly, you should, as an exercise, modify it to conform more closely to the stylistic standards outlined earlier. If you have a printer on-line, you may wish to use the print option to obtain a copy of the program trace to study at your leisure.

```
/* *******************************************************
                          TREE.PRO

   A program to illustrate depth-first and breadth-first
   searching for a goal in a hierarchically organized
   knowledge base.


   *******************************************************


   SEGMENT 1 PROGRAM DECLARATIONS


   ******************************************************* */


   /* TRACE */

   DOMAINS

    contents = record(string,char,char,char)

   PREDICATES
    run
    record(string,char,char,char)
    case(string,char,char)
    continue
    depth_first(char,char)
    depth_first_search(contents,char)
    breadth_first_search(char,char)
    descendant(contents,contents)
    child(contents,contents)

   GOAL
    run.

   CLAUSES
```

(continued)

```
/* *******************************************************

   SEGMENT 2 USER INTERFACE

   ******************************************************* */
   run :-             % Driver rule
    write("\n\t\Depth-First Search =   D\n"),
    write("\tBreadth-First Search = B\n"),
    write("\n\t\t Enter D or B: "),
    readln(Answer),nl,
    case(Answer,'A','O'),
    continue.

   continue :-
    write("n\n\tTry again?  Y/N: "),
    readln(Reply),
    Reply = "Y",
    run.
   continue :-
    exit.

   case(Type_Search,Search_from,Search_for) :-
    Type_Search = "D",
    write("Depth-first Search from ",Search_from," for ",
         Search_for),nl,
    depth_first(Search_from,Search_for),
    write("at which I found GOAL ",Search_for)
    ;
    Type_Search = "B",
    write("Breadth-First Search from ",Search_from," for ",
         Search_for),nl,
    breadth_first_search(Search_from,Search_for),
    write("I found GOAL: ",Search_for)
    ;
    Type_Search = "_",
    exit.

   /* *********** End USER INTERFACE SEGMENT *********** */

   /* *******************************************************

   SEGMENT 3 DEPTH-FIRST SEARCH ENGINE

   ******************************************************* */

   depth_first(Search_from,Search_for) :-
    record(Name,Left,Search_from,Right),
    depth_first_search(record(Name,Left,Search_from,Right),
         Search_for).
```

```
    depth_first(Search_from,Search_for) :-
     write("\n\n\tSearching from Node ",Search_from),
     write("\n\tI failed to find Node ",Search_for).

    depth_first_search(record(_,_,Search_for,_),Search_for).
    depth_first_search(record(_,Left,_,_),Search_for) :-
     record(A,B,Left,C),
     write("I visited ",Left),nl,
     depth_first_search(record(A,B,Left,C),Search_for).
    depth_first_search(record(_,_,_,Right),Search_for) :-
     record(A,B,Right,C),
     write("I visited ",Right),nl,
     depth_first_search(record(A,B,Right,C),Search_for).


/* ************ End DEPTH-FIRST SEARCH **************** */

/* ****************************************************


     SEGMENT 4 BREADTH-FIRST SEARCH ENGINE


   **************************************************** */

    breadth_first_search(Search_from,Search_for) :-
     Search_from = Search_for.
    breadth_first_search(Search_from,Search_for):-
     descendant(record(_,_,Search_from,_),
          record(_,_,Search_for,_)).

     descendant(record(_,_,Search_from,_),
                    record(_,_,Search_for,_)) :-
      child(record(_,_,Search_from,_),
            record(_,_,Search_for,_)).
     descendant(record(_,_,Search_from,_),
                    record(_,_,Search_for,_)) :-
      descendant(record(_,_,Search_from,_),record(_,_,X,_)),
      write("I visited ",X),nl,
      child(record(_,_,X,_),record(_,_,Search_for,_)).

    child(record(_,_,Search_from,_),
                   record(_,_,Search_for,_)) :-
     record(_,Search_for,Search_from,_).
    child(record(_,_,Search_from,_),
                    record(_,_,Search_for,_)) :-
     record(_,_,Search_from,Search_for).

/* ************* End BREADTH-FIRST SEARCH ***************
```

The following is the knowledge base of hierarchically organized facts containing successor node information. The facts take the form

```
record(Node_Name,Left_successor,Parent_node,Right_successor)
```

The letter u is used in leaf nodes to designate the nil condition of no children.

```
***********************************************************

SEGMENT 5 KNOWLEDGE BASE

*********************************************************** */

   record("Node A",'B','A','I').
   record("Node B",'C','B','F').
   record("Node C",'D','C','E').
   record("Node D",'u','D','u').
   record("Node E",'u','E','u').
   record("Node F",'G','F','H').
   record("Node G",'u','G','u').
   record("Node H",'u','H','u').
   record("Node I",'J','I','M').
   record("Node J",'K','J','L').
   record("Node K",'u','K','u').
   record("Node L",'u','L','u').
   record("Node M",'N','M','O').
   record("Node M",'u','N','u').
   record("Node M",'u','O','u').

/* ****************** End TREE.PRO *********************** */
```

4.1.4 More on Structures

As we have seen, Turbo Prolog structures can be quite complex and expressive. To solicit information from a Prolog knowledge base of compound facts, however, the user must know precisely how the data is structured. The user must then enter a well-formed query with strategically placed variables to instantiate to the desired information. This is asking quite a bit from most users. Certainly you will want to write programs that are more friendly and less demanding.

To simplify use of a Prolog knowledge base containing compound objects, the programmer can write a front end. This front end will interact with the user to determine what information is needed. The program will also contain *meta-rules* that "understand" how information is represented in the knowledge base. These rules serve to map user queries onto the data structures in the knowledge base and report findings to the user. This is termed *data abstraction*.

Refer to the airline fact in Figure 4.1. Imagine a large knowledge base of such facts. Now consider the following rule for obtaining departure and arrival information on airline flights.

```
flight_info(City1,City2) :-
    db(Airline,depart(City1,Time1),arrive(City2,Time2)),
    write("Airline is ",Airline," leaving ",City1, " at ",
          Time1," and arriving at ",City2," at ",Time2).
```

All the user need do is provide the program with departure and destination cities and this rule will return information on all vendor airlines and relevant times for departure and arrival of flights.

Knowing how to write such rules will allow you to get the most out of Turbo Prolog's powerful searching, pattern matching, and inferencing capabilities as you build your own applications.

4.2 REPRESENTING KNOWLEDGE USING LISTS

A list is a special kind of structure in Turbo Prolog. A list is a collection of elements somewhat similar to an array except that an array has a fixed number of elements. Elements in a list may be any number of variables, constants, structures, or even other lists. As shown here, the elements of a list are enclosed in square brackets and separated by commas.

```
[element_1,element_2,...,element_n]
```

A list, like an English sentence, may be of any length. Unlike an English sentence, however, the list may be empty and contain no elements. The empty list is shown here.

```
[]
```

Here is an example where lists are used as arguments in a structure.

```
census([smith,joan],[145,cypress],[southport,ct]).
```

Each of the three lists contains exactly two elements. You can retrieve lists, or elements in lists, by forming queries with strategically placed variables. The following queries will produce two versions of Joan Smith's address.

```
census([smith,joan],X,Y).
census([smith,joan],[Number,Street],[City,State]).
```

The first query will instantiate the two lists in which the address information is located to X and Y. The second query will return the address information as elements instantiated to the variables Number, Street, City, and State.

You could produce the addresses of all the smiths in the knowledge base with the following external query.

```
census([smith,_],[Number,Street],[City,State]).
```

The census information can also be represented as follows:

```
census([[smith,joan],[cypress,ave],[southport,ct]]).
```

Notice the subtle but important difference in this example! The difference is the extra pair of brackets surrounding the three lists. This makes the argument of the predicate census a single list that is, in turn, comprised of three sublists.

Consider the structure

```
studies(joan,[psych_103,math_201,computer_sci_112]).
```

Here the functor takes two arguments. The first is a symbol and the second is a list of courses.

Let's say that we want to create a knowledge base of student schedules. The first argument will be the student's name. Some people have two names, others have three, or even more names. We could deal with the variable number of names by using a list. The second, third, and fourth arguments will be lists of all the social science, math/science, and humanities courses the student is taking this semester.

```
schedule([abt,jim,a],[],[calculus,geology],[ethics,literature]).
```

This fact tells us that this semester Jim Abt is taking two courses each in the math/science and humanity divisions, but he is not taking any social sciences courses. We know this because the second argument slot is occupied by an empty list.

As you can see, retrieving information from lists again requires that the user know quite a bit about how the information is structured. We shall need an efficient technique for processing the variable number of elements that may be contained in our lists.

4.2.1 List Processing

The big advantages in using lists are that related information need not be redundantly entered into a knowledge base as separate facts and we can represent elements in a list without worrying about how many there are. Take a moment now and refer back to the AUTO_2 program. Note that the caused_by() relation is entered twice to declare two causes of brake squeal (hard_linings and worn_linings). For certain types of auto malfunction, there could be a very large number of causes. Using binary facts to represent this information, a fact would be needed for each and every relation. However, using the list, we can represent a many-to-one relation between multiple causes and an effect. In fact, let's add wet_linings to the brake_squeal list now.

```
caused_by(brake_squeal,[hard_linings,worn_linings,wet_linings])
```

Enter the following program:

```
                          Editor
                  /* LIST_1.PRO
             /*  A program to learn about lists
                 and how to declare list domains.   */
DOMAINS
  list_of_causes = symbol* % Asterisk means list.
PREDICATES
  caused_by(symbol,list_of_causes)
CLAUSES
  caused_by(brake_squeal,[hard_linings,
       worn_linings,wet_linings]).
```

4.2.2 Declaring List Domains

Before querying this program to illustrate the uses of the list, let's spend a moment on the declarations required for lists. As was the case with the structure, the list also requires both PREDICATES and DOMAINS declarations. Whenever structures of either type are used as terms, Turbo Prolog requires a hierarchical declaration of data type. Here the procedure is a two-step process.

1. As you declare your predicates in the PREDICATES section, enter a user-defined name for the list, for example:

   ```
   PREDICATES
      caused_by(symbol,list_of_causes)
   ```

2. Declare the user-defined name (list_of_causes) in a DOMAINS section using the appropriate system data type for the elements of the list. In this example the type is a symbol.

Notice that the elements must be of the same domain. If you want to mix elements in lists you must use structures as elements. Each structure can then be declared to contain objects of a different data type. This technique is outlined in the Turbo Prolog Manual.

As shown, the list requires that you add an asterisk at the end of the domain type. The asterisk tells Turbo Prolog to expect a list of zero or more objects of the stated type.

```
DOMAINS
list_of_causes = symbol*
```

Now try the queries

```
caused_by(Effect,Causes).
caused_by(Effect,[Cause_1,Cause_2,Cause_3]).
```

To the first query, Turbo Prolog will return the list of all three causes enclosed in brackets. In the second query, the three causes will be picked out of their brackets. If we happen to be interested only in the first and last causes, we could use the following query:

```
caused_by(_,[X,_,Y]).
```

Turbo Prolog would return

```
X = hard_linings
Y = wet_linings
```

The anonymous variables in the query allow us to discard the unneeded information.

However, as pointed out earlier, what if we do not know in advance how many elements to expect in a list? Let's say we want the causes of an auto malfunction one at a time, but we do not how many there might be. This means we cannot use variables to instantiate to information since we don't know how many to include in the query. Furthermore, we do not want to have Prolog return an entire list enclosed in brackets. Fortunately, there are techniques that will allow us to process lists of varying length.

First, we will look at list notation and then we will cover techniques for processing information in lists to deal with the problems we have posed.

4.2.3 List Notation

All lists have as their final, and usually invisible, element the empty list `[]`. In fact, since a list is a recursive compound object, it can be represented as a tree with the empty list as the terminal node. Examine Figure 4.9, where the

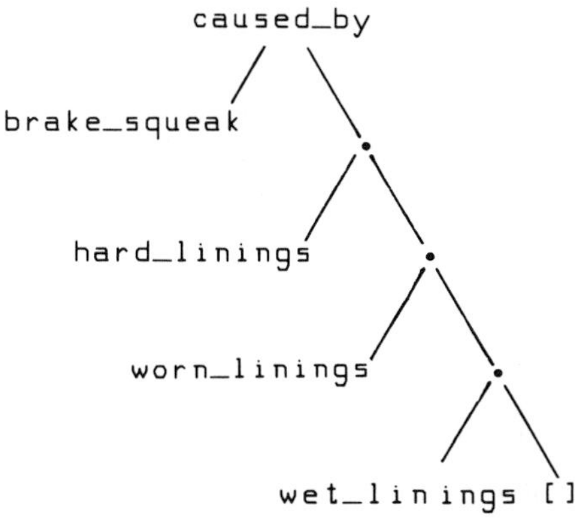

Figure 4.9 The caused_by fact displayed in tree form.

caused_by structure is portrayed as a tree. Notice the list shown as the right subtree. (I will not go into an explanation here but a list in the bracket notation has an invisible predicate represented by the period. See Appendix B.)

Lists can be split into two components called the head and the tail. The head is the first element and the tail is a list of all the remaining elements. The list constructor | in Prolog has the special job of splitting and joining the head element and the tail list.

Remember that all lists are made up of zero or more members. Any list with one or more members can be split into a head and a tail. The empty list with zero members is indivisible. Any attempt to split an empty list using the list constructor will fail.

Consider now a list with four elements, [1,2,3,4]. Using the list constructor [1|2,3,4], we can split off and remove the first element (the head), leaving a list of all the remaining elements in the tail.

```
HEAD    TAIL
  1    [2,3,4]
```

Taking the tail as a new list, we can again split off the first element [2|3,4].

```
HEAD    TAIL
  2     [3,4]
```

Next, we can split the list [3,4] into a head and tail with [3|4].

```
HEAD    TAIL
  3     [4]
```

As we know, a list always has as its last element an invisible empty list, so the preceding could be written

```
HEAD     TAIL
  3      [4|[]]
```

Splitting off the last element leaves the indivisible empty list.

```
HEAD     TAIL
  4       [[]]
```

Using the list constructor, four elements have been removed one at a time from the list. We can use the list constructor and the idea of recursively slicing the head from a list as a basic strategy for list processing. This will be illustrated again when I define the `member()` rule.

The list constructor can also be used to join lists. If the variables `L1` and `L2` are instantiated to lists, the following will hold:

```
L1 has the value [this,is,list1,and]
L2 has the value [list2,concatenated,together]
[L1|L2] = [this,is,list1,and,list2,concatenated,together]
```

Now try the following practice program.

```
Editor

                    /* LIST_2.PRO   */
      /*  Another program to learn about lists
            and how to declare list domains.      */

DOMAINS
  list_of_lists  =  list_of_courses*
  list_of_courses  =  symbol*
PREDICATES
  schedule_is(symbol,list_of_lists)
CLAUSES
  schedule(joan,[[soc,psych],[trig,calc],
            [phil,lit]]).
```

The DOMAINS declaration is a bit more complex in this example. Because this example employs nesting of lists (lists within a list) the declaration procedure requires an additional step.

The first argument in the structure is a person's given name. This is a simple object and can be declared directly as a symbol in the PREDICATES declaration.

The second argument is a list of lists. This is declared using the user-defined name `list_of_lists` again in the PREDICATES section. Next `list_of_lists` is declared as `list_of_courses*` in the DOMAINS section. Here the declarations inform Turbo Prolog that `list_of_courses` is made up of zero or more components that are themselves compound objects. `list_of_courses` is likewise declared as a list of zero or more symbols in the DOMAINS section.

Check the values of the following variables:

```
schedule_is(X,Y).
X = joan, Y = [[soc,psych],[trig,calc],[phil,lit]]

schedule_is(joan,[X|Y]).
X = [soc,psych], Y = [[trig,calc],[phil,lit]]

schedule_is(joan,[[X|Y]|Z]).
X = soc, Y = [psych], Z = [[trig,calc],[phil,lit]]

schedule_is(joan,[X,Y,Z]).
X = [soc,psych], Y = [trig,calc], Z = [phil,lit]

schedule_is(joan,[[X1,X2],[Y1,Y2],[Z1,Z2]]).
X1 = soc, X2= psych, Y1 = trig, Y2 = calc, Z1 = phil, Z2= lit
```

The first query asks Turbo Prolog to instantiate the values in the first and second argument slots to `X` and `Y`. In the second example, the first argument is provided by the user, and Turbo Prolog is directed to split off the first sublist as the head and leave the remaining two sublists as the tail of a list.

In the third example, the first sublist is again the head, but it is split into a head and a tail. This leaves the remaining two lists as a new list. Note that element 1 in sublist 1 is out of its brackets.

In the next query, Turbo Prolog instantiated the three elements (sublists) of the list to three variables. In the last query, all the elements of the sublists have been picked out of their brackets.

4.2.4 Defining List Membership

The `member()` rule is a useful list processing tool for relatively short lists and is found as a primitive in many implementations of Prolog. The `member()` rule allows the programmer to ask direct questions such as "Is `dog` a member of the list of elements `[cat,canary,goldfish,dog]`?" Prolog can answer the question by recursively slicing off the head of the list of elements until either the desired element or the empty list is reached. If the item is found in one of the slices, Turbo Prolog answers `True`; if not, it answers `False`. With such a recursive rule Prolog can sort through any list of unknown length and determine if a specified element is a member.

For an example, we might want to direct Prolog to search through a database of student schedules to find the names of students who are enrolled in a particular course. How might we proceed? The first step is to break the problem down into elements and apply list notation. Let's use X to represent a course we are looking for in a student's schedule. We can say "A student is taking course X, if X is a member of the list of the student's courses." Breaking this list down into a head and a tail, Prolog can conclude that the student is enrolled in course X if X is equal to the head of the list of courses. This can be written as follows:

```
member(X,[Y|_]) :- X = Y.
```

However, because of the unification mechanism discussed earlier, this rule can be rewritten more simply as an unconditional rule:

```
member(X,[X|_]).
```

Two forms of the rule will arrive at exactly the same conclusions because Prolog's unification algorithm will automatically perform the necessary matching and testing. Thanks to this feature, the programmer can often avoid unnecessary tests for the equality of terms by performing tests directly as done here. One such example is a predicate to test equality of terms, that is,

```
equal(X,X)
```

instead of

```
equal(X,Y) :- X = Y.
```

The anonymous variable is used in our member rule to instantiate to the tail of the list because we are interested, for the moment, only in the head. The rule states "X is a member of a list if X is equal to the head of that list." If it is equal, we have found what we are looking for and we are done. If it is not, what about the tail? X may be a member of what's left over in the tail, so another member() rule is needed to check there.

```
member(X,[_|Y] :-
          member(X,Y).
```

The second member() rule says "X is a member of a list if it is a member of the tail of that list." To prove that X is a member of the tail, we recursively invoke the first member() rule, which now takes the tail and splits off another head and checks it for equality against X. If this fails, member() will continue recursive splitting and checking until it either succeeds or reaches the empty list, where it must fail.

4.2.5 Recursion

Now you have seen a recursive rule in operation. Any rule is recursive when it must execute an image of itself as a condition of proof. In other words, the body of the rule contains a call to itself as a condition. In a tail-recursive rule, the recursive call is the last of the conditions. We will see soon that tail-recursive rules have some benefits in terms of efficient use of memory.

Note that in the second `member()` rule, the anonymous variable was used once again. This is because here we are interested only in the tail of the list. The first rule represents the *boundary condition* to recursion. A boundary condition produces success or failure and terminates what would otherwise lead to endless recursion (or a stack overflow followed by program termination). All recursive rules should have (1) a boundary condition and (2) procedures that produce that condition, if they are ever to terminate recursive looping.

The `member()` rule and other such user-defined rules, along with the primitive string processing tools provided by the system, make Turbo Prolog a highly effective list processing language.

4.2.6 Using the `member()` Rule

Add the `member()` rules to the LIST_1 program along with the necessary declarations and call it LIST_3.PRO. Take note that this declaration is not identical to the previous list declaration. This is because the object being declared is a list and not a list of lists.

```
                              Editor

/*                          LIST_3.PRO
          A program to try recursion in rules
        and to learn about declaring list domains
 */
DOMAINS
  namelist = name*
  name = symbol
PREDICATES
  member(name,namelist)
CLAUSES
  member(Name,[Name|_]).
  member(Name,[_|Tail]) :-
      member(Name,Tail).
```

Run the program and enter this goal.

```
member(c,[a,b,c])
```

To solve for this goal, Turbo Prolog must determine if `c` is a member of the list of symbols `[a,b,c]`. To solve this query, Turbo Prolog matches the query to the first `member()` rule,

```
member(X,[X|_]).
```

The rule now reads

```
member(c,[a|[b,c]]).
```

This fails, and Turbo Prolog drops down to the second rule.

```
member(c,[_|[b,c]]) :-
        member(c,[b,c]).
```

Turbo Prolog has recursively called the first `member()` rule, but this time the arguments take on the values

```
member(c,[b|[c]]).
```

Again, it fails and drops down to the second rule,

```
member(c,[_|[c]]) :-
        member(c,[c]).
```

The recursive call to `member()` now reads

```
member(c,[c|[]]).
```

This succeeds.

Another example to illustrate the use of recursion to process lists will be useful at this point. Consider a situation in which a program writes to the terminal many lines of text to provide information to the user. The `write()` primitive in Turbo Prolog accepts multiple arguments, but for many implementations of Prolog this would require a series of `write()` statements such as

```
help :-
 write("This is a help screen."),
 nl,
 write("It contains information "),
 nl,
```

```
write("needed by the user in order"),
nl,
write("to use a program successfully."),
nl,
write("A number of prompts can follow.").
```

The `print()` rule defined here uses recursion to process a list of text strings.

```
Editor

DOMAINS
  list = string*
PREDICATES
  print(list)
CLAUSES
  print([]) :-!.
  print([X|Y]) :-
    write(X),nl,
    print(Y).
```

Using `print()`, the help rule now looks as follows:

```
help :-
   print([
   "This is a help screen.",
   "It contains information ",
   "needed by the user in order",
   "to use a program successfully.",
   "A number of prompts follow."]).
```

Invoking `help()` causes Turbo Prolog to attempt to prove the `print()` rule, which has as an argument a list of elements. Each element is a string of words enclosed in quotes. The first `print()` rule invoked is not a match since the argument passed to `print()` is a list of elements and not (as yet) an empty list. The second `print()` rule is a match, however. X is instantiated to the head (first message) and Y to the tail (all the rest of the messages) contained in the list. X is printed to the screen and discarded, and Y is passed recursively back to the first `print()` rule. The list is still not empty so Turbo drops down to the second rule once again with X instantiated to the second message of the original list and Y to the remainder of the messages. In this fashion the list is pared down incrementally as each string is printed to the screen.

Eventually the empty list is reached, causing the first `print()` rule to succeed. The condition of this rule is a cut (!). The cut, you will remember, always succeeds the first time and then prevents backtracking. The first print() rule has succeeded, so Turbo Prolog returns to the help() rule, which now also succeeds.

Tail Recursion Optimization. Turbo Prolog has been optimized for maximal performance on microcomputers with limited memory. Partly, this has been accomplished through procedures that optimize tail-recursive rules. As you know, recursion occurs when a rule calls itself as one of the conditions in the body of that rule. In order to keep a record of what remains as unfinished work for the calling procedure and what alternatives are yet to be tried in solving for a goal, recursive rules add addresses to a pushdown stack on each loop of the recursion. Maintaining stacks of such records can pose a problem for systems with limited RAM. Since tail-recursive rules call themselves as the last condition, they do not need to keep records of what is left to do next. For this reason, Turbo Prolog converts tail recursion to the more memory-efficient process of iteration. (See the discussion on tail recursion and iteration in Covington, et al., 1988. pp 106–12.)

4.2.7 The append() Rule

Another useful recursive tool for list processing is the append() rule. append() is predisposed to backtracking, so many Prolog implementations provide more efficient primitives for appending elements to lists and our user-defined append() rule is not really needed. However, append() is presented here to illustrate a general approach to concatenation employing recursion.

To join two lists to form a third list, define the following pair of rules.

```
append([],List,List).
append([X|List1],List2,[X|List3]) :-
                    append(List1,List2,List3).
```

The first argument slot is occupied by a variable representing the first list to be joined. The second slot is occupied by a variable representing the second list to be joined. The third slot is filled by a variable that will instantiate to the new list made up of the two lists concatenated.

The first append() is the boundary condition and will succeed when an attempt is made to join the empty list to another list. It reads "If you append the empty list to another list you wind up with the same list you started with so stop."

The second rule introduces the recursion necessary to build the new list out of a successive splitting off of the head of the list and joining it to a new list. The rule reads "Take the head X from the first list and join it to the second list, making a third list with a head X and a tail made up of the tail of the first list and the entire second list." The head of the first list is, then, always the head of the new concatenated list. In sum, the second `append()` rule works by performing the following functions:

1. The first element of the first list, namely, the `X` in `[X|List1]`, is always to be the first element in the third list, namely, the `X` in `[X|List3]`.
2. The tail of the first list, namely, `List1`, will always have `List2` appended onto it to form the tail of the third argument, namely, `List3`. This is done by the recursive calls to `append()`.
3. The first rule will succeed when the first list has been reduced to the empty list by the splitting off of the head and the concatenation is complete.

Enter the `append()` rules, their declarations, the following two facts, and the two rules into LIST_2.PRO and call it LIST_4.PRO.

Editor

```
/*                    LIST_4.PRO
            A program to experiment with append
 */

DOMAINS
 list = elements*
 elements = symbol
PREDICATES
 append(list,list,list)
 fall_sched(list)
 spring_sched(list)
 schedule(list)
CLAUSES
 fall_sched([psy_1,calc_1,phil_1]).
 spring_sched([soc_1,trig_1,lit_1]).
 schedule(X) :-
   fall_sched(Y),spring_sched(Z),append(Y,Z,X).
 append([],List,List).
 append([X|List1],List2,[X|List3]) :-
   append(List1,List2,List3).
```

Try these queries.

```
fall_sched(X).
X = [psy_1,calc_1,phil_1]

spring_sched(X).
X = [soc_1,trig_1,lit_1]
```

```
schedule(X).
X = [psy_1,calc_1,phil_1,soc_1,trig_1,lit_1]

append([a,b,c,d],[e,f,g],X).
X = [a,b,c,d,e,f,g]

append(X,[e,f,g],[a,b,c,d,e,f,g]).
X = [a,b,c,d]
```

Notice that `append()` is invertible. This means that it can be used to find the value of any one of the three arguments. For example, if the rule is supplied with the second list and the appended list, it will return the value of the first list. Or, if the first and third arguments are provided, `append()` will return the value of a variable placed in the second slot. If all three values are correctly provided, `append()` will return `True`.

4.2.8 Other List Processing Tools

The following rule permits the programmer to determine the number of elements in, or length of, a list. Study this rule until you understand the principles used. Do you understand the boundary condition here?

```
list_length([],0).
list_length([_|Tail],Number) :-
      list_length(Tail,Count),
      Number = Count + 1.
```

Here recursion is introduced earlier in the rule. The program loops until the boundary condition is reached, then unwinds, incrementing the counter at each loop. When the last loop has been unwound, the rule succeeds with the variable `Number` now equal to the length of the list. Trace this one until you understand what is happening.

In some instances, a list of elements is constructed during program execution. Lists are built by adding a new element (the head) to an existing list (the tail). For example, the element `X` can be added to `List` using the `add_element()` predicate.

```
add_element(X,List,[X|List]).
```

Using this predicate in a recursive rule, a program could build a list of elements. However, the list will be constructed by adding elements to the head of the list. This means that items entered first would be retrieved (by the member rule) last. This is like a stack (first in, last out).

The programmer might wish to print the list of elements in the order in which they were added to the list. The `reverse_list()` predicate uses `append()` to reverse the order of the elements in a new list.

```
reverse_list([],[]).
reverse_list([Head|Tail],List) :-
      reverse_list(Tail,X),
      append(X,[Head],List).
```

In sum, recursive rules work because they process information and then pass that information to a copy of themselves in a series of loops. The process stops when a boundary condition is reached. In the recursive rules illustrated in this chapter, the boundary condition is defined as encountering an empty list. The programmer must take care in assuring that recursive rules have a boundary condition and have conditions in the body of the rule that will eventually produce this boundary condition.

Now that you have learned the basics of list processing, we can write a program to show off Prolog's list processing capabilities. The following program uses lists to represent family members. This will allow us to store and retrieve information for families where the numbers of spouses and children can vary. Remember that problem?

```
/* *****************************************************

                    FAMILY.PRO

 A program to illustrate the use of structures and lists

   *****************************************************   */

  DOMAINS
   spouses = parents(symbol,list)
   offspring = children(list)
   list = symbol*

  PREDICATES
   family(spouses,offspring)
   print(list)
   run

  GOAL
   run.


  CLAUSES
   family(parents(smith,[elizabeth,albert]),
                         children([diane,john])).
```

(*continued*)

```
family(parents(jones,[june,bill]),children([alice])).
family(parents(blake,[laura,harry]),children([sam])).
family(parents(blake,[carol,harry]),children([])).
run :-
 clearwindow,
 write("Enter family name: "),
 readln(Name),nl,
 family(parents(Name,List1),children(List2)),
 write("\nThe parents are \n"),
 print(List1),
 write("\nThe children are \n"),
 print(List2),
 fail.


print([]) :- !.
print([X!Y]) :-
write(X),nl,
print(Y).

/* ********************************************************** */
```

Examine the declarations in this program. The first step is to declare, using a user-defined type for each, the two compound objects that comprise the arguments of the `family` relation.

```
family(spouses,offspring)
```

The `parents()` structure is declared with the user-defined name `spouses`. The first term in `parents()` is a symbol and it is declared as such. The second term is a list and is declared using the user-defined type `list`. `list` is then defined as a list of zero or more symbols.

The `children()` structure is declared with the name `offspring`. The only argument in this structure is a list of symbols. We can save ourselves some trouble here and reuse the type list we have already declared.

Notice that making declarations is a backward process of working from the global structure down to its elements using user-defined types until you get to the atomic elements, which are then defined in one or more of Turbo Prolog's six data domains.

4.3 SUMMARY

Concepts covered

Binary trees
Breadth-first search

Depth-first search
DOMAIN declarations
Lists
  List constructor
  List membership
  Notation
  Processing
Recursion
  Boundary condition
  member() and append() rules
Structures

Prolog is not limited to processing simple objects and their relations. The objects of predicates may be compound. When complex objects are used as arguments, the terms are called structures. A structure has a name and terms enclosed in parentheses. Terms may be simple or compound objects.

Compound objects can also be represented as trees in Prolog. The binary tree is an easily implemented structure that has been widely used in the design of microcomputer database systems. A binary tree is composed of a root node, which can be any object including the null object. The root has a left subtree and a right subtree. The subtrees must themselves be binary trees.

Lists of objects are a special form of Prolog structure. A list is a series of zero or more objects surrounded by brackets, with the objects separated by commas. The list may be a member argument in a structure. The list constructor | splits or joins lists into a head and a tail, which is a list of the remaining objects in the list. The objects of a list may be constants, variables, integers, or other lists. The empty list cannot be divided. To access lists of varying length, several list processing tools are available or can easily be defined as procedures (rules).

Many user-defined list processing tools use recursion as a basic strategy. Recursive rules must satisfy a copy of themselves to succeed. Although at times necessary and effective, recursion in programs has the disadvantage of placing a drain on system RAM. For purposes of optimization of resources and performance, Borland has built-in methods for elimination of tail recursion.

The user-defined member() rule uses recursion and permits the programmer to determine if a selected object is a member of a given list. The user-defined append() rule is also recursive and serves to concatenate two lists.

4.4 EXERCISES

1. Enter the following clauses; then enter the declarations. Test your work by entering a query as an external goal and as an internal goal. Trace the program. Try changing the order of conditions in the buyer_needs rule. What happens? Why? Represent the program in tree form.

```
CLAUSES
can_sell(X) :-
   tool(X),
   buyer_needs(X),
   buyer_can_afford(X).
buyer_needs(X) :-
   buyer_has_job(Y),
   good_for_job(X,Y).
buyer_can_afford(X) :-
   price(X,Y),
   buyer_has_cash(Z),
   Z >=Y.
good_for_job(X,Y) :-
   applications(X,Z),
   member(Y,Z).

member(X,[X|]).
member(X,[_|Y]) :- member(X,Y).
tool(power_saw).
tool(power_drill).
applications(power_saw,[build_boat,
                        build_house,make_furniture]).
applications(power_drill,[build_boat,hobby,build_house]).
buyer_has_job(build_house).
buyer_has_cash(300).
price(power_saw,200).
price(power_drill,49.95).
```

2. Create your own personal knowledge base for friends, associates, and relatives. Include names, addresses, phone numbers, and other data. Use structures including the list to "package" the information. Write some rules to permit you to access the information. Declare the domains of the predicate objects; debug, and run the program.
3. Write a sports program based on the one in Chapter 2. Include a clause that requires that the preferred sport be a team sport. Add facts to the knowledge base that describe the various sports as team or individual. Use the list to represent team and individual sports. Run and trace the program.
4. Write an airline schedule program using the data structure discussed in this chapter but with added information about departure day, stopovers, and flight number.

Chapter 5
Turbo Prolog's Tool Kit

CHAPTER OBJECTIVES

Study of this chapter should enable you to do the following:

1. Use the Turbo Prolog Manual's catalog of primitives.
2. Understand the flow patterns that govern the functioning of primitives in programs.
3. Write simple procedures for string analysis, composition, and decomposition.
4. Write procedures for random and sequential I/O in files.
5. Use primitives that perform tests, conversions, and math operations in programs.
6. Enhance programs with windows, sound, and graphics.
7. Add DOS services to programs.
8. Write a procedure to add or subtract an element from a list of elements.
9. Write procedures for trapping entry errors.
10. Combine files at compile time.

IMPORTANT TERMS AND PHRASES

Catch rules
Devices
Evaluating expressions
File handling
Floating-point arithmetic
Formatting output
Input and output stream
Integer arithmetic
Memory management
Modularizing programs
Predicate flow patterns
Predicate invertibility
Program mode
Random I/O
Sequential I/O
String processing
Trapping errors

5.1 BUILT-IN PREDICATES

The Turbo Prolog system is a powerful and highly accessible dialect of the Prolog programming language. This is due to the integrated programming environment, which, in addition to the high performance made possible by the optimized compiler, provides the programmer with a wide range of programming tools. This chapter will introduce and explain many of the built-in predicates known as primitives that you will be using in developing your knowledge-based programs.

Be sure to take whatever time is necessary to practice with each primitive as it is introduced, and do not hesitate to experiment. Do proceed with caution when trying out the DOS system predicates, as some affect the status of files and the operating system environment.

A number of the system predicates are invertible. This means the primitive can have more than one function. Practice using these commands in alternative ways to accomplish different goals. The discussion on flow patterns will be instructive regarding the complementary uses of primitives.

Primitive commands can be entered by the user at the goal prompt without any need for declarations or a program. Primitives have been already defined and declared by the system designers. The restrictions on argument domain types and the binding of variables outlined in the manual and discussed below in the flow patterns section must be observed.

5.1.1 String Processing Tools

Much of the work that is done by knowledge-based software involves processing information in the form of strings. In this chapter, several predicates useful for manipulating strings as well as characters, numeric data, and files will be introduced.

In Turbo Prolog, a *string* is a sequence of ASCII characters surrounded by double quotation marks. The quotation marks allow the system to handle the string as an atom. Strings may be up to 250 characters in length. Turbo Prolog provides several predicates that permit the programmer to process strings in programs. The ability to analyze, compose, and decompose strings in programs is essential to the development of knowledge-based software. Single quotes are used to delimit an individual character that in Turbo Prolog is of the `char` data type.

5.1.2 Tools for Building Strings

To build `String_3` out of `String_1`, appended to the front of `String_2`, the programmer must have a tool for concatenating strings. The user-defined pair of recursive `append` rules discussed in Chapter 4 can be used. However, the `concat()` primitive provided by Turbo Prolog will do the same job more efficiently.

```
concat(String_1,String_2,String_3)
```

If `concat()` is called with `String_1` and `String_2` both instantiated to strings, it will return `String_3` with the value of `String_1` concatenated onto the front of `String_3`. To understand the function of `concat()`, as well as the other Turbo Prolog primitives, the programmer must understand predicate flow patterns.

5.1.3 Flow Patterns

In an earlier discussion a distinction was made between free and bound variables. Free variables do not have a value at the time of a call to the clause in which they reside. Bound variables do have a value; that is, they are instantiated or share a value with another variable. The characters `i` and `o` appearing in flow pattern statements represent the binding status of variables at the time the predicate is called. An `i` indicates that a variable is bound going into the call and an `o` indicates that a variable is free going in and bound coming out of the call.

Generally speaking, if a primitive has an arity of 1, it may have two possible flow patterns at the time it is used in a program. If a primitive has an arity of 2, it has four possible flow patterns for variables at the time of a call. The possible flow patterns for the binary relation are shown in Figure 5.1.

Primitives that can be called using any one of numerous patterns of variable instantiation can be used to perform multiple functions. Other primitives are extralogical and have but a single flow pattern and therefore but one function. For example, the various read primitives (`readln()`, `readchar()`, `readint()`, and `readreal()`) are used with a free variable and a flow pattern of (`o`) because their only job is to instantiate to input.

Examine the flow patterns of the `concat()` command. One primary use of this primitive is to produce a concatenated string out of two substrings. To accomplish this, the `(i,i,o)` flow pattern is used. Using this flow pattern, the programmer provides the two strings in the first two argument slots, and the primitive joins these two strings into a third string and instantiates it to the variable in the third argument slot.

At other times the programmer might use `concat()` to test that `String_3` has the value of two known substrings joined together `(i,i,i)`. If the string in slot 3 is the result of joining `String_1` and `String_2`, then this call will succeed. Yet another application would be to produce a substring value when one substring and the concatenated string are known at the time of the call to `concat()`, that is, `(i,o,i)` or `(o,i,i)`.

```
(Variable 1, Variable 2)          (Status 1, Status 2)
        (i, i)                       (bound, bound)
        (i, o)                       (bound, free)
        (o, i)                       (free, bound)
        (o, o)                       (free, free)
```

Figure 5.1 Illustration of the possible flow pattern bindings for a binary relation.

The flow patterns for all system predicates along with the permissible data types (domains) for arguments are found in the predicate definitions in the SYSTEM PREDICATE section of the Turbo Prolog Manual. The information for `concat()` in Figure 5.2 tells the programmer four things:

1. The predicate name, which symbolizes its function and serves as a mnemonic aid for remembering it
2. The predicate has three parameters, and all three must be of the `string` domain.
3. With the binding `(i,i,o)`, the first two variables must be instantiated to strings when the predicate is called.
4. The third variable will be instantiated to the output value produced by the action of the predicate.

Invoke Turbo Prolog and enter the external goal,

```
concat("This is string 1"," joined to string 2.",String_3).
```

Turbo Prolog will return

```
String_3 = "This is string 1 joined to string 2."
```

Try the other flow patterns as an exercise.

The two primitives

```
free(Variable)    (<variable>) : (o)
bound(Variable)   (<variable>) : (o)
```

will prove handy for checking the current bindings of predicate variables in programs. For example, if a predicate with an `i` flow pattern is called with a free variable, the program will generate an error message. Using `bound()` as a precondition to such a call can help eliminate problems such as these.

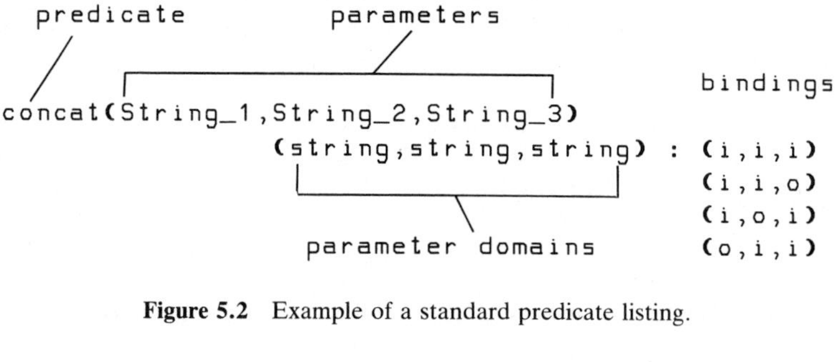

Figure 5.2 Example of a standard predicate listing.

5.1.4 Splitting Strings

Often it is necessary to split a string into a component token and a substring. You may use `concat()` but `fronttoken()` may be a better choice in this application.

```
fronttoken(String,Token,Reststring)
(string,string,string) : (i,o,o)(i,i,o)(i,o,i)
                         (i,i,i)(o,i,i)
```

`fronttoken()` splits strings into tokens which are names, that is, ASCII characters (except the nonprinting space), and a valid string representation of an integer or real number. It has multiple flow patterns and thus multiple functions. The following are examples.

`(i,o,o)` is equivalent to the call

```
fronttoken("This is a string",Token,Reststring)
Token = This
Reststring = is a string
```

`(i,i,o)` is equivalent to the call

```
fronttoken("Another example","Another",Reststring)
Reststring = example
```

`(i,o,i)` is equivalent to the call,

```
fronttoken("Try it again",Token,"it again")
Token = Try
```

`(i,i,i)` is equivalent to the call,

```
fronttoken("Prolog is great","Prolog","is great")
True
```

`(o,i,i)` is equivalent to the call,

```
fronttoken(Us,"me"," plus you")
Us = me plus you
```

5.1.5 Analyzing strings

```
frontstr(NumberOfChars,String_1,StartStr,String_2)
        (integer,string,string,string) : (i,i,o,o)
```

`frontstr()` splits a string in two components. `StartStr` is instantiated to the portion of `String_1` defined by `NumberOfChars`. The remaining characters in `String_1` are instantiated to `String_2`.

```
frontstr(4,"Incredible",Startstr,String_2)
StartStr  = Incr
String_2  = edible
```

To check for the length of a string, use

```
str_len(String,Length)     (string,integer) : (i,o)(i,i)
```

Try

```
str_len("How many characters are there here?",Length)
Length = 35
```

Notice that nonprinting spaces and punctuation are counted along with alphanumeric characters.

```
str_len("How many characters are there here?",35)
True
```

The `isname()` predicate is used to test if a string is a contiguous sequence of characters, digits, and underscores that start with a lowercase letter.

```
isname(String)    (string) : (i)
```

`isname()` will fail if the instantiated value of `String` is not a Turbo Prolog name.

```
isname(my_name)
True

isname(my name)
error

isname("my name")
False
```

5.1.6 Changing Case

There are times when the programmer must change the case of characters in strings. For example, the user may be prompted to answer `YES` if he or she wishes to continue with a program. Let's say that the program then performs the test

`Response = YES` in order to initiate branching based on the user's response. Inevitably someone who wishes to continue will answer `Yes` and the program test will fail since for the computer `Yes` does not equal `YES`.

To trap entry errors of this kind, `upper_lower()` is used. This predicate will convert user responses to either uppercase or lowercase characters; thus any test the program may make can be made in all uppercase or lowercase format. As you can see from the flow patterns for `upper_lower()`, it will either test the equality of two strings or convert the case of one or the other string format.

```
upper_lower(Upper_String,Lower_string)
                        (string,string) : (i,i)(i,o)(o,i)
```

Here is an example rule illustrating the use of the case-changing predicate:

```
continue :-
  write("Do you wish to continue - yes or no?"),
  readln(Response),
  upper_lower(Response,Lower_string),
  Lower_string = "yes",
  do_something,!.
continue :-
  do_something_else.
```

5.1.7 Reading and Writing

To process input and output in programs, the predicates `readln(String)` and `write(Arg1,Arg2,...ArgN)` are used. The optional number of arguments to `write()` may be instantiated variables, strings, constants, or a combination thereof. The argument to `readln()` is an unbound variable that will instantiate to user input terminated by a carriage return. Turbo Prolog also provides predicates for reading input in numeric and `char` data domains.

The `readreal()` predicate must be used when processing real-number input into programs. A real number is a decimal number in the range 1.0E−308 to 1.0E+308.

```
readreal(RealVariable)    (real) : (o)
```

The `readint()` primitive accepts integer (nondecimal) input in the range −32,768 to 32,767.

```
readint(IntVariable)    (integer) : (o)
```

`readchar()` reads a single character from the current input device.

```
readchar(CharVariable)    (char) : (o)
```

`readchar()` does not require that the user press the Enter key to conclude input as is the case with the other `read` primitives.

The keyboard and the screen are the default input and output devices and the only ones considered so far in our example programs. Soon, however, we will explore the use of files as a source of input and a destination for output.

When other devices, such as files on disk, printers on the parallel port, and modems on the serial port, are to be used for reading or writing, it is the programmer's job to notify Turbo Prolog by changing the default device. The programmer must also remember to change back to the standard device when finished with a programming task. I will show you how to do this soon.

Formatting output is a common function in programs. Using `writef(FormatString,Arg1,Arg2,...,ArgN)`, the programmer can tailor output to meet almost any specific format requirements. For example, the command

```
writef("Name %-15 Age %-6 Income $%10.2f.\n","John Jones",38,27450.00)
```

produces the nicely formatted output

```
Name John Jones       Age 38      Income $   27450.00.
```

Figure 5.3 shows how this primitive works. This predicate, much like `printf()` in the C language, gives the programmer fine control over the appearance of output. The arguments must be constants or variables of the standard domains. The format

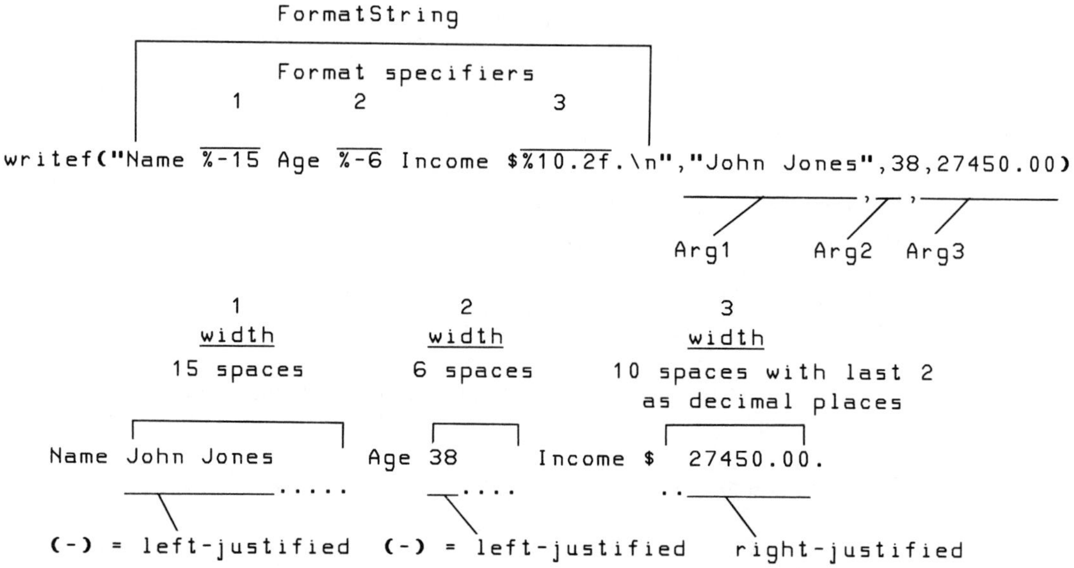

Figure 5.3 Use of the `writef()` primitive.

identifier will be printed without any changes. The percent sign % is the operator that signals to Turbo Prolog that a format specification field follows. The format specifier field is terminated by a space, as shown in the example. Formatting within each field is controlled by the following optional symbols:

- \- A hyphen indicates that the value of the corresponding argument will be left-justified in the format field. Right justification is the default.
- N{x} N is an integer that specifies the width of the field in which the argument will be printed. The x represents a qualifier of one of the forms:

  {f} for real numbers in fixed decimal notation
  {e} for real numbers in exponential notation
  {g} directive to use the shortest format (the default).

The best way to master this predicate is to use it. Starting with the example provided, try a few variations on the format specifications and study each resulting output. Use the print option to obtain a hard copy if you have a printer on-line. Using the hard copy, study the effect of each format specification on the output.

5.1.8 Interacting with DOS

One of the attractive features of the Turbo Prolog language is the easy trap door to DOS and all its resources. Without leaving Turbo Prolog, the program can invoke a DOS shell to obtain data on the system resources, make changes in directories, and handle files. There follows a listing of primitives that are particularly useful for communicating with DOS without leaving Prolog. Experiment with these at the external goal prompt.

```
system(Any_DOS_Command_String)     (string) : (i)
system("DIR C:\\Your_directory")
```

This command will return the requested directory listing. Notice that two backslash characters are required. Turbo Prolog interprets the first as a control character, and only the second backslash is passed on to the system as part of the command. It is recommended that you create a full-screen window before using this command, as output will erase your menu interface.

The command

```
system("")
```

will invoke a DOS shell as long as there is a copy of COMMAND.COM in a directory available to the Turbo system. You can then perform any normal DOS commands. To return to Turbo Prolog, type exit at the DOS prompt.

The command

```
dir(Path,File,SelectedFile)
              (string,string,string) : (i,i,o)
```

will be useful. This command allows the user to select a file with the cursor and Enter keys. The location of this file can then be passed to a Prolog procedure for processing. For example, the following command will produce a complete directory listing, and the complete path to the file chosen by the user will be instantiated to `My_Selection`.

```
dir("a:\\","*.*",My_Selection)
```

To rename a file while within a Turbo Prolog program, use

```
renamefile(OldDosName,NewDosName)
                      (string,string) : (i,i)
```

Other predicates accessing system functions are `time()` and `date()`.

```
time(Hours,Minutes,Seconds,Hundredths)
   (integer,integer,integer,integer) : (i,i,i,i)(o,o,o,o)

date(Year,Month,Day)
         (integer,integer,integer) : (i,i,i)(o,o,o)
```

Try

```
time(Hours,Minutes,Seconds,Hundredths)
time(1400,37,25,00)
date(Year,Month,DAY)
date(1988,10,6)
```

The first goal will return the current clock time. The second goal will reset the clock to 2:37.25.00 P.M. If you try this one, be sure to reset the time. The third goal will return the current calendar date, and the last goal will reset the system date to October 6, 1988.

In some instances the programmer needs to check on the current allocation of memory by Turbo Prolog.

```
storage(Stack,Heap,Trail)  (real,real,real) : (o,o,o)
```

`storage()` will return the current size in bytes of the primary partitions (stack, heap, and trail) used for memory management by Turbo Prolog.

The *stack* is the memory area where parameter transfer takes place. Prolog, as you have seen, does a lot of this. In particular, heavy demands are made on the stack by programs that use recursion. The setup option in Turbo Prolog allows the user to adjust the amount of memory allocated to the stack. Try 2048 when using the `Trace` facility.

The *heap* is used for several purposes. It is the place where facts are stored when inserted into the internal database. It is also the storage repository (a stack within the heap) for strings and structures used in programs and for user allocation of memory to other partitions. The heap takes whatever memory that remains unallocated to other partitions.

The default allocation of memory to the *trail* is zero. This area of memory is used only in special circumstances where reference variables are used in programs. Reference variables have to do with conditions where unbound variables are passed around from one subgoal to another, until they eventually become bound.

To remove unneeded files without exiting Turbo Prolog, use

```
deletefile(DOS_Filename)        (string) : (i)
```

Be careful experimenting with this one! It will remove files just as permanently as does `del` at your DOS system prompt.

To save files, use

```
save(DOS_Filename)              (string) : (i)
```

This command saves all the facts currently in the default internal database in a text file called `DOS_Filename`. We will see later that `save/2` is used to save facts currently in a named internal database in a text file called `DOS_Filename`. The file is ASCII and can be edited, but it is important not to make any syntax errors. Such errors in a file will cause any program that attempts to open it or to load it to crash. Soon we will see how files you have saved can be consulted or loaded back into working memory.

5.2 HANDLING FILES

Files may be treated as both input and output devices. Turbo Prolog can read or write information from or to a file as easily as it can using the keyboard and the screen (see Figure 5.4).

If you wish to write programs that will use a large number of facts, you can run out of RAM. One solution to this problem is to store the facts in files. Now the program can conserve RAM by opening files and reading into the program

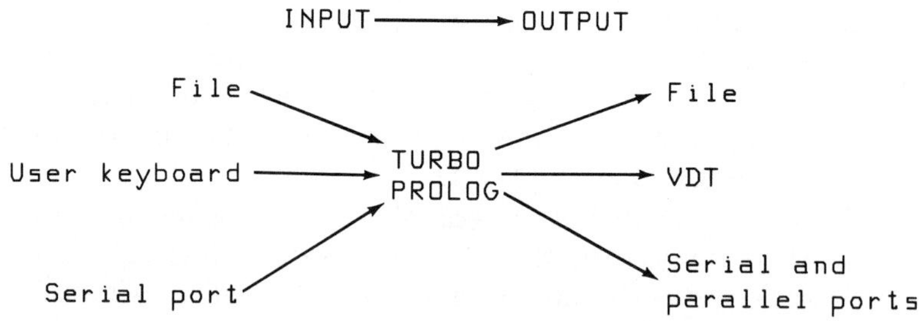

Figure 5.4 Input and output devices in Turbo Prolog.

only that information that is needed to solve a particular goal. If facts in the files are to be asserted or retracted, then appropriate DATABASE declarations must be used.

Several predicates are provided for using files as sources for program input and as destinations for program output. A program employing several of these primitives will be developed later in the chapter. A knowledge base management program KBMS.PRO will be developed in Chapter 8 to illustrate the full range of Turbo Prolog's file-handling capabilities.

5.2.1 Opening Files

To use a file in a program, it must first be opened. Several files may be open at the same time. The manner in which a file is opened is determined by the operations that are to be performed on the file. These operations may be reading, writing, modifying, or appending. A file that is opened in order to perform writing, modifying, or appending must be closed upon completion of the operation and before termination of the program. If the file is not properly closed, information may be lost. Closing files is not required when they are opened for reading only.

When a file is to be opened in a program, it must be given a symbolic name that Turbo Prolog will use internally when referencing the file. This name must be an atom, and no extension is permitted. The name must not be a reserved or restricted name, and it must be different from the name by which DOS knows the file. The `DOS_FileName.ext` also required in many I/O predicates may include a path and an extension. The DOS name and any optional path must all be enclosed in double quotes. If `DOS_FileName` is an atom with no extension or path attached, the quotes may be omitted.

The following are predicates used in handling files. Notice that the first argument slot contains the user-defined name for the file that is declared as FILE domain.

```
openread(Your_Filename,"DOS_Name.ext") (file,string) : (i,i)
openwrite(Your_Filename,"DOS_Name.ext") (file,string) : (i,i)
openappend(Your_Filename,"DOS_Name.ext") (file,string) : (i,i)
```

```
openmodify(your_Filename,"DOS_Name.ext") (file,string) : (i,i)
closefile(your_Filename)  (file) : (i)
```

The `eof()` primitive succeeds when it reads the end of file characters lurking at the end of every file. The `eof` is added by the system to the end of a file as it is closed or saved. This `eof` mark is a Ctrl Z or ASCII 26. It looks like & when you load a program into a word processor such as Wordstar. The `eof` mark is necessary because when reading files, Turbo Prolog needs to know when it has reached the end of the file. The `flush` primitive purges the contents of a buffer into the named file. This flushing of buffers is normally performed automatically by Turbo Prolog.

```
eof(Your_Filename)   (file) : (i)
flush(Your_Filename) (file) : (i)
```

5.2.2 Random Reading and Writing in Files

Once a file has been opened, the programmer must decide where in the file to perform read or write operations. Immediately after the file is opened, the default position, for all but the `openappend()` primitive, is at the beginning of the file. As you might guess, the default position is at the end of a file opened with `openappend()`. However, the programmer may wish to alter position within a file. In reading a file, it is clearly more efficient to go directly to desired information than it is to read sequentially all the file contents that precedes the relevant information. This process of nonsequential reading and writing is called *random I/O*.

After a read or a write operation has been performed in a file, Turbo Prolog will not automatically return to the beginning of the file in preparation for the next read or write operation. If a change in file position is desired, the programmer must issue a command to do so.

To change position in a file, use

```
filepos(Your_Filename,File_Position,Mode)
                    (file,real,integer) : (i,i,i)(i,o,i)
```

`File_Position` is a real number set according to Mode (see Table 5.1). A file position of 100 with a mode of 0 will direct Turbo Prolog to read or write at a point 100 bytes into the file from the beginning of the file. A position of 100 with a mode value of 1 will advance the file pointer 100 bytes farther into the file from the current position. Notice that `filepos()` can be used to locate the current position in the file as well `(i,o,i)`. Here `File_Position` will instantiate to the byte value of the location. Table 5.1 lists mode values.

Once a file is opened and a file position selected, a primitive is needed to read the fact contained at that file position. For reading in files, Turbo Prolog

TABLE 5.1 MODE SETTINGS FOR READING AND WRITING IN FILES.

Mode	Relative to:
0	The beginning of the file
1	The current position in the file
2	The end of the file

provides the `readterm()` predicate. `readterm()` will read any term that can be written by the `write()` predicate.

```
readterm(Domain,Term)    (<name>,<variable>) : (o,i)
```

`readterm()` will attempt to read the first fact encountered in the file, and if the fact does not match the template provided by the second argument, it will fail.

Performing multiple reads in a file. To direct `readterm()` to read all the facts in a file, a mechanism for repeating the call to `readterm` must be provided by the programmer. Examine the `check()` predicates in the RECORDS.PRO program in section 5.2.3. After entering and running this program, do a trace to observe the `check()` predicates at work. Notice how these rules will, through backtracking, cause `readterm()` to read all the facts in a file until either the search ends with success or the `eof` marker is encountered.

When files are to be opened in a program, this must be announced to Turbo Prolog by declaring the user-defined (symbolic) file name in the DOMAINS section. This, along with other file-handling principles, is illustrated in RECORDS.PRO.

The INCLUDE compiler directive permits the programmer to name a source file in a program and have the compiler link that file to the program at compile time. Examples of the use of the INCLUDE will be provided in several demonstration programs.

5.2.3 Devices

After opening a file for reading or writing, the programmer must reassign the input or output stream from the default of the keyboard or screen to the file:

```
readdevice(Your_Filename)   (symbol) : (i) (o)
```

If the file `Your_Filename` has been properly opened for reading, the input stream will be redirected from the keyboard to the file. Remember to reassign the current input back to the keyboard when you are finished.

```
readdevice(keyboard)
writedevice(screen)
```

In this fashion the input and output streams can be efficiently directed and redirected within programs.

Reading	Writing
readdevice(keyboard)	writedevice(screen)
readdevice(Your_File)	writedevice(Your_File)
readdevice(com1)	writedevice(printer) {parallel port}
	writedevice(com1) {serial port}

Devices are automatically defined in the file domain and must not be redeclared by the programmer. If the appropriate devices are not active on the serial or parallel ports, the program will hang, requiring a <ctrl Break> keychord to continue. Also, if the program fails to return to the keyboard as the current input device, the program will also hang! This is a common error, so be wary.

Type in the two example programs and experiment with them. Use the trace facility to follow the flow of the program. Pay particular attention to the function of the check predicates. Note that the program will crash if the file `my_data.dba` does not exist in the current directory. Try entering duplicate facts in `my_data.dba`.

Editor

```
/*                          RECORDS.PRO
   A personal database program. The program illustrates
   how to declare files and read facts from a separate
   data file. The program can be easily extended to
   accommodate larger stores of information.
 */
DOMAINS
 name,address,phone,note = string
 record = info(name,address,phone,note)
 file = data_records % Here is a file declaration!
PREDICATES
 setup
 person(name)
 check(file)
 run
 continue
GOAL
 setup.
CLAUSES
 setup :-
  existfile("my_data.dba"), /* check file is present */
  openread(data_records,"my_data.dba"),/* open for read */
  run.
```

(continued)

```
run :-
  filepos(data_records,0,0),    /* start at beginning */
  clearwindow,
  write("Enter Name: "),      /* program is interactive */
  readln(Name),nl,
  person(Name),
  continue.

person(Name) :-
  readdevice(data_records), /* read from the file    */
  check(data_records),
  readterm(record,info(Name,Address,Phone,Note)),
  writef("Name:        %-18\nResidence: %-30\nPhone:      %10
      \nNote:       %-60",Name,Address,Phone,Note),!.
person(Name) :-
  write(\nSorry, no information on ",Name),
  write("Please check that entry is in order.").

 /* Give user a chance to continue to search
    for more information.                              */

continue :-
  readdevice(keyboard),       /* back to the keyboard   */
  write("\n\nDo you wish to continue? y/n "),
  readchar(R),
  R = 'y',
  run
  ;
  closefile(data_records).

check(_).
check(File) :-
  not(eof(File)),
  check(File).
```

Editor

```
  /*                        my_data.dba
        Format of data file for RECORDS.PRO.
      Create this file before you run RECORDS.PRO.
  */
info("Tom Smith","12 Wyse Road, Westport, CT","345-6780")
info("Laura Blake","344 Jeffrey Ave, Bangor, ME","567-3212")
etc..  % Complete the database.
```

5.2.4 Trapping Entry Errors

A problem often encountered in programs is dealing effectively with unexpected user input. In fact, the programmer must assume that all programs will be used in some unorthodox manner that can result in a run time problem. This is particularly the case in Turbo Prolog, which uses primitives with data type requirements for arguments.

If a user violates the restriction on input data type, we do not want our programs to misbehave. Good programs are robust and do not crash. There are techniques that you can use for occasions when either the program expects one type of data and the user enters another or a search for information fails. The approach used in RECORDS.PRO is quite simple but effective. The program contains "catch" rules. If a rule cannot execute for reasons of improper user input, a catch rule can handle the result.

In the case of the RECORDS.PRO program, the second `person()` rule is provided for instances where either the data requested is not present in the knowledge base or the user has misspelled the keywords used by the programs in searching for information. If the first rule fails, the program drops down to the second, where the user is informed of both possibilities and then is given a chance to review the entry and to continue. Had this catch rule not been included, the program would terminate without explanation after incorrect input, leaving behind a bewildered user.

Other methods for protecting programs from user-produced run-time errors will be demonstrated in subsequent programs.

5.2.5 Consulting Files in Programs

For some programming tasks it may be desirable to load an entire file from disk into memory. This can increase program efficiency since processing will take place at the speed of memory, which is, of course, much faster than repeated accessing of even the fastest hard disk.

To do this, you use `consult/1`.

```
consult(DOS_Filename) (string) : (i)
```

Don't forget the quotes around DOS_Filename if it is not an atom. This loads a syntactically correct file into memory. If there is a syntax error in the file, `consult/1` will fail. Files stored with the `save/1` predicate should be OK, but if a file is created using a word processing program, be sure to use the ASCII or nondocument mode and be careful to avoid syntax mistakes. The facts listed in `my_data.dba` are in correct syntactic form.

The `consult/1` standard predicate has a two-argument sibling that allows the programmer to name a database domain and load facts selectively from named external databases.

When files are of modest size, it may be advisable to keep all the information in memory. RECORDS.PRO can be rewritten to use `consult/1` rather than opening the file, redirecting input, and reading successive terms to search for the desired information and once again redirecting input.

The following is a program that allows the user conveniently to list, select, open, and browse files. It uses procedures for determining the current path, listing, and selecting a file in a named directory with a bounce-bar menu.

```
disk(Directory)
dir(Directory,Files,Choice)
```

The selected file is displayed by

```
file_str(File,String)
```

Once the file is displayed, the arrow, PgUp, and PgDn keys are used to move around in the file.

The README1.PRO program uses three window primitives: `makewindow/8`, `clearwindow`, and `removewindow`. These primitives and others will be covered in Chapter 6. In the meantime, this program will serve to demonstrate the use of these primitives and the ease with which you can build useful utility programs in Turbo Prolog.

```
/* *************************************************************

                    README1.PRO
           A utility for browsing files.

   ************************************************************ */
PREDICATES
 run
 continue

GOAL
 run.

CLAUSES
 run :-
 clearwindow,
 makewindow(1,112,112,"SELECT OPTION",10,25,6,20),
 write("\n 1) Read a file\n"),
 write(" 2) Exit to DOS\n "),
 readchar(Choice),
 Choice = '1',
 removewindow,
 continue
 ;
 clearwindow,
```

```
removewindow,
exit.

continue :-
makewindow(2,112,48,"README",0,0,24,80),
write("Enter Directory: "),
readln(Directory),
disk(Directory),
dir(Directory,"*.*",File),
file_str(File,String),
display(String),
removewindow,
run.
/* ******************************************************* */
```

5.3 MATH AND TURBO PROLOG

Prolog is primarily a symbol processing language; however, Turbo Prolog supports floating-point calculations and a wide range of arithmetic predicates and functions reminiscent of Turbo Pascal.

5.3.1 Evaluating Expressions

Turbo Prolog can perform all the basic arithmetic operations on integer and real numbers, including addition (+), subtraction (−), multiplication (*), and division (/). Integers and reals can be mixed in expressions, with the system accepting responsibility for sorting things out. Table 5.2 shows the result of using mixed numeric types in expressions.

Turbo Prolog also permits calculations using hexadecimal numbers, which are identified by being preceded by a dollar sign.

Table 5.2, adapted from the Turbo Prolog 1.xx Manual, shows that if an expression uses integers only and does not involve division, which has the nasty habit of generating fractional components, the system will save resources by de-

TABLE 5.2 ARITHMETIC OPERATIONS IN TURBO PROLOG.

If the first number is:	and the Operator is:	and the second Number is:	the result is:
integer	+, −, *	integer	integer
real	+, −, *	integer	real
integer	+, −, *	real	real
real	+, −, *	real	real
integer or real	/	integer or real	real

faulting to integer calculations. Under all other circumstances, the system will default to real-number calculations in order to handle fractions and maintain maximum accuracy of results.

The programmer must be aware of the manner in which Turbo Prolog solves expressions. Consider the expression

```
X = 3 + 4/2 - 6 * (3 * (2 + 9/3))
```

Turbo Prolog will solve for X using the following rules:

- In expressions where there are nested subexpressions, solutions to the most deeply nested subexpressions will be solved for first, for example, (2 + 9/3).
- Working from left to right, division and multiplication will precede subtraction and addition: (2 + 9/3) becomes (2 + 3) which becomes (5)

The complete step by step process is as follows:

```
X = 3 + 4/2 - 6 * (3 * (2 + 9/3))
X = 3 + 4/2 - 6 * (3 * (2 + 3))
X = 3 + 4/2 - 6 * (3 * (5))
X = 3 + 2 - 6 * 15
X = 3 + 2 - 90
X = 5 - 90
X = -85
```

5.3.2 Arithmetic Predicates and Functions

`sqrt(X)` Turbo Prolog provides other math primitives such as the square root function `sqrt()`.

```
X = sqrt(A_Number)
```

X will be bound to the result and return the value. Try some examples, such as

```
Goal: X = sqrt(9)
      X = 3
```

`X mod Y` Z = X mod Y will bind the remainder of X divided by Y to Z.

```
Goal: Z = 14 mod 4
      Z = 2
```

`X div Y` — `Z = X div Y` will bind the quotient of `X` divided by `Y` to `Z`.

```
Goal: Z = 14 div 4
      Z = 3
```

Turbo Prolog provides trigonometric, exponential, and logarithmic functions. If you so desire, refer to the manual and experiment with these:

```
cos(X)
sin(X)
tan(X)
arctan(X)
exp(X)
ln(X)
log(X)
```

In some programs it is useful to introduce a principle of randomness. Selecting people randomly from a database as part of an experiment is one such use. To do this, each person would be assigned a unique number, and random numbers generated to assure that selections are made without bias. Turbo Prolog provides two versions of a random-number generating primitive.

`random(X)` — `random/1` binds its argument to a random number between 0 and 1. `random/2` produces random numbers within a specified range.

`round(X)` — `round(X)` returns the rounded value of `X`.

`trunc(X,Y)` — This new standard predicate in Version 2.0 will truncate a real to an integer number.

The programmer may define other arithmetic predicates as needed. The following predicates are not needed, but they will illustrate techniques for building such predicates.

```
add(X,Y,Z) :- Z = X + Y.
subtract(X,Y,Z) :- Z = X - Y.
divide(X,Y,Z) :- Z = X/Y.
multiply(X,Y,Z) :- Z = X * Y.

square(X,Z) :- Z = X * X.

maximum(X,Y,X) :- X >= Y, !.
maximum(_,Y,Y).
```

5.3.3 Making Comparisons in Turbo Prolog

There are times when a programmer needs to make comparisons of objects as part of a test. The relational operators permit such tests on numeric values. As defined in section 5.3.2, `maximum()` is an example of a user-defined predicate that performs such a test on two numbers and returns the value of the larger using the built-in relational operator `>=`.

Tests can also be performed using characters and strings, as the system can evaluate the ASCII values of the characters. Turbo Prolog matches and tests character by character the numerical ASCII values of two characters or pairs of successive characters in strings.

Examine the relational operators in Table 5.3. Observe that Turbo Prolog evaluates the string `success` as greater than the string `money`. Turbo Prolog performs tests based upon the ASCII values of the characters making up the two words. The ASCII value of `s` is 115 and the value of `m` is 109, and 115 is greater than 109. Had the first two characters been identical, Prolog would have matched the next pair, and so on.

TABLE 5.3 RELATIONAL OPERATORS IN TURBO PROLOG

Operator	Function	Examples of Use
<	less than	`3 < 7 is TRUE; 3 < 2 is FALSE; 'a' < 'b' is TRUE; bill < sam is TRUE`
<=	less than or equal to	`8 <= 12 is TRUE; 12 <= 12 is also TRUE`
=	equal	`9 = 9 is TRUE; success = money Prolog knows this is FALSE`
>	greater than	`3.12 > 3.11 is TRUE; success > money is TRUE`
>=	greater than or equal to	`56 >= 23 is TRUE and so is 56 >= 56`
<> or ><	different from	`3 <> 7 is TRUE`

5.3.4 A Calculator Program

Let's apply some of the arithmetic predicates and build a small calculator program. The program will perform addition, subtraction, multiplication, and division on user-entered numbers and then return the answer. This program will be enhanced in Chapter 6.

```
/* ************************************************************

                         CALC.PRO
                   A calculator program.

************************************************************ */

DOMAINS
 list = string*

PREDICATES
 start
 ask_about(integer)
 compute(integer,real,real)
 report(real)
 print(list)

GOAL
 start.

CLAUSES
start :-        % Illustrates building a menu
 clearwindow,
 print(["Welcome to the Electronic Abacus!\n",
       "Select desired operation from menu;",
       "              1) addition",
       "              2) subtraction",
       "              3) multiplication",
       "              4) division",
       "              5) exit"]),
write("Enter Choice: "),
 readint(Choice),
 Choice <= 4,
 ask_about(Choice) ;
 write("\nBye").

ask_about(Choice) :-
 write("Enter number: "),
 readreal(First_Number),nl,
 write("Enter number: "),
 readreal(Second_number),nl,
compute(Choice,First_Number,Second_Number).

report(Result) :-
 write("The answer is ",Result,"."),
 write("\nDo you wish to continue?  y/n "),
```

(continued)

```
 readchar(Request),nl,
 Request = 'y',
 start.

print([]) :- !.
print([X|Y]) :-
 write(X),nl,
 print(Y).

/* ********************************** */

compute(1,First_Number,Second_Number) :-
 Result = First_Number + Second_Number,
 report(Result).
compute(2,First_Number,Second_Number) :-
 Result = First_Number - Second_Number,
 report(Result).
compute(3,First_Number,Second_Number) :-
 Result = First_Number * Second_Number,
 report(Result).
compute(4,First_Number,Second_Number) :-
 Result = First_Number / Second_Number,
 report(Result).

/* ***************************************************** */
```

Review the logic of CALC.PRO and then trace the execution of the program. Outline ways in which you would like to improve upon this program.

5.4 SUMMARY

Concepts covered:

Accessing DOS
Arithmetic standard predicates
Changing case
Comparison operators
Error trapping
File handling
Flow patterns
Formatting output
Random and sequential I/O
Reading and writing in files and internal database

This chapter reviewed some of the major tools provided with the Turbo Prolog programming environment. The tool kit includes a variety of primitives for manipulating strings, files, numbers, and other data. The programmer uses these predefined predicates to build more complex tools for use in solving problems.

To get the most out of the tool kit provided with the language, the programmer must understand the flow patterns of variables in each predicate. The flow pattern specifies the bindings of variables at the time the predicate is called or used. The flow pattern `(i,o,i)` states that the values of the first and third variables of the predicate must be known (instantiated) at the time of the call. The predicate will perform its function and return the value instantiated to the second variable. Each predicate also places restrictions on the domains of objects that can be legally instantiated to each variable. The unwary programmer may use a predicate improperly and cause syntactical rather than logical failure of the goal in which the predicate exists as a condition.

File handling permits the programmer to read from and write to files as well as from and to the internal database. This permits programs to access huge amounts of knowledge far in excess of the limits of RAM in the current generation of microcomputers.

Turbo Prolog supports floating-point arithmetic and a wide assortment of useful math functions.

5.5 EXERCISES

1. Add a square root function to the calculator program.
2. Define the function of the cut `!` in the second person rule of the RECORDS.PRO program. Try removing it after predicting the outcome.
3. Write a small interactive program to read input from the keyboard and then write it to the file `my_data.dba`. How are you going to insert the `eof` character?
4. Answer the following with *True* or *False* after reviewing a table of ASCII values:
   a. `'!' > '&'`
   b. `Prolog >= prolog`
   c. `Lisp = Prolog`
   d. `Fortran <> Prolog`
   e. `'x' > 'T'`
5. Using `writef()`, produce the following output:

```
Name:  John Smith  Title: manager   Shift: night
Co. :  Ajax, Inc.  Prod : Frangits  Cost :$ 9.95
```

6. The RECORDS.PRO program would fail to find any requested information if the user (a) entered last name and then the first name or (b) failed to enter a name using the proper case. Rewrite the program to prevent these malfunctions.
7. Discuss the differences in function between `concat()` and `fronttoken()`.
8. Trace the `maximum()` procedure in section 5.32. Why is the anonymous variable used in the second rule?

Chapter 6
The Software Interface: Windows, Sound, and Graphics

CHAPTER OBJECTIVES

Study of this chapter should enable you to do the following:

1. Discuss the problem of computer accessibility and the issues surrounding good software interface design.
2. Use windows effectively in programs.
3. Read and write in windows using the full assortment of window primitives.
4. Use sound, color, and graphics effectively in programs.
5. Use the `INCLUDE` directive to merge programs.
6. Write useful utility and decision-making programs making effective use of software interface tools.

IMPORTANT TERMS AND PHRASES

Color palettes
Comline commands
Computer accessibility
Counter procedures
Default procedures
Human-computer interface
Logo programming language
Merging programs
Metalevel programming
Turtle graphics
Trace directives
Window attributes

> I believe that fifty years from now people will look back on the latter part of the 20th century as a quaint era when computers were designed to act like humans and some people believed that computers would soon match human intelligence. Even as computer systems increase in sophistication, we will more clearly discriminate between human capabilities, needs, and aspirations and the computer's tool-like nature. We must remember that producing computer systems is not a goal in itself, but merely a means of increasing the kinship among people.
>
> [Ben Shneiderman, *Software Psychology*, p. xii]

6.1 THE HUMAN-COMPUTER INTERFACE

The quotation serves to remind us that the key to success in developing computer systems, or any technology for that matter, lies in the accessibility of the technology. This means that people must come to regard computers as helpful tools rather than technological wizardry. Accessibility also means more than the mere proximity of a microcomputer in the workplace, school, or home. To be accessible, computers must have a human-machine interface that caters to the cognitive requirements of users, novice and expert alike. Such an interface will provide pop-up menus, clear, nonthreatening, and unobtrusive error messages, and "I think I know what you want" default procedures for the novice and command line shortcuts around time-consuming menu systems for the expert.

The KBS developer must be concerned with the functionality of programs as well as the confidence, ease, and comfort with which they can be understood and used. Windows, sound, and graphics are basic tools that you will be using in creating software interfaces for your programs. This chapter will introduce you to these tools as well as some basic methods for using them effectively in designing your program interfaces.

Several demonstration programs are included in this chapter for you to study and enhance. You should by now have mastered fundamental Prolog programming skills, and it is time for you to begin working with more ambitious programs. Study each of the demonstration programs carefully. Use both mental and program traces until you understand them completely; then modify them to suit your interests and application needs.

6.2 BUILDING WINDOWS AND SOUND INTO PROGRAMS

The Turbo Prolog system makes it easy for programmers to subdivide the CRT screen into independent areas using a variety of standard predicates. Turbo Prolog distinguishes between two types of screen subdivisions, windows and viewports. Windows are used when the system hardware is in text mode and viewports are used for graphics operations. I will explain the use of window predicates in this section. Viewport predicates will be covered in the graphics section that follows.

Partitioning the screen into windows and viewports is useful because it permits the system designer to segment program functions, and thereby divide and conquer the inherent complexity of many software applications. By subdividing program functions into windows and viewports that appear and disappear as needed, it is possible for the user to process accurately complex information while maintaining a better understanding of what is happening at any given moment. The trick is to use these tools to best advantage in achieving the goal of maximizing computer system accessibility through effective interface design.

The use of windows, much like any technique in programming, can be poorly implemented. For example, too many windows on a screen can add to the user's cognitive burden and decrease performance, so use windows only for necessary program functions such as prompts, explanations, help messages, and program output.

Also avoid use of bright color combinations in your windows, except perhaps where you must attract user attention for some important purpose. Select foreground and background colors with care, as too little contrast between text and background can cause eye fatigue and induce errors.

Sequence windows where possible by making and removing them as needed by the program. Do not allow information that is not currently needed to compete for user attention with information that is important to a task at hand. Windows should draw the eye to the material contained in them, but not to the point of being distracting to the user.

6.2.1 Making Windows

Turbo Prolog provides several standard predicates that permit easy control over the creation, appearance, and removal of windows. If you happen to have a color adapter card and color display installed in your system, you have a full palette of hues to use. Programs that you write should be adaptable to the user's particular hardware configuration. A technique for allowing the user to adapt windows to color or monochrome attributes will be demonstrated below.

To create a window, use

```
makewindow(WindowNumber,ScreenAttribute,FrameAttribute
                WindowLabel,Row,Column,Height,Width)
(integer,integer,integer,string,integer,integer,integer
                integer) : (i,i,i,i,i,i,i,i)
```

`makewindow/8` creates a window with an identifying number (`Window Number`). Using this standard predicate the programmer can create window screens and frames with colors, normal or high brightness level, blinking, inverse video, and underlining. These attributes are specified by `ScreenAttribute` and `FrameAttribute` values in `makewindow/8`. Using color attributes, of course, assumes that the target system is configured with a color adapter card and display.

Making monochrome windows. The following is a step-by-step procedure for selecting values for `ScreenAttribute` and `FrameAttribute` on a monochrome system. The attribute value 0 produces black foreground characters on a black background (a blank screen). To produce white characters on a black background, use the value 7. For inverse video (black characters on a white background) use the value 112. Starting with one of these values, add 1 to have the characters underlined in the foreground attribute. Add 8 to produce a high intensity white foreground, and add 128 to produce blinking characters.

The command

```
makewindow(1,7,240,"Demo",10,20,10,30)
```

will produce on your screen the window in Figure 6.1.

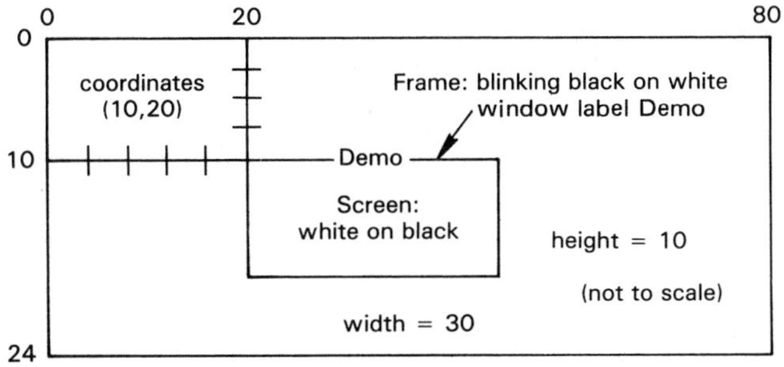

Figure 6.1 A sample window produced with `makewindow/8`.

The `ScreenAttribute` value 7 created the white foreground on a black background screen. `FrameAttribute` 240 (112 + 128) produced the blinking black-on-white frame. The parameters 10 and 20 refer to the x/y coordinates of the upper-left corner of the window. The parameters 10 and 30 refer to the height and width of the window, respectively.

The procedure for sizing windows can be a source of many errors for beginners. With a little practice, however, you will soon become proficient. As is the case with most skills, improvement comes with practice, so be sure to spend some time experimenting with these primitives.

The window label, in this example `Demo`, may be any string whose overall length is at least 3 less than the width value for the window. The window label, like any string, is enclosed in double quotes. If you enter a pair of quotes without any enclosed spaces or characters, the window will not be assigned a label. The label will be truncated if the label is too long.

The procedure for selecting correct location and size values for the `makewindow/8` command is as follows: (1) Set the upper left window coordinates with values for the `Row` and `Column` arguments. (2) Select a size for the window with values for the `Height` and `Width` arguments. (3) The `Row` and `Height` values must sum to no more than the available height of the screen (e.g., 25);

TABLE 6.1 FOREGROUND AND BACKGROUND COLOR VALUES

Foreground Color	Foreground Value	Background Color	Background Value
Black	0	Black	0
Blue	1	Blue	16
Green	2	Green	32
Cyan	3	Cyan	48
Red	4	Red	64
Magenta	5	Magenta	80
Brown	6	Brown	96
White	7	White	112
Gray	8		
Light Blue	9		
Light Green	10		
Light Cyan	11		
Light Red	12		
Light Magenta	13		
Yellow	14		
White (high intensity)	15		

similarly, the values for `Column` and `Width` must sum to no more than the width of the screen (e.g., 80). (4) Finally, if the planned window size produces values larger than those permitted, return to step 1 and adjust the upper-left corner and/or size coordinates accordingly. After creation of a window, it becomes by default the currently active window.

`makewindow/11` (Version 2.0) adds three arguments that allow the programmer to clear the window on creation and vary the position of the header in the frame and the characters used to draw the frame. By not clearing the window on creation, information currently on the screen can be captured in the new window.

Making Color Windows. To calculate screen color and frame attribute values for use with the `makewindow/8` predicate, apply the following simple rule. Select one foreground color value and one background color value from Table 6.1. Add the two integer values. The sum is the number required. Add 128 to this sum to make everything blink. Blinking screens can be very annoying to some users, so use this attribute selectively.

Manipulating Windows

```
shiftwindow(WindowNumber)  (integer) : (i),(o)
```

`shiftwindow()` allows the programmer to select which window will be the currently active window. Since the currently active window is by default the last one created, the programmer must issue a `shiftwindow()` command to shift control to another designated window. If a variable is used in `shiftwindow()`, the number of the currently active window will be returned.

```
removewindow(WindowNumber,Refresh)  (integer,integer) : (i) (i)
```

The `removewindow()` predicate erases the currently active window and makes the last window created the currently active window. If there is no currently active window, a call to `removewindow()` will cause a run-time error and the program will abort. Refresh allows the programmer a choice as to whether or not to refresh the screen behind the window.

```
clearwindow
```

This predicate is useful in performing housecleaning in windows by removing unneeded information. It fills the screen with the background color, thus erasing any foreground text.

```
window_attr(NewAttributeValue)  (integer) : (i)
```

`window_attr()` allows the programmer to change the attribute of a window on the fly during execution. This may be useful in situations where more than one window is present and the program needs to attract user attention to a particular one.

```
existwindow(WindowNum)
```

This predicate tests to determine if a numbered window exists.

```
resizewindow
resizewindow(StartRow,NumRows,StartCol,NumCols)
    (integer,integer,integer,integer) : (i,i,i,i)
```

These two predicates provide control over window size in programs. `resizewindow/0` places the window in the system-resize mode. The user then uses the arrow keys to alter the windows and presses Enter to continue. `resizewindow/4` is used by the programmer to alter window size to specified dimensions on the fly.

```
scroll(NumLines)  integer : (i)
```

This command will cause the text in the current window to scroll a number of lines determined by the value of `NumLines`.

6.2.2 Reading and Writing in Windows

Reading and writing in windows is not fundamentally different from what you have already learned about screen I/O. However, the programmer has the responsibility of shifting control to the currently active window prior to a read or write operation.

Turbo Prolog does provide some special predicates for use in window I/O.

```
window_str(StringInWindow)  (string) : (i),(o)
```

The `window_str()` predicate will bind `StringInWindow` to the contents of the window. If `window_str` is called with a string argument, the string will be written in the window. Consult the manual for more details on this one.

```
scr_char(Row,Column,Character)
                    (integer,integer,char) : (i,i,i), (i,i,o)
```

`scr_char()` writes or reads a character to or from the specified `Row` and `Column` coordinates in the currently active window.

```
scr_attr(Row,Column,Attribute)
                (integer,integer,integer) : (i,i,i), (i,i,o)
```

`scr_attr()` sets or returns the attribute of a character at the Row and Column coordinates.

```
field_str(Row,Column,Length,String)
     (integer,integer,integer,string) : (i,i,i,i), (i,i,i,o)
```

`field_str()` specifies a field defined by `Row`, `Column`, and `Length` integers. If a field of the specified `Length` can fit within the currently active window, this predicate can be used to read and write strings of the specified `Length` beginning at the location defined by Row and Column. If the string in the window is longer than the value of `Length`, it will be truncated to the value of `Length`. If the string is shorter than the value of `Length`, the field will be padded with spaces.

```
field_attr(Row,Column,Length,Attribute)
     (integer,integer,integer,integer) : (i,i,i,i), (i,i,i,o)
```

The `field_attr()` predicate is similar in function to `field_str()` except that it is used to set or return the attribute value of the field.

6.2.3 Two Demonstration Programs

The following two programs illustrate window procedures and many of the predicates that are most useful for window I/O. The README.PRO program allows the user to browse a file selected from any directory on a disk. The program uses three windows: One prompts to browse a file or to quit the program, another accepts target file directory information, and the third is used for browsing the file.

The user selects the file by typing the file path and name in a "protected field" created using `field_attr()`. The program accepts user input (up to a length defined in `field(Number)`) using `continue`, `check()`, and `process()`. If the user enters input incorrectly, or the path entered is to an empty directory, the program will fail. The process procedure assures that the user does not write beyond the limits of the protected field.

Using the Trace Facility. README.PRO is a simple program but one you should spend some time tracing. You can perform traces in programs in a variety of ways. To trace the entire program, enter the `TRACE` directive at the head of the program. The F10 key steps you through program execution. The directive `SHORTTRACE` also traces programs but produces less output and may be less confusing for the beginner. Tracing can always be turned on and off with an Alt T keychord. If you wish to trace only a particular portion of a program, you can insert `trace(on)` and `trace(off)` commands into the program code. To trace a rule or procedure, you can issue the directive `TRACE rulename` at the head of the program.

Note that the `storage` primitive is used in this program to document program use of memory.

```
/* ****************************************************

                     README.PRO

    A file-browsing utility program.  This program
    illustrates use of protected data entry fields
    and a counter procedure.

    **************************************************** */

PREDICATES
 run1
 run2(char)
 continue
 quit
 process(integer)
 check(integer,integer)
 field(integer)

GOAL
 run1.

CLAUSES
 run1 :-
  clearwindow,
  makewindow(1,112,112,"SELECT OPTION",0,0,8,20),
```

(continued)

```
  makewindow(2,112,112,"DIRECTORY",0,20,8,60),
  makewindow(3,112,112,"README",8,0,16,80),
  shiftwindow(1),
  storage(S,_,_),
  write("Stack = ",S),nl,nl,
  write(" 1) Read a file\n"),
  write(" 2) Exit to DOS\n "),
  readchar(Choice),
  run2(Choice).

run2(Choice) :-
  Choice = '1',
  continue.
run2(Choice) :-
  Choice = '2',
  quit.
run2(_) :-
  continue.

quit :-
  shiftwindow(1),
  removewindow,
  shiftwindow(2),
  removewindow,
  shiftwindow(3),
  removewindow,
  exit.

continue :-
  shiftwindow(2),
  write("\n\n Enter directory path to file: "),
  cursor(X,Y),
  field(Length),
  field_attr(X,Y,Length,7),
  field(Number),
  process(Number),
  field_str(X,Y,Number,Directory),
  shiftwindow(3),
  dir(Directory,"*.*",File),
  file_str(File,String),
  display(String),
  !,
  run1.

process(Length) :-
  not(Length = 0),
  cursor(X,Y),
```

```
    readchar(Char),
    char_int(Char,Int),
    check(Int,Length),
    scr_char(X,Y,Char),
    Length1 = Length - 1,
    Y1 = Y + 1,
    cursor(X,Y1),
    process(Length1).
    process(_).

    check(Int,_) :-
      Int >= 92,
      Int <= 122,
      !.
     check(Int,_) :-
      Int >= 48,
      Int <= 58,
      !.
     check(_,_) :-
     fail.

    field(26).

/* ************************************************* */
```

The next study program is a notepad utility. It incorporates windows, the `comline()` standard predicate for experts to use in avoiding menus, menus for novice users, protected data entry fields that employ a `counter` procedure, and DOS commands for changing directories and listing and selecting files using a "bounce-bar" menu.

The `comline()` predicate in compiled programs reads a command line argument and passes it on to the `go()` procedure, thus circumventing the menu. Compile NOTEPAD.PRO to disk as an EXE file and try this feature using these command line arguments.

`A:> notepad`	Invokes notepad, and user makes program choice at the main menu
`A:> notepad write`	Invokes the program and goes directly to the editor for writing
`A:> notepad read`	Invokes the program and goes to the `read` prompt

The Turbo Prolog editor is integrated into the program for entry of notes using all the support facilities. If `prolog.err` and `prolog.hlp` files are present in the working directory, the program will provide Turbo Prolog help and error messages.

Be sure to trace these two programs and study them in detail before moving on to new material.

```
/* ***********************************************************

                        NOTEPAD.PRO

     A utility for organizing notes by cross-indexing.

   *********************************************************** */

   CODE = 2000

   DOMAINS
    list = string*
    file = fl

   DATABASE
    count(integer)

   PREDICATES
    go(string)
    read_note
    continue2
    process(integer)
    check(integer,integer)
    counter
    run
    select(integer)
    write_note
    get_keywords(string,string)
    check2(string,string)
    print_note
    help

   GOAL
    comline(Command),
    disk(Current),
    makewindow(1,112,112,"SELECT OPTION",0,0,24,80),
    go(Command).

   INCLUDE "MENU.PRO"

   CLAUSES

    /* rules to handle command line calls, or if there are
       none, program will default to the run predicate */
```

```
go(Command) :-
 Command = " write",
 write_note,
 run.
go(Command) :-
 Command = " read",
 read_note,
 run.
go(Command) :-
 Command = " print",
 print_note,
 run.
go(Command) :-
 Command = " help",
 help,
 run.
go(_) :-
 run.


run :-
 clearwindow,
 storage(X,_,_),
 write(X),
 menu(2,4,["WRITE A NOTE",
           "READ A NOTE",
           "PRINT A NOTE",
           "HELP WITH PROGRAM",
           "EXIT NOTEPAD"],
            ANSWER),
 select(Answer),
 run.

select(1) :-
 write_note.
select(2) :-
 read_note.
select(3) :-
 print_note.
select(4) :-
 help.
select(5) :-
 removewindow,
 exit.
```

(continued)

```
/* write note rules */

write_note :-
 makewindow(1,112,15,"NOTEPAD EDITOR",0,0,24,80),
 write("\n\n Enter home directory for note: "),
 cursor(X,Y),
 field_attr(X,Y,26,7),
 asserta(count(0)),
 process(26),
 count(N),
 field_str(X,Y,N,Directory),
 retract(count(_)),
 disk(Current),
 disk(Directory),
 clearwindow,
 Note_in = " ",
 edit(Note_in,Note),
 clearwindow,
 sound(2,900),
 write("Enter source: "),
 readln(Source),
 makewindow(2,112,15," ENTER KEYWORD OR QUIT",18,10,5,35),
 get_keywords(Note,Source),
 disk(Current),
 removewindow,
 !.
write_note :-
 clearwindow,
 sound(1,900),
 cursor(10,0),
 write(" Error in writing!  Most likely you entered a
                                              bad path."),
 write("\n             Press any key to return to menu: "),
 readchar(_),
 run.

get_keywords(Note,Source) :-
 write(" Keyword: "),
 readln(Reply),
 not(Reply = "q"),
 not(Reply = "Q"),
 not(Reply = "quit"),
 not(Reply = "QUIT"),
 check2(Reply,Reply1),
 openappend(fl,Reply1),
 writedevice(fl),
 write("* * * * * * * * * * * * * * * * * * * *\n"),
 write("NOTE: ",Note,"\n\n","SOURCE: ",Source,"\n\n"),
```

```
  closefile(fl),
  writedevice(screen),
  get_keywords(Note,Source).
 get_keywords(_,_).

 check2(Reply,Reply1) :-
  concat(Reply,".not",Reply1),
  existfile(Reply1),!.
 check2(Reply,Reply1) :-
  concat(Reply,".not",Reply1),
  save(Reply1).

 /* read note rules */

 read_note :-
  cursor(3,15),
  write("\n\n Enter directory path to note: "),
  cursor(X,Y),
  field_attr(X,Y,26,7),
  asserta(count(0)),
  process(26),
  count(N),
  field_str(X,Y,N,Directory),
  retract(count(_)),
  disk(Current),
  disk(Directory),
  dir(Directory,"*.not",File),
  file_str(File,String),
  clearwindow,
  display(String),nl,
  clearwindow,
  disk(Current),!.
 read_note :-
  clearwindow,
  sound(1,900),
  cursor(10,0),
  write(" Error in reading!  Most likely no note files
                                             in directory."),
  write("\n            Press any key to return to menu: "),
  readchar(_),
  run.

 process(Length) :-
  not(Length = 0),
  cursor(X,Y),
  readchar(Char),
  char_int(Char,Int),
```

(continued)

```
  check(Int,Length),
  scr_char(X,Y,Char),
  Length1 = Length - 1,
  Y1 = Y + 1,
  cursor(X,Y1),
  counter,
  process(Length1).
  process(_).

  check(Int,_) :-
   Int >= 92,
   Int <= 122,
   !.
  check(Int,_) :-
   Int >= 48,
   Int <= 58,
   !.
  check(_,_) :-
  fail.

counter :-
 count(Number),
 NewNumber = Number + 1,
 retract(count(Number)),
 asserta(count(NewNumber)).
/* print note rules */

print_note :-
  clearwindow,
  sound(15,800),
  cursor(5,0),
  write("                    Is your printer on-line?"),nl,nl,
  write("                    1) Print a note_n"),
  write("                    2) Exit to menu_n "),
  cursor(11,14),
  readchar(Choice),
  Choice = '1',
  continue2.
 print_note :-
  run.

 continue2 :-
  write("\n\n Enter directory path to note: "),
  cursor(X,Y),
  field_attr(X,Y,26,7),
  asserta(count(0)),
  process(26),
  count(N),
```

```
   field_str(X,Y,N,Directory),
   retract(count(_)),
   disk(Directory),
   dir(Directory,"*.not",File),
   file_str(File,String),
   writedevice(printer),
   write(String),
   flush(printer),
   !,
   writedevice(screen).

  /* help rule and message */

  help :-
   makewindow(1,112,15,"NOTEPAD HELP INFORMATION",0,0,24,80),
   write("This is a simple utility program that will allow
                                        you to write,\n",
         "   store, retrieve, and print notes with very
                          little effort on your part.\n\n",
         "WRITE A NOTE\n\n",
         "You must enter directory home path for storage of
                           your note. You cannot make\n",
         "any errors here or you will be sent back to the
                          main menu. Next you type in\n",
         "your note and terminate it with an escape. F1
                      will get you help. You have all\n",
         "the edit facilities. Now enter one or more
                   keywords by which the note will be\n",
         "indexed. A 'q' or 'quit' will get you out of
                     this routine. A '.not' extension\n",
         "will be added to the note by the system. Abort note
                       with q at the keyword prompt.\n\n",
         "READ A NOTE\n\n",
         "Here again you will be asked for a home directory
                              where your note is to be\n",
         "housed. Enter it without error!\n\n",
         "PRINT A NOTE\n\n",
         "The most important point here is to make sure your
                                    printer is on-line!"),
   cursor(21,15),
   write("Press any key to continue: "),
   readchar(_),
   removewindow.

/* ********************************************************* */
```

TABLE 6.2 NOTES AND FREQUENCY VALUES

Note	Frequency
C (low)	131
C sharp	139
D	147
D sharp	156
E	165
F	175
F sharp	185
G	196
G sharp	208
A	220
A sharp	233
B	247
C (middle)	262

6.2.4 Sounding Off in Programs

Turbo Prolog provides a single predicate for introducing sound into programs.

```
sound(Duration,Frequency) (integer,integer) : (i,i)
```

`sound()` can produce all the necessary tones you will need for routine use in your programs. Notice that the difference between a chirp and a beep is simply a function of duration. Also note that the hardware you are using will affect the implementation of the `Duration` parameter. The frequency values used with this predicate are listed in Table 6.2.

There are many uses for sound in knowledge-based programs. For example, a discreet chirp or beep can help warn a user that something important is about to happen in a program. Such a situation occurs in the personal memory manager program in section 6.4.2. Here the user is given the menu option to print a record in the memory manager knowledge base. If the user's system does not have a printer or it is not turned on, selection of this option will cause the system to "hang," requiring a "warm boot" to exit. A prompt warns of this, but the beep assures that the user will notice it and avoid disruption of the program.

In some applications, however, there may be a room full of microcomputers, and the meaningful sounds produced by one program can become a stressful cacophony when multiplied several times over. If you plan consistent use of sound in a program, you might consider giving the user the option of turning it off. Providing options such as these complicate the life of the programmer, but the goal of providing for program accessibility is preeminent.

6.3 GRAPHICS

Turbo Prolog provides the programmer with two sets of graphics primitives. If you have Version 1.xx, you have modest graphics capabilities employing point, line, and turtle graphics. If you have Version 2.0, you have the graphics capabilities found in 1.xx plus a powerful new set of graphics tools called BGI (Borland Graphics Interface) as well. However, only the advanced BGI is documented in Version 2.0. I will document both systems here.

6.3.1 Version 1.xx Graphics

Admittedly, the Version 1.xx graphics are elementary, but you can use them to build higher-level procedures that can produce some interesting effects for your programs. The first step is to inform the system of your choice of screen resolution, palette of colors, and desired background color. This is accomplished with the `graphics()` command.

```
graphics(Mode,Palette,Background)
                    (integer,integer,integer) : (i,i,i)
```

Use of this primitive is guided by the type of hardware installed in the target machine. Specifically, the selected `Mode` (level of screen resolution) must be supported by the video adapter card installed in the target machine.

Table 6.3 shows the modes, screen resolutions, and necessary hardware. Table 6.4 shows the choices of palette to be used with the `graphics()` command. Table 6.5 shows the values for background colors.

The command

```
graphics(1,0,7)
```

will produce a medium-resolution graphics screen with a choice of three foreground colors (those listed for palette 0) on a white background.

TABLE 6.3 GRAPHICS SCREEN MODES AND FORMATS FOR USE WITH THE GRAPHICS PREDICATE

Mode	Columns	Rows	Adapter and resolution
1	320	200	CGA, medium resolution, 4 colors
2	640	200	CGA, high resolution, black and white
3	320	200	EGA, medium resolution, 16 colors
4	640	200	EGA, high resolution, 16 colors
5	640	350	EGA, enhanced resolution, 13 colors

CGA: The standard Color/Graphics Adapter.
EGA: The Enhanced Graphics Adapter.

TABLE 6.4 PALETTE OPTIONS IN MEDIUM RESOLUTION FOR USE WITH THE GRAPHICS PREDICATE

Palette	Color 1	Color 2	Color 3
0	green	red	yellow
1	cyan	magenta	white

TABLE 6.5 BACKGROUND COLOR VALUES FOR USE WITH THE GRAPHICS PREDICATE

0	black	8	gray
1	blue	9	light blue
2	green	10	light green
3	cyan	11	light cyan
4	red	12	light red
5	magenta	13	light magenta
6	brown	14	yellow
7	white	15	high intensity white

The command

```
text
```

will return the screen to normal text mode. If the screen is already in text mode, the command will succeed anyway.

The `dot()` command will produce a point of color specified by the value of `Color` (from the selected palette) at the intersect of the coordinates given by `Row` and `Column`.

```
dot(Row,Column,Color)
        (integer,integer,integer) : (i,i,i), (i,i,o)
```

The `line()` command will draw a colored line specified by the value of `Color` from the point defined by the coordinates of `Row1` and `Column1` to the point defined by the coordinates `Row2` and `Column2`.

```
line(Row1,Column1,Row2,Column2,Color)
  (integer,integer,integer,integer,integer) : (i,i,i,i,i)
```

The remaining primitives in Version 1.xx are turtle graphics commands. The turtle is a graphics cursor that can be commanded to move about the viewport, drawing or erasing lines. Turtle graphics originated in the work of Seymour Papert and the Logo group at MIT, and is outlined in his very interesting book *Mindstorms: Children, Computers, and Powerful Ideas* (1980). Papert created the Logo computer language and its turtle graphics to provide a medium to exploit use of the computer in the education of children. Logo was designed as a language simple enough to give children quick control over computer functions yet powerful enough to capture and hold their continuing interest.

Papert's educational philosophy is in part based in the theory of Jean Piaget, the famous Swiss developmental psychologist who advocated a constructivist view of intelligence, learning by doing, and understanding by invention. Children, using Logo and turtle graphics commands, can learn about principles of geometry by actually writing programs that produce interesting geometric forms. As children master basic concepts, they are motivated to invent higher-order concepts via metalevel programming, thus building and mastering increasingly complex concepts.

You may wish to experiment with this approach to education by reading *Mindstorms* and using Turbo Prolog graphics commands to write the higher-order graphics routines you would need for use in your own educational programs.

The turtle is activated by default in the center of the screen upon a call to the `graphics()` command. The `penup` command deactivates the turtle writing on the screen. This is useful when you wish to stop drawing in order to skip to another location on the screen without drawing a line to the new location. The command `pendown` will cause the turtle to resume drawing lines.

The turtle can be directed to move forward and backward in incremental steps specified by the `Distance` parameter. The distances used with these commands will vary with graphic mode (see Table 6.3). In medium-resolution modes, the screen is 32,000 steps wide by 32,000 steps high. The values for enhanced modes are not documented, so some experimentation will be required here. If a call to `forward()` or `back()` uses values that would result in the turtle moving off the screen, the call will fail.

```
forward(Distance)            (integer) : (i)
back(Distance)               (integer) : (i)
```

When the `graphics()` call is issued, the turtle is activated facing 12 o'clock in the center of the screen. To make the turtle turn and change direction by degrees (0–360), use the commands `left()` and `right()`.

```
left(Angle)                  (integer) : (i)
right(Angle)                 (integer) : (i)
```

The `penpos()` predicate will set the position and direction of the turtle or will return the present values.

```
penpos(RowCoordinate,ColCoordinate,Direction)
          (integer,integer,integer) : (i,i,i), (o,o,o)
```

To change the color of the pen being dragged around by the turtle, use the `pencolor()` command.

```
pencolor(Color)                (integer) : (i)
```

The basic graphics primitives can be combined into user-defined rules to create Logo-like commands. The following Turbo Prolog rule produces a square inside a window.

```
/* *************************************************************

                        TURTLE.PRO

                  Program to draw a square.

   ************************************************************* */

 PREDICATES
 to_square
 GOAL
  to_square.
 CLAUSES
 to_square :-
  graphics(5,0,1), /* Works with EGA */
  makewindow(1,7,7,"to square",1,1,23,68),
  pencolor(4),
  forward(8000),
  right(90),
  forward(8000),
  right(90),
  forward(8000),
  right(90),
  forward(8000).

/* ************************************************************* */
```

6.3.2 The Borland Graphics Interface

The Borland Graphics Interface (BGI)(version 2.0) offers some 70 predicates for development of color and monochrome graphic presentations and interfaces in your programs. BGI is a sophisticated graphics environment that includes a wide range of high-level to low-level predicates. Also included are graphics drivers for the most popular graphic adapter cards in use in PCs today (CGA, EGA, VGA, 3270, Hercules) and some excellent graphics demonstration programs.

You really must study the 2.0 manual and experiment with the BGI demonstration programs at some length if you want to master all its features. In this section I will attempt only to acquaint you with the main features and requirements of the BGI.

Using BGI, you can conveniently create one or more graphic viewports on the screen using `setviewport()`. You can then use these viewports to present elaborate three-dimensional graphics, draw and paint using a variety of fill and line styles, include text materials in a variety of fonts, manipulate images, and process input.

To use BGI you must first initialize your system using the `initgraph()` predicate. This predicate loads the appropriate graphics driver and sets the system to a graphics mode. As you cannot always anticipate how a target system will be configured, the `initgraph()` predicate can be directed to "auto detect" the system graphics adapter hardware using `detectgraph()`, and to provide the information needed to load appropriate driver software. Check the manual for a listing of files that must be available to BGI in the current directory.

Each color graphics adapter card has multiple mode settings. These settings determine pixel resolution and the colors that may be used in graphic displays. To determine the number of modes an adapter has, use `getmoderange()`. The predicate `getgraphmode()` is used to return the current mode setting. `initgraph()` and `setgraphmode()` will set the adapter card to the desired mode. `graphdefaults` returns current settings to default graphic values. The `closegraph()` predicate returns the system to default text mode settings.

Borland has simplified writing of graphics procedures by providing a file GRAPDECL.PRO that contains many useful CONSTANTS declarations for your programs. For example, this file declares PI equal to 3.14159 and color names equal to appropriate integer values. Now you can use names in programs, rather than the cryptic and difficult-to-remember integer values. Be sure to use INCLUDE to read this file into your programs.

Determining the specific colors that you can use in graphics applications is a bit complicated using the BGI. Each graphics adapter card provides the programmer with a range of pixel resolutions and a choice of color palettes at each resolution. Each palette, in turn, defines the range of foreground and background color values that can be used as arguments to the various graphics predicates. You can determine the resolution modes of any given graphics adapter using `getgraphmode()` and `getmoderange()`. You set the system to a selected resolution mode with `setgraphmode()`. Next you will select a palette of foreground and background colors values (see the Turbo Prolog 2.0 manual). With this information in hand, you are ready to begin building graphics procedures using color.

6.4 DEMONSTRATION PROGRAMS USING WINDOWS AND SOUND

Three programs, written to demonstrate Turbo Prolog programming concepts, are presented in the remainder of this chapter. The style of programming used in these programs illustrates the procedural power of Turbo Prolog. For the most part, the programs are not documented internally with comment statements because the accompanying text explains the overall design. I recommend, however, that you get in the habit of using comments liberally in your programs.

6.4.1 An Enhanced Calculator Program

The first program is an enhancement of the calculator program developed in Chapter 5. It employs new predicates for additional arithmetic functions, windows, sound, error trapping, and a `counter` procedure.

The program is designed to perform the following arithmetic functions using both standard and exponential notation: addition, subtraction, multiplication, division, and square root. The program maintains a running arithmetic total as well as an on-screen record of the last six entries. The program uses `writef()` to format input and output by aligning numbers at the decimal. The program provides an informative error message and a beep if the user enters data incorrectly. The user is given time to study the mistake; then the error is erased and the user is prompted for another entry. The user is able to clear the calculator or exit at any time.

Enter the program and run it a few times to familiarize yourself with its operation and features. It is far from bulletproof (trapping all manner of errors) and you may enjoy improving it as an exercise.

```
/***************************************************************

                          CALC_2.PRO
  An enhanced calculator program with windows, sound,
  entry error trapping, formatted I/O, and a counter.

******************** Declarations *************************/
DATABASE
 count(integer)
 op(char)
PREDICATES
 start
 compute(char,real,real,real)
 get_data(real)
 counter
 quit
GOAL
 start.
CLAUSES
 start :-
  count(X),
  retract(count(X)),
  fail.
start :-
  asserta(count(0)),
```

```
    makewindow(1,112,48,"Electronic Abacus",1,19,4,29),
    write("Programming in Turbo Prolog"),
    makewindow(2,112,48,"Entry Window",5,19,9,29),
    write("> +"),
    Number = 0.0,
    writef("%14.4f",Number),nl,
    makewindow(3,112,48,"Operators",5,1,9,16),
    write(" +   add"),nl,
    write(" -   subtract"),nl,
    write(" *   multiply"),nl,
    write(" /   divide"),nl,
    write(" s   sq root"),nl,
    write(" c0  clear"),nl,
    write(" e   exit"),
    makewindow(4,112,48,"Total",9,50,3,22),
    cursor(0,0),
    write("    ",Number),
    get_data(Number).

  get_data(Number) :-
    shiftwindow(2),
    write("> "),
    cursor(X,Y),
    readln(Op_CharNumber),
    frontchar(Op_CharNumber,Op,CharNumber),
    asserta(op(Op)),
    Op <> 'e',
    str_real(CharNumber,NewNumber),
    cursor(X,Y),
    writef("%-1 %13.4f",Op,NewNumber),nl,
    compute(Op,Number,NewNumber,Return),
    counter,
    shiftwindow(4),
    clearwindow,
    write("   ",Return),
    retract(op(Op)),
    get_data(Return)
    ;
    op(Op),
    Op = 'e',
    retract(op(Op)),
    quit.
  get_data(Number) :-
    cursor(X,Y),
    sound(10,131),
    makewindow(5,112,48,"ERROR",15,30,6,30),
    write(" Operator and number needed.\n"),
```

(*continued*)

```
    write(" Example: +103.66\n"),
    write(" To continue, press any key!\n"),
    readchar(_),
    removewindow,
    shiftwindow(2),
    X1 = X - 1,
    cursor(X1,Y),
    write("                         "),
    cursor(X1,Y),
    get_data(Number).

  compute('+',First_Number,Second_Number,Return) :-
    Return = First_Number + Second_Number.
  compute('-',First_Number,Second_Number,Return) :-
    Return = First_Number - Second_Number.
  compute('*',First_Number,Second_Number,Return) :-
    Return = First_Number * Second_Number.
  compute('/',First_Number,Second_Number,Return) :-
    Return = First_Number / Second_Number.
  compute('s',_,Second_Number,Return) :-
    Return = sqrt(Second_Number).
  compute('c',_,_,Return) :-
    clearwindow,
    Return = 0.

  quit :-
    shiftwindow(1),
    removewindow,
    shiftwindow(2),
    removewindow,
    shiftwindow(3),
    removewindow,
    shiftwindow(4),
    removewindow.

  counter :-
   shiftwindow(2),
   count(Number),
   Number <= 4,
   NewNumber = Number + 1,
   retract(count(Number)),
   asserta(count(NewNumber))
   ;
   retract(count(Number)),
   asserta(count(0)),
   clearwindow.
/**************** End Calculator Program ***************/
```

The first `start` rule cleans up any residual facts that may have been asserted to working memory in a prior use of the calculator. The second `start` rule asserts a `count(0)` to the internal database, then sets up the windows and using `writef()` aligns and initializes the running total to zero in the `Total` window. The `get_data()` rule is invoked and prompts for the first entry.

The entry is analyzed using `frontchar()`. The desired user operation is determined by `Op` and `CharNumber` and the operand is converted from a string to a real number. The operand is formatted, printed to the screen, and then passed on to the `compute()` procedure. Entry errors are trapped here, with the second `get_data()` rule providing an error message and a prompt for another entry. The user is given time to study the incorrect entry, and after pressing any key the erroneous entry is removed and the user is returned to the calculator.

A `counter` procedure keeps track of the number of entries and returns the user to the top of the window before running out of window space. Try changing the number in the `counter` rule to 10. Now when the program is run and the bottom of the window is reached, the Turbo system begins adding a line feed to the one already in the program. This produces an extra line feed, and the program begins skipping a line between entries. The counter prevents this and illustrates how to count operations in a program so that when some criterion number is reached, the program can be directed to react in some appropriate fashion.

The `counter` rule begins by reading the value of the argument of the fact `count()`. This value is initialized to zero in the `start` procedure. After each user entry and calculation the argument to `count()` is incremented by 1. When this value reaches 4, the program clears the window, thereby returning the user to the top of the window.

Study the exit procedure carefully. Note that the program is recursive until it reads the character `e` as an operator, in which case the `quit` rule is invoked. The interface design of the program is compact yet easy to read and informative. A cyan frame and white screen with black foreground has been selected for the windows. Experiment with other colors. Also add the system `setup` procedure, used in PROMOTE.PRO in section 6.4.3, to give the user the option of monochrome or color windows. The warning beep accompanying errors is unobtrusive and followed by an explanatory message that includes an example of a correct entry. The error message disappears as the user continues. The screens are all cleared away as the program terminates.

Compile the calculator program into an EXE file that can execute independently of Turbo Prolog. Now run the program from the DOS prompt.

6.4.2 A Free-form Notebook Utility

The next demonstration program is a free-form database that can be used as a personal utility. It can be used to store notes that might be forgotten if not written down. It can also be used for quick reminders, lists of things people have borrowed, addresses, telephone numbers, and birthdays.

Start by building a list of categories that will be "keys" to the information to be saved. Then write to the keys, do a sequential read of information stored by key, or print a hard copy of this information. The program does not support random access to files, but redesigning it to do so would be a good exercise, particularly after you have completed Chapter 8 of this book.

Notice that once again I have developed a program in segments. The first segment contains the setup, menu, selection, and add procedures. This segment will run independently of the remainder of the program. As each additional segment is merged with the first, a new feature is added to the program.

```
/*************************************************************

                           PMM.PRO
              A personal memory manager program

 *************************************************************

       First segment in the development of the program

 ********************** Declarations **********************/

DOMAINS

 list       = string*
 file       = info; entry
 cat        = category(string)

DATABASE

 category(string)
 note(string,string)
 exists(string,real)

PREDICATES

 setup_menu
 main_menu
 modify_mm
 list_cat
 print(list)
 call_selection(char)
 setup_modify
 check_cat(string)
 check(file)
 create_cat(cat)
```

```
GOAL

 existfile("cat.dba"),
 existfile("notes.dba"),
 setup_menu,
 main_menu
 ;
 asserta(category(" ****PMM****")),
 save("cat.dba"),
 retract(category(_)),
 save("notes.dba"),
 setup_menu,
 main_menu.

CLAUSES

/***************** Main Menu ******************/

main_menu :-
  shiftwindow(1),
  clearwindow,
  print([
  " Main Menu\n\n",
  " * Select:\n",
  " 1) Add Category\n",
  " 2) Write to Category\n",
  " 3) Read Notes\n",
  " 4) Print Notes\n",
  " 5) Exit\n",
  " "]),
  readchar(Selection),
  call_selection(Selection),
  main_menu.

/************* Call Selections **************/

call_selection('1') :-
  setup_modify,
  modify_mm.
call_selection('5') :-
  shiftwindow(2),
  removewindow,
  shiftwindow(1),
  removewindow,
  exit.
call_selection(_) :-
  main_menu.
```

(continued)

```
/*************** Setup Windows *****************/

setup_menu :-
  makewindow(1,112,48,"Memory Manager",2,1,11,28),
  makewindow(2,112,48,"Categories",1,64,23,15).

setup_modify :-
  makewindow(3,112,48,"Modify Category",4,3,7,45).

/*********** Add Categories *************/

modify_mm :-
  shiftwindow(2),
  clearwindow,
  list_cat,
  shiftwindow(3),
  clearwindow,
  write(" Enter NEW category.\n"),
  write(" Enter Category or (quit): "),
  readln(Cat),
  Cat <> "quit",
  check_cat(Cat),
  not(exists(Cat,_)),
  create_cat(category(Cat)),
  modify_mm.
modify_mm :-
  shiftwindow(3),
  removewindow,
  main_menu.

create_cat(Entry) :-
  openappend(info,"cat.dba"),
  writedevice(info),
  write(Entry,"\n"),
  closefile(info),
  writedevice(screen).

/************* Utility Rules *****************/

print([]) :- !.
print([X|Y]) :-
  write(X),
  print(Y).

list_cat :-
  shiftwindow(2),
  clearwindow,
  openread(info,"cat.dba"),
```

```
  readdevice(info),
  check(info),
  readterm(cat,category(Cat)),
  write(Cat),nl,
  fail.
list_cat :-
  closefile(info),
  readdevice(keyboard).

check(_).                % procedure forces readterm()
check(File) :-           % to read entire file to
  not(eof(File)),        % success or eof marker
  check(File).

check_cat(NewCat) :-
  openread(info,"cat.dba"),
  readdevice(info),
  check(info),
  filepos(info,Position,0),
  readterm(cat,category(Cat)),
  Cat = NewCat,
  asserta(exists(NewCat,Position))
  ;
  fail.
check_cat(_) :-
  closefile(info).

/******************* End First Segment ******************/
```

The first segment of the program produces a menu of options that the program will eventually offer. In this segment only the `add` and `exit` options are made operative in the `call_selections()` procedure. `readchar()` is used to permit single-keystroke entries. If any choice other than `add` a category or `exit` is selected the program will ignore it. This is possible because the third `call_selection()` rule using the anonymous variable traps all unrecognized responses and returns the user to the main menu. The `add` section allows the user to create a new category or to delete an existing category from the knowledge base file.

The code begins with a Declarations section in which I have listed the domains that I will be using. The `list` domain is defined as a list of strings. This will be used by `print()` to produce the menu.

The program uses separate files to store user-created categories and notes keyed to categories. These files have the internal names `info` and `entry`. The `add` procedure will be working with categories entered into and deleted from this file. This requires a DATABASE declaration, `category(string)`. The existence of categories is checked in memory, and this requires the DATABASE declaration `exists(string,real)`. The utility rules will read from and write to this file, and the object with which they will work is declared as `cat`. All the remaining relations used are declared in the PREDICATES section.

The GOAL section checks to see if the key and notes files exist. Since the files do not exist the first time the program is run, they are created by the `save/1` predicate. The GOAL also sets up the main menu and category windows and invokes the `main_menu` rule. As noted, `main_menu` offers the program options. If the user elects to `add` keys, the existing keys are listed in the category window, an `Add` window is created, and `modify_mm` invoked. A brief but informative instructional message is printed, and the user is prompted for a category name. Note that the `Add` window overlaps the options in the now inoperative main menu, thus reducing the user's cognitive load.

If the category name entered by the user exists, the user is returned to the main menu. If the category does not exist, it is added to the file and the new list of categories is printed in the window. After a category is created, the user is prompted for another category. Note the use of the file predicates in this program. Trace the program and study each of these primitives at work.

The second segment of the program adds the procedures that permit writing notes to categories. Notes are appended to the database file as follows:

```
            notes(Category,Note).
```

```
/****************** Begin Second Segment *****************/

 DOMAINS      /* Add this to the DOMAINS section */

   entry    = notes(string,string)

 PREDICATES   /* Add these to the PREDICATES section */

   setup_write
   write_mm
   write_db(entry)

 CLAUSES      /* ADD these to the CLAUSES section */

 call_selection('2') :-
   setup_write,
   write_mm.

 setup_write :-
   makewindow(3,112,48,"Write To Category",4,1,10,63).

 write_mm :-
   clearwindow,
   shiftwindow(2),
   clearwindow,
```

```
    list_cat,
    shiftwindow(3),
    write(" Enter Category or (quit): "),
    readln(Cat),
    Cat <> "quit",
    write("\n Enter notes for ",Cat,"\n : "),
    readln(Notes),
    write_db(note(Cat,Notes)).
  write_mm :-
    closefile(entry),
    removewindow.

  write_db(Entry) :-
    openappend(entry,"notes.dba"),
    writedevice(entry),
    write(Entry,"\n"),
    closefile(entry),
    writedevice(screen),
    write_mm.

 /****************** End Second Segment ********************/
```

The third segment adds the code for the `Read` option. Study the use of `readterm()` carefully. In well-designed application programs, the user is always provided the option of a quick and graceful exit. Notice how I have built an exit into each of the procedures.

```
/***************** Begin Third Segment ********************/

PREDICATES
  setup_read
  read_mm
  read_db(string)

CLAUSES

call_selection('3') :-
  setup_read,
  read_mm.

setup_read :-
  makewindow(3,112,48,"Read A Category",4,1,10,63).

read_mm :-
  listcat,
  shiftwindow(3),
```

(continued)

```
  write(" Enter Category or (quit): "),
  readln(Cat),
  Cat <> "quit",
  openread(entry,"notes.dba"),
  readdevice(entry),
  read_db(Cat)
  ;
  closefile(info),
  removewindow,
  main_menu.

read_db(Cat) :-
  check(entry),
  readdevice(entry),
  readterm(entry,note(Cat,Note)),
  clearwindow,nl,nl,
  write(Note),nl,
  readdevice(keyboard),
  write("\nPress any Key"),
  readchar(_),nl,
  clearwindow,
  fail.
read_db(_) :-
  closefile(entry),
  removewindow.

/**************** End Third Segment *********************/
```

The last segment adds the print option to the program. The sound used here will help users avoid the problem of hanging their systems by attempting to print when their printer is not on-line.

```
/*************** Begin Fourth Segment *******************/

PREDICATES

  setup_print
  print_mm
  print_db(string)

CLAUSES

call_selection('4') :-
  setup_print,
  print_mm.

setup_print :-
  makewindow(3,112,48,"Print A Category",5,5,6,43).
```

```
print_mm :-
  shiftwindow(2),
  list_cat,
  shiftwindow(3),
  write(" Be sure printer is turned on!"),nl,
  sound(5,100),
  sound(5,200),
  sound(5,100),
  sound(10,200),
  write(" Enter Category or (quit): "),
  readln(Cat),
  Cat <> "quit",
  clearwindow,
  openread(entry,"notes.dba"),
  print_db(Cat)
  ;
  closefile(info),
  removewindow.

print_db(Cat) :-
  check(info),
  readdevice(info),
  readterm(entry,note(Cat,Note)),
  writedevice(printer),
  write(Note),nl,
  flush(printer),
  writedevice(screen),
  readdevice(keyboard),
  clearwindow,
  write("Printing\n"),
  write("Press any key:"),
  readchar(_),nl,
  fail.
print_db(_) :-
  closefile(info),
  removewindow.

/*********************** End Program ***********************/
```

6.4.3 A Company Promotion Program

The final program demonstrates the use of a Turbo Prolog for decision making. The criteria used here are elementary but illustrative of this kind of application.

Some people may reject the idea of using a computer program for important personnel decisions such as promotions. However, given that additional criteria can be built into such a program, computerizing this process could be more equitable than many existing practices. Also, a program can generate explanations that can be used to justify decisions to both employer and employee. Using such programs could encourage the development of more objective, valid, and rational criteria for decision making. Records of program decisions could then become evidence of fair employment practices for the employer and useful feedback for the employee.

The program begins with an option to configure the windows to match the user's hardware. It lists the employees in the company database and prompts for last and first names of a candidate for promotion. The rules `rating_check_ok()`, `dept_cleared()`, and `time_on_job_ok()` are used to implement the test for promotion. The first part of each rule, if it succeeds, writes a positive statement to the `Explanation` window. The OR option in each rule is invoked if the employee does not meet a criterion for promotion, and a negative statement is written to the `Explanation` window and an ineligibility flag is asserted to the dynamic database. The `notify()` rule looks for ineligibility flags, and if one is found, the promotion is denied. The disjunctive portion of `notify()` succeeds if there are no negative statements, and the employee is promoted and her or his salary is incremented by the amount listed for the department in the company knowledge base.

The decision is followed by some questionable "music." An elementary explanation is given for the decision and the employee's increment in salary is computed and printed to the screen. The employee is removed from the list of eligible names, and the user prompted for a decision to continue.

```
/*************************************************************

                          PROMOTE.PRO

A knowledge-based program illustrating mechanized decisions
                    using windows and sound

*************************************************************/

DOMAINS
  known_as = name(string,string)
  residence = address(string,string)
  phone = tel_no(string)
  job = title(string)
  dept = dept(symbol)
  income = salary(real)
  history = date_hired(mo,yr)
  mo = integer
  yr = integer
  evaluation = rating(real)
DATABASE
  promotion_rating(symbol,real,real)
  ineligible(string,integer)
  promoted(integer)
```

```
PREDICATES
  setup
  promote
  continue(integer)
  list_employees
  rating_check_ok(integer)
  dept_cleared(integer)
  time_on_job_ok(integer)
  make_windows(integer)
  emp_id(integer,known_as)
  emp_address(integer,residence,phone)
  emp_job(integer,job,dept,income)
  emp_rating(integer,history,evaluation)
  promotion_cleared(symbol)
  notify(integer)
  play_cheers
  play_bummer
GOAL
  setup.
CLAUSES
  setup :-
  clearwindow,
  write("Is your system    1) color?"),nl,
  write("                  2) monochrome?"),nl,
  write("           Enter:  "),
  readint(Type),
  make_windows(Type),
  list_employees,
  promote.

make_windows(1) :-
  clearwindow,
  makewindow(1,48,15,"Company Promotion Program",0,0,12,80),
  makewindow(2,48,15,"Selections Window",12,0,13,30),
  makewindow(3,48,15,"Explanation Window",12,30,13,50).

make_windows(2) :-
  clearwindow,
  makewindow(1,112,15,"Company Promotion Program",0,0,12,80),
  makewindow(2,112,15,"Selections Window",12,0,13,30),
  makewindow(3,112,15,"Explanation Window",12,30,13,50).

promote :-
  shiftwindow(1),
  clearwindow,
  cursor(1,0),
  write("Enter last name of employee being considered\n"),
```

(continued)

```
  write("for promotion (q to quit): "),
  readln(Last_name),
  upper_lower(Last_name,Last),
  Last = "q",
  exit
  ;
  write("Enter first name: "),
  readln(First_name),
  emp_id(Id,name(Last_name,First_name)),
  rating_check_ok(Id),
  dept_cleared(Id),
  time_on_job_ok(Id),
  notify(Id),
  continue(Id).
promote :-
  sound(10,300),
  write("Entry error or employee not listed.\n"),
  write("Examine entry and press any key: "),
  readchar(_),
  clearwindow,
  promote.


list_employees :-
  shiftwindow(2),
  clearwindow,
  emp_id(Id,name(Last,First)),
  not(ineligible(_,Id)),
  not(promoted(Id)),
  write(Last,", ",First),nl,
  fail.
list_employees.


rating_check_ok(Id) :-
  emp_rating(Id,_,rating(Number)),
  emp_job(Id,_,dept(Dept),_),
  promotion_rating(Dept,Value,_),
  Number >= Value,
  shiftwindow(3),
  clearwindow,
  write("\nEmployee exceed rating for ",Dept,"!"),nl,
  shiftwindow(1)
  ;
  shiftwindow(3),
  clearwindow,
  write("\nEmployee does not have promotion rating!\n"),
  shiftwindow(1),
  asserta(ineligible(rating,Id)).
```

```
dept_cleared(Id) :-
  emp_job(Id,_,dept(Dept),_),
  promotion_cleared(Dept),
  shiftwindow(3),
  write(Dept," has promotion authorization!"),
  shiftwindow(1)
  ;
  emp_job(Id,_,dept(Dept),_),
  shiftwindow(3),
  write(Dept," not authorized for promotion."),
  shiftwindow(1),
  asserta(ineligible(frozen,Id)).

time_on_job_ok(Id) :-
  emp_job(Id,_,dept(Dept),_),
  emp_rating(Id,date_hired(_,Yr),_),
  date(Year,_,Day),
  Year >= Yr + 2,
  shiftwindow(3),
  write("\nEmployee has job tenure in ",Dept,"!"),
  shiftwindow(1)
  ;
  shiftwindow(3),
  write("\nEmployee does not have job tenure!"),
  shiftwindow(1),
  asserta(ineligible(time,Id)).

notify(Id) :-
  ineligible(_,Id),
  emp_id(Id,name(Last,First)),nl,
  write(First," ",Last," is ineligible."),
  play_bummer
  ;
  asserta(promoted(Id)),
  emp_id(Id,name(Last,First)),
  emp_job(Id,_,dept(Dept),salary(Amount)),
  promotion_rating(Dept,_,Increase),
  Increment = Amount * Increase,
  write("\nPromotion authorized for ",First," ",Last,"!"),nl,
  writef("Annual salary increased to $ %7.2\n",Increment),
  play_cheers.

play_cheers :-
  sound(5,196),
  sound(5,196),
  sound(2,175),
  sound(8,247),
```

(*continued*)

```
   sound(3,233),
   sound(8,247),
   sound(3,233),
   sound(8,247),
   sound(3,233),
   sound(8,247).

play_bummer :-
  sound(14,90),
  sound(18,70).

continue(Id) :-
  write("\nDo you wish to continue?  y/n: "),
  readchar(Answer),
  Answer = 'n',
  exit
  ;
  list_employees,
  shiftwindow(3),
  clearwindow,
  shiftwindow(1),
  promote.

 /* begin employee database */

  emp_id(101,name("Smith","William")).
  emp_id(102,name("Jones","John")).
  emp_id(103,name("Robbins","Harvey")).
  emp_id(104,name("Kendricks","Ken")).
  emp_id(105,name("Wilson","Larry")).
  emp_address(101,address("Bridgeport Conn.","765 Ivy Road"),
           tel_no("3724467")).
  emp_address(102,address("Shelton Conn.","14 Duncan Place"),
           tel_no("6228433")).
  emp_address(103,address("Trumbull Conn.","22B Condoville"),
           tel_no("4752207")).
  emp_address(104,address("Bridgeport Conn.","66 Main Street"),
           tel_no("5763344")).
  emp_address(105,address("New Haven Conn.","481 East Avenue"),
           tel_no("2234541")).
  emp_job(101,title("supervisor"),dept("shipping"),
                       salary(24530.00)).
  emp_job(102,title("accountant"),dept("finance"),
                         salary(31268.00)).
  emp_job(103,title("lathe op"),dept("manufacturing"),
                       salary(23755.00)).
  emp_job(104,title("president"),dept("administration"),
                       salary(84500.00)).
```

```
  emp_job(105,title("driver"),dept("delivery"),
                              salary(19430.00)).
  emp_rating(101,date_hired(09,1980),rating(8.5)).
  emp_rating(102,date_hired(11,1984),rating(7.5)).
  emp_rating(103,date_hired(09,1978),rating(8.5)).
  emp_rating(104,date_hired(04,1985),rating(8.0)).
  emp_rating(105,date_hired(04,1982),rating(8.0)).

 /* end employee database */

 /* begin company database */

  promotion_rating("shipping",6.5,1.10).
  promotion_rating("finance",8.0,1.25).
  promotion_rating("manufacturing",7.0,1.11).
  promotion_rating("administration",8.0,1.50).
  promotion_rating("delivery",7.0,1.085).
  promotion_cleared("shipping").
  promotion_cleared("finance").
  promotion_cleared("administration").
  promotion_cleared("delivery").

 /* end company database */

/* ****************************************************** */
```

This program represents an "all or none" approach to decision making. Alternatively, decisions could be made based on varying profiles in employee records. In one such scheme, the employee might be required to pass all of some primary criteria but only a few of some secondary ones. Another possibility is to give varying weights to the criteria. Each test would then contribute to an overall score required for promotion. Designing and implementing one or more of these alternatives is left as an exercise.

6.5 MERGING PROGRAMS

Turbo Prolog allows the programmer some control over compilation through the use of compiler directives. The directive

```
INCLUDE "DOS_filename"
```

permits the programmer to merge source code from separate files into programs at compile time. In this fashion, programs can be developed as separate files or modules and merged automatically just before compilation.

The personal memory manager program was developed in four separate steps or segments. The first of these segments is the "master" or "driver" component. The master program grows in features as you merge each of the remaining segments with the first. This program might be written using four separate and distinct files. With three `INCLUDE` directives in the first file, Prolog would locate and merge the files at compile time. To use this compiler directive, enter the keyword `INCLUDE` and the DOS filename enclosed in quotes at the top of the program along with the other keywords. The file that is called may itself have an `INCLUDE` directive in it. Files must not be called recursively, and a file may not be included more than once. The files that are called may contain DOMAINS or PREDICATES declarations but may not contain DATABASE declarations.

As an exercise, merge the personal memory manager and calculator programs into one large utility. To accomplish this, take the following steps:

1. Make a copy of PMM.PRO and call it PMM&CALC.PRO.
2. Make a copy of CALC2.PRO and call it CALC3.PRO.
3. Move the DATABASE declarations in CALC3 to PMM&CALC.
4. Enter `INCLUDE "CALC3.PRO"` just before the CLAUSES section in PMM&CALC.
5. Enter `(C)alculator\n` in the `main_menu` rule in PMM&CALC.
6. Enter the rule

```
call_selection("C") :-
    start.
```

7. Remove the internal GOAL from CALC3.

Now run the program and try the calculator.

6.6 SUMMARY

Concepts covered

Computer accessibility
Designing interfaces
Point, line, and turtle graphics
Windows, color, and sound in programs
Writing utility programs

This chapter introduced the concept of the human-computer interface and the tools provided by Turbo Prolog for implementing windows, sound, and graphics. The point was made that successful software anticipates and supports human cognitive capabilities and needs through good design and program options. Use of many of the Turbo Prolog primitives was illustrated in several demonstration programs.

6.7 EXERCISES

1. Write a `memory` option for the calculator program that will perform these tasks:
   a. Create a memory category entered by the user.
   b. List user-created memory categories.
   c. Store a user-entered number in each such category.
   d. Retrieve the number from a named category as directed by the user.
2. Write procedures for the promotion program that will do all of the following:
   a. Place a limit on the number of promotions in a department or the entire company (or both) for a specified period of time.
   b. Expand the qualifications for promotion to include some employee attributes entered by the supervisor at run time, such as initiative or contributions to community.
   c. Employ an alternative scheme such as weighting for determining eligibility for promotion.
   d. Access employee and company knowledge bases in files and retrieve addresses, criteria, salaries, and other data.
   e. Make each salary increase a permanent change in the employee record in the database (note that this will require a separate file for the knowledge base).
   f. Give the user the option of turning off the sound.
   g. Terminate the program when the employee candidate list is empty.
   h. Clear the screen before exiting.
3. Develop a procedure for deleting a category from the key file in the personal memory manager program.
4. When in `write mode` in the memory manager program, the user can enter and write to a nonexisting category. Design a procedure that will check for the existence of a category before writing.
5. Add a `change directory` option to the notepad program.

Part 3
Advanced Programming Topics

Chapter 7
Designing a Knowledge-based System

CHAPTER OBJECTIVES

Study of this chapter should enable you to do the following:

1. Discuss each of the important stages in KBS development.
2. Discuss the role of the knowledge engineer (KE).
3. Discuss techniques for knowledge acquisition.
4. Discuss the problems associated with the knowledge acquisition stage in KBS development.
5. Conceptualize, design, and code your own small KBS.
6. Build into your KBS such essential features as a windowed interface, a representative knowledge base of facts and rules, explanation facility, and context sensitive on-line help.

IMPORTANT TERMS AND PHRASES

Conceptualizing knowledge
Domain expert
Expert paradox
Feasibility study
Formalizing knowledge
How and why explanations
Knowledge engineer
Personal construct theory
Programming style
Protocol analysis
Resource identification
Role Construct Repertory Test
Stages in KBS development
System prototyping
Theoretical models of knowledge

> The evolution of an expert system normally proceeds from simple to hard tasks by incrementally improving the organization and representation of the system's knowledge. This incremental approach to development means that the system itself can assist in the developmental effort. As soon as builders acquire enough knowledge to construct even a very simple system, they do so and use feedback from the running model to direct and focus the effort.
>
> [D. A. Waterman, *A Guide to Expert Systems*, p. 135]

7.1 SYSTEM CONSTRUCTION

Building a knowledge-based system is best described as an evolutionary process. As pointed out in the quoted passage by the late Don Waterman, the development of an expert system (KBS) is an incremental process proceeding from simple to increasingly complex approximations of the desired end product. Each step in this process is fraught with pitfalls that may require revision or even major reformulation of the entire system.

While it is an oversimplification to represent the construction of a KBS as a linear series of discrete steps or procedures, it is useful to characterize the KBS development process as a series of stages (see Buchanan & Shortliffe, 1984). These stages are (1) initial identification of a feasible problem and adequate human and material resources for the completion of the project (identification stage); (2) acquiring the domain knowledge to be used in the project (knowledge acquisition and conceptualization stage); (3) the refining of knowledge into a form suitable for use in a computational system (knowledge representation and formalization stage); (4) design of an interface and inference engine followed by successive passes at building approximations of a final system (prototyping, testing, and validation stages); (5) introduction of the product to the users (deployment stage); and (6) a long-term support and updating stage. At all stages the designer and knowledge engineer will depend on the cooperation and input of administrators, experts, and end-users.

Each stage in the complex process of KBS development has been discussed in the literature by scientists who themselves have developed well-known systems (Buchanan & Shortliffe, 1984; Waterman, 1986; McDermott, 1981; Hayes-Roth, Waterman, & Lenat, 1983). The stages and the relations among them are graphically represented in Figure 7.1. The arrows in this figure illustrate how each stage in the process feeds information back to previous stages in a self-correcting loop. The circular relations between the KE and resources at the identification and conceptualization stages denote the close and continued interaction that characterizes development at these stages of the project.

It is worth noting that due to the potential economic impact of this technology, much future KBS R&D will take place in commercial environments, and advance-

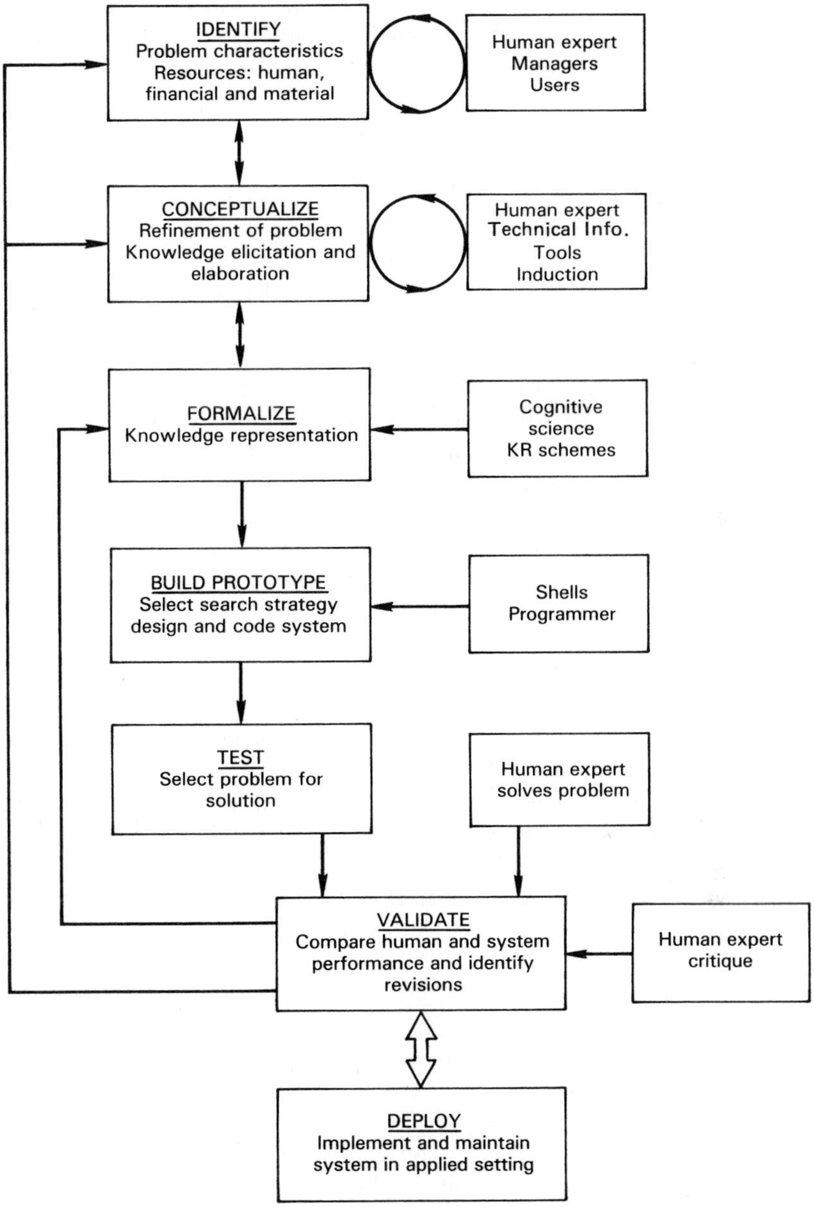

Figure 7.1 Model for incremental development of a knowledge-based system. After D. A. Waterman, *A Guide to Expert Systems* (Reading, Mass.: Addison-Wesley, 1986), p. 137.

ments in this technology will therefore be proprietary. KBS R&D is knowledge-intensive and expensive. While academicians are rewarded for sharing details of major discoveries and developments, corporations will be naturally reluctant to publish (read as "give away") valuable corporate information. To the extent that this proves true, new techniques will be sparsely reported in the literature, and the evolution of KBS technology in the coming decade may well be significantly retarded.

Numerous AI venture capital groups are currently offering a variety of tools which promise to simplify KBS development. These range from knowledge acquisition aids to full-blown expert system development environments. Some of the more extensive tools are supported only by larger computers (e.g., Vaxes, LISP machines, and AI workstations), but the trend is to offer scaled-down versions for microcomputers. Many of these tools are the result of considerable experience and research on the part of the developers and are excellent products. However, a market crowded with competing KBS tools has the potential to create further confusion in the minds of already bewildered consumers.

In the sections that follow, I will present a distillation of the development experiences reported by several researchers experienced in KBS design and implementation. I will then develop a small program to illustrate the development cycle and features of a KBS.

7.2 THE KNOWLEDGE ENGINEER

The success of any KBS project depends directly on the quality of the efforts of the knowledge engineer at each stage in the development process. Before I begin developing our demonstration program, it is appropriate to elaborate on the crucial role played by the KE in KBS development. The role of the KE is new and is evolving right along with KBS technology. Accordingly, what is said regarding the KE is, of course, subject to imminent revision.

A logical place to begin our discussion is with the qualifications of a KE. As I see it, an ideally qualified KE would have excellent interpersonal and communication skills; familiarity with management and organizational structures; a background in psychology and cognitive science; a capacity for assimilating and organizing highly technical information; the ability to formulate clearly defined concepts and goals; an understanding of the theoretical basis and procedures for coding, testing, and validating a KBS; and most important of all, patience and a great sense of humor. It would seem by these criteria that our ideally qualified KE would be a modern-day Renaissance man. Most practicing KEs are sure to demur at such hyperbole. Yet the KE, much like a Renaissance man, must be a generalist, ranging freely across technical boundaries, conceptualizing and representing expertise in new and innovative ways.

Many among the first generation of KEs were trained in AI, often to the Ph.D. level. For this reason, highly qualified KEs are in short supply. The current generation of KEs seem not to be as highly trained in AI, but gain their technical skills through on-the-job experience.

There are exciting opportunities in this field for bright people interested in the nature of knowledge, problem solving, technology, and new ideas. It will not be long before universities sense this market and begin offering programs leading to graduate degrees with a specialty in designing and implementing knowledge-intensive software systems.

7.2.1 The KE Working with the Client

I predict that the majority of future KEs will be developing systems for what has been called the end-user and mainstream markets. The end-user market consists of corporations and commercial organizations that do not attempt major software projects in-house. These companies will wish to develop KBS applications for training, maintaining knowledge bases, and product support using task-specific domain knowledge and advanced KBS techniques. The systems that they will want will be relatively small and inexpensive. That is, small systems which will require less than one worker-year to develop. The end-user market will employ outside consultants and firms specializing in AI and KBS development.

The mainstream market consists of *Fortune* 2000 companies with requirements for large systems. Here development will involve highly trained in-house staff with some help from outside consultants. These will be sophisticated and expensive programs and will be efforts measured in worker-years.

Together these two client categories represent a significant potential market and will generate a large demand for individuals with KE skills to serve as independent consultants and in-house R&D staff. It is clear that the market for KBS development support tools will also flourish in the 1990s.

Common to both these markets is the client, a commercial organization (large and small) with a tight budget and an increasingly pragmatic attitude regarding AI. This means eliciting management's continuing support by articulating the validity and feasibility of systems and by setting concrete and realistic goals for development.

A major danger in working with such organizations will be promising more than can be delivered. Management will have to be educated about the realities of KBS development without diminishing enthusiasm and support for these projects. This will require effective planning and communication—skills expected of top executives but not always associated with scientists and technical types.

7.2.2 The KE Working with End Users

The individual end user, too often forgotten, must also be considered by the KE. The end user is the practitioner in the field who needs the problem-solving expertise encoded within the KBS to perform her or his daily functions. If the person who will use the system lacks faith in the project, even the best KBS can be a failure.

McDermott (1981) recounts the importance of efforts to gain end-user acceptance in the early days of R1 (a.k.a XCON), the well-known Vax system configuration expert system. Had the end users not come to accept R1, it would not be numbered among the most successful commercial systems in daily use today.

A very good strategy for getting people interested in a project is (1) to convince them that the project will not threaten them personally, (2) to permit them to exercise some modicum of control over the implementation and deployment of the project into their daily activities, and (3) to convince them that the project will simplify rather than complicate their lives.

People must perceive themselves to be in control of any new system, or they will conclude that they will inevitably be controlled by it. The proper perception can be achieved by involving the end users early in the project, permitting them to contribute to the development of the system. And, if necessary, it is better to make concessions early than to scrap an expensive but unused system later. The KE must be skilled in applied psychology to succeed in this stage of development.

7.2.3 The KE Working with Experts

Once a project is approved and budgeted, the KE must identify the resources necessary for the successful completion of the project. Chief among these is the human expert who will provide the domain knowledge and expertise. The KE will then begin the difficult task of soliciting and maintaining the expert's cooperative participation in the project. This can be a very difficult task, for several reasons.

The KE must be able to convince management that a significant portion of the expert's valuable time must be dedicated to the project on a regular basis and for a protracted period. The expert should perceive management as solidly behind the project. The KE must also convince the expert that the project justifies time spent away from the important business of solving problems. Here the KE will need tact and continuing intellectual stimulation to avoid losing the expert's cooperation.

Many KEs recommend implementing a prototype as soon as is reasonably possible for the expert to critique. Skillfully done, this can demonstrate the importance of the expert's participation in the development process and the validity of the project as well as KBS technology, and it can serve to pique the expert's curiosity and interest. Undue haste in prototyping, however, is ill-advised. To be useful, the prototype must be a provisional yet veridical working model of the desired end product. Also, a failure at this stage can be disastrous for the project.

Most people would accept the commonsense definition of an expert as "an unusual person who knows how to solve difficult and important problems in some special area of knowledge." This definition is correct as far as it goes—but its simplicity masks a paradox. The paradox is that experts, while superior to the rest of us in solving problems, are also in another way very much like us; they rarely articulate what they do. In fact, the more expertise someone has, the more likely it is that he or she will not be able to describe the conceptual representations or even the procedures used in solving problems with the requisite degree of clarity.

The reason for this paradox is that through years of study and experience, experts compile their knowledge into highly functional units. The functionality of their knowledge stresses application and not articulation. The KE's most difficult job, then, is to assist the expert in expressing, or "reverse-compiling," this expertise. The KE must not allow this difficult process to become unpleasant, threatening, or dull lest the expert physically or psychologically withdraw from the project. A mistake at this crucial point of knowledge acquisition can irreparably damage or delay the project. Here the KE must use sensitivity and diplomacy while patiently and persistently pursuing the expert until success is achieved.

On some projects the KE may have to work with more than one expert. While working with more than one expert can be beneficial, it can also complicate the knowledge acquisition task. According to McGraw and Seale (1988, p. 31) "If knowledge acquisition for an expert system with a single expert can be described as a bottleneck [Hayes-Roth, et al., 1983], acquisition from multiple experts, especially in a group setting, has the potential to become a log-jam." Refer to Mittal and Dym (1985) for a detailed discussion of the pros and cons of knowledge acquisition working with multiple experts.

Large-scale and complex projects may require the efforts of two KEs. Rolandi (1986) proposes an interesting model where one KE would assume primary responsibility for debriefing the expert while another acts as a "quality control" monitor of the effectiveness of the debriefing procedures.

7.3 PROCEDURES FOR KNOWLEDGE ACQUISITION

The position taken here is that expertise is embodied in representations accumulated over a lifetime of domain experience. With the possible exception of those who teach, few experts spend very much time articulating their knowledge. To coax knowledge out of the expert, the KE must first understand the ways in which the expert represents objects, relationships, conditions, constraints, and events within the problem domain. Here the KE may use a wide variety of tools, including interviews, protocol analysis, simulations, and theoretical conceptions such as Kelly's personal construct theory (see Kidd, 1987; Hart, 1986; Gammack & Young, 1985; Waterman, 1986; Hoffman, 1987; Prerau, 1987; Hayes-Roth et al., 1983).

7.3.1 Interviewing Techniques

Despite extensive research by psychologists, interviewing techniques are still a long way from being reduced to a body of facts and rules. Human personality, communication, and social behaviors are, after all, extraordinarily complex phenomena. This means that there is as yet no substitute for interviewing experience. In addition to experience, good interviewers are able to select from among a range of techniques those that are most appropriate to the situation and the individual being interviewed. The following are some useful general suggestions for the interviewer KE drawn from the research literature (see Hart, 1986).

1. Try not to allow the discussion to remain too long at a general or abstract level. Discussing generalities may be necessary initially to get an expert to warm up to the task, but the KE must bring the discussion down to the more difficult level of specific problems and methods used for solutions in order to generate useful information. Some experts will resist all attempts to accomplish this.

2. Do not ask the expert to represent his or her thinking in ways that are not familiar or natural. For example, do not encourage an expert to use a decision tree if the expert never uses that particular representational method in his or her daily work.

3. Resist the temptation to interrupt the expert's train of thought. The KE must be patient and not rush or unduly press the expert. Some experts will tend to ramble on. Others will repeat or even contradict themselves. After the expert has finished talking, the KE must sift through what has been said and then direct the interview back to important points for review and in-depth discussion.

4. Record information carefully. An interview may contain information that at the moment seems unimportant. Later, in reviewing a record of the interview, the KE may discover that this information is significant. Most KEs recommend the use of tape recorders; some warn against video recording, which may make the expert unduly self-conscious and reticent.

5. Tune in to the way the expert applies knowledge. The surface or explicit content of the interview may mask other important information that is implicit and less obvious. This can include the order in which points are covered or the relative emphasis given to them by the expert.

6. Try to remain flexible. The KE must avoid investing in a premature hypothesis about the structure of the expertise and resist the tendency to hold on to a favorite hypothesis even when it has proved unusable. The KE must always remain receptive to new information and better ways of representing knowledge.

7.3.2 Protocol Analysis

Protocol analysis is often used as an adjunct to the interview. It involves asking the expert to describe solutions to problems solved in the past or to work through a set of representative problems designed by the KE. The expert is encouraged to recount interesting cases and critical incidents surrounding the procedures used in solving these problems. The KE may question the expert about details of procedures. Analysis of several such case histories often enables the KE to identify patterns of expert response to underlying features of problems. Analysis may also focus on specific behavioral aspects of the task.

Experts, again very much like the rest of us ordinary people, often say one thing yet do quite another. A KE must be careful to check rules obtained from interviews against observations made of actual performances. Rolandi (1986) suggests that application of techniques developed by behavioral psychologists may have merit in such an objective empirical analysis of expert performance.

In a behavioral analysis, the KE presents the expert with a sample of problems to solve. The KE records frequencies of the various behaviors evidenced by the expert in solving the problem set. This frequency data would help the KE to define the types and priority values of various categories of solutions. The KE would, in this approach, focus attention on a descriptive analysis of the environmental setting (discriminative stimuli) of the problem, the expert's behaviors (responses), and the environmental consequences (reinforcing stimuli) instrumentally contingent on the expert's behaviors. Observed regularities among these three components of any problem situation could assist the KE in constructing empirically based rules that will accurately model what the expert does behaviorally when solving problems.

7.3.3 Theoretical Models

Historically, psychologists have attempted to explain aspects of human nature by relating the multiplicity of observed daily behavior to a relatively smaller number of underlying structures. Freud, for example, explained a wide variety of adult temperament by speculating about the dynamic interrelations of a small number of hypothetical personality constructs and intervening variables (id, ego, superego, libido). George Kelly (1955), an important figure in the early days of the cognitive psychology movement, similarly attempted to explain human behavior by employing theoretical constructs. Disenchanted with the psychoanalytic view of motivation stressing unconscious sexual drives, Kelly viewed man as a cognizing creature with a drive to interpret and understand what is in fact a very personal world. To explain how people go about the important process of understanding their personal worlds, Kelly postulated an underlying cognitive structure that he termed the *personal construct.*

According to personal construct theory, all people (experts, KEs, you, and I included) attempt to understand their world by interpreting events in terms of personalized minitheories or constructs derived from past experiences. We are all in this sense scientists. We make predictions based on hypotheses generated from our personal constructs and then, more or less, check the results against subsequent inputs from reality. In this fashion, we gradually build our theories of the world. To understand any person's behavior, Kelly suggests that we must first fathom the depth and variety of the individual's personal constructs.

The conclusion that should be drawn from personal construct theory is that understanding how an individual applies his or her expertise requires that one learn about the expert's personal constructs as they relate to the problem domain. One must answer the question, "What are the theories the expert is using to perceive and interpret a problem?" It is interesting that in this connection the KE must guard against his or her own premature formulation of constructs. We all run the risk of becoming attached to our preconceptions, that is, our own personal constructs. The KE cannot afford to make this kind of error. He or she must remain open to the continual revision or even abandonment of all hypotheses about how an individual expert is applying knowledge to solve a particular problem.

To assist in the process of debriefing people regarding their constructs, Kelly devised an instrument he called the Role Construct Repertory Test. This test elicits from people the constructs they use in interpreting significant events in their lives. The client is asked to list important elements (e.g., people, features of a problem) in his or her daily experiences. The client then groups these elements in clusters of three showing how two are similar to each other and at the same time different from the third. In this fashion the personal constructs used by the client in perceiving similarity among events are gradually revealed. Continuing this process yields a multidimensioned set of personal concepts used by each individual in interpreting classes of events.

Several KBS researchers have found personal construct theory and the Rep Test a useful approach to debriefing experts (Shaw, 1981). These techniques can be a valuable aid to the KE in defining precisely how experts discriminate and interpret dimensions of problem situations.

Bolstered by this cursory background in knowledge engineering, we will now move on to the construction of a small KBS, attempting to apply as much as possible what has been learned thus far in the book.

7.4 PROTOTYPING A PRODUCT LIABILITY INSURANCE CLAIMS KBS

The problem I have chosen to illustrate the development cycle of a prototype KBS is product liability claims evaluation and is based upon the example given by the late Don Waterman in Chapter 15 of *A Guide to Expert Systems* (1986). Complete coverage of the complexities of the evolutionary process of a KBS is well beyond the scope and intent of this book. In particular, to fully document the knowledge acquisition process here would require far more space than we can afford. Also, the selection of representation and inferencing schemes will not be detailed, as Turbo Prolog and its built-in depth-first searching and backward chaining inference engine will be used.

7.4.1 Identifying the Problem

Let's begin by assuming that you are president of an independent consulting firm specializing in designing small-scale KBSs for the insurance industry. (Why not begin at the top?) You receive a call from the VP for claims settlement at Small Hands, Inc., a company that writes product liability policies. The VP expresses interest in the potential of AI software for helping her company respond to claims more efficiently. What she means by more efficiently is left undefined for the moment, and you agree to meet with her to discuss the matter in more detail.

The next afternoon you discuss the project in some depth with the client. The client knows little about AI or KBS, but she does know the insurance business and her company's needs very well. It seems that the company is worried about the rising cost of settling claims. Management is concerned that many of the company's adjusters are ineffective in factoring all settlement variables in their large caseload of claims so as to respond in a timely fashion with estimates that are neither so low as to prompt costly litigation nor so high as to be wasteful of company resources. The board has authorized the VP to explore the AI approach and has provided a small budget for the project.

The company has one adjuster who seems to stand head and shoulders above the rest in his department. He is very efficient in making claims settlements and effective in training new personnel. This individual, however, is close to retirement age, and the company is worried that it may not be able to replace his expertise. The company would like very much to model his performance in a computer program for its training program and for possible implementation as a computerized assistant for adjusters in several of its field offices.

You discuss the feasibility of a KBS with the VP, stressing the need for resources, including the expert's time, and establishment of reasonable goals for development of the system. You agree to do a feasibility study and to submit a written proposal.

As part of the feasibility study, you interview the expert at length to assess his capabilities and to determine his attitudes about the potential of KBS. You also attempt to get an overview of the problem and the ways in which the expert determines the value of a claim. Others in the claims department are interviewed to assess levels of expertise, as well as attitudes about using computers to solve problems.

After some study you conclude that the resources at Small Hands are adequate, the problem is amenable to operational definition and emulation in a small-scale KBS, and the end users are open to use of computerized aids. You discover that the company mainframe will not be available and that the scope of the problem really lends itself to a more portable microcomputer-based system. You submit your report along with a proposal for a three-month development project for a working prototype dealing with one aspect of claims settlement, claims associated with product failure and related injuries. You outline specific goals you expect to achieve during the development period as well as detailed requirements for commitment of resources by the company. Your proposal is accepted and you begin the next step in the process.

7.4.2 Conceptualizing the Problem

This stage involves a great deal of time spent with the expert. You interrogate the expert to identify major working concepts involved in making a claim settlement. You discuss your tentative definitions with the expert and revise them according to the expert's critique. You also do a protocol analysis of the last 10 cases handled by the expert to determine the procedures he used. Out of an extended process of conceptualizing and reconceptualizing major aspects of the problem, you arrive at the working concepts that are essential to settling a claim.

1. *Plaintiff losses* attributable to current and future costs associated with product-caused injury
2. *Plaintiff responsibility* for damages
3. *Defendant liability* for damages
4. *Plaintiff trauma*
5. *Subjective characteristics* surrounding the case that are collectively known to affect the size of settlements determined through litigation

More specifically, you determine that the expert estimates a claim by assigning a value in each of these categories. The claim's value is the multiplicative total of these values as shown in this formula:

$$\text{Claim value} = \text{Plaintiff loss} \times (1 - \text{plaintiff responsibility}) \times \text{defendant liability} \times \text{plaintiff trauma} \times \text{subjective case characteristics}$$

1. *Plaintiff loss* is a dollar value determined in a straightforward manner by adding together values for various costs directly associated with the product failure. These are special damages (e.g., hospital costs and lost income), general damages (costs associated with property loss), and future damages (future lost income). These values are determined in part from the case history and in part by an estimate of future lost income provided by the expert when evaluating the claim.

2. *Plaintiff responsibility* is an estimate of the amount of responsibility the plaintiff has for damages associated with the product failure. For example, the brakes on a car may be documented as faulty, but if the plaintiff was intoxicated at the time of an accident the plaintiff shares, to some degree, responsibility for the losses incurred.

You discover after an analysis of several cases that the expert typically uses six categories for assessing plaintiff responsibility: very high, high, moderate, low, very low, and none. Use of descriptive verbal categories is common among experts when working with uncertain knowledge. Problem solving using such fuzzy categories will be discussed in more detail in Chapter 10.

Each of these categories is then assigned a value by the expert. If, for example, plaintiff responsibility is estimated as very high, plaintiff loss is reduced by the inverse of the value given to this category. At the other end of the scale, if the expert estimates plaintiff responsibility to be nil, plaintiff loss is unaffected in its value.

3. The expert estimates the degree of *defendant liability* in a similar fashion, using five categories this time. The nil category is omitted here because the claim would not be honored in instances where there was no product liability. The value obtained using the first two variables is multiplied by the value associated with the estimated degree of defendant liability.

4. The expert states that he also considers *plaintiff trauma* in determining a claim's value. Upon probing further you learn that plaintiff trauma is in fact made up of two components: injury trauma (pain and suffering associated directly with the product failure event) and future trauma (a prediction of the likelihood of illness and disability causally related to the present trauma). The expert uses special tables prepared by medical and actuarial specialists to help him establish this value. The value obtained from the first three steps is multiplied by the value obtained for injury trauma and then by the value of future trauma.

5. *Subjective case characteristics* represents public opinion and an estimate of any potential bias a jury might have for either the plaintiff or the defendant. For example, a large, rich, and impersonal corporation with a history of producing shoddy and dangerous products is likely to be subject to high punitive awards in jury trials. The expert estimates this by using indirect measures of public opinion of both plaintiff and defendant. If, in the mind of the expert, these subjective characteristics favor the plaintiff, the claim value is increased by a factor the expert has gleaned from experience. If the characteristics favor the defendant, the claim value is reduced in a similar fashion.

7.4.3 Formalizing the Knowledge

Your task is now defined well enough for you to begin coding a prototype program. This prototype will help you to validate your tentative model for claims evaluation by having the expert critique estimates made by the program. You are also hopeful that the program will pique the expert's interest and renew what you perceive to be his flagging motivation for continuing with the project.

You decide to prototype the program in Turbo Prolog. Most important to this decision is the fact that the problem seems well represented as Turbo Prolog facts and rules. The decision is also prompted by the rapid prototyping capabilities of the language. In addition, Turbo Prolog provides good control over the user interface and permits easy access to large related files that will be needed in various claims evaluations. In thinking about the client's small budget, you recall that a Turbo Prolog system can be compiled into fast stand-alone EXE form and used on many PCs without payment of royalties or fees for run-time software.

7.4.4 Implementing the System

You next proceed to design the prototype. You start by drawing up a list of specifications you want to build into the program.

1. You recognize that this program is the first component of a larger program that will model value estimation in additional categories of claims. Each section of this larger program will be written and tested independently and later merged into one system. Modularization will permit the large program to run on PCs.

It will also help simplify development and debugging. Developing a module at a time will demonstrate incremental progress to the client and sustain corporate support. As many of the facts used by the program are dynamic and will require regular editing, they will be maintained in separate files for information security and convenience in updating.

2. The program must explain its behavior to the user by providing why and how explanations as requested. Why explanations are offered to users who want to know why the program is behaving in the manner that it is at any particular moment. Why questions are often of the form "Why are you asking me for this information?" A KBS program often accomplishes this by telling the user where it is in the problem solution process and what rule it is attempting to prove.

How explanations are offered to users to explain the conclusions arrived at by the program. A typical how answer justifies the logic of a conclusion by tracing the firing of all the rules that led up to proving the conclusion. A how explanation must be instructive and model the expert's procedural solution to a specific problem. In this fashion, an expert system can be used as a tutor—solving problems and then demonstrating the logic used in the solution.

3. The program must solicit necessary data and react to missing, incomplete, or incorrect data by searching tables or synonym files. If the data are still deficient, the program must ask the user for clarification and then return to the task.

4. The program must perform robustly and not terminate unless directed to do so by the user.

5. The program must provide help when asked. It must also trap errors and provide help automatically when the user makes an error or attempts to use the program improperly.

6. The program must have a professional-looking windowed interface that makes all program functions clearly and easily accessible to the user.

7. The program will be implemented on microcomputers with limited RAM and must therefore use system resources very efficiently.

8. Last and most important, the program must accurately emulate the processes used by the expert in estimating claims.

Next you spend several days coding the following prototype program.

```
/* ****************************************************
                       CLAIMS.PRO

    Product liability program for Small Hands project.
   ****************************************************
             DECLARATIONS, GOAL, AND INCLUDE SEGMENT
   **************************************************** */

DOMAINS
values = integer*
```

```
list = record(values)
entry = injury(string) ; cause_of(string) ; severity(real)

DATABASE
help_msg(integer)
fired(list)
case_hist(string,string)
case_values(string,real)
dict(entry,entry)
synonym(string,string)

PREDICATES
run
select(integer)
solicit(string,symbol)
record(string,symbol)
claim_value(integer)
explanation
get_info
show_info
reply(integer)
build_hist
save_hist
help
error
erase_all
help_message(integer,string)
plaintiff_loss(integer,real)
special_damages(integer,real)
general_damages(integer,real)
future_damages(integer,real)
plaintiff_trauma(integer,real)
injury_trauma(integer,real)
future_trauma(integer,real)
check_synonyms(string,string)
plaintiff_responsibility(integer,real)
defendant_liability(integer,real)
case_characteristics(integer,real)
favor_plaintiff(integer,real)
favor_defendant(integer,real)
compute_claim_value(real,real,real,real,real,real)
notify(real)
show_how
list_out(values)
list_desc(values)
why(integer)
rule_table(integer,string)
p_index(integer,real)
```

(continued)

```
d_index(integer,real)
f_d_index(integer,real)
p_s_index(integer,real)

GOAL
makewindow(1,112,15,"Product Liability Claims Assistant",
     0,0,25,80),
run.

INCLUDE "MENU.PRO"   % read in Borland's bounce-bar menu

/* *****************************************************
                PROGRAM MAIN MENU SEGMENT
   ***************************************************** */

CLAUSES
run :-
 clearwindow,
 storage(S,_,_),                       % Check stack and
 write("Stack = ",S," bytes"),         % inform programmer
 menu(8,23,["Load/Create Case History","Display Case History",
 "Determine Claim Value","Explanation of Claim Value",
     "Help File",
 "Exit Program"],Answer),
 select(Answer).

select(1) :-                 % Procedure to invoke user option
 get_info.
select(2) :-
 show_info.
select(3) :-
 claim_value().
select(4) :-
 explanation,
 erase_all.
select(5) :-
 help.
select(6) :-
 erase_all,
 removewindow,
 exit.

/* *****************************************************
                LOAD/CREATE CASE HISTORY SEGMENT
   ***************************************************** */

get_info :-
 erase_all,
```

```
 menu(8,23,["Create Case History","Load Case History"],Ch),
 reply(Ch),
 run.

reply(1) :-
 clearwindow,
 makewindow(2,112,15,"Case History",5,4,15,70),
 build_hist,
 save_hist.
reply(2) :-
 makewindow(3,112,15,"Directory",2,27,21,20),

% Make menu of case history files for user to select from

 dir("c:\prolog\turbo\pro","*.dba",File),
 consult(File),
 removewindow.
                                 % Procedure for collecting
build_hist :-                    % case history information
 record(X,Y),
 solicit(X,Y),                   % Needed to handle data typing
 fail.
build_hist.

 solicit(X,is_string) :-          % Solicit string information
  write("\tEnter ",X,": "),
  readln(Answer),
  assertz(case_hist(X,Answer)).

solicit(X,is_real) :-             % Solicit real information
  write("\tEnter ",X,": "),
  readreal(Answer),
  assertz(case_values(X,Answer)).

 save_hist :-
  write("\tDo you wish to save this history?  y/n: "),
  readchar(Reply),
  Reply = 'y',
  write("\n\n\tEnter filename with no extension: "),
  readln(File),
  concat(File,".DBA",File_ext),
  save(File_ext),
  removewindow
  ;
  erase_all,     % OR if case not to be saved, then erase it
  removewindow.
```

(continued)

```
erase_all :-            % Procedure for erasing asserted facts
 retract(case_hist(_,_)),
 fail.
erase_all :-
 retract(case_values(_,_)),
 fail.
erase_all :-
 retract(fired(record(_))),
 fail.
erase_all.


 /* ******************************************************
                    DISPLAY CASE HISTORY SEGMENT
    ****************************************************** */


  show_info :-            % Has user loaded a case history?
   not(case_hist(_,_)),nl,
   asserta(help_msg(1)),
   error,                 % If not, provide an error message
   run.
  show_info :-            % If loaded, display it
   makewindow(4,112,15,"Display Case History",2,10,20,60),
   case_hist(Category,Fact),nl,
   write("\t",Category,": ",Fact),
   fail.
  show_info :-
   case_values(Category,Fact),nl,
   write("\t",Category,": ",Fact),
   fail.
  show_info :-
   case_hist(_,_),
   nl,write("\n\tPress any key to continue: "),
   readchar(_),
   removewindow,!,        % cut set to limit building stack
   run.

  error :-         % Procedure used by other segments as well
  makewindow(13,112,15,"Help",11,18,5,45),
  help_msg(Number),
  help_message(Number,Message),
  write("  ",Message),nl,
  write("  You may wish to review the help file."),nl,
  write("      Press any key to continue: "),
  readchar(_),
  removewindow.
```

```
/* ***********************************************************
                    DETERMINE CLAIM VALUE SEGMENT
   *********************************************************** */

claim_value(1) :-  % Check to see if case history is loaded
 not(case_hist(_,_)),
 asserta(help_msg(2)),
 error,                        % If not, give error message
 run
 ;                               % OR do claim evaluation
 makewindow(5,112,15,"Claim Evaluation",0,0,24,80),
 consult("m_dict.dba"),
 plaintiff_loss(2,P_L),
 plaintiff_trauma(6,P_T),
 plaintiff_responsibility(9,P_R),
 defendant_liability(10,D_L),
 case_characteristics(11,Index),
 compute_claim_value(Value,P_L,P_R,D_L,P_T,Index),
                          % Make record of fired rules and
                        % set cut to limit growth of stack
 asserta(fired(record([1,2,6,9,10,11]))),!,
 notify(Value).

plaintiff_loss(2,P_L) :-
 special_damages(3,S_D),
 general_damages(4,G_D),
 future_damages(5,F_D),
 P_L = S_D + G_D + F_D,
                              % Make record of fired rules
 assertz(fired(record([2,3,4,5]))).

special_damages(3,S_D) :-
 case_values("Plaintiff's Lost Income",Lost),
 case_values("Plaintiff's Hospital Costs",Costs),
 S_D = Lost + Costs.

general_damages(4,G_D) :-
 case_values("Plaintiff's General Damages",G_D).

future_damages(5,F_D) :-
 menu(8,23,["Estimate Future Lost Income 0%",
            "Estimate Future Lost Income 5%",
            "Estimate Future Lost Income 10%",
            "Estimate Future Lost Income 30%",
            "Estimate Future Lost Income 50%",
            "Estimate Future Lost Income 70%",
```

(continued)

```
            "Estimate Future Lost Income 100%",
            "Why ask this question?"],Estimate),
  not(Estimate = 8),              % User not asking why
  case_values("Plaintiff's Age",Age),
  case_values("Plaintiff's Salary",Income),
  Earning_years = 70 - Age,
  f_d_index(Estimate,Index),
  F_D = Earning_years * (Index * Income),
  assertz(case_values("Plaintiff's Future Lost Income",F_D))
  ;
  why(5),                         % OR give a why explanation
  future_damages(5,F_D).

plaintiff_trauma(6,P_T) :-
 injury_trauma(7,I_T),
 future_trauma(8,F_T),
 P_T = I_T + F_T,
                                  % Make a record of fired rules
 assertz(fired(record([6,7,8]))).

injury_trauma(7,I_T) :-
  menu(8,23,["Plaintiff Pain & Suffering Very High",
             "Plaintiff Pain & Suffering High",
             "Plaintiff Pain & Suffering Moderate",
             "Plaintiff Pain & Suffering Low",
             "Plaintiff Pain & Suffering None",
             "Why ask this question?"],Estimate),
 not(Estimate = 6),
 p_s_index(Estimate,I_T),
 assertz(case_values("Plaintiff's Pain & Suffering",I_T))
 ;
 why(7),
 injury_trauma(7,I_T).

future_trauma(8,F_T) :-
 case_hist("Type of Injury",Injury),
 dict(injury(Injury),cause_of(Future_Disease)),
 dict(injury(Future_Disease),severity(Index)),
            % Medical dictionary recognizes "injury"
 F_T = Index.
               % Rule to cover unrecognized injuries
future_trauma(8,F_T) :-
 case_hist("Type of Injury",Injury),
 check_synonyms(Synonym,Injury),  % Is there a synonym?
 dict(injury(Synonym),cause_of(Future_Disease)),
 dict(injury(Future_Disease),severity(Index)),
 F_T = Index.
```

```
check_synonyms(Synonym,Injury) :-
 synonym(Synonym,Injury).
           % First rule succeeds if there is a synonym
                   % drop down to the second rule and
              % ask for info if there is no synonym
check_synonyms(Synonym,Injury) :-
 makewindow(6,112,15,"Query the User",10,15,6,45),
 write("  I do not know about ",Injury),nl,
 write("  Please rephrase: "),
 readln(New_Injury),       % Change to rephrased injury
 retract(case_hist("Type of Injury",Injury)),
 assertz(case_hist("Type of Injury",New_Injury)),
 removewindow,
 synonym(Synonym,New_Injury)
                    % Check to see if this is a synonym
   % This logic requires that a word be its own synonym
 ;                           % OR if not, ask again
 case_hist("Type of Injury",New_Injury),
 check_synonyms(Synonym,New_injury).

plaintiff_responsibility(9,P_R) :-
 menu(8,23,["Plaintiff Responsibility Very High",
           "Plaintiff Responsibility High",
           "Plaintiff Responsibility Moderate",
           "Plaintiff Responsibility Low",
           "Plaintiff Responsibility Very Low",
           "Plaintiff Responsibility None",
           "Why ask this question?"],Estimate),
 not(Estimate = 7),
 p_index(Estimate,P_R),
 assertz(case_values("Plaintiff's Responsibility",P_R))
 ;
 why(9),
 plaintiff_responsibility(9,P_R).

defendant_liability(10,D_L) :-
 menu(8,23,["Defendant Liability Very High",
           "Defendant Liability High",
           "Defendant Liability Moderate",
           "Defendant Liability Low",
           "Defendant Liability Very Low",
           "Why ask this question?"],Estimate),
  not(Estimate = 6),
 d_index(Estimate,D_L),
```

(continued)

```
 assertz(case_values("Defendant's Liability",D_L))
 ;
 why(10),
 defendant_liability(10,D_L).

case_characteristics(11,Index) :-
 makewindow(7,112,15,"Case Characteristics",5,5,10,70),
 favor_plaintiff(12,Index),
 removewindow.
case_characteristics(11,Index) :-
 clearwindow,
 favor_defendant(13,Index),
 removewindow.
case_characteristics(11,Index) :-
 removewindow,
 Index = 1.00,
 assertz(fired(record([11,14]))),
 assertz(case_values("Case Characteristics Are Neutral",
     Index)).

favor_plaintiff(12,Index) :-
 write("\n\tAre one or more of the following statements
     true?\n"),
 write("\t\tMedia favor plaintiff."),
 write("\n\t\tPublic opinion is against defendant."),
 write("\n\t\tDefendant has lost similar cases in the past."),
 write("\n\n\tAnswer y/n: "),
 readchar(Answer),
 sound(2,800),
 Answer = 'y',
 Index = 1.2,    % Value if public opinion favors plaintiff
 assertz(fired(record([11,12]))),
 assertz(case_values("Case characteristics favor plaintiff.",
     Index)).

 favor_defendant(13,Index) :-
 write("\tOK.  Now answer the following:"),
 write("\n\tAre one or more of these statements true?\n"),
 write("\t\tMedia favor defendant."),
 write("\n\t\tPublic Opinion is against plaintiff."),
 write("\n\t\tDefendant has won similar cases in the past."),
 write("\n\n\tAnswer y/n: "),
 readchar(Answer),
 Answer = 'y',
 sound(2,800),    % Sound used here because screen looks
                  % like previous one and might confuse user
 Index = 0.8,
```

```
 assertz(case_values("Case characteristics favor defendant.",
     Index)),
 assertz(fired(record([11,13]))).

                     % Master rule to compute claim value
compute_claim_value(Value,P_L,P_R,D_L,P_T,Index) :-
 Value = P_L * (1 - P_R) * D_L * P_T * Index,
 assertz(case_values("Claim Value",Value)).

notify(Value) :-                   % Notify user of value
 makewindow(8,112,15,"Claim Value Estimate",10,15,6,48),
 writef("   Claim value is estimated at $%9.2f\n",Value,"."),
 write("\n    Press any key to return to main menu."),
 readchar(_),
 removewindow,
 run.

/* ********************************************************
                 EXPLAIN CLAIM VALUE SEGMENT
   ******************************************************** */

explanation :-      % Check to see if a claim evaluation
 not(fired(record(_))),                 % has been done
 asserta(help_msg(3)),
 error,
 run
 ;
 makewindow(9,112,15,"Explanation of Claim Value",0,0,25,80),
 show_how,
 write("\n\n\t\tPress any key to continue: "),
 readchar(_),
 removewindow,
 run.

show_how :-
 fired(record(X)),  % Pick up each record of fired rules
 list_out(X),
 fail.
show_how.

list_out([]).         % First rule in list is an ancestor
list_out([X|Y]) :-
 rule_table(X,Z),
 write("\n\n To prove ",Z),            % Format and print
 list_desc(Y).
```

(continued)

```
list_desc([]).         % Subsequent rules are descendants
list_desc([X|Y]) :-
 rule_table(X,Z),
 write("\n I had to prove ",Z),      % Format and Print
 list_desc(Y).

why(X) :-
 rule_table(X,Z),
 makewindow(10,112,15,"WHY Explanation of Claim Value",
     3,3,8,74),
 write("I need information to prove\n\t ",Z),
 write("\n\n\tPress any key to continue: "),
 readchar(_),
 removewindow.

/* ******************************************************
                     HELP SEGMENT
   ****************************************************** */

help :-
 not(existfile("helpfile.hlp")),
 asserta(help_msg(4)),
 error,
 run
 ;
 makewindow(11,112,15,"Instructions for Using Help File",
     0,0,3,80),
 write("UP:up arrow & PgUp\t\tDOWN:down arrow & PgDn\t\tEXIT:
     Esc"),
 makewindow(12,112,15,"Help File",3,0,22,80),
 file_str("helpfile.hlp",String),
 display(String),
 removewindow,
 removewindow,
 run.


/* ******************************************************
             INDEX, HELP, RECORD, & RULE TABLES

   Could be in a separate file to facilitate editing and
   program security!
   ****************************************************** */

 % Help messages used in error messages

 help_message(1,"First create or load a case history.").
 help_message(2,"To determine claim value load case history.").
```

```
help_message(3,"First you must do a claim evaluation.").
help_message(4,"I cannot find helpfile.hlp").

% Pain & Suffering values

p_s_index(1,1.30). /* Very High-increase claim by 33% */
p_s_index(2,1.20).
p_s_index(3,1.15).
p_s_index(4,1.10).
p_s_index(5,1.00).     % None, so no increase in claim

% Plaintiff Responsibility values

p_index(1,0.50).     /* Very High-decrease claim by 50% */
p_index(2,0.40).
p_index(3,0.30).
p_index(4,0.20).
p_index(5,0.10).
p_index(6,0.00).      % None-claim value not affected

% Future Damages values

f_d_index(1,0.00).  % No future losses, so no increase
f_d_index(2,0.05).
f_d_index(3,0.10).
f_d_index(4,0.30).
f_d_index(5,0.50).
f_d_index(6,0.80).
f_d_index(7,1.00).% Increase by full amount of losses

% Defendant Liability values

d_index(1,1.40).% Liability very high-increase by 40%
d_index(2,1.20).
d_index(3,1.10).
d_index(4,0.95).
d_index(5,0.80). % Liability very low-decrease by 20%

% Facts for the solicit procedure
record("Plaintiff's Name",is_string).
record("Plaintiff's Age",is_real).
record("Plaintiff's Salary",is_real).
record("Type of Injury",is_string).
record("Plaintiff's Hospital Costs",is_real).
record("Plaintiff's Lost Income",is_real).
record("Plaintiff's General Damages",is_real).
```

(continued)

```
 record("Defendant's Name",is_string).
 record("Product Name",is_string).

 % Rule Table - used by explanation procedures

 rule_table(1,"Claim Value = Plaintiff Loss (R2) * Plaintiff
     Trauma (R6)\n\t * (1 - Plaintiff Responsibility (R9)) *
     Liability (R10)\n\t * Case Characteristics (R11)").
 rule_table(2,"R2:  Loss = Special + General + Future Damages").
 rule_table(3,"R3:  Special Damages = Lost Income + Hospital
     Bill").
 rule_table(4,"R4:  General Damages = Property Lost").
 rule_table(5,"R5:  Future Damages = Estimated Lost Future
     Income").
 rule_table(6,"R6:  Trauma = Injury Trauma + Future Disease").
 rule_table(7,"R7:  Injury Trauma = Estimated Pain &
     Suffering").
 rule_table(8,"R8:  Future Disease = Index of Related
     Illness").
 rule_table(9,"R9:  Proof by User Estimate of Plaintiff
     Responsibility").
 rule_table(10,"R10: Proof by User Estimate of Defendant
     Liability").
 rule_table(11,"R11: Case Subjective Characteristics").
 rule_table(12,"R12: Case subjective characteristics favor
     plaintiff").
 rule_table(13,"R13: Case subjective characteristics favor
     defendant").
 rule_table(14,"R14: Case subjective characteristics
     neutral").

/* ***************** END CLAIMS.PRO ****************** */

/* ************************************************** */
                       M_DICT.DBA

      A medical knowledge base consulted by CLAIMS.PRO.
      It supports causal medical relations and synonyms
      for trauma disorders supplied by medical experts.
      Severity indices would be reviewed by an insurance
      claims expert as well.
/* ************************************************** */

dict(injury("head trauma"),cause_of("blurred vision")).
dict(injury("back trauma"),cause_of("arthritis")).
dict(injury("arthritis"),severity(1.35)).
dict(injury("blurred vision"),severity(1.75)).
```

```
synonym("head trauma","head trauma").
synonym("head trauma","concussion").
synonym("head trauma","fractured skull").
synonym("back trauma","back trauma").
synonym("back trauma","back problem").
synonym("back trauma","backache").

/* ****************** END M_DICT.DBA ****************** */

/* **************************************************** */
                    KLUTZ.DBA

      A sample case history file created using CLAIMS.PRO
    and saved as a separate file to be consulted as needed.
/* **************************************************** */

case_hist("Plaintiff's Name","Ken Klutz")
case_hist("Type of Injury","back trauma")
case_hist("Defendant's Name","Limber Ladders, Inc.")
case_hist("Product Name","Shakey 12 Footer")
case_values("Plaintiff's Age",41)
case_values("Plaintiff's Salary",24500)
case_values("Plaintiff's Hospital Costs",3750)
case_values("Plaintiff's Lost Income",4575)
case_values("Plaintiff's General Damages",280)

/* *************** END SAMPLE CASE HISTORY ************* */


/* **************************************************** */
                        HELPFILE.HLP
                  A help file for CLAIMS.PRO.
/* **************************************************** */

MENU OPTIONS                   INFORMATION
************                   ***********

MAIN MENU           The main menu is a bounce-bar menu. Move the
                    bar up or down with the up and down arrow keys.
                    Press the Enter key to select the highlighted
                    option.

LOAD/CREATE
CASE HISTORY        Selecting this option produces a second bounce-ba
                    menu with two choices: Create Case History and Loa
```

(*continued*)

Case History. See below for explanations of each of these options.

CREATE CASE HISTORY — Selecting this option produces a window with prompts for entering a new case history. Follow the prompts as you would filling in a paper form. After you have created the case history, it is automatically loaded and you may then opt to display the case history or run a claims estimate.

LOAD CASE HISTORY — Selecting this option displays the case history files in the current directory in a bounce-bar menu. Move the bar with the up and down arrow keys. Select the file to be loaded by pressing the Enter key. Once a case history is loaded you may choose to display it or run a claim evaluation. See below for explanation of these options.

DISPLAY CASE HISTORY — This option displays the currently loaded case history. If you have not loaded a case history, the program will beep and tell you so. Pressing the Enter key returns you to the main menu, where you may load a case history.

DETERMINE CASE VALUE — Selection of this option causes the program to run a claim evaluation on the currently loaded case history. If you have not loaded a case history, the program will beep and notify you of this. Pressing Enter will return you to the main menu, where you can load the necessary case history. Then select this option once again and the program will provide the claim evaluation.

EXPLAIN CASE VALUE — This option provides you with a trace of the actual program logic used in arriving at the claim evaluation. The trace of rule execution will vary with the case parameters.

HELP FILE — This option produces the file you are reading.

EXIT — This option returns you to the operating system.

/* ******************** End Help File ********************** */

A walk through the program

Main Menu

The program is driven by a main menu that permits the user to easily review and then select the desired option:

```
Load/Create Case History
Display Case History
Determine Claim Value
Explanation of Claim Value
Help
Exit
```

The bounce-bar menu system provided by Borland is used by issuing the directive `<INCLUDE "menu.pro">` in the DECLARATIONS section at the head of the program. This means that the code for the menu program is merged with your program source code before compilation. The `INCLUDE` directive may be used more than once and may be located anywhere in a program it is legal to use a keyword. The file that is included may itself contain `INCLUDE` directives. The programmer may not, however, include files recursively.

By using the arrow keys to highlight the desired option and then pressing Enter, the user makes a selection. An integer representing the user's selection is bound to `Answer` and passed as a parameter to the `select()` rules. Note that the first entry in the menu list always binds the `Answer` variable to the integer 1, the second binds to 2, and so on.

Option Selection and Execution

The `select()` rules invoke procedures for each of the six program functions. Each of these procedures lives in its own program segment. Procedures such as `erase_all` and `error` are used by more than one program segment and could be collected together and housed in a utilities segment or even a separate file. In this program, utilities are located in the segment that first uses them.

With the exception of the exit option, the user is recursively returned to the main menu after each procedure has concluded. If the user attempts to select procedures out of logical order (e.g., display a case history before one is created or loaded), an informative message is provided, and the user is prompted to return to the menu, where more help is available as an option.

A running check on stack usage is provided in the upper-left corner of the screen to assist in development of the program.

The program automatically cleans house at some (not all) logical junctures. For example, working memory is cleared of all assertions by `erase_all` before the user is allowed to build a new case history or exit or after each explanation is given. This prevents case history accretion in the global database.

Loading or Creating a Case History

After selecting the `LOAD/CREATE` option, the user is presented with a submenu offering two choices. This could have been avoided by including both choices in the main menu; however, to illustrate the use of submenus, this design option was selected.

If the user selects `CREATE` in the submenu, he or she is prompted through a procedure for building a new file. Study this procedure carefully. It demonstrates how to use rules [e.g., `build_hist` and `solicit()`] for prompting for user input and asserting answers to the global database instead of a long series of `readln()` and `assert()` statements. The facts that store the prompts and their data type can be kept in a separate file. This file of prompts would be easily altered without any danger of an editing error affecting the performance of the program.

A prompt asks for a `y/n` decision to save the file. This allows a file to be thrown away if the user so desires. If the file is to be saved, the user is prompted for a name. The file is then saved to disk with a `.DBA` extension added automatically by the program using `concat()`.

If the user selects the `LOAD` option, the program displays all the `.DBA` files in the default directory in a bounce-bar menu. The user can also name a directory. The user then selects the desired file, which is loaded into memory.

Displaying a Case History

The `DISPLAY` option first checks to see that a case file is currently in memory and then prints the information to the screen. If the internal database does not contain relevant information, the user is provided with an informative error message and returned to the main menu, where a file can be created or loaded. A cut is included in this segment to limit backtracking and stack building. Try removing this cut. Run the program. Observe the stack message in the upper-left corner of the screen and watch the stack grow.

Determining a Claim's Value

The `DETERMINE CLAIM VALUE` option is, of course, the heart of the program. `claim_value()` is the master rule that calls each procedure in turn to determine needed values. `compute_claim_value()` does the calculations, and `notify()` informs the user of the computed value. This segment contains all the expertise extracted from the claims expert. Study this segment carefully.

Providing Why Explanations

Note that as each rule succeeds, a record is asserted to the global database, where it can be used later by the `explanation` rules. Study the method used to implement why explanations. In each rule, the integer value of the why selection is introduced as a test. If the user selects this option, the test succeeds, and the rule defaults to the disjunctive option which calls `why()` with a rule identification parameter. `why()` looks up the rule descriptor in the rule table and informs the user, using this description, that it is attempting to prove this rule.

Providing Needed Information

The program has the capacity to recover from a failure to find needed data during execution. The first `future_trauma()` rule may fail if the medical dictionary does not recognize the type of injury recorded in the case history. In this event, the second rule tries to find a synonym for the injury that it can recognize. It uses `check_synonym()` for this check. If this fails, the second `check_synonym()` rule recursively asks the user to rephrase the injury until an injury is entered that the program does recognize. These rules are pretty smart, but there is much room for improvement. Try to make some improvements.

Providing How Explanations

The `EXPLANATION` option provides the user with a trace of program execution and thus a how explanation. The formatting of the trace to distinguish between rules and subrules is accomplished by `show_how`, `list_out()`, and `list_desc()`.

Starting at the top of the database, which reflects the order of program execution, `show_how` passes each record of rule execution to `list_out()`. Each of these records may contain a list of one or more rule identification numbers. If there was but one rule number in the record, it means that this rule was the only one used in a proof. When the record contains a list of more than one rule, it means that the first rule listed called the remaining rules to complete a proof. To distinguish between single and multiple rule proofs the prompts state

```
To prove (a primary rule here)
   I had to prove (a secondary rule here)
```

`list_out()` prints the primary prompt and rule description and `list_desc()` prints recursively the secondary prompt and rule description.

Providing Help

The `help` option is implemented using the primitives `file_str()` and `display()`. This permits the user to key throughout the entire `help` file—hitting the Escape key to return to the main menu. The primitive

```
file_str(DOS_file,String)
```

reads a file named `DOS_file` (up to 64K in size) out on disk and binds its contents to the variable `String`. The primitive

```
display(String)
```

then presents the file contents and permits the user leisurely perusal.

Exiting the Program

The `exit` option does just what it promises. Before exiting, however, the program cleans house (i.e., retracts all assertions to the internal database). This is necessary because Turbo Prolog does not do it, and if the program is run again without exiting the compiler or editing the source code, the global database will still contain the data from the previous consultation.

The interface is designed to be intuitive and easy for both novice and expert to understand and use. Liberal use is made of windows with labels that are informative as to the nature of their contents. Notice that the windows overlap to occupy the central portion of the available space on the screen. The locations quickly become predictable, minimizing effort in making responses. The windows are removed when they are no longer needed.

Improving efficiency. Try removing the two cuts in the program. Run the program and observe the stack data in the upper-left corner. Sample data for my 512K IBM AT are reproduced in Table 7.1. Without the cuts in place, the stack builds inexorably such that one could run out of space if the program is used

TABLE 7.1 AUDIT OF STACK DURING PROGRAM EXECUTION.

Stack	Change in Stack (bytes)	Program Function	Cuts
45842	0	Value at GOAL	0
45834	8	Run	0
45824	10	Load case history	0
45768	56	Display history	0
45144	624	Determine claim value	0
45068	76	Explain evaluation	0
Subtotal	774		
45058	10	Load new case history	0
45002	56	Display history	0
44378	624	Determine claim value	0
44302	76	Explain evaluation	0
Total	1540		
45842	0	Values at GOAL	2
45834	8	Run	2
45824	10	Load case history	2
45824	0	Display history	2
45824	0	Determine case value	2
45814	10	Explain evaluation	2
Subtotal	28		
45804	10	Load new history	2
45804	0	Display history	2
45804	0	Determine case value	2
45794	10	Explain evaluation	2
Total	48		

repeatedly to evaluate a number of consecutive claims. The stack information informs about the magnitude of the problem and provides an indication as to where program design is least efficient. Program redesign and setting cuts are possible alternatives.

The question is where to place the cuts in a program. Beyond appeals to black magic, there is no simple answer to this question, and several techniques can be used in setting cuts. Most obvious among the possibilities is to study the logic of the program and then set cuts where nondeterministic rules send Turbo Prolog off on a backtracking binge.

One can also use the TRACE compiler directive. For help in locating nondeterministic rules, insert a DIAGNOSTICS directive at the beginning of the program. Turbo Prolog will then list out information on all predicates, whether they are rules and facts, whether deterministic or nondeterministic, and the size of the code along with flow patterns. The CHECK_DETERM directive will list only the rule determinacy information, and in Version 1.xx only, CHECK_CMPIO will warn the programmer whenever predicates with compound flow patterns are being used in program.

7.4.5 Debugging and Testing the System

Turbo Prolog helps the programmer discover syntax bugs by aborting compilation and returning to the editor at the approximate point of an error. The error messages are mildly helpful also. The trace facility is helpful in that it enables the programmer to follow the program flow of control step by step. There is, however, no built-in mechanism for spotting errors in logical design. Here the programmer may have to go back to the design stage. The more time you spend on designing your programs before you sit down at the computer, the better.

Testing a program requires a systematic trial of all functions using every possible type of user response. Be systematic! Cycle through the program recording input and program output until the program is bulletproof. Use the diagnostics and storage predicates freely in your code to identify procedures where memory is being used inefficiently. If you find that the program is behaving inefficiently, try to redesign the offending procedures or set a cut or two.

Once the program has been performance-tested, it is time to show it to the expert for criticism, revision, and then more testing. This is the first, but certainly not the last, loop in the development cycle. Good luck!

7.5 SUMMARY

The development of a KBS is an evolutionary process. The complex and knowledge-intensive nature of this software has proved traditional systems analysis techniques to varying degrees inadequate for guiding development, although this issue is the subject of much research and debate. The role of KE has evolved to replace the more familiar conventional software systems analyst.

The KE must apply a wide range of skills to the task of building a KBS. These skills blend psychology and computer science; management; planning; knowledge elicitation, acquisition, and representation; and designing, coding, and testing. Above all, the KE must be able to work effectively with people.

As the role of the KE evolves, new tools are being developed to assist in the acquisition and representation of knowledge. The interview, protocol analysis, and theoretical models were discussed in this chapter.

A model program was developed to illustrate each of the stages of KBS development:

1. Identification
2. Conceptualization
3. Formulation
4. Prototyping
5. Testing
6. Validation
7. Deployment

The model KBS provided in this chapter illustrates a variety of functions usually expected in fifth-generation software:

- Modeling of expert performance
- How and why explanations for program behavior
- Handling of insufficient data by search and querying the user
- Use of a professional windowed environment
- Error handling

Techniques for handling uncertain or fuzzy knowledge will be covered in Chapter 10.

7.6 EXERCISES

1. Add why explanations to the claims program at points where the user is prompted for yes or no responses to questions.
2. Limit program stack building during explanations by placing another cut in the program.
3. Alter the synonym facts to include a list of names for each type of injury. Write a procedure that will search the list to determine if an unrecognized injury entered in a case history has a medical name (synonym) known to the `m_dict` knowledge base.
4. Rewrite the program so that all the various tables are kept in separate files. Open this file and use the `readterm` primitive to obtain information as needed by the program.

5. Does the `erase_all` procedure completely erase all asserted facts from the global database? If not, correct this omission.
6. Rewrite CLAIMS.PRO so that the user may execute two consecutive claim evaluations on the same case without accumulating assertions from each evaluation in the internal database.
7. Rewrite CLAIMS.PRO so that the user can do consecutive claims evaluations on a single case and then compare the two settlements for (a) likelihood of plaintiff acceptance of settlement and (b) cost effectiveness of settlements for Small Hands, Inc.

Chapter 8
Relational Database and Turbo Prolog

CHAPTER OBJECTIVES

Study of this chapter should enable you to do the following:

1. Discuss the features and benefits of database management systems.
2. Discuss the organization and benefits of the hierarchical data model.
3. Declare the procedures needed to conduct binary searches in a hierarchically organized database.
4. Discuss the organization and benefits of the network data model.
5. Declare the facts and rules necessary to conduct searches in networked data.
6. Discuss the organization and benefits of the relational data model.
7. Implement procedures to perform reading, writing, deleting, and modification of data organized as relations in a Prolog database.
8. Write heuristic rules to serve as an intelligent front end to a Prolog relational database system.

IMPORTANT TERMS AND PHRASES

Balanced tree
Binary dictionary
Binary tree
B+ tree
Database management
Data consistency
Data dictionary
Data fields
Data integrity
External database
Hash bucket
Hashing
Hierarchical model
Internal database
Key field
Network model
Nonsequential search
Normalization
Pack procedure
Records
Relation
Relational model
Table
Tuple

8.1 DATABASE MANAGEMENT SYSTEMS

Today, individuals and organizations depend more than ever before upon up-to-date and accurate information in order to cope with the problems of daily affairs. Our intensifying collective appetite for information has transformed us into what George Miller (1984) colorfully describes as a society of "informavores." Over the past two decades computer database technology has evolved into a primary provider for our information needs. Efficient and accessible database management systems for desktop microcomputers is one of the most lucrative and competitive of today's software markets.

8.1.1 Overview

A database is a set of interrelated data. A database must be organized to provide for efficient entry, storage, maintenance, and accessibility of the data it contains. Three schemes for data organization are most often used in the design of contemporary databases: the hierarchical, network, and relational data models.

We will begin by considering the hierarchical and network data models as they apply to database design. With this information as background, we will next consider the relational data model in more detail. The relational model will then be the basis for development of a demonstration knowledge-based management system called KBMS.PRO. This program will illustrate basic features of both fourth-generation database and fifth-generation knowledge base technologies.

A database management system (DBMS) provides the tools needed for secure and relatively easy tailor-made development of user database applications. The design of a DBMS involves (1) selection of a suitable data structure in which to represent information and to guide searches in the database, (2) an interface to assist the user in formulating queries and for the structuring of system answers to user requests for data, (3) a data dictionary used for checking information to be added to the database and in translating user requirements into appropriate system commands, and (4) a set of common procedures to implement management operations on the contents of the database. In reference to the last point, DBMSs typically use standardized procedures in effecting all additions, modifications, and deletions in the database to assure that all changes are made consistently throughout the system.

It may be helpful to envision a DBMS as a layer of software serving in the role of mediator between the user's application and the procedures that operate upon the data store (see Figure 8.1).

8.1.2 Advantages

Multi-user DBMSs offer many advantages that collectively justify the high costs often associated with implementing these complex computer systems. Advantages include the following:

1. Using a DBMS, a company can centralize all information in one secure lo-

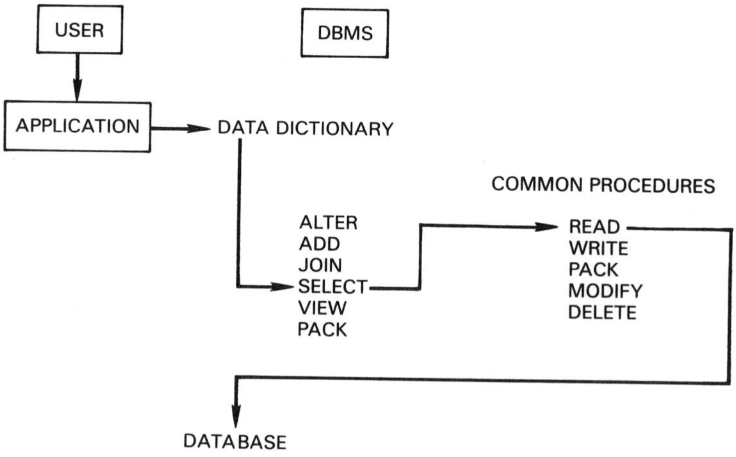

Figure 8.1 Schematic view of a DBMS.

cation. Updates to data are uniform, thus assuring consistency of data throughout the organization. Local area networks (LANS) are used to provide accessibility and to distribute data conveniently from a centralized location.

2. Constituencies with differing information requirements can readily solicit services from a centralized source.
3. Centralized systems minimize the need for duplication of data. Data redundancy can be very costly due to the complexities of maintaining data consistency and security in disparate locations.
4. Users are protected by the DBMS from many of the complexities inherent in computerized data management.
5. In centralized systems, data security and integrity are enhanced as users provide and receive only those data needed to perform their authorized functions.
6. In many companies, centralization of data management functions represents a significant economy of scale. In part, these economies are possible because a well-designed DBMS minimizes costs associated with redundancy of data storage.

On the down side, centralized systems can crash, causing loss of valuable data; however, regular backups are typically scheduled to protect against this contingency.

While single-user database management systems for the IBM PC are less powerful, sophisticated, and costly than systems developed for minis and mainframes, they are nonetheless a very important business tool. In fact, the appearance of the 80386 and 68020 based desktop systems, together with local area networks and multiuser operating systems, will make it practical for microcomputer systems of the future to rival the functionality of present mini and mainframe systems.

8.2 ADDING INTELLIGENCE TO DATABASE MANAGEMENT SYSTEMS

An issue of current interest is how DBMSs might be enhanced through the addition of inferencing capabilities that depend on symbolic processing to generate, through a chain of inference, new information and intelligent conclusions. Such hybrid systems are called knowledge-based management systems (KBMSs). There is a growing body of research directed to solving the many problems inherent in combining database and knowledge base technologies (Brodie & Mylopoulos, 1986; Kerschberg, 1986).

A small demonstration KBMS will be presented in this chapter to illustrate the use of Turbo Prolog in implementing these systems. The Prolog language is a good choice for developing a KBMS because it is database oriented with powerful pattern matching, clause indexing, and inferencing all built in free of charge.

Using Prolog to build an intelligent database system may be approached from several directions. One strategy is to start with an existing DBMS and then layer on top of this a front-end Turbo Prolog program. The front end allows the user to receive deductive answers to queries using the facts provided in the DBMS. This approach, however, presents the problem of linking programs written in different computer languages. This problem, though complex, is not insoluble. Several current Prolog implementations, including Turbo Prolog, allow for calls to procedures written in one or more "foreign" languages, (e.g., C, Pascal, Assembler).

A simpler and more direct strategy is to design and build a KBMS using Turbo Prolog for all components (database, access procedures, interface, and heuristics). This approach will be used in developing our demonstration KBMS program.

8.3 DATA MODELS FOR KBMSs

The first task in designing a KBMS is to select a suitable data model for the system. As mentioned, most database systems use one of three designs, the hierarchical, network, and relational data models. The relational model, largely attributable to the work of E. F. Codd at IBM, is the newest of the three schemes and is gaining favor among many system designers (see Martin, 1977; Date, 1983). The relational model will be our choice for our demonstration KBMS. However, before we begin, let's briefly survey the hierarchical and network designs as a conceptual foundation for the task ahead.

8.3.1 The Hierarchical (Tree) Model

In a Turbo Prolog knowledge base, facts are independent declarative units arranged sequentially. The default organization of such a body of such facts is the order in which they are entered into the database. Searches for data are conducted in a top-down fashion and are blind in that no heuristics are provided to aid in shortening searches.

Top-down searches in a sequential knowledge base mean that the system will have to read on average one-half of the relevant clauses to locate desired information. If the information does not exist in the knowledge base, the system will read all the relevant clauses before the search fails. In large databases, sequential searches are far too time-consuming to be cost-effective, and nonsequential methods are used to reduce computational overhead.

The hierarchical model supports efficient nonsequential search strategies and is often used where data items or records can be readily represented as a tree. You have already met the tree structure in our discussion of compound objects in Chapter 4. A brief review, however, should help to reinforce important terms and concepts.

A tree consists of a root node portrayed at the top of the structure. If not empty, the root node, called here the parent node, branches downward to nodes called children. A parent node may have several children, but a child node may have but one parent. Only the root node lacks a parent. Nodes with the same parent are called siblings.

A set of nodes arranged as a tree may be balanced or unbalanced. In a balanced tree, each parent node at the same level in the tree has the same number of child nodes. Conversely, in unbalanced trees, nodes at the same level have differing numbers of child nodes.

Some trees are termed binary. In a binary tree, the root node may be childless or it must have exactly two children. Each child node must itself be a binary tree. Note that there are procedures that are used to operate on and transform tree data structures. These procedures are beyond the scope of this book; however, you may review these techniques in Clocksin and Mellish (1984), Bratko (1986), Giannesini, et al. (1986), Martin (1977), and Amsbury (1985).

Examine Figure 8.2, which contains a record of student data. Note that there

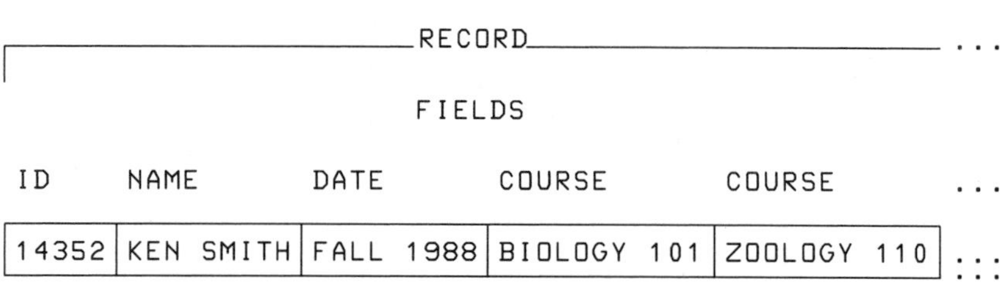

Figure 8.2 A student record with repeating data for courses.

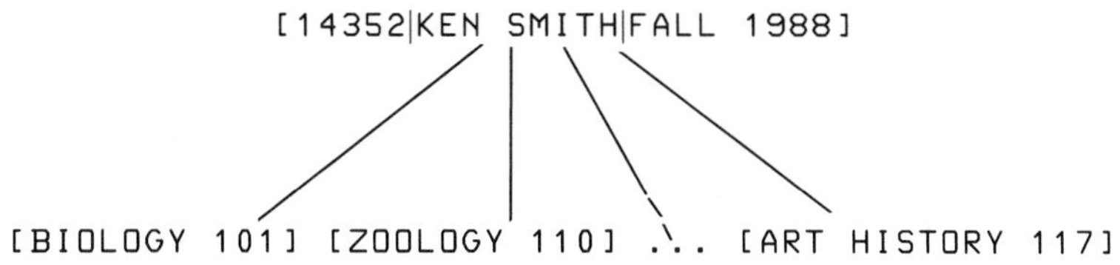

Figure 8.3 Tree representation of a one-to-many relation between a student and courses in the current semester.

is a one-to-many relationship between the student and the courses in which he is enrolled. That is, information on a single student is accompanied by information on several courses. Figure 8.3 displays this one-to-many data relation in tree form.

In a similar fashion, a record might contain information on the student enrollment in a course (see Figure 8.4). Here the one-to-many relation is expressed between a course and the enrolled students. This relation between a course and the student enrollment is shown as a tree in Figure 8.5.

Because of the hierarchical nature of tree-structured data, it is possible for the programmer to implement a variety of searches for data stored in nodes. The programmer directs searches (navigates) through a tree structure using the pathways that link parent and child nodes and information contained at the nodes. One kind of nonsequential search technique is the binary search.

The binary search significantly reduces the average time needed to find records in a large database. Later in this chapter we will see how version 2.0 of Turbo Prolog uses a close relative of the binary search to reduce search time in databases. The binary search method requires that each node contain a unique and quantifiable identifier field called a *key*. These key fields must be arranged in either ascending or descending order, and the total number and values of the key fields must be known to the system. This latter information is needed for the system to compute the root node of the binary tree.

An example of a unique key is the student ID number shown in Figure 8.2. No two students are allowed to have the same ID number; therefore, this field, and the record in which it is housed, is made unique in the database.

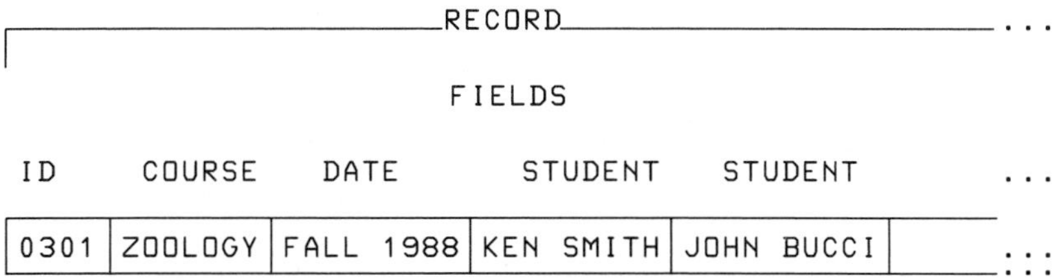

Figure 8.4 A course record with repeating data for students.

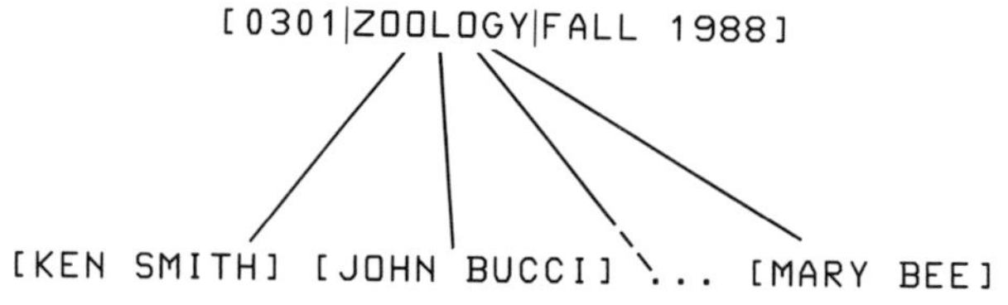

Figure 8.5 Tree representation of a one-to-many relation between a course and the current semester enrollment of students.

To illustrate a binary search, let's create a student database of 15 records with each record containing a unique ID number. Figure 8.6 displays this set of 15 records with ID numbers arranged as a binary tree. Information in this form is referred to as a binary dictionary.

A binary search for a desired record starts at the root node. Three tests are made at the root node. If the value of the root node ID is equal to the desired record ID, the search is over and the record has been found. If the desired value is less than that of the root node, the search is continued in the left subtree. In this case the right subtree is discarded and the search space is reduced by half. If the desired value is greater than the node value, the search is continued in the right subtree. In this case the left subtree is discarded and the search space again has been reduced by half. This process is repeated at each subtree root node until the number is located or the search fails because the record number is not to be found in the database.

Let's initiate a search for student ID 1000. The search starts at the root node, which has the value 800. The first test (1000 = 800) fails, so the root is not the record sought. The second test (1000 < 800) also fails, and the left subtree is discarded. The third test (1000 > 800) succeeds, and the search is directed to the right successor node, which is now the root node of the reduced tree.

Again three tests are performed. The equality test (1000 = 1200) fails, and the root node is not what we are looking for. The next test (1000 < 1200) succeeds,

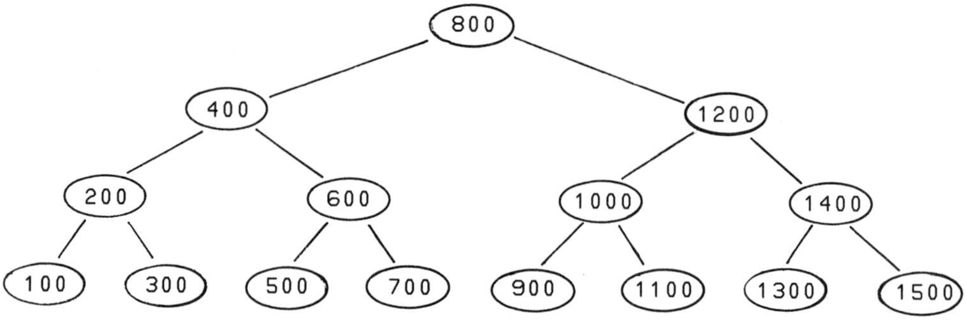

Figure 8.6 A binary dictionary of 15 student ID numbers.

and the left subtree is selected. The equality test at this new root node (1000 = 1000) succeeds. The desired record has been located, and the search is concluded.

The savings made possible by the binary search of this small tree may seem trivial. However, consider a tree made up of 15,000 student records. Suppose that you are searching for a record with ID number 10,000. A sequential search of a random database would examine on average thousands of records. A depth-first search, called in the database world a *preorder traversal*, of this binary tree would require visiting approximately 10,000 nodes. Our binary search requires visiting just three nodes.

The efficiency of binary searches reflects the fact that the length of a search is proportional to the height of the tree, where the height of the tree is the length of the longest path between the root and a leaf node. The longest binary search in the tree displayed in Figure 8.6 is four nodes, as the height of this tree is four levels of nodes.

Let's begin with a practical example. We will represent each node in a tree using the following Turbo Prolog fact:

```
student(Left_Subtree,Node_Value,Right_Subtree,Student_Data)
```

Each of our facts will contain a student ID number (`Node_Value`), a left successor node value (`Left_Subtree`), a right successor node value (`Right_Subtree`), and pertinent student information. Given the value of the root node of the tree (this value is normally computed by the system using a procedure not shown here) and a valid student ID number provided by the user, a binary search can be made to locate the ID node and of course the accompanying student data. Three rules will be used to perform a binary search in our hierarchically organized knowledge base.

```
b_search(ID,student(_,Root,_,Data)) :-
                    ID = Root,
                    write(Data).
```

This first rule is passed the desired ID value by the user. If the test of equality succeeds, the root is the node sought, and the student data would be printed to the screen. If this rule fails, the second rule is invoked.

```
b_search(ID,student(Left,Root,Right,_)) :-
            ID < Root,
            b_search(ID,student(_,Left,_,_)).
```

The second rule tests to determine whether the ID value is less than the value of the root. If so, the left successor node is selected, and a recursive call to the first rule is made to perform the test for equality. Following a successful test, the student data are printed on the screen. If the test in the second rule fails, the right side of the tree is tested using the third rule.

```
b_search(ID,student(Left,Root,Right,_)) :-
                    ID > Root,
                    b_search(ID,student(_,Right,_,_)).
```

The following program (adapted from TREE.PRO) illustrates a binary search of a tree-structured knowledge base. As in TREE.PRO, a few conveniences are added to assist you in tracing and understanding program execution.

```
/* ***********************************************************

                      B_SEARCH.PRO

                 A binary search program

   ********************************************************* */

DOMAINS
 record = student(integer,integer,integer,string)

PREDICATES
 b_search(integer,record)
 student(integer,integer,integer,string)
 root(integer)
 run
 continue

GOAL
 run.

CLAUSES

 run :-
  clearwindow,
  root(Root),
  write("Enter ID#: "),
  readint(ID),
  student(Left,Root,Right,Name),
  b_search(ID,student(Left,Root,Right,Name)),
  continue.

 continue :-
  write("\n\n\tContinue?  y/n: "),
  readchar(Answer),
  Answer = 'y',
```

```
 run
 ;
 exit.

b_search(ID,student(_,Root,_,Name)) :-
 write("\n\tI tried ",Root,"."),
 ID = Root,
 write("\n\n\tI found ",Name,"."),!.
b_search(ID,student(Left,Root,_,_)) :-
 ID < Root,
 student(New_Left,Left,New_Right,New_Name),
 b_search(ID,student(New_Left,Left,New_Right,New_Name)).
b_search(ID,student(_,Root,Right,_)) :-
 ID > Root,
 student(New_Left,Right,New_Right,New_Name),
 b_search(ID,student(New_Left,Right,New_Right,New_Name)).
b_search(_,_) :-
 sound(1,800),
 write("\n\n\tRecord not found.").

root(800). /* Root node value provided for system.   */
           /* A procedure could compute it as would  */
           /* be required in a changing database.    */

/* A whimsical database */

student(0,1500,0,"Clark Kent").
student(1300,1400,1500,"Charlie Brown").
student(0,1300,0,"Lois Lane").
student(1000,1200,1400,"Jimmie Olsen").
student(0,1100,0,"Green Hornet").
student(900,1000,1100,"Popeye").
student(0,900,0,"Dagwood").
student(400,800,1200,"Olive Oyl").
student(0,700,0,"Wimpy").
student(500,600,700,"Blondie").
student(0,500,0,"Peanuts").
student(200,400,600,"Superman").
student(0,300,0,"Spiderman").
student(100,200,300,"Dick Tracy").
student(0,100,0,"Snoopy").

/* ****************** END B_SEARCH.PRO ***************** */
```

Any working KBS is dynamic and is constantly changing as information in the knowledge base is added, modified, and deleted. However, the structure of the information must be maintained as a binary dictionary if the system is to continue to conduct maximally efficient searches. Methods for adding and deleting records as leaf nodes to a binary tree are relatively simple. However, techniques for adding and deleting records as internal nodes in a tree are more complex. Refer to Bratko (1986) for coverage of these advanced procedures.

8.3.2 The Network Model

The tree, as we have seen, organizes data hierarchically so that any child node can have but one parent. Knowing a student ID, for example, one can direct a search from that node for a course in which the student is enrolled. In this knowledge base, one-to-many relations exist between parent nodes and child nodes.

At times relations among data elements are not adequately expressed as a tree. Where many-to-many relations exist among data elements is an example. In this case the tree data structure rule that a child node can have but one parent is violated. Here the network data model is used.

For example, one might wish to represent in a single database the relationships among (1) individual students and the courses in which they are enrolled and (2) individual courses and the students enrolled in each. That is, one might want the answers to the questions "In which courses is John Jones enrolled?" and "Which students are enrolled in Physics 101?" To answer these kinds of questions without adding new relations, nodes in the database must be represented in many-to-many relations.

Figure 8.7 illustrates such a many-to-many or network relation. Notice that the arrows point in both directions in the network model. This means that one can start with a student and search for courses in which that student is enrolled or, conversely, start with a course and search for students enrolled in that course.

The network model is based in the concept of sets whereby many-to-many relations are expressed. This concept can be illustrated using a graph. Graphs, as you will remember, are networks of nodes with each pair of nodes connected by an arc.

One of the more readily understood examples of a graph is the ordinary road map. A road map of a state graphically represents the location of cities and towns (nodes) and the network of roads (labeled arcs) that connect them. The road map is a topographical model, so it also preserves the relative distance relations among the various cities and towns. Distance information is expressed as labels on the individual arcs. Figure 8.8 presents a sample network or road map.

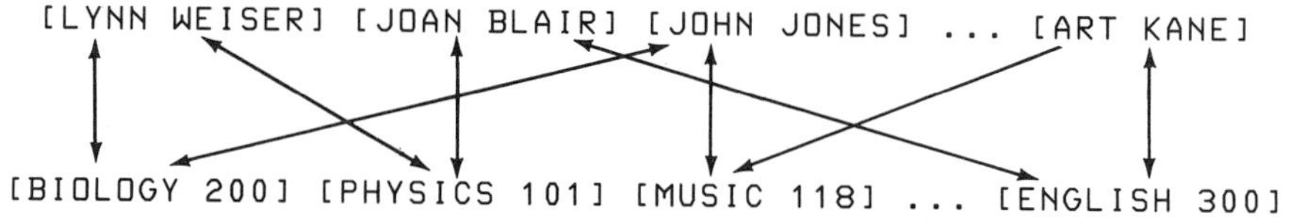

Figure 8.7 A network relation among students and courses.

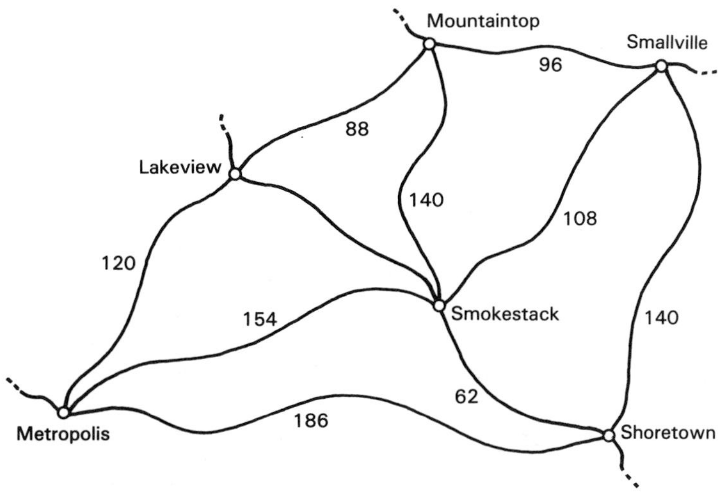

Figure 8.8 A map of cities (nodes) and roads between them with distances indicated (labeled arcs). (Not drawn to scale.)

An instructive analogy may be drawn between planning for a vacation trip on the one hand and searching for a path connecting nodes in a database on the other. Let's look more closely at the road map. Assume that we wish to find all possible routes from Metropolis to Smallville. Armed with an exhaustive list of routes, we might then wish to select a trip based on the basis of constraints such as distance, traffic level, or quality of scenery. (This is a variation on the classic problem of the traveling salesman that mathematicians have struggled with for years.)

The problem is to determine which cities are connected so that an acceptable path beginning at the start node and ending at the goal node can be identified. Such a path may be direct. In this case the start and goal cities are connected by a road with no intervening cities. An indirect route will contain sets of linked nodes. In the case of a trip starting at Metropolis and ending in Smallville, the route cannot be direct because, as the map shows, no existing road connects the two cities without intervening stopovers.

Using the map in Figure 8.8 as a basis, we can create a database of facts (set of connected nodes) to represent the cities, roads, and distances. Information on mileage and traffic can be included in each fact so that later we can introduce constraints on trips. One such fact is illustrated here. The integer value in the fourth argument slot represents moderate traffic on a 10-point scale.

```
path("Metropolis","Shoretown",186,6)
```

Examining the map in Figure 8.8, you can see that several different routes connect

Metropolis and Smallville. One route, represented as a list of cities, is

```
["Metropolis","Lakeview","Smokestack","Smallville"]
```

Rather than tracing all the alternatives by hand, we can write a Turbo Prolog path-finding program that will operate upon the database to find all possible routes from any starting point to any goal. The program will also compute the total distance of each trip. A specific route can be selected to conform to constraints or heuristics that the user may care to build into the program ("Which trip will have the least traffic?" "Which is the shortest trip?" "Which trip optimally combines low traffic, low mileage, and minimum stopovers?").

The completed program is shown here.

```
/* ************************************************************


                        TRAVEL.PRO

   A program to illustrate path finding in a graph.  This
   program identifies trips and computes distances.  Traffic
   data is provided in the database for use in adding
   constraints.

 * ************************************************************ */

DOMAINS
 itinerary = string*
 miles = integer*

PREDICATES
 run
 route(string,string,itinerary,miles)
 adjacent(string,string,integer,integer)
 go(string,string)
 member(string,itinerary)
 neighbor_cities(string,string,integer)
 reverse(itinerary,itinerary)
 append(itinerary,itinerary,itinerary)
 print(itinerary)
 sum(miles,integer)
 continue

GOAL
 clearwindow,
 run.
```

```
CLAUSES
run :-
 write("\n\tEnter Starting City: "),
 readln(Here),
 write("\tEnter Destination City: "),
 readln(There),
 go(Here,There),
 continue.

 go(Here,There) :-
  route(Here,There,[Here],[]),
  write("\n\tLook for another route?  y/n "),
  readchar(Answer),
  clearwindow,
  Answer = 'n',
  continue.
 go(_,_).

route(City,City,Visited,Miles) :-
    reverse(Visited,Itinerary),
    sum(Miles,Distance),
    write("\n\tRoute is: \n"),
    print(Itinerary),nl,
    write("\n\n\tDistance is ",Distance).
route(City_1,City_2,Visited,Miles) :-
    neighbor_cities(City_1,City_3,Z),
    not(member(City_3,Visited)),
    route(City_3,City_2,[City_3|Visited],[Z|Miles]).

reverse([],[]).
reverse([Head|Tail],List) :-
    reverse(Tail,New_List),
    append(New_List,[Head],List).

append([],List,List).
append([X|List1],List2,[X|List3]) :-
    append(List1,List2,List3).

print([]) :- !.
print([X|Y]) :-
    write("\t\t",X),nl,
    print(Y).

sum([],0).
sum([X|Y],Distance) :-
     Sum(Y,Z),
     Distance = Z + X.
```

(continued)

```
neighbor_cities(X,Y,Z) :-
    adjacent(X,Y,Z,_).
neighbor_cities(X,Y,Z) :-
    adjacent(Y,X,Z,_).

continue :-
  sound(1,800),
  write("\n\n\tThat's all!  Plan another trip?  y/n "),
  readchar(Response),
  Response = 'y',
  clearwindow,
  run
  ;
  exit.

member(X,[X|_]).
member(X,[_|T]) :-
    member (X,T).

/* adjacent(City_1,City_2,Miles,Traffic)
   For traffic values: low=1 hi=10) */

adjacent("Metropolis","Lakeview",120,6).
adjacent("Metropolis","Smokestack",154,9).
adjacent("Metropolis","Shoretown",186,6).
adjacent("Lakeview","Mountaintop",80,4).
adjacent("Lakeview","Smokestack",108,4).
adjacent("Mountaintop","Smallville",96,3).
adjacent("Mountaintop","Smokestack",110,4).
adjacent("Smallville","Shoretown",140,4).
adjacent("Smokestack","Smallville",128,5).
adjacent("Smokestack","Shoretown",82,8).

/* ***************** END TRAVEL.PRO ******************** */
```

In explaining TRAVEL.PRO, I will not review the amenities once again included for user convenience in observing program behavior. Rather, the discussion will focus on the rules that are used in governing the path-finding behavior of the program. The best way to analyze the function of these rules is to run the program with a `TRACE route` directive. Start by requesting a trip from Metropolis to Metropolis. This may seem a strange request, but the program can handle any legal trip including this one. Besides, this trip will allow the first `route()` rule to succeed, and this will be helpful in understanding the operation of this procedure. You will note that the first `route()` rule is invoked as

```
"route("Metropolis","Metropolis",["Metropolis"],[])
```

This goal succeeds because the two `City` arguments share the same name. The first `sum()` rule then returns a 0 distance value, and everything is printed to the screen. This rule says, "If where you are is where you want to go, stay there, as there are no more ways to get there and the distance is minimal." This is a boundary condition in which all legal trips will ultimately terminate.

Next try planning a trip from Metropolis to Smallville. The first itinerary returned will be

```
Metropolis
Lakeview
Mountaintop
Smallville
Distance is 296 miles.
```

In this example, the first `route()` rule initially fails, and the second `route()` rule is invoked as

```
route("Metropolis","Smallville",["Metropolis"],[]) :-
```

The `neighbor_cities()` condition matches with the head of a rule. The `adjacent_city()` condition of this rule searches in the knowledge base for the next city in the itinerary. The rationale for this seemingly extra step in searching for an arc from Metropolis to the next city in the chain is that the program must to be able to travel in any direction. The knowledge base as presently constructed declares connections as arcs between cities in one direction only. The two `neighbor_cities()` rules permit the program to look both ways when checking for an arc.

The next city listed as adjacent to Metropolis is Lakeview. `City_3` now has the value Lakeview, and `Z` is instantiated to the mileage (120) between Metropolis and Lakeview. `Lakeview` is checked against the list of visited cities because we do not want any backtracking or looping through cities we have already visited. The final condition now looks like this:

```
route("Lakeview","Smallville",["Lakeview"|"Metropolis"],[120])
```

`route()` recursively calls itself with these new values as arguments. Note that `Lakeview` has been added to the head of the list of visited cities and the mileage added to the odometer list.

The first `route()` rule checks to see if the two cities have the same name. Remember that when the program has established a connection with the destination city, this rule will succeed. The first `route()` fails again, and a link from Lakeview is sought by the second `route()`. The next city is Mountaintop. As we have not been here before, it too is added to the head of the cities list. The mileage is added to the odometer list of values. The first rule checks once again to determine if we are where we wish to be. The rule fails, and the next arc is sought. This city is Smallville. We have not been here either, so it too is added to the cities list. The mileage list is again incremented. The first `route()` rule is recursively called, and this time the first rule succeeds. We have arrived at our destination.

All that remains is to print the list of cities and sum the mileage. As the visited list was built by adding cities to the head of the list, a `reverse()` procedure is used to reorder the list. `sum()` adds up the mileage and everything is printed to the screen.

Designing and maintaining complex hierarchical and network-based DBMSs require considerable expertise. The relational model, more or less the new kid on the database block, has been designed with simplicity and ease of management in mind.

8.3.3 The Relational Model

As we have seen, a hierarchical database uses a tree structure. Network databases represent data as sets. The relational model organizes data more naturally and directly as two-dimensional tables or relations. Lacking any hierarchical structure, searches in a relational database are free of any dependency on paths.

Tables are two-dimensional rectangular arrays made up of rows called records (i.e., tuples) and columns containing fields (i.e., attributes). All records in a relational database must have the identical number of fields, and no field may contain more than one value. Each column has a name that declares the domain of the data entered into fields in that column. In a relational system, one column is selected to serve as a unique primary key. Other fields may serve as additional keys. The unique data entered into the primary key distinguishes the record from all other records in the relation.

Navigation in a relational system is guided by the values of the attributes in the table. The relational model does not require that the programmer organize the data around a path mechanism or pointers as is the case with network and hierarchic systems.

It will reassure those who suspect that the simple relational method of data representation may not be as complete and expressive as the more complex hierarchical and network models to know that noted authorities in this field (Codd, 1970; Date, 1983; and Martin, 1977) have shown that any data represented as either a tree or a network can also be represented in a relation or table. The proofs of this are based in relational algebra and symbolic logic and are well beyond the purposes of this book. However, the process of transforming trees and networks into relations (a process called normalization) guarantees that all information is expressed with minimal redundancy. Consider the student information arranged in hierarchical form in Figure 8.9. The same information can be accommodated in tabular form using methods outlined below.

A sample student table is illustrated in Figure 8.10. In Turbo Prolog this student table can be represented as a collection of facts in the following form.

```
student(4523,"JOHN JONES","MALE","BODINE",500)
```

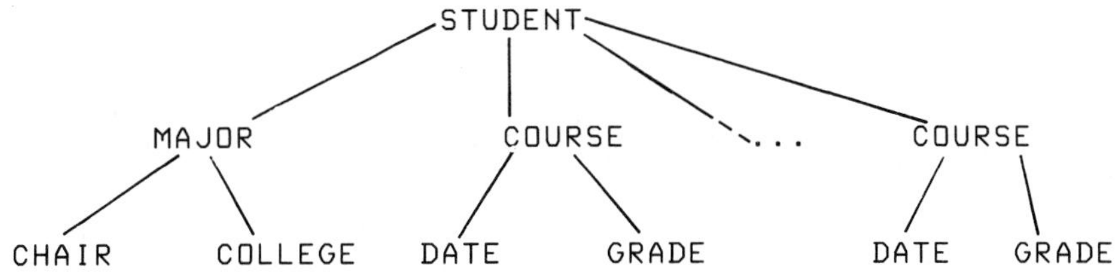

Figure 8.9 Student data in tree form.

Here you can see the strong family resemblance between relational database and Prolog.

To qualify as relational, entries in a table must satisfy 12 requirements, among them these:

1. The entries in any row may not contain repeated groups. The following record is not allowed in a relational database because the `Course` and `Grade` fields comprise a repeated group.

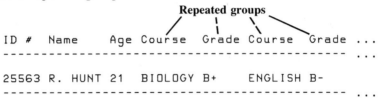

Repeated groups

```
ID #   Name      Age  Course   Grade  Course   Grade  ...
--------------------------------------------------------- ...

25563  R. HUNT   21   BIOLOGY  B+     ENGLISH  B-
--------------------------------------------------------- ...
```

```
       Col 1  Col 2        Col 3  ...........

                                  ---> n-attributes or fields

       ID#    Name         Sex    Dorm    Major Code
       ------------------------------------------
```

	ID#	Name	Sex	Dorm	Major Code
Row 1	4523	JOHN JONES	MALE	BODINE	500
Row 2	6782	BILL SMITH	MALE	SCHINE	700
Row 3	2672	JOAN HARRIS	FEMALE	SEELEY	200
.	4653	SUE BLAKE	FEMALE	COOPER	600
.	3447	LAURA CANE	FEMALE	SEELEY	900
.	8453	KIM WILSON	FEMALE	SEELEY	300
.	3378	SANDRA LEWIS	FEMALE	SEELEY	500
.	8577	KEN NORRIS	MALE	BODINE	300
	6448	MARY ISAACS	FEMALE	COOPER	500
	7113	LEN HUBBARD	MALE	SCHINE	400

Table or Relation

V **n-tuples or records**

Figure 8.10 A student table or relation.

2. The entries in any column must be of the same domain (e.g., the `ID` domain includes any four-digit integer number, and the `Sex` domain is either `M` or `F`). Further, each of the columns must be assigned a distinctive name. The records below violate this rule as the `Sex` field contains mixed entries (`MALE` instead of `M`; note also that Turbo Prolog would not approve of mixing `char` and `string` domains). Also, two of the fields are titled `Name`, which is not allowed in a relational system. One of the fields must serve as a unique primary key. In these records, the primary key is the `ID #`.

```
ID #   Name            Sex            Major        Name
--------------------------------------------------------
6778   LOU SAMUELS     F              BIOLOGY      BODINE
7882   KEN BLOCK       MALE           ECONOMICS    SEELEY
--------------------------------------------------------
```

3. No two rows or records in the table may be identical. Records 1 and 3 violate this rule.

```
Dorm      Address      Sex
--------------------------
SEELEY    MAIN ST      F
BODINE    PARK AVE     M
SEELEY    MAIN ST      F
--------------------------
```

When these requirements have been met, the relation is said to be in *first normal form*. Remember that the order of records in the table is of no consequence in a relational database system. The order selected for columns in a relation is also entirely a matter of programmer design. That is, the semantics of the information content in a relational system is unaffected by the order in which rows and columns are read.

Using the relational data model, we will build a prototype KBMS for teacher use in processing student data. Our KBMS will include the functions that are typically found in data base systems for adding, removing, reading, and modifying data. This program will also include a `consult()` procedure to illustrate the deductive capabilities of such a system.

We will begin by structuring the data required as a set of relations. The relations will be designed to minimize data redundancy and to conform to the stated requirements of relational database design. Each of these relations will be kept in a separate file. The program will open and close these files as needed during program execution for reading, writing, deleting, and modifying data.

The relations are as follows:

```
student(Stud_ID,Stud_Name,Sex,Address,Maj_ID)
major(Maj_ID,Maj_Name,Req_Credit,Coll_ID,Chair_Name)
```

```
transcript(Stud_ID,Course_ID,Date,Grade)
enroll(Course_ID,Stud_ID,Attendance)
```

All the student information that could have been organized as a tree is represented here in four tables or relations.

Notice that each relation has an ID field to serve as a primary key. The ID numbers serve to tie the relations together. Knowing a student ID, one can obtain the student's major ID code. The major ID code can then be used to read information about the student's major. Information about the major is kept in its own table and not mixed in with the student information. When all nonkey information in records relates to the key, the relation is said to be in *third normal form*. The name of a major relates to that major's ID and not to the student ID; therefore, it belongs where it is in the major relation. *Second normal form*, where nonkey fields must relate to the entire key (a group of fields serving collectively as a key), is not relevant to our example.

User selection of program functions. KBMS.PRO will employ the Borland bounce-bar menu program provided on the program disk that came with the compiler to simplify the process of user selection of program functions. Be sure that MENU.PRO is located in your working directory. Basic techniques for development of a natural language command processor for KBMS.PRO that will allow the user to enter commands in restricted English-sentence form will be discussed in Chapter 10. You may wish to add natural-language processing features to KBMS.PRO after reading this chapter.

The main menu segment lists the major functions of the program: writing, reading, deleting, modifying, consulting, obtaining help, and exiting. When the user selects one of these functions, a bounce-bar submenu appears listing the specific procedures for this function that are operational in this version of the program. A variety of procedures have been included to document many of the basic operations one might expect to find in a KBMS. Use this program as a prototype for modification and further development.

Standardized procedures for reading, writing, and deleting information are used, where feasible and consistent with instructional objectives, in the various program functions to assure that data consistency is maintained throughout the system knowledge bases.

Writing information to the knowledge base

1. ENTER A STUDENT RECORD. The `write` submenu lists several procedures for entering data into the knowledge base. The first selection is used to enter a student record into the student relation.

The `write_stud()` rule illustrates basic writing procedures. The program prompts the user for student ID number, name, sex, dorm address, and major code number. The `kb_write()` rules are an example of a standardized procedure. As you examine the program, you will see that these rules are used in several places for entering data into knowledge-base tables.

The `write_stud()` procedure performs several functions:

- Checks to see that the file to be written to exists on disk.
- If the file exists, it is opened for appending with `openappend()`; if the file does not exist, the second rule will create a new file and open it for writing.
- The file is named as the `write` device and the current output stream is redirected from the screen to the file.
- The position of the file pointer is noted.
- The term passed to `write_stud()` is written at the noted pointer position in the file.
- The screen is named as the `write` device.
- The file is closed.

You may have been wondering about efficiency of searches in a relational database where the data records do not contain any path information that can be used in navigational schemes. The next condition in the `write_stud()` rule invokes a `write` procedure, `kb_write_hash()`, which provides a mechanism for reducing search time.

Hashing

Assume that the student record just entered using `kb_write()` is located at the end of a long file containing thousands of records. When an attempt is made to access this record at some later time, the program will have to search through all these records to find it. The records are not organized as a tree or a network, so a sequential search is required. Turbo Prolog Version 2.0 provides built-ins for indexing in a binary tree and speeding up searches that we will consider soon. For now, let's learn how to develop a scheme of our own using *hashing*.

The Turbo Prolog primitive `filepos()` permits the programmer to direct a read or write operation at a specific location in a file providing the basis for random rather than sequential input/output. If we had an index of where in the file a particular student record is located, we could go directly to that point to perform a `read` or a `write` operation. This index, much like the index in a book, allows us to go directly to a subject rather than reading sequentially until we discover the material for which we are searching.

What is needed, then, is an index table with a record of student ID numbers and the corresponding file location value for each student record. As you may have surmised, nothing is gained if the program must do a complete search through all the student numbers to find the file position value. Hashing is one simple technique that permits the programmer to exploit the savings provided by direct addressing.

The `kb_write_hash` rule uses a simple hashing technique for reducing the number of reads in the index file. The technique is to divide the student ID, which is an integer number, by 10, using the `mod` operator. This returns the remainder of the division. This value will be an integer number between 0 and 9. The student ID and file position of the student's record are stored in a file called a *hash bucket*, named with the appropriate number 0 through 9. When performing a search for a student record, the program hashes the student number and then looks in the relevant hash bucket for the required file position data. As each of these hash buckets holds approximately 10 percent of all the index information, searches are reduced accordingly. Admittedly, hashing is not as efficient as would be a binary search of tree-structured nodes (tuples of ID numbers and file position values) or some other elaborate indexing scheme; nonetheless, hashing can be used to good advantage in many KBMS programs.

The last condition of `write_stud()` is a recursive call to itself. This provides the mechanism for making multiple entries into the knowledge base. A zero entry returns the user to the `write` submenu, where other `write` procedures may be invoked.

2. `ENTER STUDENTS INTO A COURSE.` The next main menu `WRITE` option is a mechanism for entering students into a course using `write_stud_co()`. The course file name is produced by a concatenation of the prefix `enr` and the user-provided course ID number. The `kb_write()` procedure is used to enter the student data into this file. Recursion is employed for multiple entries, and a zero entry terminates the procedure.

3. `ENTER A STUDENT GRADE.` This procedure creates a transcript file for each student and enters the date and a course grade. Once again `kb_write()` is used.

4. `ENTER COURSE ATTENDANCE.` This procedure is a bit more complex. It enters attendance data for each student listed in the course enrollment file. Trace the execution of the `write_attend()`, `get_stud()`, and `record()` rules and you will understand the logic.

5. `HELP WITH THE PROGRAM.` The HELP procedures are not operational in this program. When developed, these procedures would give the user context-sensitive information.

6. `RETURN TO THE OPERATING SYSTEM.` Selection of this option returns the user directly to Turbo Prolog without going back to the main menu. In the case of an EXE version of this program, which is executable independent of the Turbo Prolog compiler, the user is returned to the operating system prompt.

Reading information in a knowledge base. As was the case with the `write` functions, the `read` functions use standardized procedures for accessing information in files.

1. `READ STUDENT RECORD.` Selecting this option invokes `read_stud` _rec(). The user is prompted for a student ID number. The rule kb_read_hash() performs the following actions:

- It hashes the ID number using mod.
- It opens the index file designated by the hash.
- It sets the input stream to the file.
- It uses readterm() to read the index record containing the ID and the file position of the student record.
- It closes the file.
- It redirects input to the keyboard.
- It calls kb_read().

The kb_read() rule then performs these actions:

- It opens the student record file.
- It directs input to the file.
- It sets the file position to the location of the desired record.
- It reads the record.
- It redirects input to the keyboard.
- It closes the file.
- It returns the data to the read_stud_rec() rule, where it is formatted and printed to the screen.

2. READ STUDENTS IN A MAJOR. This option invokes read_stud_in_maj(), which does the following:

- It uses a bounce-bar menu for user selection of a major.
- It opens the student records file.
- It redirects input to the file.
- Using read_majors(), it prints the data on all students with the selected major.

3. READ STUDENTS AND MAJOR IN A COURSE. The read_stud_co() rule prompts for a course number. The enrollment file is consulted, and read_enrollment() selects each student's data from the student table and prints it to the screen. HELP and EXIT options are also provided.

Deleting information in a knowledge base

1. DELETE A STUDENT RECORD. Deleting records in Turbo Prolog requires a more complex process than either reading or writing. Consider the fact that each student record in the student file has an address. This address, along with the student's ID, is located in one of 10 hash files. Adding or removing even

a single byte from the student file will alter the addresses of all records, rendering the hash useless. In fact, all deletions in files must be done with great care so as to maintain the structural and syntactic integrity of the file. Deleting of records is accomplished using `delete_stud_rec()`.

The `delete_stud_rec()` procedure hashes the ID number and invokes `kb_delete_hash()`. This procedure opens the relevant hash bucket and locates the index record. It then divides the ID by 10 using the `div` operator. This reduces the ID number by one decimal place. The procedure then adds a minus sign to the beginning of the number and rewrites the record with the new minus value ID. The minus value is instantiated to the variable `Eraser`. Notice that we have not added or subtracted a single byte from the file using this process. As the program will ignore any ID with a minus value, the index record has been effectively erased. The `kb_delete()` rule is passed the eraser and the student record file position. The student record is then similarly erased.

Repeated use of this deletion procedure will produce a file with a substantial number of deactivated records occupying considerable space on the disk. Many DBMSs provide a batch procedure called `pack` to remove garbage records from files.

Implementing a `pack` procedure in this program will require rewriting the entire student records file along with all the hash bucket files. Nonetheless, a `pack` procedure can be added to KBMS.PRO quite easily. Be sure that you maintain a complete set of backup files on separate media until the procedure is perfected. Begin by designing a procedure to perform the following operations:

1. Erase the hash bucket files.
2. Open a renamed copy of the student file.
3. Erase the old student file.
4. Read the first record in the renamed copy of the student file.
5. Check the ID value of the record.
6. If the ID value is less than 1, read the next record.
7. If the ID value is greater than 1, hash the ID.
8. Write the student record in a new student file, noting the record's file position.
9. Add the ID and file position to an appropriately named new hash file.
10. Repeat this procedure for all records in the renamed student file.
11. Erase the renamed student file.

Modifying information in a knowledge base. This program function permits the user to change current information in the knowledge base. The modification process involves reading, writing, and deleting functions.

1. `CHANGE A STUDENT MAJOR.` This option invokes `modify_major()`. The user is prompted for a student ID and a new major code number. The rule hashes the ID and reads the location of the record. An eraser is created as before, and `kb_delete_hash()` negates the index record. `kb_delete()` is invoked to negate the student record. `kb_write()` enters the record with the new major code in the student file. `kb_write_hash()` records a new index entry.

2. CHANGE A STUDENT GRADE. Selection of this option invokes `modify_grade()`. This is a recursive rule that allows for multiple changes. The user is prompted for an ID number. The number is converted to a string and concatenated with a string `t` to generate the unique transcript file name for the student. This file will exist if the student has been previously assigned a grade for a course. If the file does not exist, the user is returned to the menu. The user is then prompted for a course ID number and a new grade (an integer value). The transcript file is opened and the old record located. The new record is written over the old. The file is closed and the transaction reported to the user.

Consulting the knowledge base.

3. PROCEDURE FOR STUDENT ABSENCE. This procedure uses student information gleaned from all the relations in the knowledge base. `procedure_for_absence()` prompts for the course and student ID numbers. Note that the program will crash if this information is incorrect. The course enrollment file is read and the student attendance data retrieved. The list of ones and zeros representing attendance and absence is converted to a number by `process()`. The student record is read into RAM. The `recommendation()` procedure evaluates the level of absence and returns expert advice on appropriate action.

With three or more absences, the student's major is used to identify the chairperson of that department. The student's dorm address and major are used to search for a peer with the same address and major. If there is no peer, a recommendation for change of dorm is made. Otherwise, the instructor is advised to notify the resident adviser, the dean, and the peer. This procedure is an example of the kind of heuristic rules that can be built into what is otherwise a straightforward database program.

The completed program is listed here.

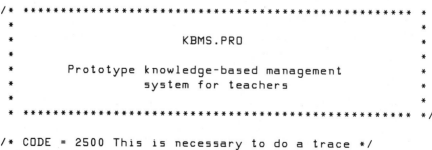

```
/* ****************************************************** *
 *                                                        *
 *                     KBMS.PRO                           *
 *                                                        *
 *       Prototype knowledge-based management             *
 *                system for teachers                     *
 *                                                        *
 * ****************************************************** */

/* CODE = 2500 This is necessary to do a trace */
NOWARNINGS % Replace named variables with anonymous
           % variables and you can delete directive
```

```
DOMAINS

 list = integer*

 file = stu_file ; grade_file ; maj_file ;
        index_file; enroll_file

DATABASE

/* ******************************************************
 *                          TABLES                      *
 *                                                      *
 *        S_ID    S_NAME    SEX  ADDRESS M_ID          */
 student(integer,string,string,string,integer)

/*       M_ID     M_NAME CREDITS CO_ID  CHAIR          */
 major(integer,string,integer,integer,string)

/*            S_ID     C_ID     DATE     GRADE          */
 transcript(integer,integer,integer,integer)

/*        C_ID     S_ID                                 */
 enroll(integer,integer,list)

/*  S_ID  POSITION                                      */
 h(integer,real)

 count(integer)

PREDICATES
 append(list,list,list)
 check(file)
 consult_kb
 delete_kb
 delete_stud_rec
 get_major(integer)
 get_peer(string,string,integer,string)
 get_student
 help
 kb_read_hash(dbasedom,integer,file,string)
 kb_read(dbasedom,file,string,real)
 kb_write(dbasedom,integer,real,file,string)
 kb_write_hash(integer,real)
 kb_delete_hash(dbasedom)
 kb_delete(dbasedom,real,file,string)
 main_menu
 modify_kb
```

(continued)

```
 modify_major
 modify_grade
 procedure_for_absence
 process(list)
 read_stud_rec
 read_stud_in_maj
 read_majors(integer)
 read_stud_in_co
 read_enrollment
 read_enrollment2(integer)
 read_kb
 recommendation(integer,string,string,string,string,string)
 record(string,integer,integer,list)
 eraseall
 select(integer)
 select_read(integer)
 select_write(integer)
 select_major(integer,integer)
 select_delete(integer)
 select_modify(integer)
 select_consult(integer)
 write_kb
 write_attend
 write_stud
 write_stud_in_co
 write_stud_grade

INCLUDE "menu.pro"     % Be sure this file is in your
GOAL                   % working directory.
 existfile("majors"),
 makewindow(1,112,15,"KBMS",0,0,25,80),
 main_menu
 ;
 clearwindow,
 sound(1,800),
 write("\n\n\tFiles MAJORS & COURSES not in directory.\n"),
 write("\tPlease create these files before running KBMS.").

CLAUSES

 /* ******************** MAIN MENU ******************** */

 main_menu :-
 clearwindow,
 cursor(6,33),
 write("MAIN MENU"),nl,
 menu(8,19,["WRITE INFORMATION TO KNOWLEDGE BASE",
           "READ INFORMATION IN KNOWLEDGE BASE",
```

```
            "DELETE INFORMATION FROM KNOWLEDGE BASE",
            "MODIFY INFORMATION IN KNOWLEDGE BASE",
            "CONSULT KNOWLEDGE BASE",
            "HELP WITH THE PROGRAM",
            "RETURN TO OPERATING SYSTEM"],Answer),
 select(Answer).

select(1) :-
 clearwindow,
 write_kb,!,
 main_menu.
select(2) :-
 clearwindow,
 read_kb,!,
 main_menu.
select(3) :-
 clearwindow,
 delete_kb,!,
 main_menu.
select(4) :-
 clearwindow,
 modify_kb,!,
 main_menu.
select(5) :-
 clearwindow,
 consult_kb,!,
 main_menu.
select(6) :-
 clearwindow,
 help,!,
 main_menu.
select(7) :-
 removewindow,
 exit.

/* ****************** END MAIN MENU ******************* */

/* *********************** WRITE *********************** */

write_kb :-
 clearwindow,
 cursor(6,34),
 write("WRITE MENU"),nl,
 menu(8,25,["ENTER A STUDENT RECORD",
            "ENTER STUDENTS INTO A COURSE",
            "ENTER A STUDENT GRADE",
            "ENTER COURSE ATTENDANCE",
```

(continued)

```
            "HELP WITH THE PROGRAM",
            "RETURN TO THE MAIN MENU"],Answer),
 select_write(Answer).


select_write(1) :-
 clearwindow,
 write_stud,
 write_kb.
select_write(2) :-
 clearwindow,
 write_stud_in_co,
 write_kb.
select_write(3) :-
 clearwindow,
 write_stud_grade,
 write_kb.
select_write(4) :-
 clearwindow,
 write_attend,
 write_kb.
select_write(5) :-
 clearwindow,
 help,
 write_kb.
select_write(6) :-
 clearwindow,
 main_menu.

write_stud :-
 clearwindow,
 Write("\n\tTo quit, enter 0 at the ID# prompt!"),
 write("\n\n\tEnter Student ID#: "),
 readint(ID),
 not(Id = 0),
 write("\tEnter Student Name: "),
 readln(N),
 write("\tEnter Sex: "),
 readln(S),
 write("\tEnter Student Dorm Building: "),
 readln(A),
 upper_lower(D,A),
 write("\tSelect Major: "),
 get_major(M),
 kb_write(student(ID,N,S,D,M),ID,Position,stu_file,
                                          "students"),
 kb_write_hash(ID,Position),
```

```
 write_stud
 ;
 write_kb.

get_major(M) :-
menu(8,22,[ "ART",
            "BIOLOGY",
            "BUSINESS",
            "CHEMISTRY",
            "COMPUTER SCIENCE",
            "ENGINEERING",
            "HISTORY",
            "PHILOSOPHY",
            "PSYCHOLOGY"],Answer),
 select_major(Answer,M).

 select_major(1,100).
 select_major(2,200).
 select_major(3,300).
 select_major(4,400).
 select_major(5,500).
 select_major(6,600).
 select_major(7,700).
 select_major(8,800).
 select_major(9,900).

write_stud_in_co :-
 clearwindow,
 Write("\n\tTo quit, enter 0 at the Course ID# prompt!"),
 write("\n\n\tEnter Course ID#: "),
 readint(C_ID),
 not(C_ID = 0),
 write("\tEnter Student ID#: "),
 readint(S_ID),
 str_int(String,C_ID),
 concat("enr",String,F_Name),
 kb_write(enroll(C_ID,S_ID,[]),S_ID,_,enroll_file,F_Name),
 write_stud_in_co
 ;
 write_kb.

write_stud_grade :-
 write("\n\tTo quit, enter 0 at the student ID# prompt!"),
 write("\n\n\t\tEnter Student ID #: "),
 readint(ID),
 not(ID = 0),
```

(*continued*)

```
 str_int(String,ID),
 concat("t",String,Name),
 write("\n\t\tEnter Course ID#: "),
 readint(C_ID),
 write("\n\t\tEnter Grade as an integer: "),
 readint(Grade),
 date(Year,_,_),
 kb_write(transcript(ID,C_ID,Grade,Year),ID,_,grade_file,
                                                   Name),
 write_stud_grade
 ;
 write_kb.

write_attend :-
 clearwindow,
 write("\n\n\tTo quit, enter 0 at the Course ID# prompt!"),
 write("\n\n\tEnter Course ID#: "),
 readint(C_ID),
 not(C_ID = 0),
 str_int(X,C_ID),
 concat("enr",X,Name),
 existfile(Name),
 consult(Name),
 get_student,
 save(Name),
 eraseall.
write_attend.

get_student :-
 enroll(C_ID,S_ID,List),
 write("\n\tStudent ",S_ID," in attendance? y/n: "),
 readln(Answer),
 upper_lower(X,Answer),
 record(X,C_ID,S_ID,List),
 fail
 ;
 write("\n\n\tPress any key to continue: "),
 readchar(_).

record("Y",C_ID,S_ID,List) :-
 append([1],List,NewList),
 retract(enroll(C_ID,S_ID,List)),
 asserta(enroll(C_ID,S_ID,NewList)).
record("N",C_ID,S_ID,List) :-
 append([0],List,NewList),
 retract(enroll(C_ID,S_ID,List)),
 asserta(enroll(C_ID,S_ID,NewList)).
```

```
kb_write(Term,ID,Position,Sym_File,Dos_File) :-
 existfile(Dos_File),
 openappend(Sym_File,Dos_File),
 writedevice(Sym_File),
 filepos(Sym_File,Position,0),
 write(Term),nl,
 writedevice(screen),
 closefile(Sym_File).
kb_write(Term,ID,Position,Sym_File,Dos_File) :-
 openwrite(Sym_File,Dos_File),
 writedevice(Sym_File),
 filepos(Sym_File,Position,0),
 write(Term),nl,
 writedevice(screen),
 closefile(Sym_File).

kb_write_hash(ID,Position) :-
 Hash = ID mod 10,
 str_int(Bucket,Hash),
 existfile(Bucket),
 openappend(index_file,Bucket),
 writedevice(index_file),
 Term = h(ID,Position),
 write(Term),nl,
 writedevice(screen),
 closefile(index_file).
kb_write_hash(ID,Position) :-
 Hash = ID mod 10,
 str_int(Bucket,Hash),
 openwrite(index_file,Bucket),
 writedevice(index_file),
 Term = h(ID,Position),
 write(Term),nl,
 writedevice(screen),
 closefile(index_file).

append([],L,L).
append([X|L1],L2,[X|L3]) :-
 append(L1,L2,L3).

eraseall :-
 retract(enroll(_,_,_)),
 fail.
eraseall.

/* ***************** END WRITE PROCEDURES ************* */
```

```
/* ************************** READ ********************** */

read_kb :-
 clearwindow,
 cursor(6,34),
 write("READ MENU"),nl,
 menu(8,21,["READ STUDENT RECORD",
            "READ STUDENTS IN A MAJOR",
            "READ STUDENTS & MAJOR IN A COURSE",
            "HELP WITH THE PROGRAM",
            "RETURN TO MAIN MENU"],Answer),
 select_read(Answer).

select_read(1) :-
 clearwindow,
 read_stud_rec,
 read_kb.
select_read(2) :-
 clearwindow,
 read_stud_in_maj,
 read_kb.
select_read(3) :-
 clearwindow,
 read_stud_in_co,
 read_kb.
select_read(4) :-
 clearwindow,
 help,
 read_kb.
select_read(5) :-
 clearwindow,
 main_menu.

read_stud_rec :-
 write("\n\n\tEnter Student ID#: "),
 readint(ID),
 kb_read_hash(student(ID,Name,Sex,Dorm,Maj),ID,stu_file,
                                              "students"),
 write("\n\n\tNAME:  ",Name,"   SEX: ",Sex),
 write("\n\tDORM:  ",Dorm,"\n\tMAJOR: ",Maj),
 write("\n\n\tPress any key to continue: "),
 readchar(_).

read_stud_in_maj :-
 write("\n\n\n\n\tSelect Major: "),
 get_major(M),
 clearwindow,
 openread(stu_file,"students"),
```

```
 write("\n\tStudents with major code ",M),nl,
 readdevice(stu_file),
 read_majors(M).
read_stud_in_maj :-
 readdevice(keyboard),
 closefile(stu_file),
 write("\n\n\tPress any key to continue: "),
 readchar(_).

read_majors(M) :-
 check(stu_file),
 readterm(dbasedom,student(ID,Name,_,Address,M)),
 ID > 0,
 write("\n\t",Name," ",Address),
 fail.

read_stud_in_co :-
 clearwindow,
 write("\n\n\tEnter Course ID#: "),
 readint(C_ID),
 not(C_ID = 0),
 str_int(String,C_ID),
 concat("enr",String,F_Name),
 openread(enroll_file,F_Name),
 write("\n\tStudents & Major in Course ",C_ID),nl,
 existfile(F_Name),
 consult(F_Name),
 openread(stu_file,"students"),
 readdevice(stu_file),
 read_enrollment.
read_stud_in_co :-
 closefile(stu_file),
 closefile(enroll_file),
 eraseall,
 readdevice(keyboard),
 write("\n\n\tPress any key to continue: "),
 readchar(_).

read_enrollment :-
 enroll(_,S_ID,_),
 filepos(stu_file,0,0),
 read_enrollment2(S_ID),
 fail.

read_enrollment2(S_ID) :-
 check(stu_file),
```

(continued)

```
 readterm(dbasedom,student(S_ID,Name,_,_,Major)),
 S_ID > 0,
 write("\n\t",Name," ",Major).

kb_read_hash(Term,ID,Sym_File,Dos_File) :-
 Hash = ID mod 10,
 str_int(Bucket,Hash),
 openread(index_file,Bucket),
 readdevice(index_file),
 check(index_file),
 readterm(dbasedom,h(ID,Position)),
 closefile(index_file),
 readdevice(keyboard),
 kb_read(Term,Sym_File,Dos_File,Position).
kb_read_hash(student(ID,"null","null","null",0),ID,_,_) :-
 sound(1,800),
 readdevice(keyboard),
 closefile(index_file).

kb_read(Term,Sym_File,Dos_File,Position) :-
 openread(Sym_File,Dos_File),
 readdevice(Sym_File),
 filepos(Sym_File,Position,0),
 readterm(dbasedom,Term),
 readdevice(keyboard),
 closefile(Sym_File).

 check(_).
 check(File) :-
 not(eof(File)),
 check(File).

/* ***************** END READ PROCEDURES ************ */

/* *********************** DELETE ****************** */

delete_kb :-
 clearwindow,
 cursor(8,33),
 write("DELETE MENU"),nl,
 menu(8,28,["DELETE STUDENT RECORD",
           "HELP WITH THE PROGRAM",
           "RETURN TO MAIN MENU"],Answer),
 select_delete(Answer).

select_delete(1) :-
 clearwindow,
 delete_stud_rec,
```

```
 delete_kb.
select_delete(2) :-
 clearwindow,
 help,
 delete_kb.
select_delete(3) :-
 clearwindow,
 main_menu.


delete_stud_rec :-
 write("\n\n\tEnter Student ID# to Be Deleted: "),
 readint(ID),
 kb_read_hash(student(ID,Name,_,_,_),ID,stu_file,"students"),
 not(Name = "No Record!"),
 kb_delete_hash(h(ID,Position)),
 openread(stu_file,"students"),
 filepos(stu_file,Position,0),
 readdevice(stu_file),
 readterm(dbasedom,student(ID,N,S,A,M)),
 X = ID div 10,
 Y = -X,
 Eraser = student(Y,N,S,A,M),
 closefile(stu_file),
 kb_delete(Eraser,Position,stu_file,"students"),
 write("\n\n\t",ID," Deleted"),
 write("\n\n\tPress any key to continue: "),
 readchar(_)
 ;
 write("\n\n\tNo record for this ID#."),
 write("\n\n\tPress any key to continue: "),
 readchar(_).

kb_delete_hash(h(ID,Position)) :-
 Hash = ID mod 10,
 str_int(Bucket,Hash),
 openmodify(index_file,Bucket),
 readdevice(index_file),
 check(index_file),
 filepos(index_file,Location,0),
 readterm(dbasedom,h(ID,Position)),
 filepos(index_file,Location,0),
 X = ID div 10,
 Y = -X,
 Eraser = h(Y,Position),
 writedevice(index_file),
 write(Eraser),
```

(*continued*)

```
 writedevice(screen),
 readdevice(keyboard),
 closefile(index_file).

kb_delete(Eraser,Position,Sym_File,Dos_File) :-
 openmodify(Sym_File,Dos_File),
 filepos(Sym_File,Position,0),
 readdevice(Sym_File),
 filepos(Sym_File,Position,0),
 writedevice(Sym_File),
 write(Eraser),
 writedevice(screen),
 readdevice(keyboard),
 closefile(Sym_File).

/* *************** END DELETE PROCEDURES ************ */


/* *********************** MODIFY ****************** */

modify_kb :-
 clearwindow,
 cursor(6,33),
 write("MODIFY MENU"),nl,
 menu(8,27,["CHANGE A STUDENT MAJOR",
           "CHANGE A STUDENT GRADE",
           "HELP WITH THE PROGRAM",
           "RETURN TO THE MAIN MENU"],Answer),
 select_modify(Answer).

select_modify(1) :-
 clearwindow,
 modify_major,
 modify_kb.
select_modify(2) :-
 clearwindow,
 modify_grade,
 modify_kb.
select_modify(3) :-
 clearwindow,
 help,
 modify_kb.
select_modify(4) :-
 clearwindow,
 main_menu.

modify_major :-
 write("\n\n\tEnter Student ID#: "),
 readint(ID),nl,
```

```
 write("tEnter New Major Code #: "),
 readint(Code),nl,
 kb_read_hash(student(ID,N,S,A,M),ID,stu_file,"students"),
 not(N = "No Record!"),
 X = ID div 10,
 Y = -X,
 Eraser = student(Y,N,S,A,M),
 kb_delete_hash(h(ID,Position)),
 kb_delete(Eraser,Position,stu_file,"students"),
 kb_write(student(ID,N,S,A,Code),ID,Location,stu_file,
                                              "students"),
 kb_write_hash(ID,Location)
 ;
 write("\n\n\tNo record for that ID#."),
 write("\n\n\tPress any key: "),
 readchar(_).

modify_grade :-
 write("\n\tTo quit, enter 0 at the Student ID# Prompt!"),
 write("\n\n\t\tEnter Student ID#: "),
 readint(Id),
 not(Id = 0),
 str_int(String,Id),
 concat("t",String,Name),
 existfile(Name),    /* If no file return to menu */
 write("\n\t\tEnter Course ID#: "),
 readint(C_Id),
 write("\n\t\tEnter New Grade as an Integer: "),
 readint(Grade),
 openmodify(grade_file,Name),
 readdevice(grade_file),
 check(grade_file),
 filepos(grade_file,Position,0),
 readterm(dbasedom,transcript(Id,C_Id,Old_Grade,Year)),
 write("\n\t\tOld Grade is ",Old_Grade,"."),
 write("\n\t\tNew Grade is ",Grade,"."),nl,nl,
 filepos(grade_file,Position,0),
 writedevice(grade_file),
 Term = transcript(Id,C_Id,Grade,Year),
 write(Term),nl,
 closefile(grade_file),
 writedevice(screen),
 modify_grade
 ;
 modify_kb.

/* ************** END MODIFY PROCEDURES ************* */
```

(continued)

```
/* ********************* CONSULT ******************** */

consult_kb :-
 clearwindow,
 storage(S,_,_),
 write("Stack = ",S),
 cursor(6,32),
 write("CONSULT MENU"),nl,
 menu(8,24,["STUDENT ABSENCE RECOMMENDATION",
           "HELP WITH THE PROGRAM",
           "RETURN TO THE MAIN MENU"],Answer),
 select_consult(Answer).

select_consult(1) :-
 clearwindow,
 procedure_for_absence,
 retract(count()),
 consult_kb.
select_consult(2) :-
 clearwindow,
 help,
 consult_kb.
select_consult(3) :-
 clearwindow,
 main_menu.

procedure_for_absence :-
 /* Get Course ID# */
 write("\n\n\tEnter Course ID#: "),
 readint(C_ID),
 str_int(X,C_ID),
 concat("enr",X,F_Name),
 existfile(F_Name), /* check that course exists */
 /* Get Student ID#. Note that program crashes if user- */
 /* selected student is not enrolled in the course */
 write("\n\tEnter Student ID#: "),
 readint(S_ID),
 /* Read enrollment data for selected student */
 openread(enroll_file,F_Name),
 readdevice(enroll_file),
 check(enroll_file),
 readterm(dbasedom,enroll(_,S_ID,List)),
 readdevice(keyboard),
 closefile(enroll_file),
 /* Get data on student */
 kb_read_hash(student(S_ID,S_Name,_,Address,M_ID),
                             S_ID,stu_file,"students"),
 asserta(count(0)),
 /* Determine number of absences */
```

```
 process(List),
 count(N),
 /* Get chair of student's major */
 openread(maj_file,"majors"),
 readdevice(maj_file),
 check(maj_file),
 readterm(dbasedom,major(M_ID,M_Name,_,_,Chair)),
 readdevice(keyboard),
 closefile(maj_file),
 /* Get a peer in same dorm and with same major */
 get_peer(S_Name,Address,M_ID,Peer),
 /* Make recommendation based on number of absences */
 recommendation(N,S_Name,Address,M_Name,Chair,Peer).
procedure_for_absence :-
 write("\n\n\t\tNo such course."),
 write("\n\t\tPress any key: "),
 readchar(_),
 consult_kb.
process([]) :- !.
process([X|Y]) :-
 X = 0,
 count(N),
 N1 = N + 1,
 retract(count(N)),
 asserta(count(N1)),
 process(Y).
process([X|Y]) :-
 process(Y).

get_peer(S_Name,Address,M_ID,Peer) :-
 openread(stu_file,"students"),
 readdevice(stu_file),
 check(stu_file),
 readterm(dbasedom,student(_,Peer,_,Address,M_ID)),
 not(S_Name = Peer),
 readdevice(keyboard),
 closefile(stu_file).
get_peer(S_Name,Address,M_ID,"None") :-
 readdevice(keyboard),
 closefile(stu_file).

recommendation(N,S_Name,Address,M_Name,Chair,Peer) :-
 N <= 2,!,
 write("\n\n\t",S_Name," has ",N," absence(s)."),
 write("\n\tNo action required at this time."),
 write("\n\n\tPress any key to continue: "),
 readchar(_).
```

(continued)

```
recommendation(N,S_Name,Address,M_Name,Chair,Peer) :-
 N >= 3,
 not(Peer = "None"),!,
 sound(1,800),
 write("\n\n\t",S_Name," has ",N," absence(s)."),
 write("\n\n\tI recommend that you take the following
                                                steps."),
 write("\n\n\t\tNotify Resident Adviser at ",Address,"."),
 write("\n\t\tRA may wish to talk with a fellow major: ",
                                                 Peer,"."),
 write("\n\t\tNotify ",Chair," Chair of ",M_Name,"."),
 write("\n\n\tPress any key to continue: "),
 readchar(_).
recommendation(N,S_Name,Address,M_Name,Chair,Peer) :-
 sound(1,800),
 write("\n\n\t",S_Name," has ",N," absence(s)"),
 write("\n\n\tI recommend that you take the following steps."),
 write("\n\n\t\tNotify Resident Adviser at ",Address,"."),
 write("\n\t\t",S_Name," does not have any fellow majors"),
 write("\n\t\tin the same dorm. Recommend change of dorm."),
 write("\n\t\tNotify ",Chair," Chair of ",M_Name,"."),
 write("\n\n\tPress any key to continue: "),
 readchar(_).

/* ************** END CONSULT PROCEDURES ************ */

/* *********************** HELP ******************** */

help :-
 cursor(10,25),
 write("Help Screen Here!"),
 cursor(12,25),
 write("Press any key to continue: "),
 readchar(_).

/* ********************* END HELP ***************** */

/* ******************* MAJORS FILE **************** */

major(900,"Psychology",33,16,"Anna Lytical")
major(500,"Computer Science",39,10,"E. S. Oteric")
major(300,"Business",33,18,"Ed Wharton")
major(100,"Art",33,16,"Ben Smith")
major(200,"Biology",36,10,"Norma King")
major(400,"Chemistry",39,10,"Ulysses Jenkins")
major(600,"Engineering",42,10,"Frank Schmidt")
major(700,"History",33,16,"Will Halperin")
major(800,"Philosophy",33,16,"John Locke")

/* ********************************************** */
```

```
/* ****************** COURSES FILE ***************** */

course(901,3,16,"Intro. to Psychology","K. Teft")
course(902,3,16,"Cognitive Science","L. Teft")
course(903,4,16,"Statistics","J. Leonard")
course(501,3,10,"Pascal Programming","K. Grant")
course(502,3,10,"Expert Systems","S. Hart")
course(503,3,10,"Artificial Intelligence","H. Willis")
course(301,3,18,"Intro to Business","F. Allen")
course(302,3,18,"Marketing","L. Hunt")

/* ********************************************** */
```

8.4 DATABASE FACILITIES IN TURBO PROLOG VERSION 2.0

In version 2.0, Borland International has made significant improvements to the database capabilities of Turbo Prolog. Version 2.0 adds several database primitives that make it easy to manipulate facts in internal and external databases. These extensions to Turbo Prolog make it possible for the programmer to write very efficient programs that can access multiple large databases in RAM, EMS, and on disk. Databases in Turbo Prolog are of two types, internal and external.

8.4.1 Internal Database

The internal database in Turbo Prolog is a home for facts associated with a program. To add or remove facts from the internal database, you must first declare the predicates in the DATABASE section of the program. You can then dynamically add facts into the program by asserting them (using `asserta/1-2` and `assertz/1-2` at either the goal prompt or as a condition within the program), by using `consult/1-2` to read an entire file of facts, or by reading individual facts from a file using `readterm()`.

The `save/1-2` predicate can be used to save the current internal database in memory or on a disk file. Facts may be removed from the internal database using `retract/1-2` or `retractall()`. Dynamic facts may not contain free variables and keep in mind that, unlike standard Prolog, Turbo does not provide facilities for dynamic manipulation of rules in databases.

Turbo Prolog permits a program to have several working internal databases. The single arity database predicates are used with the default internal database called dbasedom. The binary database primitives permit the programmer to access and manipulate facts in programmer-defined internal databases.

Version 2.0 allows the programmer who is developing a large modular project to declare dynamic predicates as local or global. Globally defined predicates are available to all modules, whereas locally defined predicates are known only to programmer-defined modules. The default dbasedom should be used for globally defined predicates.

The Turbo Prolog 2.0 manual provides handy procedures for extending internal databases onto disk files.

8.4.2 External Database

The external database is provided for easy manipulation and efficient accessing of large databases (collections of terms not directly a part of a program) exceeding in size the DOS limitations on RAM (640K). External databases require special declarations.

Terms (facts, integers, reals, strings, symbols, and compound objects) in an external database are stored on disk or in extended memory as chains. An external database may contain any number of chains, and each chain may contain any number of terms.

To illustrate this method of storage, imagine that you are building a book loan program for a large library. This program would require several large relational databases containing information about books and members. Let's say you want to have three relations in one external database to represent book information (index numbers, titles, and author names). In a Turbo Prolog external database, this information would be stored as three separate chains of terms, one for each set of data. Also, each chain is given a name (a string to describe the relation) that is used in procedures that will access the chain and the elements contained within it.

Several system database primitives are provided to: manipulate an entire database [`db_copy()` and `db_open()`], to add elements to chains [`chain_inserta()`, `chain_insertz()`, and `chain_insertafter()`], to delete chains [`chain_delete()`], to manipulate terms in a chain [`term_delete()`, and `term_replace()`], and to collect terms during backtracking through chains [`chain_terms()`].

8.4.3 B+ Trees

It should be obvious that for large applications, chains will be quite long and an efficient method will be required for processing elements in chains. For this purpose, Borland has added to version 2.0 two features: term referencing and the B+ tree. (The B+ tree is a close relative of the binary tree you have already met in this chapter; however, one important difference is that the B+ tree stores data a little differently and always remains balanced.) Here is a general description of how you go about using these features to process elements in chains.

As you construct an internal database, you work out a procedure for creating a key (hashing perhaps) for each term you will be inserting into a chain. As the term is added to the chain, the Turbo Prolog system automatically assigns to it a reference number (address) that can be used to directly access that term. You then add the key and the reference number for the term to the B+ tree housed in another database.

When you want to access a term in a chain you first determine the key. Next you use the key to perform an efficient binary search for the reference number of the term. Finally, the reference number is used to directly access the term in the chain.

Reference numbers of terms can be accessed using the following primitives: (`chain_first()`, `chain_last()`, `chain_next()`, and `chain_prev()`). The reference number can then be used in retrieving, modifying, or retracting terms in a chain.

Several primitives are provided with version 2.0 for operating on B+ trees. To update the tree, use `key_insert()` and `key_delete()`; to position the pointer at a specific place in the B+ tree, use `key_first()`, `key_last()`, `key_next()`, `key_prev()`, and `key_search()`. To determine where the pointer is in the B+ tree and to retrieve reference numbers, use `key_current()`; and finally, to determine the name of the B+ tree, use `db_btree()`.

8.5 SUMMARY

Concepts covered

Advantages of DBMSs
Attribute
B+ trees
Binary dictionary
Binary search
Database
    External
    Internal
Database management systems (DBMSs)
Data models for DBMS
    Hierarchical model
    Network model
    Relational model
Field
Graphs
Hashing
Keys
Normal forms
Record or tuple
Relations or tables
Sequential and nonsequential searching

Database management is of primary concern in today's information-driven society. The database management system (DBMS) is one effective solution to the many problems associated with data management. The DBMS is a layer of software between the user's application and the procedures that operate on the data stored in databases.

Major advantages of DBMSs include enhanced efficiency, maximal data security and integrity, reduction of data redundancy and costs associated with the maintenance of data in several locations, and user ease and convenience in obtaining services. Adding heuristic reasoning capabilities to DBMS is a burgeoning area of interest and research.

Three data models—hierarchical, network, and relational—are most often used in the design of DBMS. The hierarchical model employs the tree data structure. The tree model permits the system designer to organize data in one-to-many relations. That is, a parent node may have zero to many child nodes, but a child node may have only one parent node.

The definition of a binary tree is in part recursive. A binary tree may be empty. If not empty, the tree is comprised of a root node, which may have exactly two child nodes. Each child node must itself be a binary tree. Using data organized as a binary tree, a DBMS can conduct highly efficient nonsequential binary searches for data records in a database.

The network model employs the concept of data sets and can express more complex data relationships, represented as many-to-many relations. Navigation in a network system is through a series of nodes and arcs connecting them.

The relational model is conceptually the simplest of the three schemes. Data is organized as two-dimensional tables or relations. Each row or tuple in the table is a record. The columns are called fields or attributes. The form and content of a table must conform to rules derived from mathematical principles (such as normalization). Navigation in a relational database is guided by the values of attributes and not by pointers or other structures added to the records. Hashing is a technique that uses a unique identifier field (a key) and an index to shorten the time needed to search for records. Other more sophisticated direct addressing techniques are also used in place of the generally more time-consuming sequential search.

8.6 EXERCISES

1. Write a `pack` procedure for KBMS.PRO that will remove erased records from the student file and include it as a main menu option.
2. Trace KBMS.PRO and identify inefficient procedures. Set cuts to minimize use of stack space.
3. Write a rule for the `ENTER STUDENT RECORD` procedure in KBMS.PRO that will check to determine if a user-entered student ID number already exists.
4. Rewrite TRAVEL.PRO to select and print only the shortest trip from start to destination.
5. Rewrite TRAVEL.PRO to select the trip with the least average traffic.
6. If you have Turbo Prolog 2.0, rewrite KBMS.PRO to use external databases for all facts.
7. Rewrite KBMS.PRO to use term referencing and the B+ tree facilities of version 2.0.

Chapter 9
Representing Uncertain Knowledge

CHAPTER OBJECTIVES

Study of this chapter should enable you to do the following:

1. Discuss the problem of representing uncertain knowledge in logic-based programs.
2. Discuss the use of probability theory for handling uncertainty in KBS.
3. Discuss the use and implementation of certainty factors in KBSs.
4. Discuss fuzzy logic and methods for implementing this approach to imprecise and uncertain knowledge in programs.

IMPORTANT TERMS AND PHRASES

Bayes' rule
Certainty factors
Combining certainty factors
Confidence in conclusions
Fuzzy logic
Probability theory
Reasoning with uncertain evidence

Inexact reasoning is common in the sciences. It is characterized by such phrases as "the art of good guessing," the "softer aspects of physics" (or chemistry, or any other science), and "good scientific judgment." By definition, inexact reasoning defies analysis as applications of sets of inference rules that are expressed in the predicate logic. Yet it need not defy all analysis.

[E. H. Shortliffe and B. G. Buchanan, "A Model of Inexact Reasoning in Medicine," in Buchanan & Shortliffe, *Rule-based Expert Systems*, p. 233]

9.1 LOGIC AND UNCERTAINTY

In the first eight chapters you have learned to represent domain knowledge as Prolog clauses. You have used such knowledge, together with Prolog's built-in inferencing system, to develop KBSs that can manage information and provide conclusions based on data, perform useful procedural tasks, and model the decision-making behavior of experts.

All of our work so far has been rooted in the assumptions of predicate logic. Specifically, we have assumed that all knowledge in our programs is immutably true. However, the quote from Buchanan and Shortliffe serves to remind us that in the real world experts regularly use uncertain knowledge, changing "facts", and approximate reasoning in solving problems. For example, expert physicians attempting to diagnose patient disorders are often confronted with uncertain and incomplete information about symptoms and conditions, yet accurate diagnoses are routinely made.

Consider the following heuristic concerning the relationship between cigarette smoking and lung cancer:

> Older persons who have smoked cigarettes heavily for a long time are at significantly greater risk of developing lung cancer, emphysema, and heart disease than similarly aged persons who are have never smoked cigarettes.

Notice the nature of the knowledge embodied in this heuristic. It states the health consequences of long-term cigarette smoking in probabilistic terms. That is, the phrase *significantly greater risk* implies differences in the odds associated with health outcomes for smoking and nonsmoking groups. Notice also that it is not clear what sets of objects are denoted by the predicates in the heuristic. We do not know with certainty what specific class of people is referenced by the predicate "older". Also, we cannot state with precision either the duration of a long time or what level of consumption constitutes heavy smoking. Predicates that lack crisp definition have what linguists call an *open texture*. Such predicates are fuzzy in meaning and denote objects that are termed members of *fuzzy sets*.

All of this uncertainty raises the interesting question: "How can we use Prolog, which is based in axiomatic truth, to develop programs that simulate the reasoning behavior of human experts solving problems using tentative, uncertain, and incomplete knowledge?" We will see that, while this is a difficult question, it need not defy all analysis.

What we need to do is find a way to extend Prolog's methods for logical knowledge representation and deductive inference to include the uncertain knowledge that is so much a part of real-world reasoning and problem solving. Among the techniques that have been used in dealing with the uncertainty problem are probability theory, certainty factors, and fuzzy logic (see Buchanan & Shortliffe, 1984; Clancey & Shortliffe, 1984; Marcus, 1986; Negoita, 1985; and Pearle, 1984).

9.2 PROBABILITY THEORY

The first candidate for dealing with the certainty problem is probability theory. Probability theory comes first to mind because it is a well-developed mathematical system that forms the foundation of inferential statistics and therefore much of the empirical sciences. Probability theory is discussed extensively in many texts, so I will not attempt systematic coverage of the subject here. However, a few examples will help to illustrate the relationship between probability theory and some of the issues surrounding uncertainty of evidence and conclusions in KBSs.

9.2.1 Estimating the Likelihood of Outcomes

A probability represents the percentage of the time that some outcome will be true. For example, if you toss a fair coin, the probability of the outcome "head" being true is 1 in 2. Since probabilities are expressed as either a fraction or a decimal number between 0 and 1, we can say the odds are 1/2 or .50 that a head will be the outcome.

To calculate the probability associated with the event "three heads" {H,H,H} in three successive tosses of a coin, all we need do is count the number of occurrences of the specified event {H,H,H} in the set of all possible outcomes. The total number of possible outcomes is calculated by taking the number of possible outcomes on a single toss and raising it to a power determined by the number of tosses ($2^3 = 8$).

As you can see from Table 9.1, three heads in three successive tosses is one of eight possible outcomes, and the probability of its occurrence is therefore 1/8, or .125. The probability of all the remaining events is 7/8, or .875.

We can specify the probability of drawing a king of hearts from a standard deck of cards as 1/52. The odds of drawing a king of any one of the four suits in the standard deck is 4/52. The odds of drawing any king or any jack is determined by using the additive rule, which states that the probability of either one event or another event occurring is equal to the sum of their independent probabilities. The probability of two events occurring together (e.g., drawing a king and a jack

TABLE 9.1 SET OF ALL POSSIBLE OUTCOMES PRODUCED BY TOSSING A COIN THREE SUCCESSIVE TIMES

First Toss	Second Toss	Third Toss
H	H	H
H	H	T
H	T	H
H	T	T
T	H	H
T	H	T
T	T	H
T	T	T

in two successive draws with replacement) is found by calculating the product of their independent probabilities.

9.2.2 Representing Probabilities in Turbo Prolog

We will turn now to the issue of how we might represent probabilistic knowledge in Turbo Prolog. To illustrate our method we will use an auto example. Let's start by agreeing that the last argument slot in `relations` will be reserved for a value that will represent the odds of the relation holding true for its arguments.

Let's say that the odds of observing faulty brakes in a car selected at random are 2 in 100, or .02. We can then assert the fact

```
faulty(brakes,0.02).
```

If we discover by empirical observation that 40 percent of cars that have faulty brakes have worn linings and another 27 percent have bad hydraulic seals, then we can write the pair of rules in this way:

```
faulty(brakes,0.40) :-
     brake_linings(worn,1.0).

faulty(brakes,0.27) :-
     hydraulic_seal(leaks,1.0).
```

Here we see examples of conditional probabilities. That is, one thing happening is conditional on another thing happening. The left side conclusion of faulty brakes will happen 40 percent of the time if it is certain that the linings are worn, and 27 percent of the time if it is certain that the hydraulic seal is leaking. Notice that these two rules constitute an `or` relation with the precondition of each rule stated with certainty.

The following is an example of a rule with `and'ed` conditions.

```
faulty(brakes,0.90) :-
    brake_linings(worn,1.0),
    sound(screech,1.0),
    pull(side,1.0).
```

Often it is not possible to collect certain evidence in support of a conclusion in rules. This can occur when recognizing and categorizing evidence for a conclusion depends upon expert judgment and experience. In these cases the evidence may carry a probability to reflect inherent inaccuracies of observation and assessment. For example, the mechanic who inspected the brake linings may be inexperienced in making determinations (or trying to generate business) about what constitutes worn linings and may make incorrect judgments some percentage of the time.

```
repair(brakes,Probability) :-
    brake_linings(worn,Probability).
```

This rule states that the probability that the brakes should be repaired is equal to the probability that the diagnosis of their worn condition is accurate.

If we were actually to build a brake-repair diagnostic program, we would want to combine the probabilities from many proven facts and rules into a single probability indicating the odds associated with the conclusion (hypothesis) that repair is needed. Some of the successful rules would carry probabilities indicating their predictive validity. Some conclusions would have probabilities computed by the system from rules with `and'ed` or `or'ed` conditions. Other rules would have probabilities derived from a combination of values associated with both conclusions and with `and'ed` or `or'ed` conditions.

I will reserve discussion of specific techniques for ranking conclusions based upon combined values from multiple rules and their evidence for the next section, in which we will discuss a special type of probability called certainty factors. The techniques used with certainty factors are very similar to those used with objective probabilities. In this section I will also develop a program to illustrate the use of these techniques.

In some problems, however, we may rank a series of conclusions generated by a program using conditional probabilities and Bayes' theorem. Let's use a medical example and begin by assigning the symbol `H` to the hypothesis that a person has a viral infection. We will assign the symbol `E` to the presence of a symptom (evidence of a high temperature). The probability that a person has a viral infection can be expressed as

```
P(H)
```

The probability that this person has a high temperature given that the patient has a viral infection is

$$P(E|H)$$

(The vertical bar is read as "given".) What we want to find out is the probability that the patient has a viral infection given that she or he has a high temperature. To obtain the answer we use Bayes' rule as shown here:

$$P(H|E) = \frac{P(E|H)P(H)}{P(E)}$$

Applied to this example, Bayes' rule states that the probability that a patient has a viral infection, given that the patient has a high temperature, is equal to the ratio of the probabilities that the patient has both a temperature and a viral infection to the probability that the patient has a high temperature.

In order to use Bayes' theorem in this particular application, a medical diagnosis program would need knowledge about the frequencies in the general population of viral infections with and without regard for symptoms. As you can see, Bayes' theorem requires that the system have available a lot of conditional information. Probability theory has not been widely used in KBSs in part because all too often a system cannot be provided with needed up-to-date and accurate information concerning relevant conditional and unconditional probabilities. Another important reason for not using probability theory in KBSs is that evidence from studies in cognitive psychology indicate that the reasoning of human experts conforms rather poorly to the objective probability model.

9.3 CERTAINTY FACTORS

Shortliffe and Buchanan, known for their work in development of the MYCIN medical expert system, recognized the need for an alternative to the formal probability model. They developed a model employing subjective probabilities that they call *certainty factors* (CFs) (Shortliffe & Buchanan in Buchanan & Shortliffe, 1984).

Unlike probabilities, which are rooted in a formal mathematical model, CFs reflect more closely the ways human experts actually handle uncertainty of knowledge and evidence while drawing conclusions. Like probability theory, CFs provide a method for obtaining quantitative estimates of the relative strength of a conclusion drawn from uncertain premises using approximate inference.

CFs, like probabilities, are expressed as a number between 0 (uncertainty) and 1 (certainty). We can use CFs to represent a certainty estimate for both conclusions and conditions in rules. When an expert assigns CFs to the goal portion of a rule, it indicates the confidence the expert has in a conclusion drawn from the conditions of that rule. CFs attached to the conditions denote confidence estimates of the evidence for a condition.

Once again, let's imagine we are building an expert car-repair program containing a set of rules that will draw conclusions and make recommendations about various malfunctions. If, for example, the engine fails to turn over, one diagnosis could be a fault in an electrical component of the car (e.g., the battery). Here we might use the following rule

```
inoperative(battery,0.80) :-
        inactive(starter_motor),
        noisy(solenoids),
        age(battery,AGE_IN_MONTHS),
        AGE_IN_MONTHS > 36.
```

In the conclusion of this rule, the auto expert is expressing confidence at the .80 level in the conclusion that a battery is inoperative if the starter motor is inactive, the solenoids are noisy, and the battery is more than 36 months old. This is not a probability, in that it does not reflect odds derived from empirical study of samples of randomly inspected cars. The value is merely a measure of the expert's confidence in the conclusion drawn by the rule.

CFs can also be assigned to the conditions of a rule to reflect uncertainty about the evidence supporting a conclusion. Consider the case where the car owner provides the answers to queries about symptoms. Most owners are not experts and are more or less unsure of the information they provide. The evidence for rules and the CF associated with conclusions should reflect this uncertainty. To accomplish this, each condition in a rule is assigned a CF and the overall CF for the conclusion supported by these conditions is computed from these values. The following rule illustrates this process.

```
inoperative(battery,CF) :-
   inactive(starter_motor,0.65),
   noisy(solenoids,0.80),
   age(battery,AGE_IN_MONTHS,0.50),
   AGE_IN_MONTHS > 36,
   combine(CF,[0.65,0.80,0.65]).
```

One approach to computing a CF for a conclusion assumes that a rule is only as good as its weakest evidence. Using this logic, we can combine CFs by using the weakest CF to represent all the conditions. The rule now looks like this:

```
replace(battery,0.50) :-
  inactive(starter_motor,0.65),
  noisy(solenoids,0.80),
  age(battery,AGE_IN_MONTHS,0.50),
  AGE_IN_MONTHS > 36,
  minimum([0.65,0.80,0.50],0.50).
```

A procedure for selecting the minimum CF value in a list of values is as follows:

```
minimum([X],X).
  minimum([X,Y|Z],Min) :-
  minimum([Y|Z],Min_R),
  min(X,Min_R,Min).

min(X,Y,X) :- Y >= X.
min(X,Y,Y) :- Y <  X.
```

In some cases the expert may opt for a conservative approach and decide that the maximum CF for the conditions should be selected to represent the confidence placed in a conclusion. The following rule demonstrates how this is accomplished.

```
replace(tire,CF) :-
  worn(treads,0.95),
  mileage(Value,0.80),
  Value > 30000,
  bruised(belting,0.85),
  maximum([0.95,0.80,0.85],CF).

maximum([X],X).
maximum([X,Y|Z],Max) :-
  maximum([Y|Z],Max_R),
  max(X,Max_R,Max).

max(X,Y,X) : - Y <= X.
max(X,Y,Y) : - Y > X.
```

Yet another method for assigning a CF to a conclusion involves combining the CFs of the conditions with the CF assigned to the rule. In this situation, the procedure is to assign the CF obtained from the product of the CF of the rule and the minimum (or maximum, depending on your strategy) CF of all the conditions.

```
battery(weak,Rule_CF=0.85,Overall_CF) :-
  starter_motor(inactive,0.65),
  solenoids(clicking,0.80),
  battery(AGE_IN_MONTHS,0.50),
  AGE_IN_MONTHS > 36,
  minimum([0.65,0.80,0.65],Min_CF),
  Overall_CF  = Min_CF * Rule_CF .
```

The methods for assigning CFs are summarized in Table 9.2. In actual practice, conclusions are drawn from the combined action of several rules. In this

TABLE 9.2 METHODS FOR ASSIGNING A CONFIDENCE FACTOR TO A RULE

1. The confidence factor is assigned to the goal portion rule by the expert.
2. Confidence factors may be assigned to the conditions of the rule and the minimum (maximum) of these confidence factors assigned to the goal of the rule.
3. The product of a confidence factor assigned to the goal of rule and the minimum (maximum) Confidence Factor of the conditions may be assigned to the conclusion of the rule.

fashion, confidence in a program's conclusion can accumulate through the action of several rules. For example, confidence in a diagnosis of the electrical origin of an auto malfunction could be increased if additional rules prove that the car has other related problems that are electrical in origin (a short in the ignition system with a CF of .90). In such cases, CFs from all successful rules are propagated through the system and the maximum of these CFs is assigned to the conclusion.

9.4 FUZZY LOGIC

A KE frequently works with knowledge expressed in subjective linguistic categories rather than quantitative values. Usually this means that the set of objects denoted by a predicate is not sharply defined. Fuzzy logic (Zadeh, 1975) is an approach to approximate reasoning where the truth value of a conclusion is defined as a possibility distribution carrying linguistic rather than numeric labels. To illustrate the distinction between linguistic and quantitative labels, take the example of describing an individual's height. We can apply both kinds of labels and say a person is 6 feet 3 inches and is tall. We do not have any trouble with the statement of height expressed in inches. We all know what an inch is and, even if we don't, there is always a ruler handy. But how tall is "tall"? There are no generally accepted rulers that measure linguistic categories such as this. Is a person who is 5 feet 11 inches also tall?

Let's see how we can use fuzzy logic to answer questions such as these. In Table 9.3, "tall" is represented as a distribution of quantitative values (feet and inches) along with another value (assigned by an expert physical anthropologist, perhaps), which indicates the degree to which each category belongs to the fuzzy set "tall." Reading this table, we can see that a person who is 5 feet 0 inches in height is not a member of the "tall" fuzzy set. A person who stands 5 feet 4 inches is tall to the degree (.09), while a 7-footer is, we are confident (1.00), a member of the "tall" set.

Using fuzzy set theory, we can say that a person is tall and express quanti-

TABLE 9.3 DISTRIBUTION OF QUANTITATIVE HEIGHT CATEGORIES AND ASSOCIATED DEGREE OF MEMBERSHIP IN THE FUZZY SET "TALL"

Height	Inclusion in Fuzzy Set "Tall"
5′0″	.00
5′4″	.09
5′8″	.35
6′0″	.55
6′4″	.84
6′8″	.98
7′0″	1.00

tatively our degree of confidence in this fact. Now we can write a Prolog rule to express our confidence in the membership of a person in the tall set.

```
tall(Person,CF) :-
  height(Person,Inches),
  tall_table(Inches,CF).

tall_table(60,0.00).
tall_table(64,0.09).
tall_table(68,0.35).
...
...
```

You can see that to include fuzzy logic in Turbo Prolog programs, you must employ a procedure for mapping the linguistic labels onto a numeric distribution that reflects expert estimates of the degree of membership of values in fuzzy categories. Once this is done, you can perform all the operations outlined in the discussion on confidence factors in computing CFs for the conclusions of a program. For output in programs, you map the numeric values back onto the linguistic categories and report the appropriate descriptive linguistic labels to the user.

Procedures for use of CFs and fuzzy sets are illustrated in detail in the following demonstration program.

9.5 DEMONSTRATION PROGRAM: COLLEGE ADMISSIONS

To detail the procedures for using CFs and fuzzy logic in Turbo Prolog programs, we present a program designed to help high school students and their counselors select colleges where admission at each can be assigned a certainty factor.

9.5.1 Modeling the College Admission Process

In order to write our program, we must first consider the variables involved in the college admissions procedure. Some of these variables describe the student, and some pertain to the institution.

Student variables. Admissions officers evaluate student records containing the following information:

- Performance in coursework
- Cumulative performance on standardized tests
- Class percentile rank
- Recommendation of a teacher

Institutional variables. Each college sets its own standards for student performance. In days of dwindling enrollments, however, some colleges will consider a candidate qualified if the candidate meets minimum levels in four areas:

- Grade average
- Total SAT score
- Class rank
- Personal recommendation

Colleges differ widely in the range of information that they require to make an admissions decision. As mentioned, some colleges are content with conclusions or decisions based on acceptable performance in the criteria listed. Other schools will look more deeply into the students' applications. They will also require personal interviews seeking indices of motivation, character, leadership potential, self-confidence, and other traits. For these institutions, a decision based on the listed criteria is tentative and to some degree uncertain. As a result, simply meeting minimum requirements at these schools is far from a guarantee of admission.

The COLLEGE.PRO program models these differences using rules for student qualification and institutional minimal standards. Differences in certainty for the qualification rules reflect the fact that selective schools are looking more closely at subjective variables not assessed by the program.

Remember that there are no hard and fast rules for dealing with uncertain knowledge in programs, so don't be afraid to experiment and innovate. The real test is how well the program performs in modeling the problem-solving behavior of the expert and the statistical realities of the domain.

9.5.2 The College Selection Program

The program begins by making the windows needed by the program to prompt for user input, for explanations, and to report selections. The `start` rule calls `eraseall` to clean up any leftover facts asserted to the dynamic database in a previous consultation. The `start` rule then calls `get_student_info`, which uses `ask_for()` to solicit relevant information from the student or counselor. This rule also builds a list of states in which the student would like to study if the student does not select the `all states` option. Study this procedure carefully, for it shows you how to use a few lines of code to solicit a wide variety of typed input.

Errors in user input are trapped, and the user is given an opportunity to get information in the `Explanation` window. The user can also obtain information by entering ? at most of the prompts. The recommendation procedure solicits fuzzy input and uses `rating()` to map the linguistic categories onto a numeric distribution that is compatible with the CF scheme.

The `run` rule selects the first college in the database, calls `select_college()` to evaluate the students credentials, and returns the results of the analysis in the form of a CF along with the college name to the user. The `fail` causes `run` to track through the entire database of colleges.

The `select_college()` rules check the college to see that it is in the desired location and offers the student's intended major course of study. It then calls `qualified_for()` to perform the actual analysis of student credentials. The `qualified_for()` rules reflect the admissions procedures and certainty assignments at four levels. Level 1 institutions check student credentials against their requirements and use the "weakest link" approach to assign a rather stringent CF. If the student fails to meet the minimal standards for grade average and SAT score, these schools default to a low CF. The strategy is essentially the same for level 2 and 3 schools, which are less stringent in their admissions policies. Level 4 schools service a different student population and accordingly use the "strongest link" philosophy and assign CFs on the basis of the most impressive component of the students' credentials.

Type in the program and experiment with it. Study the ways in which the rules model the admissions philosophies of the fictitious colleges. Modify the rules and CF and study the results.

```
/* **********************************************************
                        COLLEGE.PRO

               A college selection program

   ********************************************************** */

   CODE = 2500

   DOMAINS
   list = string*
   values = real*
```

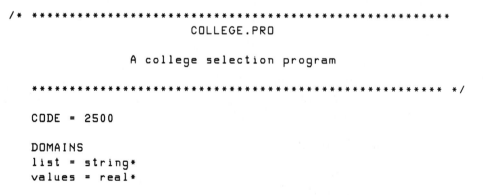

```
DATABASE
 student_info(string,string)
 student_data(string,real)
 preferred_states(list)

PREDICATES
 start
 run
 get_student_info
 select_college(string,integer,real)
 ask_for(string)
 types(string,symbol)
 input(string,symbol)
 input_states
 member(string,list)
 append(list,list,list)
 explain(string)
 show(string,symbol)
 college(string,integer)
 college_data(string,string,real)
 college_majors(string,list)
 college_location(string,string)
 qualified_for(string,integer,real)
 has_grade_average(string,integer,real)
 has_class_rank(string,real)
 has_sat_scores(string,integer,real)
 is_recommended(real)
 minimum(values,real)
 maximum(values,real)
 min(real,real,real)
 max(real,real,real)
 compute_min_CF(real,values)
 compute_max_CF(real,values)
 rating(string,integer)
 eraseall

INCLUDE "Menu.pro"

GOAL
 makewindow(1,112,15,"College Selection Program",
                                           0,0,15,80),
 makewindow(2,112,15,"Selections Window",15,0,10,40),
 makewindow(3,112,15,"Explanation Window",15,40,10,40),
 start.
```

(continued)

```
CLAUSES

start :-
 eraseall,
 get_student_info,
 run.

run :-
 student_data("recommendation",CF1),
 college(College,Level),
 select_college(College,Level,CF),
 shiftwindow(2),
 clearwindow,
 student_info(name,Name),
 upper_lower(Name_U,Name),
 write(Name_U,", Here are my findings:"),
 write("\n   COLLEGE         CERTAINTY FACTOR"),
 write("\n\n    ",College,"          ",CF),
 write("\n\n Press any key for another selection: "),
 readchar(_),
 fail
 ;
 write("\n\tNo more selections.\n\tPress any key: "),
 readchar(_),
 removewindow,
 removewindow.

/* Get student information */

get_student_info :-
 shiftwindow(3),
 cursor(2,2),
 write("Enter  ?  for information."),
 shiftwindow(1),
 ask_for("name"),
 ask_for("grade average"),
 ask_for("sat score"),
 ask_for("rank in class"),
 ask_for("intended major"),
 ask_for("recommendation"),
 ask_for("preferred state").

/* Procedure for soliciting and inputting info */

ask_for(Info) :-
 shiftwindow(1),
 write(" Enter ",Info,": "),
```

```
 types(Info,Value),
 input(Info,Value).

types("name",is_string).
types("grade average",is_real).
types("sat score",is_real).
types("rank in class",is_real).
types("intended major",is_string).
types("recommendation",is_fuzzy).
types("preferred state",is_list).

input(Info,is_string) :-
 readln(Data),
 upper_lower(Data,Lower_data),
 not(Lower_data = "?"),
 assertz(student_info(Info,Lower_data))
 ;
 shiftwindow(3),
 clearwindow,
 explain(Info),
 ask_for(Info).
input(Info,is_real) :-
 readreal(Data),
 assertz(student_data(Info,Data))
 ;
 shiftwindow(3),
 clearwindow,
 explain(Info),
 ask_for(Info).
input(Info,is_fuzzy) :-
 menu(3,50,["Very Favorable",
           "Favorable",
           "Moderately Favorable",
           "Moderately Unfavorable",
           "Unfavorable",
           "Very Unfavorable"],Rating),
 rating(Info,Rating),nl.
input(Info,is_list) :-
 write("\n Select ",Info," by\n          1) state\n"),
 write("          2) select all states\n"),
 write(" Choice: "),
 readint(Reply),
 Reply = 1,
 write(" Enter state: "),
 readln(Response),
 upper_lower(Response,State),
```

(continued)

```
 asserta(preferred_states([State])),
 input_states.
input(_,_) :-
 asserta(preferred_states(["all"])).

rating(Info,1) :-
 assertz(student_data(Info,0.90)).
rating(Info,2) :-
 assertz(student_data(Info,0.75)).
rating(Info,3) :-
 assertz(student_data(Info,0.60)).
rating(Info,4) :-
 assertz(student_data(Info,0.45)).
rating(Info,5) :-
 assertz(student_data(Info,0.30)).
rating(Info,6) :-
 assertz(student_data(Info,0.15)).

input_states :-
 write(" Enter state: "),
 readln(Response),
 upper_lower(Response,State),
 not(State = q),
 preferred_states(List),
 append([State],List,New_list),
 retract(preferred_states(List)),
 asserta(preferred_states(New_list)),
 input_states.
input_states.

member(X,[X|_]).
member(X,[_|Y]) :- member(X,Y).

append([],X,X).
append([X|Y],Z,[X|Y1]) :- append(Y,Z,Y1).

eraseall :-
 student_data(_,_),
 retract(student_data(_,_)),
 fail.
eraseall :-
 student_info(_,_),
 retract(student_info(_,_)),
 fail.
eraseall :-
 preferred_states(_),
 retract(preferred_states(_)),
 fail.
eraseall.
```

```
/* Procedure to catch type errors and to prompt for
   and give how and why explanations.  */

explain(Info) :-
 clearwindow,nl,
 write("\n  If you did not press ? you have"),
 write("\n  made an entry error. Type how to"),
 write("\n  see correct data entry format."),
 write("\n\n  If you entered ? type:\n   'why' for
                                  reason for question,"),
 write("\n   'how' for format for answer\n Enter: "),
 readln(Answer),
 Answer = why,
 clearwindow,nl,
 show(Info,why)
 ;
 clearwindow,nl,
 show(Info,how).

show(Info,why) :-
 clearwindow,nl,
 write("\n   I need your ",Info," so that"),
 write("\n   I can evaluate your credentials"),
 write("\n   and identify colleges to which"),
 write("\n   you may qualify for admission."),
 write("\n\n    Enter ?  for more information.").
show("name",how) :-
 write("\nEnter name like this: John Smith"),
 write("\n\n Enter ?  for more information.").
show("grade average",how) :-
 write("\nEnter your grade average as a real"),
 write("\nnumber.  Examples are: 82.0 or 91.7"),
 write("\n\n Enter ?  for more information.").
show("sat score",how) :-
 write("\nEnter your SAT score as an integer"),
 write("\nnumber.  Example:   1127"),
 write("\n\n Enter ?  for more information.").
show("intended major",how) :-
 write("\nEnter your intended major as follows"),
 write("\nExamples: psychology, biology.  "),
 write("\n\nEnter ?  for more information.").
show("rank in class",how) :-
 write("\nEnter your percentile rank in class as an"),
 write("\ninteger.  Example: 86 "),
 write("\n\n Enter ?  for more information.").
```

(*continued*)

```
/* Procedure for selecting colleges by preferred
   location and intended student major */

select_college(College,Level,CF) :-
 preferred_states([X]),
 X = "all",
 college_majors(College,Majors),
 student_info("intended major",Discipline),
 member(Discipline,Majors),
 qualified_for(College,Level,CF).
select_college(College,Level,CF) :-
 college_location(College,State),
 preferred_states(List),
 member(State,List),
 college_majors(College,Majors),
 student_info("intended major",Discipline),
 member(Discipline,Majors),
 qualified_for(College,Level,CF).

/* Procedures for evaluating student qualifications
   for admission */

qualified_for(College,Level,CF) :-
 Level = 1,
 has_grade_average(College,Level,CF_HGA),
 has_class_rank(College,CF_HCR),
 has_sat_scores(College,Level,CF_HSAT),
 is_recommended(CF_R),
 compute_min_CF(CF1,[CF_HGA,CF_HCR,CF_HSAT,CF_R]),
 CF = CF1 * 0.75.
qualified_for(College,Level,CF) :-
 Level = 2,
 has_grade_average(College,Level,CF_HGA),
 has_class_rank(College,CF_HCR),
 has_sat_scores(College,Level,CF_HSAT),
 is_recommended(CF_R),
 compute_min_CF(CF1,[CF_HGA,CF_HCR,CF_HSAT,CF_R]),
 CF = CF1 * 0.85.
qualified_for(College,Level,CF) :-
 Level = 3,
 has_grade_average(College,Level,CF_HGA),
 has_class_rank(College,CF_HCR),
 has_sat_scores(College,Level,CF_HSAT),
 is_recommended(CF_R),
 compute_min_CF(CF1,[CF_HGA,CF_HCR,CF_HSAT,CF_R]),
 CF = CF1 * 0.90.
```

```
qualified_for(College,Level,CF) :-
 Level = 4,
 has_grade_average(College,Level,CF_HGA),
 has_class_rank(College,CF_HCR),
 has_sat_scores(College,Level,CF_HSAT),
 is_recommended(CF_R),
 compute_max_CF(CF1,[CF_HGA,CF_HCR,CF_HSAT,CF_R]),
 CF = CF1 * 0.95.

has_grade_average(College,Level,CF_HGA) :-
 Level = 1,
 student_data("grade average",Student_score),
 college_data(College,"grade average",Desired_score),
 Student_score >= Desired_score,
 CF_HGA = 0.60.
has_grade_average(College,Level,CF_HGA) :-
 Level = 1,
 student_data("grade average",Student_score),
 college_data(College,"grade average",Desired_score),
 Student_score < Desired_score,
 CF_HGA = 0.20.
has_grade_average(College,Level,CF_HGA) :-
 Level = 2,
 student_data("grade average",Student_score),
 college_data(College,"grade average",Desired_score),
 Student_score >= Desired_score,
 CF_HGA = 0.70.
has_grade_average(College,Level,CF_HGA) :-
 Level = 2,
 student_data("grade average",Student_score),
 college_data(College,"grade average",Desired_score),
 Student_score < Desired_score,
 CF_HGA = 0.30.
has_grade_average(College,Level,CF_HGA) :-
 Level = 3,
 student_data("grade average",Student_score),
 college_data(College,"grade average",Desired_score),
 Student_score >= Desired_score,
 CF_HGA = 0.80.
has_grade_average(College,Level,CF_HGA) :-
 Level = 3,
 student_data("grade average",Student_score),
 college_data(College,"grade average",Desired_score),
```

(continued)

```
 Student_score < Desired_score,
 CF_HGA = 0.40.
has_grade_average(College,Level,CF_HGA) :-
 Level = 4,
 student_data("grade average",Student_score),
 college_data(College,"grade average",Desired_score),
 Student_score >= Desired_score,
 CF_HGA = 0.95.
has_grade_average(College,Level,CF_HGA) :-
 Level = 4,
 student_data("grade average",Student_score),
 college_data(College,"grade average",Desired_score),
 Student_score < Desired_score,
 CF_HGA = 0.50.

has_class_rank(College,CF_HCR) :-
 student_data("rank in class",Student_score),
 college_data(College,"class rank",Desired_score),
 Student_score >= Desired_score,
 CF_HCR = 0.90.
has_class_rank(College,CF_HCR) :-
 student_data("rank in class",Student_score),
 college_data(College,"class rank",Desired_score),
 Student_score < Desired_score,
 CF_HCR = 0.50.

has_sat_scores(College,Level,CF_HSAT) :-
 Level = 1,
 student_data("sat score",Student_score),
 college_data(College,"sat score",Desired_score),
 Student_score >= Desired_score,
 CF_HSAT = 0.80.
has_sat_scores(College,Level,CF_HSAT) :-
 Level = 1,
 student_data("sat score",Student_score),
 college_data(College,"sat score",Desired_score),
 Student_score < Desired_score,
 CF_HSAT = 0.40.
has_sat_scores(College,Level,CF_HSAT) :-
 Level = 2,
 student_data("sat score",Student_score),
 college_data(College,"sat score",Desired_score),
 Student_score >= Desired_score,
 CF_HSAT = 0.85.
has_sat_scores(College,Level,CF_HSAT) :-
 Level = 2,
 student_data("sat score",Student_score),
```

```
 college_data(College,"sat score",Desired_score),
 Student_score < Desired_score,
 CF_HSAT = 0.50.
has_sat_scores(College,Level,CF_HSAT) :-
 Level = 3,
 student_data("sat score",Student_score),
 college_data(College,"sat score",Desired_score),
 Student_score >= Desired_score,
 CF_HSAT = 0.90.
has_sat_scores(College,Level,CF_HSAT) :-
 Level = 3,
 student_data("sat score",Student_score),
 college_data(College,"sat score",Desired_score),
 Student_score < Desired_score,
 CF_HSAT = 0.60.
has_sat_scores(College,Level,CF_HSAT) :-
 Level = 4,
 student_data("sat score",Student_score),
 college_data(College,"sat score",Desired_score),
 Student_score >= Desired_score,
 CF_HSAT = 0.95.
has_sat_scores(College,Level,CF_HSAT) :-
 Level = 4,
 student_data("sat score",Student_score),
 college_data(College,"sat score",Desired_score),
 Student_score < Desired_score,
 CF_HSAT = 0.70.

is_recommended(CF) :-
 student_data(recommendation,CF).

/* Procedures for computing CFs */

compute_min_CF(CF,List) :-
 minimum(List,Min),
 CF = 0.90 * Min.

compute_max_CF(CF,List) :-
 maximum(List,Max),
 CF = 0.90 * Max.

minimum([X],X).
minimum([X,Y|Z],Min) :-
 minimum([Y|Z],Min_R),
 min(X,Min_R,Min).
```

(continued)

```
min(X,Y,X) :-
 Y >= X .
min(X,Y,Y) :-
 Y < X.

maximum([X],X).
maximum([X,Y|Z],Max) :-
 maximum([Y|Z],Max_R),
 max(X,Max_R,Max).

max(X,Y,X) :-
 Y <= X .
max(X,Y,Y) :-
 Y > X.

/* College database.  */

college("Prestige U",1).
college("Ivy U",2).
college("State U",3).
college("Community College",4).

college_data("Ivy U","grade average",90).
college_data("Ivy U","sat score",1150).
college_data("Ivy U","class rank",88).
college_data("Prestige U","grade average",93).
college_data("Prestige U","sat score",1250).
college_data("Prestige U","class rank",92).
college_data("State U","grade average",80).
college_data("State U","sat score",1000).
college_data("State U","class rank",65).
college_data("Community College","grade average",75).
college_data("Community College","sat score",875).
college_data("Community College","class rank",50).

college_majors("State U",["art","accounting","biology",
                       "computer science","psychology"]).
college_majors("Ivy U",["art","biology","psychology",
                       "literature","computer science"]).
college_majors("Prestige U",["art","biology","history",
          "literature","computer science","psychology"]).
college_majors("Community College",["art","accounting",
                      "biology","history","psychology"]).

college_location("Ivy U","connecticut").
college_location("Prestige U","massachusetts").
```

```
college_location("State U","pennsylvania").
college_location("Community College","florida").

/* ****************************************************** */
```

9.6 SUMMARY

Concepts covered

Certainty and confidence factors
Fuzzy logic
Handling inexact and uncertain knowledge in a KBS
Probability theory

This chapter covered methods used in knowledge-based programs for dealing with uncertain and inexact knowledge. Three approaches to handling uncertainty and imprecision in programs are most often used in KBSs: probability theory, CFs, and fuzzy logic. Methods for inexact reasoning are still very much a question of research, and no hard and fast rules currently exist for dealing with uncertainty in either knowledge representation or inferencing.

Probability theory has to date been least widely used as a method for modeling domain expert behavior. The reasons for this are very complex, but chief among them are that the information needed to compute conditional probabilities are often not available and the formal probability model conforms rather poorly to ways in which studies show experts actually solve real-world problems.

CFs were developed by Shortliffe and Buchanan and their colleagues as an alternative to probability theory in modeling uncertainty in the medical diagnosis program MYCIN. Certainty factors are numeric values somewhat similar to probabilities in that they are often expressed as a fractional component of 1. They differ in that they emulate more closely the manner in which human experts actually process and evaluate evidence in the process of producing conclusions.

CFs may be attached to the goal portion of rules. Such rules, when fired, are accompanied by the expert's degree of confidence in that goal. CFs may also be attached to conditions of rules. The rule may then fire using the minimum (or maximum) CF of the conditions. In some cases, overall confidence in a conclusion is expressed as the product of the goal CF and the minimum CF of the conditions. CFs generated by rules "collaborating" in the production of a conclusion are most often generated by selecting the minimum (or maximum) of the rule CFs.

Fuzzy logic is based on the fact that much human reasoning involves descriptive categories that lack numeric precision. People, experts included, most typically respond to dimensions and attributes of their experience using imprecise verbal categories ("very," "little," "almost," "sometimes," "frequently"). Fuzzy logic, as used in some KBSs, involves mapping these inexact English-language categories onto numeric dimensions so that confidence in evidence and conclusions can be expressed with more precision.

9.7 EXERCISES

1. Write an explanation module for COLLEGE.PRO that will explain the logic used by the program in selecting colleges and in determining confidence values.
2. Write procedures for COLLEGE.PRO that will evaluate the student's estimates of the success of interviews at various colleges and will incorporate this into the selection process.
3. Write a procedure that reports the degree of confidence the program has in admission at a particular college using fuzzy categories rather than numeric CFs.

Chapter 10
Programming for Natural Language

CHAPTER OBJECTIVES

Study of this chapter should enable you to do the following:

1. Discuss the importance of teaching computers to understand and generate natural language.
2. Discuss the computational steps involved in natural-language processing.
3. Explain the techniques used for tokenizing natural-language input.
4. Write a simple parser using either finite-state or phrase structure grammars.
5. Explain the differences in efficiency between parsers based on the `append()` rule and those using difference lists.
6. Discuss the problem of context dependency and methods for dealing with this problem using Turbo Prolog.
7. Use Backus-Naur form to define a set of grammar rules.
8. Convert rules from Backus-Naur form to Turbo Prolog clauses.
9. Discuss the issues surrounding syntactic and semantic analysis of sentences and text.

IMPORTANT TERMS AND PHRASES

Artificial language
Augmented transition network
Backus-Naur form
Chart parsing
Conceptual dependency
Context-free parsing
Difference lists
Finite-state grammar
Garden path sentences
Natural-language front end
Natural-language processing
Natural-language understanding
Lexicon
Noise-word disposal
Parsing
Phrase structure grammar
Pragmatics
Rewrite rules
Semantic analysis
State transition
Syntactic analysis
Terminals
Tokens
Transition network

> Much of the work in computer science has been pragmatic, based on a desire to produce computer programs that can perform useful tasks. But the design of computational systems also has a theoretical side, which is often called "cognitive science." The same concepts of program and data that serve as a framework for building and understanding computer programs can be applied to the understanding of any system carrying out processes that can be understood as the rule-governed manipulation of symbols. Computational theories are the basis for the current studies in many areas of psychology related to language.
>
> [T. Winograd, *Language as a Cognitive Process*, p. 2]

10.1 INTRODUCTION TO NATURAL-LANGUAGE PROCESSING

A long-standing goal of AI research has been to teach computers to process (to understand and to generate) natural-language productions. As used here, *natural language* refers to the native human dialects that have evolved over many generations of use and with which people communicate ideas, feelings, needs, and intentions. Artificial languages are also symbolic systems for communication; however, unlike natural languages, they have been invented for the specific purpose of enhancing the precision of knowledge representation and communication in some specialized domain. Mathematics, computer command interpreters, and programming languages such as Turbo Prolog are examples of artificial languages.

An immediate consequence of having computers able to process natural language is that we would be able to converse with our computers and applications software without having to learn difficult artificial languages. Natural-language understanding in computers would serve to bridge the gap between the richness and expressiveness of human languages and the precision of the artificial languages of the computer. We are, however, a long way from achieving this goal. While acquiring natural language is generally an easy task for children, teaching it to computers turns out to be extraordinarily difficult. Many find it an interesting paradox that the things that we humans find easiest to do (such as learning language) are the very things that are the most difficult to teach the computer.

For many reasons, some of which we will discuss in a moment, computers continue to require that we communicate with them using awkward artificial languages. This problem is being ameliorated for users of some popular application packages through the appearance of natural-language front-end programs. Lotus Corporation's HAL is one such program. HAL permits Lotus 1-2-3 spreadsheet users to carry out complex program functions using commands expressed in limited English-sentence form. Microrim's Clout performs a similar role as an interface to the popular R:BASE database program. Intellect from Artificial Intelligence, Inc., is a powerful natural-language front-end system that has been adapted to several mainframe database systems.

Although natural-language front-end programs represent progress toward the day when machines will understand queries, directives, and discourse expressed in everyday English, they are still far from a final solution. These programs circumvent, but do not solve, the really intractable problems inherent in representing natural language in a computer. That is, they work well only because they limit the user to a small subset of English words and sentence structures, and each program understands only the relatively few English words and sentence structures that are essential to performing functions within the domain served by the applications program.

In processing natural language, a computer system performs certain basic operations, which typically include these:

1. Tokenizing the user's natural-language sentence or text input
2. Performing a lexical and syntactic analysis of the structure of the sentence input
3. Performing a semantic analysis to determine the meaning of the sentence and text input
4. Representing meaning in some appropriate form usable by the machine
5. Mapping the intent of the input onto application and operating system command syntax for processing
6. Generating pertinent natural-language output. (Step 6 is actually quite complex and will not be treated in this chapter.)

10.2 TOKENIZING NATURAL-LANGUAGE INPUT

Tokens are the smallest elements that a computer system can understand. In the Turbo Prolog language, variables, constants, and integers are examples of tokens. In sentences these tokens, called grammatical morphemes, are words or parts of words that add meaning to the sentence. The words *run* and *laugh*, the prefix *non-*, and the suffixes *-s* and *-es* are examples of morphemes. For the sake of simplicity, the programs developed in this chapter will process only word tokens, although the principles used can easily be extended to include morphological analysis of prefixes, suffixes, and other word components as well.

When the user types a command at the DOS prompt and presses the Enter key, the computer reads a string of ASCII values, one for each printing or nonprinting character in the command. Before the command can be executed, however, the command interpreter must convert these ASCII characters into tokens it can understand, (e.g., `DIR`, `DEL`, `*.*`, `..`, `\`, the nonprinting space).

Similarly, the natural-language processing (NLP) programs developed in this chapter require procedures for converting sentences entered in the form of strings of ASCII characters into lists of English words.

CONVERT.PRO will serve as our tokenizer for all our NLP programs. It accepts a sentence string from the user and converts it into a list of words with all spaces and punctuation removed.

```
/* ***********************************************

                    CONVERT.PRO

   A program to tokenize a sentence string into
   a list of words.

   *********************************************** */

PREDICATES

 convert(string)
 word(string,string)
 add_word(string)
 add(string,list,list)
 reverse(list,list)
 append(list,list,list)
 word_end(string,integer,integer)
 strip(string,string)

CLAUSES

 convert(S) :-
   word(S,S2),
   convert(S2).
 convert(_).

 word(S,S2) :-
   word_end(S,Count,0),
   Count > 0,
   frontstr(Count,S,W,S3),
   add_word(W),
   strip(S3,S2).

 word_end(S,Count,C) :-
   frontchar(S,Ch,S2),
   Ch <> ' ',
   Ch <> '.',
   C2 = C + 1,
   word_end(S2,Count,C2).
 word_end(_,Count,Count).

 strip(S,S2) :-
   frontchar(S,Ch,S2),
   Ch = ' '.
```

```
strip(S,S2) :-
  frontchar(S,Ch,S2),
  Ch ='.'.
strip(S,S).

add_word(W) :-
  wordlist(L),
  add(W,L,L2),
  retract(wordlist(L)),
  assert(wordlist(L2)).

add(W,L,[W|L]).

reverse([],[]).
reverse([Head|Tail],List) :-
  reverse(Tail,New_List),
  append(New_List,[Head],List).

append([],List,List).
append([X|List1],List2,[X|List3]) :-
  append(List1,List2,List3).

/* ********************************************** */
```

Enter and save this program to disk as CONVERT.PRO so it will be available to the parsing programs that follow. In these parsing programs, a sentence entered at the keyboard by the user will be read by `readln()` as a string and passed to the `convert()` procedure. `convert()` calls `word()`, which together with `word_end()` reads the string a character at a time until a delimiter (either a space or punctuation) is reached. The delimiter is discarded by `strip()` and the word is added to the word list by `add_word()` and `add()`. This process continues recursively until there are no more characters and therefore no more words in the string to read.

As the list of words is constructed by adding words to the front of a list, the list must then be reversed to return the words to correct sentence order. The `reverse()` and `append()` procedures will be used to perform this function.

Now we can represent the sentence in a form that can be used in the next step in NLP.

10.3 SYNTACTIC ANALYSIS

Syntax has to do with the rules that define acceptable sequences of words in sentences. Grammars define both the elements of lexical categories of a language, (e.g., the token *boy* is a *noun*) and the rules governing the valid arrangements of these elements in sentences. The syntactic step in natural-language processing stresses the grammatical analysis of the sentence word list. This procedure is called *parsing.* A parser is simply a program that can recognize the structure of a sentence and determine if this structure is grammatically correct.

To implement a parser, the first task is to formalize acceptable orderings of elements in a sentence as a set of rules or productions. Once these rules are stated, they can be transposed into Turbo Prolog clauses and then into an executable program. Keep in mind that parsers are, in and of themselves, of little practical use. A parser can only tell us if a given sentence can or cannot be analyzed according to the rules of its grammar. The problems of determining the meaning or intent of the sentence, mapping that meaning onto the computer's artificial language, and generating appropriate output must yet be addressed.

10.3.1 A Finite-State Grammar and Parser

A finite-state syntax assumes that humans produce sentences one word at a time. The syntax is based on a left-to-right grammar consisting of constraint rules that limit the words that can be selected for use at any point in the production of a sentence. For example, after choosing one word, a person's choices for the next word are constrained by the choice already made. If the initial word is a determiner, the next word is very likely to be either an adjective or a noun, and it is unlikely that the next word will be a preposition. This choice in turn limits the range of candidate words for the next choice. If a noun was chosen as the second word, it is likely to be followed by a verb. On the other hand, if an adjective was selected as the second word, the third choice is most likely to be a noun or possibly another adjective. This word selection process continues until the sentence is completed.

In the finite-state grammar (FSG) approach, sentence production and analysis are viewed as a transition through a series of states. These states are represented in diagrams as nodes. The transitions between states are termed arcs and are represented as arrows. Collectively, the legal states and transitions define the finite-state grammar. Figure 10.1 illustrates a small sample FSG.

The FSG is often called a *transition network.* The nodes represent syntactic categories. The directed arcs indicate legal transitions to the next state. The broken arrow pointing to a node designates it as a legal initial state. The label "Jump" means that the node may be skipped. For example, a sentence may begin with a determiner or the determiner may be skipped and a beginning made with any of the legal states that follow the determiner node. A broken arrow pointing away from a node designates legal terminal states. For example, a sentence may end with a noun, verb, or adverb, but not a determiner or preposition. The loop over the adjective node indicates that a grammatical sentence may have a sequence of one or more adjectives.

Using a finite-state approach, let's see how we would parse the sentence "The small boy went to the store." The procedure begins with the parser accepting the

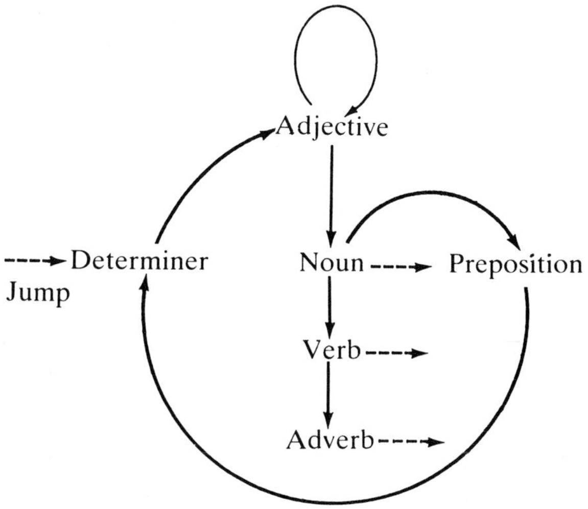

Figure 10.1 Diagram of a finite-state grammar expressed as a collection of states (nodes) and legal transitions (arcs). Such a collection of nodes and arcs is often referred to as a transition network.

first word, "The." The parser would check its lexicon and ascertain that the first word is a determiner. The parser would next check its grammar knowledge base to validate that a determiner is a legal initial state. If the check returns `True`, the state of the system is established as "determiner." The parser would then accept the next word in the sentence, *small*, and determine that it is an adjective. The parser would next check its grammar rules to determine if a transition from determiner to adjective is legal. If the check returns `True`, the system state is now adjective. The next word, "boy," is accepted, found to be a noun, and thus a legal transition from an adjective, and the system is now in a noun state. This process continues until the last word is accepted and found to be a legal terminal state. The sentence has been parsed and is found to be grammatical.

You may have noticed that the problem of parsing this sentence resembles the travel problem presented in Chapter 8. In that problem we were given a set of nodes with arcs connecting pairs of nodes (the map of cities). The task was to find all possible paths from a user-defined start node to a user-defined finish node. In the parsing problem, the task is to test the validity of a path, this time represented by a series of words from a sentence using a transition network of nodes and arcs.

The following is a Turbo Prolog finite-state grammar parsing program that will perform all the procedures just outlined. The program includes the CONVERT.PRO program to convert the sentence entered at the keyboard into a list of words with all embedded spaces and punctuation removed. The `reverse()` procedure restores the list to the proper order.

The tokenized list of words is passed to `parse()`. `parse()` calls `get_word()` to fetch the first word from the list. The word's state is checked in the lexicon. The word is also checked to determine if its state is a legal initial state.

If this call succeeds, the state and remainder of the list are passed to the recursive `parse2()`. If the remainder list is not empty, the first two `parse2()` rules will fail. The third rule uses `get_word()` to return the next word in the list. The states of the last word and of this new word are checked using the transition rule to determine if the grammar supports a transition to the new state. This process continues until the remainder list is empty, in which case the first `parse2()` rule is checked. If the last word belongs to a valid final state, the program terminates a successful parse. If the state of the last word is not a valid final state, the parse will fail.

The PARSE_1 program includes a lexical knowledge base containing information on words and the syntactic categories to which they belong. A grammar knowledge base declares all the transitions supported by this tiny grammar. The program also includes information on valid initial and final states.

This program includes several `write()` statements to assist the reader in following the program design. Without these statements, the program will return only `True` or `False` to indicate that the parse has either succeeded or failed. To help you follow program execution, I have once again introduced this pedagogical aide. After you understand the program, remove the write statements from the `parse()` and `parse2()` procedures as an exercise.

```
/* ***********************************************************

                        PARSE_1.PRO

                  A Finite-State Parser

   *********************************************************** */

DOMAINS

 list = string*

DATABASE

 wordlist(list)

PREDICATES

 parse(list)
 parse2(string,list)
 initial_state(string)
 transition(string,string)
 dict(string,list)
 final_state(string)
 get_word(string,list,list)
```

```
INCLUDE "Convert.pro"

GOAL
 asserta(wordlist([])),
 clearwindow,
 write("Enter a sentence: "),
 readln(S),
 convert(S),
 wordlist(L),
 reverse(L,L2),
 parse(L2),
 retract(wordlist(_)).

CLAUSES

 parse(S) :-
   get_word(Word,S,Remainder),
   dict(State,[Word]),
   initial_state(State),
   write("\nInitial state = ",State),
   write("\nWord = ",Word),
   write("\nRemainder = ",Remainder),
   parse2(State,Remainder).
 parse(_) :-
   sound(1,900),
   write("\n\nParse failed.  ").

 parse2(State,[]) :-
   final_state(State),
   write("\nFinal state ",State,"\n\nParse OK.").
 parse2(State,[]) :-
   write("\nFinal state ",State,"\n\nParse failed.").
 parse2(State,List) :-
   get_word(Word,List,Remainder),
   dict(Category,[Word]),
   transition(State,Category),
   write("\nTransition = ",State," to ",Category),
   write("\nWord = ",Word),
   write("\nRemainder = ",Remainder),
   parse2(Category,Remainder).

  get_word(Word,[Word|Remainder],Remainder).

 /* grammar knowledge base */
```

(*continued*)

```
transition("determiner","adjective").
transition("adjective","noun").
transition("determiner","noun").
transition("noun","verb").
transition("verb","preposition").
transition("verb","determiner").
transition("preposition","determiner").

initial_state("determiner").
initial_state("noun").

final_state("verb").
final_state("noun").

/* lexicon knowledge base */

dict("determiner",["The"]).
dict("determiner",["the"]).
dict("adjective",["small"]).
dict("adjective",["old"]).
dict("noun",["boy"]).
dict("noun",["store"]).
dict("noun",["man"]).
dict("noun",["old"]).
dict("noun",["boats"]).
dict("verb",["ran"]).
dict("verb",["man"]).
dict("preposition",["to"]).

/* ************************************************** */
```

As you can see, an FSG parser works its way through a tokenized sentence one word at a time in left-to-right order. As each word is parsed, there is a transition to a new state or lexical category. A failure to parse a word requires that the system backtrack and retest the current state. Without Turbo Prolog's built-in backtracking mechanism, this FSG parser could not process what are called "garden path" sentences.

In human discourse, garden path sentences seduce the reader into making incorrect state transitions by encouraging assignment of words to syntactic categories based solely on the strength of word associations determined by past experience. To illustrate this type of sentence, consider the following garden path sentences taken from Sanford (1985).

- The steel ships are transporting is expensive.
- The old man the boats.

You may have stumbled for a moment when reading these sentences. This was because you made transitions from one state to another based solely on the strength of the past associations between pairs of words (steel and ships, old and man). In the second sentence, you probably assigned *man* to the noun category because of the frequency of association between *old* and *man* in such sentences as "My old man likes baseball." You then expected a verb (just as our parser would), and finding none, you backtracked, reassigned *man* to the verb category. You then completed the sentence and correctly interpreted its meaning.

10.3.2 Limitations of an FSG Parser

Try a trace on the parser program with a few legal sentences and you will come to appreciate the importance and power of backtracking in the parsing procedure. Yet even though backtracking can assure that a grammatical sentence will ultimately parse, the efficiency of the process is problematic, particularly in applications to unrestricted natural languages.

This is because an FSG parser requires that all the legal state transitions and word memberships in lexical categories be represented in the system. And we know, many words belong to several lexical categories. For example, *old* can be an adjective or a noun. The sheer size and complexity of the English language would obviously require a prohibitively large grammar knowledge base in order to represent all the possible transitions and syntactic categories. In practice, this introduces problems of both storage and searching. FSG parsers are useful, therefore, only in applications where the natural-language input can be restricted to a small and manageable subset of English.

Another criticism of the finite-state approach to grammar was raised by Chomsky (1957), the noted theoretical linguist. Chomsky pointed out that any sentence in the English language can be extended by embedding within it another structure or sentence. The sentence "The mouse ran into its hole" can be extended by including within it the sentence, "The cat knows," as in "The cat knows the mouse ran into its hole." This can be extended even further as in "The cat the dog chased knows the mouse ran into its hole." In fact, this process of embedding structures within structures and producing grammatically correct sentences can go on indefinitely. Although such complex sentences may not often be used in practice, they are nonetheless theoretically possible, and any valid grammar must have the capacity to formalize the processes involved. Chomsky has argued convincingly that because a finite-state grammar is not recursive, it is inadequate to this task.

This aspect of Chomsky's critique of finite-state grammars can be addressed by a grammar that can analyze sentences from the top down using structures (phrases) as well as terminals and has the capability of making recursive calls to other transition networks as part of the process for reducing intermediate structures into terminals. A grammar with this feature is the phrase structure grammar (PSG) or augmented transition network (ATN).

10.3.3 A Phrase Structure Grammar and Parser

The Phrase Structure Grammar is based on the work of the linguist Zelig Harris (1951), who conceived of sentences as composed of structures such as noun, preposition, and verb phrases. The parsing of such structured sentences requires a top-down recursive analysis of the component structures until terminal elements (words) are reached. The syntax rules of the grammar govern the ways in which these structures may be composed.

To illustrate the phrase structure approach to parsing, consider the simple sentence "John liked the old books." It is composed of a noun phrase, *John* and a verb phrase, *liked the old books*. In order to parse this sentence, a computer program must identify the grammatical structure to which each word in the sentence belongs. The parse of the sentence can then be represented as a parse tree as shown in Figure 10.2.

The root of the tree is the sentence. Intermediate nodes in the tree represent component structures such as noun and verb phrases. The terminal nodes or leaves are the component words of the phrase structures.

The structures of a PSG can be expressed as "rewrite rules," as shown in Figure 10.3. The arrow in each rule stands in the place of the phrase *may be rewritten as*. In a rewrite rule, the single structure on the left side of the arrow is rewritten into components on the right side. The components on the right side

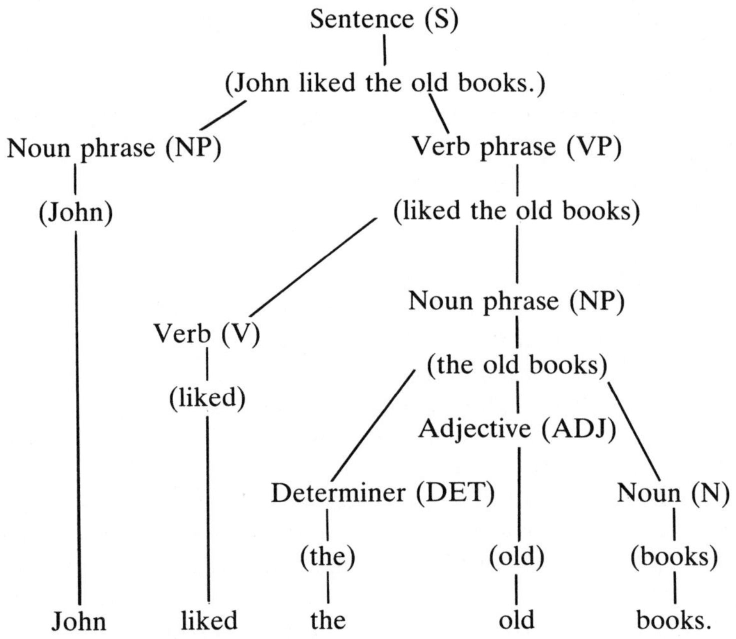

Figure 10.2 Tree diagram of the structure of the sentence "John liked the old books."

```
Rule 1  S   ⟶ NP + VP
Rule 2  VP  ⟶ V
Rule 3  VP  ⟶ V + NP
Rule 4  NP  ⟶ N
Rule 5  NP  ⟶ DET + N
Rule 6  NP  ⟶ ADJ + N
Rule 7  DET ⟶ the ¦ a
Rule 8  V   ⟶ threw ¦ ran
Rule 9  N   ⟶ john ¦ books
Rule 10 ADJ ⟶ old ¦ small ¦ pretty
```

Figure 10.3 Rewrite rules for a small PSG.

may themselves be either structures or terminals. Structures require further rewriting to be reduced into terminals. Terminals are tokens (words in a lexicon) that cannot be further rewritten. The vertical bar indicates alternative terminal choices.

Components of grammar can also be described using what is called *Backus-Naur form* (BNF). BNF is used to describe the grammars of programming languages. (The reference guide in Chapter 12 of the Turbo Prolog Manual shows the BNF syntax of the Turbo Prolog language.) In BNF syntax, a structure or any nonterminal is surrounded by a left and right angle bracket, as in <SENTENCE>. The left and right sides of a rule are separated by `::=` rather than by an arrow as in the rewrite rule. Terminals or tokens are displayed using lowercase letters, as in <NOUN> ::= books. The asterisk is used to indicate a series of zero or more terminals or nonterminals, as in <NOUN_PHRASE> ::= <DETERMINER> <ADJECTIVE>* <NOUN>. The vertical bar stands for *or*, the plus sign + is used to designate one or more repetitions of a terminal or nonterminal symbol in a rule, and brackets or braces surround optional elements. To illustrate the use of these symbols, consider the BNF syntax of the Turbo Prolog variable as defined in Chapter 12 of the manual.

A name in Turbo Prolog begins with a letter followed by zero or more optional letters or digits.

```
<NAME> ::= (<LETTER> | _) { <LETTER> | <DIGIT>}*
```

A letter may be uppercase or lowercase:

```
<LETTER> ::= <LOWER-LETTER> | <UPPER-LETTER>

<LOWER-LETTER> ::= a | b | c | d | e | f | .........

<UPPER-LETTER ::= A | B | C | D | E | F |........
```

Similarly, a digit is defined as one of the terminals

```
<DIGIT> ::= 0 | 1 | 2 | 3 | 4 | 5 | 6 | 7 | 8 | 9
```

A variable starts with an uppercase letter or an underscore, which can be followed by an optional name.

```
<VARIABLE> ::= (<CAPITAL-LETTER> | _ ) [<NAME>]
```

The rewrite rules of Figure 10.3 transposed into BNF are shown in Figure 10.4.

```
Rule 1  <SENTENCE> ::= <NP> <VP>
Rule 2  <VP> ::= <V>
Rule 3  <VP> ::= <V> <NP>
Rule 4  <NP> ::= <N>
Rule 5  <NP> ::= <DET> <N>
Rule 6  <NP> ::= <ADJ> <N>
Rule 7  <DET> ::= the | a
Rule 8  <V> ::= threw | ran
Rule 9  <N> ::= john | books
Rule 10 <ADJ> ::= old | small | pretty
```

Figure 10.4 BNF syntax for the PSG.

It is a simple matter now to convert either rewrite or BNF rules into Turbo Prolog clauses.

```
/* Rule 1 */
sentence(X) :-
      append(Y,Z,X),
      noun_phrase(Y),
      verb_phrase(Z).

/* Rule 2 */
 verb_phrase(X) :-
      verb(X).

/* Rule 3 */
 verb_phrase(X) :-
      append(Y,Z,X),
      verb(Y),
      noun_phrase(Z).

/* Rule 4 */
 noun_phrase(X) :-
      noun(X).

/* Rule 5 */
 noun_phrase(X) :-
      append(Y,Z,X),
      determiner(Y),
      noun(Z).
```

```
/* Rule 6 */
 noun_phrase(X) :-
      append(Y,Z,X),
      adjective(Y),
      noun(Z).

/* Rule 7 */
 determiner("the").
/* Rule 8 */
 verb("liked").

/* Rule 9 */
 noun("John").
 noun("books").

/* Rule 10 */
 adjective("old").
```

Notice that I have used `append()` to split the sentence word list into individual tokens. (You may wish to review the discussion of the `append()` rule in Chapter 5 before continuing.)

Each of these 10 rules has both declarative and procedural meanings. Declaratively, the `sentence()` rule says "*X* is a sentence if it is comprised of a noun phrase *Y* and a verb phrase *Z*." A procedural reading of this rule is "To prove that *X* is a sentence, split *X* into two components, *Y* and *Z*, where *Y* can be proved to be a noun phrase and *Z* proved to be a verb phrase."

The phrase structure grammar presented is the top-down and recursive approach to syntactic analysis we were looking for to handle Chomsky's criticism of finite-state grammars. The program starts with a large structure, the sentence. It processes the sentence into an NP. The NP is further processed into terminals (words) by calls to DET, ADJ, and N. Next the ATN VP is called to check the sentence for a verb phrase. Calls to V and NP produce a verb and a determiner, adjective, and noun, respectively.

Here is the completed program. Run it and study it closely. Be sure to put a trace on each of the `parse()` rules!

```
/* **************************************************
                    PARSE_2.PRO

         Phrase structure parsing using append

   ************************************************** */

DOMAINS

 list = string*
```

(continued)

```
DATABASE

 wordlist(list)

PREDICATES

 sentence(list)
 noun_phrase(list)
 verb_phrase(list)
 prep_phrase(list)
 prep(list)
 noun(list)
 determiner(list)
 adjective(list)
 verb(list)

INCLUDE "Convert.pro"

GOAL
 asserta(wordlist([])),
 clearwindow,
 write("Enter a sentence: "),
 readln(S),
 convert(S),
 wordlist(L),
 reverse(L,L2),
 sentence(L2),
 retract(wordlist(_)).


CLAUSES
 sentence(X) :-
   append(Y,Z,X),
   noun_phrase(Y),
   write("NP is ",Y),nl,
   verb_phrase(Z),
   write("VP is ",Z),nl.

 noun_phrase(X) :-
   noun(X).
 noun_phrase(X) :-
   append(Y,Z,X),
   determiner(Y),
   noun_phrase(Z).
 noun_phrase(X) :-
   append(Y,Z,X),
   adjective(Y),
   noun_phrase(Z).
```

```
verb_phrase(X) :-
  append(Y,Z,X),
  verb(Y),
  noun_phrase(Z).
verb_phrase(X) :-
  append(Y,Z,X),
  verb(Y),
  prep_phrase(Z).
verb_phrase(X) :-
  verb(X).

prep_phrase(X) :-
  append(Y,Z,X),
  prep(Y),
  noun_phrase(Z).

/* lexicon knowledge base */

determiner(["The"]).
determiner(["the"]).
determiner(["a"]).

adjective(["little"]).
adjective(["old"]).

noun(["boy"]).
noun(["girl"]).
noun(["ball"]).
noun(["man"]).
noun(["store"]).

verb(["ran"]).
verb(["threw"]).
verb(["man"]).
prep(["to"]).

/* ********************************************** */
```

10.3.4 Increasing Parse Efficiency with Difference Lists

PARSE_2.PRO uses `append()` to split the sentence list into individual words, passed one at a time to the syntax rules for testing. In a small parser such as this one, this is quite adequate. However, the `append()` rule attempts nondeterministically to produce all possible candidate words even though most of these words do not satisfy the noun phrase rule constraints. (Do a trace of `append()` and see for yourself.) A large parser would be severely taxed by the backtracking behavior of `append()`.

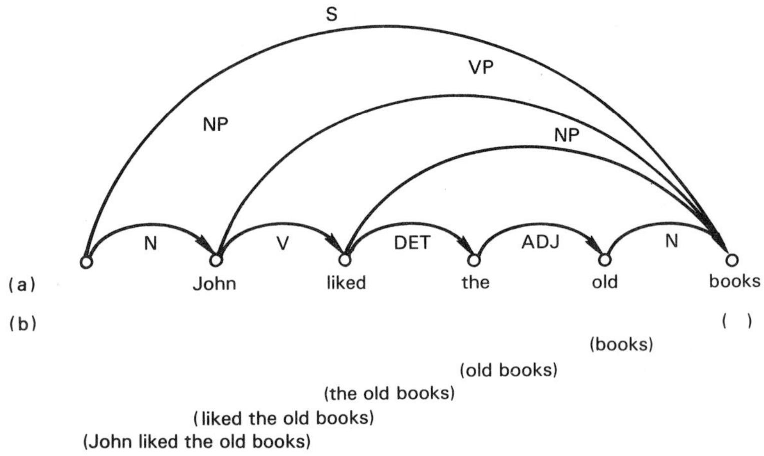

Figure 10.5 Chart representations of the sentence "John liked the old books." (a) The words are seen as labels for nodes, collections of which in turn represent phrases. (b) The nodes are labeled by the list of words that lie to the right of each node.

A more efficient approach to producing candidate words from the list of words is based on the concept of the *difference list*. The difference list approach to ATNs can be understood by contrasting the tree representation of a parsed sentence with that of the chart shown in Figure 10.5. In the tree, each leaf is a terminal or word (a). In the chart, the terminal nodes represent lists of sentence components (b).

Each word in the tokenized sentence

```
[john,liked,the,old,books]
```

can be represented as the difference between two lists. For example, the word *John* can be seen as the difference between these two lists

```
[john,liked,the,old,books]
     [liked,the,old,books]
```

The word *old* may be defined as the difference between

```
[old,books]
```

and

```
    [books]
```

The difference between two lists can be expressed more generally as

```
[john,liked,the,old,books|X]
```

and

X

and

[old,books|X]

and

X

Consider now the following difference list parse clauses

```
sentence(X,Z) :-
  noun_phrase(X,Y1),
  verb_phrase(Y1,Z),
noun_phrase(X,Z) :-
  determiner(X,Y1),
  adjective(Y1,Y2),
  noun_phrase(Y2,Z).
noun_phrase(X,Z) :-
  noun(X,Z).

verb_phrase(X,Z) :-
  verb(X,Y),
  noun_phrase(Y,Z).

/* Lexicon */
determiner([The|X],X).
determiner([the|X],X).
adjective([old|X],X).
noun([john|X],X).
noun([books|X],X).
verb([liked|X],X).
```

Applying the difference list concept to the sentence rule, we can say that a sentence is the difference D1 between two lists X and Z if there exists a noun phrase that is the difference D2 between the two lists X and Y1 and there is a verb phrase that is the difference D3 between the two lists Y1 and Z.

	X	= [john,liked,the,old,books|Z]
Sentence	Z	= []
	D1	= [john,liked,the,old,books|Z]
	X	= [john,liked,the,old,books|Y1]
Noun phrase	Y1	= [liked,the,old,books]
	D2	= [john|Y1]

	Y1	= [liked,the,old,books!Z]
Verb phrase	Z	= []
	D3	= [liked,the,old,books!Z]

Furthermore, for the noun phrase rule (the second `noun_phrase` rule applies here), we can say that a noun phrase is the difference between two lists X and Z if there is a noun X.

	X	= [john!Z]
Noun phrase	Z	= []
	D	= [john!Z]
and	noun([john!Z],Z).	

For the verb phrase rule, we can say that a verb phrase is the difference between two lists X and Z if there is a verb that is the difference between the lists X and Y and a noun phrase that is the difference between Y and Z.

	X	= [liked,the,old,books!Y]
Verb	Y	= [the,old,books]
	D	= [liked!Y]
and	verb([liked!Y],Y).	

For the noun phrase, we can say that a noun phrase is the difference between two lists X and Z if there is a determiner that is the difference D1 between the two lists X and Y1, there is an adjective that is the difference D2 between the two lists Y1 and Y2, and there is a noun that is the difference D3 between the lists Y2 and Z.

	X	= [the,old,books!Y1]
Determiner	Y1	= [old,books]
	D	= [the!Y1]
and	determiner([the!Y1],Y1).	
	Y1	= [old,books!Y2]
Adjective	Y2	= [books]
	D2	= [old!Y2]
and	adjective([old!Y2],Y2).	
	Y2	= [books!Z]
Noun	Z	= []
	D3	= [books!Z]
and	noun([books!Z],Z).	

A call to this program with "The boy liked the old books." would parse and return `True`. Enter PARSE_3.PRO and prove it with a trace. A parser based on the difference list data structure will parse much more efficiently than one relying on `append()`. You may wish to undertake rewriting the conversion procedures in CONVERT.PRO using difference lists as an exercise.

```
/* **************************************************

                    PARSE_3.PRO

          Parsing with difference lists

   ************************************************** */

DOMAINS

 list = string*

DATABASE

 wordlist(list)

PREDICATES

 sentence(list,list)
 noun_phrase(list,list)
 verb_phrase(list,list)
 prep_phrase(list,list)
 remainder(list,list)
 verb(list,list)
 noun(list,list)
 pronoun(list,list)
 determiner(list,list)
 adjective(list,list)
 conjunction(list,list)
 preposition(list,list)
 adverb(list,list)
 print(list)

INCLUDE "Convert.pro"

GOAL

 asserta(wordlist([])),
 clearwindow,
 write("Enter a sentence: "),
```

(*continued*)

```
 readln(S1),
 upper_lower(S1,S),
 convert(S),
 wordlist(L),
 retract(wordlist(L)),
 reverse(L,L2),
 sentence(L2,_),
 write("\tThe sentence \" "),
 print(L2),
 write("\"\n\tis grammatically correct.");nl,nl
 ;
 sound(10,750),
 write("\nThe sentence does not parse!").

CLAUSES

 /* Parse sentence */

 sentence(X,Y) :-         /* Declarative sentence */
   noun_phrase(X,Z1),     /* The man ran quickly to the */
   verb_phrase(Z1,Z2),    /* house with the ball.  */
   remainder(Z2,Y).

 sentence(X,Y) :-
   noun_phrase(X,Z1),     /* The small boy and the pretty */
   remainder(Z1,Z2),      /* girl ran quickly to the large */
   verb_phrase(Z2,Z3),    /* house with the ball.  */
   remainder(Z3,Y).

 sentence(X,Y) :-         /* Imperative sentence */
   verb_phrase(X,Y).      /* Run quickly to the house */
                          /* with the ball. Or a question: */
 noun_phrase(X,Y) :-      /* Can the man run to the house */
   determiner(X,Z),
   noun(Z,Y).
 noun_phrase(X,Y) :-
   determiner(X,Z),
   adjective(Z,Z1),
   noun_phrase(Z1,Y).
 noun_phrase(X,Y) :-
   adjective(X,Z),
   noun(Z,Y).
 noun_phrase(X,Y) :-
   noun(X,Y).

 verb_phrase(X,Y) :-
   verb(X,Z),
   adverb(Z,Y).
```

```
verb_phrase(X,Y) :-
  verb(X,Z),
  noun_phrase(Z,Y).
verb_phrase(X,Y) :-
  verb(X,Y1),
  prep_phrase(Y1,Y).
verb_phrase(X,Y) :-
  verb(X,Y).

prep_phrase(X,Y) :-
  preposition(X,Z),
  noun_phrase(Z,Y).

remainder([],[]) :- !.
remainder(X,Y) :-
  prep_phrase(X,Y),
  remainder(Y,_).
remainder(X,Y) :-
  adverb(X,Y),
  remainder(Y,_).
remainder(X,Y) :-
  conjunction(X,Y1),
  noun_phrase(Y1,Y).

print([]) :- !.
print([X|Y]) :-
  write(X," "),
  print(Y).

/* Lexicon */

determiner(["the"|X],X).
determiner(["The"|X],X).
determiner(["a"|X],X).

adjective(["good"|X],X).
adjective(["pretty"|X],X).
adjective(["small"|X],X).
adjective(["large"|X],X).
adjective(["quick"|X],X).
adjective(["rich"|X],X).
adjective(["old"|X],X).

noun(["boy"|X],X).
noun(["girl"|X],X).
noun(["store"|X],X).
```

(*continued*)

```
noun(["ball"|X],X).
noun(["man"|X],X).
noun(["house"|X],X).
noun(["dog"|X],X).
noun(["cat"|X],X).

noun(X,Y) :- pronoun(X,Y).

pronoun(["I"|X],X).
pronoun(["we"|X],X).
pronoun(["they"|X],X).

verb(["ran"|X],X).
verb(["threw"|X],X).
verb(["ran"|X],X).
verb(["can"|X],X).
verb(["go"|X],X).
verb(["run"|X],X).
verb(["built"|X],X).
verb(["sold"|X],X).
verb(["gave"|X],X).
verb(["bought"|X],X).
verb(["eat"|X],X).

preposition(["to"|X],X).
preposition(["with"|X],X).
preposition(["by"|X],X).

conjunction(["and"|X],X).

adverb(["quickly"|X],X).

/* ************************************************ */
```

10.3.5 Limitations of a Phrase Structure Parser

One basic problem with PARSE_3 is that it does not check parts of the sentence for agreement in either number or tense. For example, a singular subject and a plural form of verb would be considered by this parser to be grammatically correct. The sentences "Every child plays" and "Every child play" are equally grammatical to a parser that looks only at the syntactic categories of the words and not at number agreement between the sentence components.

The reason for this is that the parsers we have constructed thus far have been context-free. Context-free means that parsing of one structure or element in a sentence does not affect the way the rest of the sentence is parsed. As you can see, the PSG system is context-free since it does not have a mechanism for passing context information on agreement between NP and VP structures in a sentence.

10.3.6 Adding Contextual Information to the PSG Parser

Adding context dependency to the parser can be accomplished by affixing arguments to the parse rules and to the lexicon of word facts. Context information for number agreement (N) and tense (T) can be appended as follows:

```
sentence(N,T,X,Y) :-
  noun_phrase(N,X,Z1),
  verb_phrase(N,T,Z1,Z2),
  remainder(N,Z2,Y).

noun_phrase(N,X,Y) :-
  determiner(N,X,Z),
  noun(N,Z,Y).

noun(N,X,Y) :- pronoun(N,X,Y).

verb_phrase(N,T,X,Y) :-
  verb(N,T,X,Z),
  noun_phrase(N,Z,Y).

remainder(N,X,Y) :-
  conjunction(X,Y1),
  noun_phrase(N,Y1,Y).

noun(singular,["child"|X],X).
noun(plural,["children"|X],X).

determiner(singular,["every"|X],X).
determiner(plural,["all"|X],X).
verb(plural,present,["run"|X],X).
verb(singular,present,["runs"|X],X).
verb(singular,past,["ran"|X],X).
verb(plural,past,["ran"|X],X).
```

The `sentence()` rule calls the `noun_phrase()` procedure with number and tense parameters. When the `noun_phrase()` rule matches the first word (a determiner) in the lexicon, the number variable will be instantiated to either `singular` or `plural`. The call to `noun()` is now constrained by number. If the noun and determiner agree in number, the parse will continue. If they do not agree in number, the parse will fail. In like fashion, the verb must also agree in number with the determiner and noun, or the parse will fail. Tense information can similarly be built into rules to assure that the appropriate components of the sentence match in verb form.

As demonstrated in section 10.3.5, PSGs can be designed to carry context-dependent information so that components in a sentence can be checked for agreement in tense and number as part of the syntactic analysis. PSGs, however, suffer from another deficiency related to the effects of context dependency. Specifically, this has to do with the fact that words may belong to more than one lexical category.

Consider the sentence "They are cooking apples." Applying the rewrite rules, this sentence can be analyzed in two ways:

```
PARSE 1

           (NP) + (VP)
S    --->  They + are cooking apples

           (N)
NP   --->  They

N    --->  They

           (V)               + (NP)
VP   --->  are cooking       + apples

V    --->  are cooking

           (N)
NP   --->  apples

N    --->  apples

PARSE 2

           (NP) + (VP)
S    --->  They + are cooking apples

           (N)
NP   --->  They

N    --->  They

           (V)  +(NP)
VP   --->  are  + cooking apples

V    --->  are

           (ADJ)   +  (N)
NP   --->  cooking +  apples

ADJ  --->  cooking

N    --->  apples
```

As you can see, this sentence maps equally well onto two distinct phrase structures. From the point of view of a purely syntactic analysis, this sentence is ambiguous. It is not at all clear whether the word *cooking* is a verb or an adjective. If, however, this sentence could be analyzed using information contained in earlier sentences, the ambiguity could be readily resolved. Let's add two sentences leading up to the one we are analyzing.

> The chefs are peeling Rome apples. Rome apples are often used in making pies. They are cooking apples.

From this contextual information we can see that the pronoun *they* refers to the Rome apples and that *cooking* is therefore an adjective modifying *apples*.

Now consider the sentence in a somewhat different context.

> The chefs are preparing dinner. They are cooking ingredients for a sauce. They are cooking apples.

Here the pronoun *they* refers to the chefs who are cooking the ingredients for a sauce. In this context, it is clear that the word *cooking* is used as a verb.

In human discourse, ambiguity in sentences is resolved using syntactic information obtained from previous sentences, knowledge of the speaker's plans and goals, and general world knowledge. Researchers are currently exploring methods for implementing natural-language understanding systems using strategies based in varying degrees on both syntactic and semantic analysis of sentence and discourse inputs. If you are interested in exploring this topic further, Allen (1987) and Harris (1985) offer in-depth and comprehensive coverage of natural-language understanding from the point of view of computational linguistics. The psycholinguistic viewpoint is well covered in Garnham (1985). The interesting work by Schank and his associates at the Yale AI lab on semantic analysis is covered in scattered sources (see Schank & Abelson, 1977; Schank & Riesbeck, 1981; Schank & Childers, 1984; Lehnert & Ringle, 1982).

Many of the current generation of natural language processing systems deal with the problem of machine understanding of complex and ambiguous natural language by restricting inputs to a subset of English words and sentence structures. The specific subset that is selected is often determined by an empirical study of the kinds of input typically encountered in the application domain.

During the tokenizing and parsing phases of analysis, the tokens belonging to lexical categories used by the system in performing application functions are recognized and compiled into a list. Unneeded tokens are discarded. The intent of the input is realized by passing the list of tokens as an argument to rules that process the tokens and initiate procedures to realize the sense and intent of the input.

To illustrate, take the case of a natural-language front end program to a library database application. A natural-language query to this database might take the form:

Show to me the authors of all the books that were published in the year 1981.

After tokenizing, recognition of relevant words, and disposal of unnecessary words, the sentence would be mapped onto the following logical structure or template and passed to rules for processing:

```
[COMMAND,MODIFIER,FIELD,OPERATOR,VALUE]

[show,all,author,=,1981]
```

Let's continue the example and construct a natural-language front-end for a simple library database.

10.4 CONSTRUCTING A CONTEXT-FREE NATURAL LANGUAGE INTERFACE

To illustrate the design of this kind of natural-language front end, it is necessary first to construct a simple database that the system will access (see Figure 10.6). The keywords and permissible sentence structures can then be defined (see Figure 10.7).

As you can see, this small database stores information on a personal library. The PARSE_4 program will permit the user to access the database using restricted natural-language queries. The principles developed here can then be used to extend the parser to include additional sentence structures or semantic templates.

These queries have a similar structure in that after noise disposal, they all begin with a verb or command followed by an ordered sequence of keywords. The keywords the program must understand fall into several categories: `Command`, `Modifier`, `Field`, `Operator`, and `Date` (see Figure 10.8).

Words used in queries and listed in the `ignore_word()` database are treated as noise and discarded during the conversion procedure. Words that are synonyms for commands will be accepted. Words that are neither part of the

```
info(1345,"R. Abel","Man the Measure",1976).
info(3345,"L. Bloomfield","Why a Linguistic Society",1925).
info(3299,"A. Newell & H. Simon","Human Problem Solving",1972).
info(4318,"J. Fodor","The Language of Thought",1975).
info(1515,"M. Sahlins","Colors and Cultures",1976).
info(5882,"R. Harris","The Language Myth",1981).
```

Figure 10.6 A sample library database.

```
List all authors.
Show me all my titles.
List all.
Print the indexes of all of my books.
Show me all titles before 1981.
Please list out all of the titles in 1976.
May I please see a list of all the titles of
 my books that were published before 1983?
```

Figure 10.7 Sample natural-language queries.

command structure nor listed in the ignore or synonym categories will cause the system to default to a `print_all_records` condition. Procedures could easily be written to trap such unrecognized words and to have the user redefine them as either keywords, synonyms for keywords, or words to ignore. You are encouraged to undertake this conversion as an exercise.

The PARSE_4 program permits the user to input commands in a relatively normal manner. Its only requirement is that the essential command keyword along with optional modifier, field, operator, and date words can be extracted from the natural-language input and mapped to a template. If a match cannot be made,

```
CATEGORY          ACCEPTABLE WORDS

Command           list | print | show | display

Modifier          all | a | one | each | every

Field             author(s) | title(s) | index(es) |
                  date

Operator          before | in | during | after

Date              <any (integer) year>
```

(a)

```
COMMAND <modifier> <field name> (operator> <date>
```

(b)

Figure 10.8 The lexicon of PARSE_4.PRO. (a) The current list of keyword categories and words in each category that the system understands. (b) The current legal sentence structure. Both words and types of sentences may be expanded by the user.

the system defaults to a `print_all_records()` condition. This would, obviously, not be an acceptable default where databases are very large. Modify the program to default to a `restate_command` condition as an exercise.

A database of words to ignore is included so that the program can filter out commonly used but irrelevant words prior to parsing. The program produces but one field per query from either a single (the first) record or from all records in the database. This is done to keep the program as simple as possible while illustrating the important programming techniques. Add procedures to handle more complex input if you so desire.

By implementing other semantic templates, the program can easily be enhanced. The program could also be enhanced by adding multiple-field retrievals (a database `join`) to single-field retrievals (a database `select`) with additional rules and appropriate access procedures. Also, the program can be expanded to include other database command functions such as `delete` and `modify`. Before tackling these changes, the program should be redesigned and modularized, with the library maintained as a separate file opened and closed for reading and writing. These modifications are recommended as an exercise.

```
/* ************************************************

                     PARSE_4.PRO

         A natural language front-end program

   ************************************************ */


DOMAINS
 list = string*

DATABASE
 wordlist(list)

PREDICATES
 run
 query(list,list,string,string,string,string,string)
 field_phrase(list,list,string,string)
 command_phrase(list,list,string,string,string,string,
                                                  string)
 command(list,list,string)
 field_ID(list,list,string)
 field(list,list,string)
 date_phrase(list,list,string,string)
 op(list,list,string)
 synonym(list,list,string)
 year(list,list,string)
```

```
 process_with_date(string,string,string,string,string)
 modifier(list,list,string)
 process(string,string,string,string,string)
 process2(string,string,string)
 continue
 info(integer,string,string,integer)

 /* support predicates */

 convert(string)
 word(string,string)
 add_word(string)
 ignore(string)
 add(string,list,list)
 reverse(list,list)
 append(list,list,list)
 word_end(string,integer,integer)
 strip(string,string)
 print(list)

GOAL

 makewindow(1,112,112,"Natural-Language Front End",
                                          0,0,24,80),
 run.

CLAUSES
 run :-
   asserta(wordlist([])),
   clearwindow,
   storage(St,_,_),
   cursor(21,50),
   write("Stack = ",St),
   cursor(0,0),
   write("\tAt present, the program supports queries
                                       entered in"),nl,
   write("\n\tthe format:  <COMMAND> [MODIFIER] [FIELD]
                            [OPERATOR] [DATE]"),nl,
   write("\n\tEnter query: "),
   readln(S1),
   upper_lower(S1,S),
   convert(S),!,
   clearwindow,
   write("\n    Tokenized query: ",S),
   wordlist(L),
   retract(wordlist(L)),
   reverse(L,L2),
```

(continued)

```
  query(L2,_,C,M,F,O,D),
  process(C,M,F,O,D),!,
  continue.

continue :-
  write("\n\n\tDo you wish to continue?  (y/n): "),
  readchar(Answer),
  Answer = 'y',
  run
  ;
  removewindow.

query(X,Y,C,M,F,O,D) :-
  command_phrase(X,Y,C,M,F,O,D).

/* Current Templates */

command_phrase(X,Y,C,M,F,O,D) :-
  command(X,Y1,C),
  field_phrase(Y1,Y2,M,F),
  date_phrase(Y2,Y,O,D).
command_phrase(X,Y,C,M,F,O,D) :-
  M = "all",
  F = "records",
  O = "",
  D = "",
  command(X,Y,C).

field_phrase(X,Y,M,F) :-
  modifier(X,Y1,M),
  field_ID(Y1,Y,F).
field_phrase(X,Y,M,F) :-
  field_ID(X,Y1,F),
  modifier(Y1,Y,M).
field_phrase(X,Y,M,F) :-
  M = "all",
  field_ID(X,Y,F).

field_ID(X,Y,F) :-
  field(X,Y,F).
field_ID(X,Y,F) :-
  synonym(X,Y,F).

date_phrase([],[],O,D) :-
  O = "",
  D = "".
date_phrase(X,Y,O,D) :-
  op(X,Y1,O),
  year(Y1,Y,D).
```

```
/* lexicon */

modifier(["all"|X],X,"all").
modifier(["a"|X],X,"one").
modifier(["one"|X],X,"one").
modifier(["every"|X],X,"all").

field(["author"|X],X,"author").
field(["title"|X],X,"title").
field(["index"|X],X,"index").
field(["date"|X],X,"date").
field(["dates"|X],X,"date").
field(["records"|X],X,"records").
field([Name|X],X,Field) :-
 synonym([Name|X],X,Field).

command(["print"|X],X,"print").
command([Name|X],X,Comm) :-
 synonym([Name|X],X,Comm).
command([_|X],X,Comm) :-
 Comm = "print".

op(["before"|X],X,"before").
op(["in"|X],X,"in").
op(["after"|X],X,"after").

year([X|Y],Y,X).

synonym(["titles"|X],X,"title").
synonym(["fields"|X],X,"records").
synonym(["authors"|X],X,"author").
synonym(["writers"|X],X,"author").
synonym(["indexes"|X],X,"index").
synonym(["dates"|X],X,"date").
synonym(["display"|X],X,"print").
synonym(["see"|X],X,"print").
synonym(["list"|X],X,"print").
synonym(["show"|X],X,"print").

/* Ignore_word database */

ignore("my").          ignore("me").
ignore("i").           ignore("for").
ignore("please").      ignore("which").
ignore("want").        ignore("now").
ignore("you").         ignore("if").
ignore("the").         ignore("you").
```

(continued)

```
ignore("to").                 ignore("will").
ignore("of").                 ignore("thank").
ignore("out").                ignore("can").
ignore("from").               ignore("next").
ignore("published").          ignore("written").
ignore("were").               ignore("book").
ignore("books").              ignore("with").
ignore("may").                ignore("that").
/* **************** CONVERT ********************** */

convert(S) :-
  word(S,S2),
  convert(S2).
convert(_).

word(S,S2) :-
  word_end(S,Count,0),
  Count > 0,
  frontstr(Count,S,W,S3),
  add_word(W),
  strip(S3,S2).

word_end(S,Count,C) :-
  frontchar(S,Ch,S2),
  Ch <> ' ',
  Ch <> '.',
  C2 = C + 1,
  word_end(S2,Count,C2).
word_end(_,Count,Count).

strip(S,S2) :-
  frontchar(S,Ch,S2),
  Ch = ' '.
strip(S,S2) :-
  frontchar(S,Ch,S2),
  Ch = '.'.
strip(S,S).

add_word(W) :-
  not(ignore(W)),
  wordlist(L),
  add(W,L,L2),
  retract(wordlist(L)),
  assert(wordlist(L2)).
add_word(_).

add(W,L,[W|L]).

reverse([],[]).
reverse([Head|Tail],List) :-
```

```
    reverse(Tail,New_List),
    append(New_List,[Head],List).

append([],List,List).
append([X|List1],List2,[X|List3]) :-
    append(List1,List2,List3).

print([]) :- !.
print([X|Y]) :-
    write(X," "),
    print(Y).

/* ***********************************************

             DATABASE ACCESS PROCEDURES

   *********************************************** */

/* Current rules that implement templates */

process(C,M,F,O,D) :-
    not(O = ""),
    write("\n\n\tDo you wish to execute the command."),
    write("\n\t\t",C," ",M," ",F," ",O," ",D),
    write("\n\ty/n: "),
    readchar(A),
    A = 'y',
    clearwindow,
    process_with_date(C,M,F,O,D),
    write("\n\n\tPress any key: "),
    readchar(_),
    clearwindow.
process(C,M,F,O,D) :-
    O = "",
    write("\n\n\tDo you wish to execute the command."),
    write("\n\t\t",C," ",M," ",F," ",O," ",D),
    write("\n\ty/n: "),
    readchar(A),
    A = 'y',
    clearwindow,
    process2(C,M,F),
    write("\n\n\tPress any key: "),
    readchar(_),
    clearwindow
    ;
    !.

process_with_date(_,M,F,O,D) :-
    O = "in",
```

(continued)

```
    M = "all",
    F = "title",
    str_int(D,D1),
    info(_,_,T,D1),
    write("\n\t",T),
    fail.
process_with_date(_,M,F,O,D) :-
    O = "before",
    M = "all",
    F = "title",
    str_int(D,D1),
    info(_,_,T,X),
    X < D1,
    write("\n\t",T),
    fail.
process_with_date(,M,F,O,D) :-
    O = "after",
    M = "all",
    F = "title",
    str_int(D,D1),
    info(_,_,T,X),
    X > D1,
    write("\n\t",T),
    fail.

process2(print,all,author) :-
    info(_,A,_,_),
    write("\n\t",A),
    fail.
process2(print,one,author) :-
    info(_,A,_,_),
    write("\n\t",A).
process2(print,all,title) :-
    info(_,_,T,_),
    write("\n\t",T),
    fail.
process2(print,one,title) :-
    info(_,_,T,_),
    write("\n\t",T).
process2(print,all,index) :-
    info(I,_,_,_),
    write("\n\t",I),
    fail.
process2(print,one,index) :-
    info(I,_,_,_),
    write("\n\t",I).
process2(print,all,date) :-
    info(_,_,_,D),
```

```
   write("\n\t",D),
   fail.
 process2(print,one,date) :-
   info(_,_,_,D),
   write("\n\t",D).
 process2(print,all,records) :-
   info(A,B,C,D),
   write("\n\t",A," ",B," ",C," ",D),
   fail.
 process2(_,_,_).


/* ***********************************************************

                    LIBRARY DATABASE

                 info(INDEX,AUTHOR,TITLE,DATE)

*********************************************************** */

info(3299,"A. Newell & H. Simon","Human Problem Solving",
                                                      1972).
info(4318,"J. Fodor","The Language of Thought",1975).
info(1515,"M. Minsky","A Framework for Representing
                                          Knowledge",1975).
info(5882,"R. Harris","The Language Myth",1981).
info(1345,"R. Abel","Man the Measure",1976).
info(3345,"L. Bloomfield","Why a Linguistic Society",
                                                      1925).
info(2911,"M. Sahlins","Colors and Cultures",1976).
/* ********************************************************* */
```

Enter the program and experiment with it. As an exercise, try

```
TRACE convert, add_word, query, command_phrase,
      command, synonym
```

with the query

```
Please list the titles of all my books that were
 published before 1987.
```

This trace will illustrate the operation of the parser as well as the methods for ignoring words and finding and using synonyms for commands. You may also wish to remove the internal goal statements and try the program with some external goal queries.

10.6 SUMMARY

Concepts covered

Append() parsing
Augmented transition networks
Backus-Naur form
Chart parsing
Conceptual dependencies
Context dependency
Difference lists
Finite-state grammars
Front-end natural language programs
Natural versus artificial language
Noise disposal
Phrase structure grammars
Rewrite rules
Scripts
Semantics
Syntactic analysis
Tokenizing natural-language input
Transition networks

Teaching natural language to a computer presents many challenges. The sheer size and complexity of languages such as English makes it extraordinarily difficult to simulate all the mechanisms that humans use to communicate without ambiguity and misunderstanding.

Many current natural-language understanding systems combine syntactic and semantic analysis of input. In Turbo Prolog, syntactic analysis involves translating a grammar into a set of executable rules and facts called a parser that the computer can use to determine the structure of a tokenized natural-language sentence. Tokenization refers to the conversion of a natural-language "string" (in this case a string of printing and nonprinting characters entered at the keyboard by the user) into a list of words that can be processed by the parser. A lexicon is used by the system in determining the syntactic categories of words.

Semantic analysis deals with the meaning as well as the intent of the natural-language production. The lexicon and knowledge base of rules are used to map the sentence elements into structures that represent the meaning of queries. In natural-language front-end programs this meaning is mapped onto computer commands that translate the intent of natural-language productions into computer functions.

A finite-state grammar expresses syntax as nodes and arcs in a directed graph or transition network. The graph expresses the valid transitions from one syntactic category to another. The FSG approach has many limitations: (1) FSGs cannot represent structures within a sentence, (2) they are context-free and cannot check for dependency between elements of structures within a sentence, and (3) they cannot express the recursive nature of sentence productions.

Phrase structure grammars represent sentence productions as a tree. The root node is the sentence. The terminal nodes or leaves are words and intermediate nodes are phrases. A parser based on a PSG analyzes sentences by breaking structures into components that may be structures or terminals. A PSG grammar is recursive and can also represent and process context-dependent information.

To deal with the ambiguity issue, many current natural-language systems restrict the range of words and sentence structures the system understands, thus simplifying design and implementation.

10.7 EXERCISES

1. Modify CONVERT.PRO so that semicolons can be used in the body of sentences and question marks at the end.
2. Modify PARSE_4.PRO to process queries requiring extracting two fields. Specifically, make the modifications so the following query can be processed:

   Show me all the authors and titles of my books written prior to 1984.

3. Modify PARSE_4.PRO to add book records to the database.
4. Check the efficiency of PARSE_4.PRO and set cuts or redesign procedures where necessary.
5. Modify the PARSE_4.PRO tokenizing procedure to (a) trap words not found in the lexicon, (b) interrupt parsing to solicit from the user a syntactic category for these words, and (c) continue parsing either using or ignoring the words.
6. Modularize PARSE_4.PRO by separating program functions into four separate files. Use the parsing procedures as the basis for the master program, which includes both the tokenization and database processing files and opens and closes the book data file for accessing information requested by the user.
7. PARSE_4.PRO will crash if you enter two successive queries that the program cannot parse. Why? How can you modify the program to prevent this from occurring?
8. Using Backus-Naur form, define the grammar rules of PARSE_4.PRO.
9. Write a natural-language front end for the KBMS.PRO program in Chapter 8.

Appendix A
Supplements to Turbo Prolog

Borland International provides many supplemental programs for users of Turbo Prolog to study and integrate into their applications.

GEOBASE

The GEOBASE natural-language geography database program combines the two natural strengths of the Prolog language, that is, database representation and natural-language processing. GEOBASE is provided free when you purchase the Turbo Prolog package. It will be instructive for you to study this program, as it represents an interesting extension of some of the programming techniques used in Chapter 10 for the development of our natural-language program PARSE_4.

Another useful supplement (not free, however) is the Turbo Prolog Toolbox. This extensive collection of software tools and demonstration programs enables the developer to implement professional-looking useful functions in applications programs. Included are tools for development of screen layouts (data entry screens) and user interfaces (all types of menus); graphic representation of data in programs (bar and pie charts); communications protocols; importation of files from such well-known applications programs such as Lotus 1-2-3, Reflex, dBASE III, and Symphony; and a parser generator that automatically creates a compilable Turbo Prolog source code program from a grammar stated in BNF form.

The Toolbox is marketed by Borland International.

Using the GEOBASE Program. Copy GEOBASE.PRO, GEOBASE.INC, GEOBASE.HLP, and GEOBASE.DBA from the distribution disk into the directory where you keep your prolog source code programs. If you have a printer, it would be helpful if you produce hard copies of the files for reference as you study the program. However, you may not wish to print the rather lengthy GEOBASE.DBA file, as examples of each relation included in this file are provided in this appendix.

Enter Turbo Prolog, load, and compile GEOBASE.PRO. At the opening menu, select the `Load Database` option. If you get an error message, it is most likely that you have too little memory available for the program to add the database to RAM. If you have any "terminate and stay resident" programs (such as Sidekick) loaded in RAM, you will have to deinstall them before trying again. Spend some time familiarizing yourself with the menu system. Also try some of the queries listed here.

GEOBASE Functions. The GEOBASE program allows users to enter and receive answers to queries about geographic features of the United States. It provides information about states, rivers, and population.

- Area of the state in square kilometers
- Population of the state in citizens
- Capital of the state
- Which states border a given state
- Rivers in the state
- Cities in the state
- Highest and lowest point in the state in meters
- Length of rivers
- Population of the city in citizens

Here are some examples of the types of queries that GEOBASE is able to process.

- states
- give me the cities in california.
- what is the biggest city in california?
- what is the longest river in the usa?
- which rivers are longer than 1 thousand kilometers?
- what is the name of the state with the lowest point?
- which states border alabama?
- which rivers do not run through texas?
- which rivers run through states that border the state with the capital austin?

The GEOBASE Database. Eight types of geographic database relations are contained in GEOBASE.DBA. Examples of each are given here:

```
        STATE, ABBREV, CAPITAL, POPULAT, AREA, ADMIT, CITIES
state("alabama","al","montgomery",3894e3,51.7e3,22,"birmingham",
     "mobile","montgomery","huntsville")

        STATE, ABBREV, CITY, POPULATION
city("alabama","al","birmingham",284413)
```

```
          RIVER, LENGTH, STATES THROUGH WHICH IT FLOWS
river("mississippi",3778,["minnesota","wisconsin","iowa",
      "illinois","missouri","kentucky","tennessee","arkansas",
      "mississippi","louisiana","louisiana"])

          STATE, ABBREV, STATES WITH WHICH IT SHARES BORDERS
border("alabama","al",["tennessee","georgia","florida",
      "mississippi"])

          STATE, ABBREV, HIGH POINT, HEIGHT, LOW POINT, HEIGHT
highlow("alabama","al","cheaha mountain",734,"gulf of mexico",0)

          STATE, ABBREV, MOUNTAIN, HEIGHT
mountain("alaska","ak","mckinley",6194)

       ROUTE, STATES THROUGH WHICH ROUTE PASSES
road("95",["maine","new hampshire","rhode island","connecticut",
     "new york","new jersey","delaware","maryland","district of
       columbia","virginia","north carolina","south carolina",
      "georgia","florida"])

      LAKE, AREA, STATES THAT BORDER ON LAKE
lake("superior",82362,["michigan","wisconsin","minnesota"])
```

These relations represent the lowest level of GEOBASE. They represent the information that the rest of the program operates on to produce answers to queries about states, cities, rivers, mountains, major roads, and borders in the United States.

How GEOBASE Works. Load GEOBASE.INC and peruse the file in the editor as we trace GEOBASE's path of execution as it generates an answer to a query. This will give you a feel for the way all the parts of the program work together. After you have read the material that follows, you may wish to trace the program functions using some of your own queries.

GEOBASE begins with the goal `natlang()`, which produces the menu. If the user selects the `Query` option, `proces()` directs `readquery()` to prompt for and accept the user's query and then pass it on to `loop()`, where the real action begins. `scan()` tokenizes the query and returns a list of words to the `filter()` procedure, which performs punctuation and noise word disposal. The list is then passed to `pars()` for parsing. `pars()` uses the same difference list approach applied in the PARSE_4.PRO program presented in Chapter 9.

The parsing procedure `pars(List1,E,Q)` is invoked, with `List1` instantiated to the filtered word list. `E` and `Q` will return data from the parsing procedure. Try tracing this procedure with the query "How big is New York?"

You will observe that `List1` is instantiated to

```
["big","new","york"]
```

E is instantiated to

```
population
```

and Q is instantiated to

```
q_eaec("population","of","city","new york")
```

Note that in performing its duties, pars() will require assistance from other rules [s_attr(), s_minmax(), s_rest()] when parsing complex queries.

The findall() primitive then collects all the instances of

```
eval(q_eaec("population","of","city","new york"),ANSWER)
```

in the database. To do this, eval() uses db() to access the database. db() in turn calls state() for matching in the database and to return the population value. The one record that satisfies the match in the list collected by findall() returns the population of new york instantiated to ANSWER. Other facts, if any, accumulated by findall() are discarded.

What the parser has done is similar to what PARSE_4 did when the parse string was passed on to the appropriate process() rule for accessing of the database using a template that returned after matching the desired information.

Now try tracing some of your own queries. I have just scratched the surface of this instructive program. There remains much for you to discover.

The Turbo Prolog Toolbox

The Turbo Prolog Toolbox is an extensive set of development tools. These tools can be used to produce a wide variety of functions and effects. Many of these effects take programmers long hours to produce using conventional languages.

The comprehensive nature of the Toolbox demonstrates that the Borland people are interested in product support. The Toolbox does much to enhance the value of Turbo Prolog for software developers.

Two diskettes with program source code are accompanied by a manual covering all aspects of the use of these tools in application programs. Several demonstration programs are included to illustrate the use of the tools.

The 80-plus tools are divided into six categories, each of which is explained in a chapter in the manual. The manual also includes a reference guide to all the predicates that make up the tools. The reference guide describes the essential information on each tool: predicate declaration, flow pattern, function, legal parameters, and the environment required for use of the tool.

Chapter 2 discusses several menu tools that allow the programmer to use in programs all the types of menus that are currently in vogue in software: pop-up, pulldown, status line, multicolumn, long, scrolling, tree, and menus that disappear or remain active after the user has made a selection. Very professional effects can be achieved using these tools.

The programs in this book have been limited to the pop-up variety. Since I could not assume that you have access to the Toolbox, I resisted the temptation to include examples of these useful menus in the demonstration programs in this book. Those of you who purchase the Toolbox may wish to rewrite the programs so as to make use of alternative menus from the Toolbox. The use of these menus is quite straightforward, and you will have little difficulty in implementing them.

Chapter 3 covers the several screen layout tools included in the Toolbox. These tools enable the programmer to create slick data entry screens with and without protected fields. Virtual screens can also be created with the tools. A virtual screen can be of any size, though, only a monitor-sized portion can be viewed at any time.

Chapter 4 explains the graphics tools that are provided. Graphics functions can be implemented in standard and virtual screens. The IBM CGA and EGA are supported, but the Hercules monochrome graphics card is not for Version 1.xx users. The tools make it possible to draw point and line graphics. There are also tools to draw and fill with color a variety of geometric figures on screen.

The tools allow the programmer to use a variety of coordinates for drawing to the screen (e.g., virtual-screen, scaled, text, and actual coordinates referring to pixels produced by the hardware).

Using higher-level tools the programmer can implement pie charts and two- and three-dimensional bar charts in monochrome and color.

Chapter 5 discusses the communications tool predicates in the Toolbox. The first section of the chapter covers serial communications and includes several programs illustrating methods for using the predicates to build communications programs that enable the programmer to connect two PCs, to write terminal emulation programs so that a PC can be connected to a mini or mainframe system, and procedures for connecting to a Hayes-compatible modem. The next section covers modem communications programming using the tools.

Chapter 6 presents the tools used for importing data from database and spreadsheet programs (Reflex, dBASE III, Lotus 1-2-3, and Symphony). Helpful sample programs are included.

Chapter 7 covers the parser generator that comes with the Toolbox. This is a powerful tool that advanced programmers can use to develop a personalized computer language or compiler. Other versions of Prolog, using definite-clause-grammars (DCGs) can produce parsers from a user-defined grammar (see Marcus, 1986). The Toolbox parser generator adds equivalent DCG functionality to the Turbo Prolog dialect.

Appendix B
Comparing Turbo Prolog with Other Versions of Prolog

Marseilles Prolog

As mentioned earlier in this book, the Prolog language was first implemented in 1972 by Colmerauer and his colleagues of the *Groupe d'Intelligence Artificielle* in Marseilles, France. This first version of Prolog is known as Marseilles Prolog or M-Prolog. Interest in this new language quickly spread to universities in other countries, where the language underwent further development.

At Edinburgh University in Scotland, a slightly different version of Prolog was developed by David Warren for the DEC 10. A version of this DEC 10 Prolog, called Edinburgh Prolog, has evolved into the de facto standard for Prolog implementations throughout the world. The syntactic differences between the Marseilles and Edinburgh dialects are summarized in Table B.1. This table is based on material in an informative article on the Prolog language authored by Cohen and appearing in the December 1985 issue of *Communications for the ACM*. Students of Prolog will want to obtain a copy of this edition of the *Communications* as it also includes an interesting article by Alain Colmerauer, one of the original authors of the Prolog language.

As you can see from the table, syntax differences are relatively minor until you come to lists, where in the Marseilles version the empty list is explicitly represented by the symbol `nil`, the elements of the list are separated by periods rather than by commas, and the list constructor is conspicuously absent.

It was not long after the appearance of the microprocessor and the personal computer that versions of Prolog were developed to run within the limited resources of these machines. Developers of PC implementations have more or less based their syntax on the Edinburgh standard.

As we have seen, Turbo Prolog representation of rules and facts is consistent with the Edinburgh standard. However, Turbo Prolog departs from the standard

TABLE B.1 SUMMARY OF BASIC SYNTACTIC DIFFERENCES BETWEEN THE MARSEILLES AND EDINBURGH VERSIONS OF PROLOG

Variables	(M)	x	a	x'*	x1*
	(E)	X	A	Xprime	X1†
Constants	(M)	123	abc‡		
	(E)	123	abc		
Rules	(M)	a ⟶ b c;		a ⟶ ;	
	(E)	a :- b, c.		a.	
Lists	(M)	a.b.x.nil		x.y	
	(E)	[a,b,X]		[X¦Y]	

*Single letters followed by a prime or by digits.
†Identifiers starting with an uppercase letter.
‡Integers or a sequence having more than two letters.

Table B.1 reprinted with permission of Jacques Cohen and ACM. *Communications of the ACM*, Vol. 28, No. 12, December 1985.

in important ways. For one thing, it is strongly typed, whereas the others are not. This difference brings with it both advantages and disadvantages.

The advantages are that when using Turbo Prolog, compilation is very rapid, and efficient fast-running code is generated. Speed of compilation can be important to a software developer, who must compile and recompile programs many times during coding and debugging. Turbo Prolog generally runs much faster on several benchmarks than other micro-based Prologs (Shafer, 1987). Typing helps make this possible since the compiler can do a lot of strict error checking that is not possible in untyped systems. Strong typing can also be a benefit in applications where Turbo Prolog is used in developing a natural-language front end to a relational database system as it helps the programmer enforce the relational requirement that all columns in records be of the same domain.

The disadvantages to strong typing are that untyped systems allow the programmer to use predicates that can accept all data types as arguments. In fact, Edinburgh system predicates may accept rules as parameters. And the strong typing constraints of the Turbo Prolog compiler limit the programmer in executing certain kinds of symbolic programming. This is a problem that the programmer can sometimes, but not always, get around.

If you find that you cannot get the job done using Turbo Prolog, you are probably writing larger and more powerful programs requiring use of metalevel symbolic functions and the full expressive power of the standard Prolog. Since the code you have written in Turbo Prolog (sans declarations) is based on the Edinburgh syntax, you will in many cases be able to port your programs over to a full-blown Prolog Edinburgh implementation. Some difficulties will arise, however, with the use of the Turbo Prolog = operator as it means quite different things in Turbo Prolog and in Edinburgh implementations.

Use Turbo Prolog where it excels (rapid development of small to medium-sized programs), but don't hesitate to switch where desirable to a more powerful, full-featured Edinburgh version. A ready and able candidate to fill this role on the PC is the Arity Prolog system.

Arity Prolog

Arity Prolog is a superset of the C&M Standard Prolog. The Arity people have added several powerful features to what one expects to find in a standard C&M implementation. Arity Prolog was originally implemented as an interpreted language, but a compiler is now also available.

The Arity Corporation, based in Concord, Massachusetts, offers two Prolog packages. One package includes an interpreter at a price of under $100—no doubt designed to compete with Turbo Prolog. Another package offers both an interpreter and a compiler with a nice interface. Arity also offers support tools for development of expert systems and SQL-based database systems.

By offering both compiler and interpreter, Arity makes it easy for programmers to develop programs incrementally, first using the interpreter and then, after component modules are fully debugged, compiling them for maximum efficiency.

Advanced features of the Arity version of Prolog include a virtual database of up to 1 gigabyte in size. The virtual database feature makes it feasible to develop very large applications. In a virtual database system, hard disk storage is treated as an extension to RAM, and when a program occupies all available space in RAM, the system automatically uses disk space. All this is transparent to the user.

Backtracking through megabytes of data stored on disk would be unduly time-consuming, so Arity provides a partitioning scheme called Worlds. This allows the programmer to use virtual memory without sacrificing efficiency. The Arity system also has built-ins for implementing b-trees and hashing for use in databases.

The full complement of standard primitives are found in the Arity implementation. Arity supports floating-point arithmetic. In comparison, Turbo Prolog lacks some of the useful and at times essential predicates, such as `op()`, used to define new operators for the system and which can help to make programs much more readable; `functor()`, which returns a structure's name and arity; `arg()` used to unify a variable with the nth argument of a structure; and `clause()`, which returns the goals associated with the head of a given rule.

A further difference worth noting is the use of `=` in the Arity and Borland versions of Prolog. In Arity Prolog, `=` is used by the programmer to unify terms. In Turbo Prolog, `=` is a synonym for the evaluable `is` predicate in Edinburgh Prolog. Porting programs using `=` between Edinburgh and Turbo Prolog implementations may require some serious reprogramming to circumvent this difference.

Arity is weakly typed, and any manner of Prolog object (or mixture of objects) can be used as arguments in clauses. The Arity implementation is robust and provides the programmer with the full expressive power of Prolog along with the efficiency of compilation. However, on most benchmarks for current versions, Turbo Prolog outclasses Arity in speed of execution (Shafer, 1987).

For teaching, learning, ease of development of small to moderate-sized programs, and low cost, Turbo Prolog is a good choice. For development of larger programs where the full power of the standard Prolog language is needed and cost is less a factor, Arity Prolog is a better choice.

The Arity implementation is covered in detail in the well-written and fully documented manuals that accompany the system. A book on Prolog written by Claudia Marcus (1986) of the Arity Corporation features a section devoted to the details of the Arity implementation. Arity Prolog is reviewed along with 13 other Prolog implementations (including Turbo Prolog) in the June 1987 edition of *AI Expert* magazine. Arity Prolog runs on the IBM PC, XT, AT, and compatibles.

micro-PROLOG

The Imperial College in London was the locus for the development of a venerable Prolog interpreter called micro-PROLOG. The micro-PROLOG program is documented in detail in the quite readable manual and an authoritative book that accompany the product. The book, *micro-PROLOG: Programming in Logic*, was written by the implementers K. L. Clark and F. G. McCabe and includes contributions from a distinguished list of Prolog experts. The book introduces the user to a variety of Prolog programming applications and issues as well as details of the specific features of this unique implementation.

The syntax used by the micro-PROLOG command interpreter (called the Supervisor) is the list, giving programs a LISP-like appearance. The Supervisor is extensible, and users can add modules to enhance its functions. One of these modules is a front end called Simple that permits the user to interact with the Supervisor using a bounce-bar menu interface and commands expressed in either a "sugared" English-like syntax or a more standard prefix syntax. Micro is another front-end option that also has menus but supports infix syntax where the predicate is nested between arguments rather than preceding them as is the case in the prefix syntax we are used to.

Let's look at the infix syntax more closely. To add facts to the database, the user employs the built-in predicate `add(X)`, with the argument `X` being a fact stated in infix form. In the case of unary relations, the predicate follows the argument (this is postfix syntax).

```
     ARG1       RELATION  ARG2
&.add(Katherine mother-of Mary)
&.add(Henry father-of Elizabeth2)
      ARG1  RELATION
&.add(Henry male)
&.add(Katherine female)
```

Several books and articles cover the contributions of other members of the Imperial College group to the application of Prolog to a variety of domains. Robert

Kowalski, the head of the Logic Programming Group, is one of the intellectual founding fathers in the logic programming field, and his book *Logic for Problem Solving* (1979) is required reading for anyone interested in this discipline. Other works by Kowalski explore applications of logic to computation in education (1982), and database technology (1981). Richard Ennals has written extensively on the use of micro-Prolog in educational settings (Ennals, 1982, 1985). Frank Kriwaczek (1982), another member of the Imperial College group, has explored applications of Prolog to business systems, and especially decision support systems.

An expert system shell called APES (Augmented Programming for Expert Systems) can also be added to the Supervisor. This product is marketed separately and requires micro-PROLOG to execute. APES is a collection of some 60 modules that, when added to micro-PROLOG, facilitate the rapid interactive development of sophisticated logic-based programs. APES permits users with minimal programming experience to develop programs with advanced features such as explanation and query-the-user facilities. The documentation provided with APES is a bit on the skimpy side. A chapter written by P. Hammond appearing in the book by Clark and McCabe (1984) discusses the conceptual underpinnings of APES.

A third front-end module called DEC is for the user with a background in Edinburgh Prolog. Consistently austere, DEC does not provide a menu-driven interface. Other modules that can be added to the Supervisor provide editing services and support for tracing and debugging. The speed of execution is adequate for the smaller programs I have run. The program offers cursor positioning support; however, Ansi.sys support is required.

micro-PROLOG is marketed outside the United States by Logic Programming Associates for the IBM PC. A compiler called Mac-PROLOG is available for the Apple Macintosh. All U.S. marketing is handled by Programming Logic Systems of Milford, Connecticut.

Prolog/i

Chalcedony Software of La Jolla, California, has recently upgraded and enhanced its interpreted version of Prolog called Prolog-V and renamed it Prolog/i. Prolog/i supports the C&M standard along with floating-point arithmetic, excellent tracing and debugging facilities, provision for memory management, editing (Wordstar-like), execution of DOS commands from within the interpreter, and calling of coresident programs that can process and return data to Prolog/i. Programs run quite briskly in Prolog/i. Programs written in Prolog/i can use all available memory up to the DOS limit of 640K.

Chalcedony markets a utility package containing over 50 useful productivity predicates that can be integrated into user programs. The Toybox is a similar adjunct product containing puzzles and mindteasers written by an academician to help students in mastering Prolog. The people who write Chalcedony's documentation know what they are doing, and the manuals include an exceptionally well done tutorial on Prolog. Prolog/i is a good low-cost alternative to Turbo Prolog. Prolog/m runs on the Apple Macintosh.

Appendix C
Future Directions for Prolog

I will attempt to point out some of the research issues that will shape the future development of the Prolog computer language. As these issues are deeply rooted in logic and computational theory, any extensive discussion of them is well beyond the scope of this book. However, I will indicate sources where additional information can be found.

Syntax

Some experts believe that Prolog's syntax is confusing and could benefit from modifications (Fogelholm, 1984). For example, commas and periods have multiple meanings in Prolog. The comma can serve as a delimiter to separate arguments, but it can also separate subgoals in the body of a rule, where its meaning is equivalent to the logical AND. Some suggest the use of two commas , , to separate subgoals. Ambiguity can arise in the use of periods as well. Periods signal the end of clauses in the Edinburgh syntax; they are used as list predicates in the Marseilles syntax.

Other writers have suggested more fundamental changes to Prolog, including changes to the unification algorithm so as to handle with greater effectiveness Prolog's affinity for looping (Colmerauer, 1982).

Several interesting extensions to Prolog are currently being explored by researchers to enhance the functionality and efficiency of the language (Cohen, 1985; Campbell, 1984). Among these extensions are applications of Prolog to parallel processing.

Parallel Processing and Prolog

Computer scientists are constantly exploring new ways to increase the speed of computers. The many technological advances of the past several years have produced microprocessors with the capability of executing up to 5 million instructions per second (5 MIPS). There is even talk of pushing chips to a mind-boggling 30 MIPS in the next few years. Impressive as these figures are, they may still be inadequate for many future AI applications.

The Japanese are addressing this issue in their ICOT fifth-generation computer project. The fifth-generation goal is to develop a machine that can compute solutions to problems by using many processors acting in concert on components of complex problems. Parallel processing architectures for the machines of the future offer the promise of speeds measured in hundreds of millions of MIPS and millions of logical inferences per second (LIPS).

The Japanese selection of Prolog as the core language for their fifth-generation project has stimulated a good deal of interest in the potential of this language for parallel computing. Today many research labs are exploring the strengths and limitations of logic programming and extensions to Prolog in multiprocessor approaches to AI computing (see Stolfo & Miranker in The Annual Review of Computer Science, 1987; Kluzniak & Szpakowicz, 1984; Monteiro, (1984); Wise, 1987).

The structure of a Prolog program lends itself to parallel interpretation. A Prolog program consists of many rules that are evaluated sequentially during program execution. Parallel processing of Prolog programs would permit concurrent evaluation of rules, conditions to rules, and perhaps the unification procedure itself.

However, a complication for parallel processing arises from the fact that conjunctive conditions may share variables (this is called AND parallelism). In this instance, variables occurring in later conditions in a rule have to wait for values to be established by searches conducted in evaluating earlier conditions. In cases where multiple processors attempt to prove goals simultaneously, there remains the difficult problem of how to efficiently pass information regarding instantiations between processors. One candidate for information passing between processors would be the standard Prolog I/O facilities. However, this method presents its own problems of efficiency. Significant savings in processing overhead would result if unification could be performed using multiple processors operating concurrently.

In rules with disjunctive conditions (OR parallelism), parallel processing may be executed with less difficulty as only one condition need succeed and disjunctive conditions do not have variables that share values.

Monotonicity

Another problem occupying researchers concerns the monotonicity of predicate logic and Prolog. Monotonic inference is based in the assumption that if a sentence `S` (a wff in predicate logic or a fact in Prolog) is a logical consequence of a collection of sentences `A`, then it follows that `S` must also be a logical consequence of a larger set of sentences that includes `A`. Once facts are proved true in a Prolog program, new facts that are added during execution of the program cannot change the truth value of the existing facts.

The realities of everyday inferencing are that humans reason all the time, taking into account new information that may cause changes in the truth values of existing facts. This is called nonmonotonic reasoning and is illustrated in a simple example given by John McCarthy (1977):

> If you know I have a car, you may conclude you can ask me for a ride home. If I tell you the car is in the shop, you may conclude that you can't ask me for a ride. If I tell you it will be out of the shop in 2 hours, you may conclude you can ask me.

Here the conclusion you can draw about asking for a ride changes with each new piece of information that is given to you.

Take another example:

> All birds fly.
>
> Tweety is a bird.
>
> therefore:
>
> Tweety can fly.

Let's say now we discover new information that penguins and ostriches are birds but that neither can fly. Now we must represent the information that all birds fly unless the bird in question is an ostrich or a penguin. A rule for which there are such exceptions is not purely deductive and is called a default or defeasible rule.

An approach to the problem of adapting logic to inferencing where new information creates exceptions to old information is being taken by Donald Knuth at the Advanced Computational Methods Center at the University of Georgia. Knuth is offering d-Prolog, which runs on top of Arity Prolog or Prolog-1 and supports nonmonotonic reasoning using defeasible rules, presumptions, and defeaters. The ACMC also offers a list of reprints of many Prolog-related studies conducted over the past several years. It may be obtained by writing to the center.

Glossary

Algorithm A completely specified set of programmer-defined instructions to the computer as to how to perform step-by-step processing of data to assure the correctness of a result.

Argument The arguments of a function or a predicate follow the function or relation (predicate) name. A single argument of a relation is enclosed within parentheses and denotes an attribute of that relation. Multiple arguments of a relation are separated by commas. Multiple arguments of a relation denote the objects or events of a domain for which the relation is assumed to hold true.

Artificial intelligence A controversial term first proposed by John McCarthy in the 1950s to describe the general study, development, and implementation of intelligent human-like functions in nonbiological systems.

Atom An individual object in Prolog that is not reducible to component objects. For example, the constant names "john" and "mary" are not reducible to component atoms, whereas the relation `likes(john,mary)` is reducible to a predicate name and two constants.

Axiom A self-evident proposition accepted without proof as being true.

Backtracking When the user enters a query (goal) into a Prolog program, the system attempts to unify the query with a fact or head of a rule in the knowledge base. If the query is unified with the head of a rule, the conditions of that rule (along with instantiated variables) become subgoals that are added to the front of the proof list. If the system fails to find a match for one of these subgoals the system backtracks to the last successful match and, after undoing any instantiations, continues searching for another match for the query lower down in the knowledge base.

Bound variable A variable that has acquired a value during program execution through unification with a term. The variable is then said to be bound to the term.

Breadth-first search A search strategy where all the nodes of a tree are examined at each level before moving down to examine nodes at the next lower level. This strategy will find the optimal solution if one in fact exists.

Certainty factor A numeric value assigned to a rule or fact to reflect the degree of confidence placed in that rule or fact. The certainty (or confidence factor) is not to be confused with probability.

Cognitive science An interdisciplinary science that includes investigators from psychology, mathematics, linguistics, computer science, and other disciplines interested in the study of human processes of perception, thinking, reasoning and problem solving, learning and remembering, language, and general symbolic behaviors. Cognitive scientists often use the computer as an important tool in their research to simulate and study models of these processes. The cognitive psychologist is likely to use the computer to study and evaluate models of human processes, whereas the computer scientist is more likely to be interested in using knowledge about human processes to build smarter and better computer systems.

Combinatorial explosion The proliferation of choices that occurs in problems requiring resolution search strategies. Take a chess game as an example. It has been estimated that there are upwards of 10^{120} choices possible in a typical chess game. If you have 20 options for your first move and your opponent also has 20, this creates a space of 400 (20×20) possibilities. There are over 50,000 moves possible after the second pair of moves. A typical chess game may total 80 single moves, so you can see how the search space can reach staggering proportions and why a "brute force" search strategy for "best" moves is not feasible and heuristics are employed to prune the search tree.

Conflict resolution Triggering rules in the inference engine that decide the precedence order for execution of candidate rules. Such a rule might state "If more than one rule is selected, then execute them in the order of their frequency of past use." That is, the rules that are used by the system frequently in solving problems earn a higher priority in the system.

Data models In database systems, three data models are most often employed. The network model employs a structure where an *n*-to-*n* relation can hold between data elements. In the tree model, the data is hierarchically arranged so that each element is related to only one element above it and to *n* data elements below it. In the relational model, a database is organized as a collection of normalized relations in a two-dimensional table.

Debugging The art (some claim it is a black art) and science of finding and removing syntactic and logical errors from Prolog program code to enable it to perform as expected.

Declarative versus procedural knowledge representation Knowledge is represented declaratively by stating the facts and rules that hold for a domain. Declarative representation stresses what is known to be true of a domain. Procedural representation stresses how to do things in a domain expressed in program procedures.

Deductive reasoning The inferential processes by which knowledge structures held in storage are manipulated to arrive at true conclusions. If the knowledge structures are true, then conclusions drawn deductively from these premises are absolute and certain.

Default value A value needed by a program that is assumed and used by the system in the absence of static or dynamic assertion or user-provided information.

Demon A function that is automatically invoked when some current program value is changed or a new one is needed by the system.

Depth-first search In contrast to a breadth-first search, a depth-first strategy attempts complete proof of one rule (and the rules below it in the tree) before attempting proofs of other rules at the same level in the hierarchy.

Explanation module A component of an expert system that offers the user explanations for program behavior. Typically this module provides how and why explanations. A how explanation offers information on what is expected from the user as the interactive program solicits input. A why explanation provides information on program inferencing and decision-making behaviors at interactive junctures.

First-order predicate logic Logic in which variables may be used in formulas to represent objects in a domain. Propositional logic, which does not allow use of variables, is a zero-order logic. Principles of FOPL are employed in Prolog for representing knowledge and inferencing.

First principle (deep knowledge) Abstract theoretical knowledge as opposed to empirically based surface facts and heuristics.

Frame A knowledge representation method useful for expressing a frame of reference with regard to an object, situation, or event. The frame is made up of a variable number of slots that contain information related to the frame object. These slots may point to other frames and exchange information with them in an inheritance hierarchy.

Free variable A variable that is not unified with a term.

Fuzzy logic An approach to approximate reasoning in which possibilistic rather than probabilistic quantifiers and truth values are associated with propositions. This allows programs to process knowledge using propositions associated with degrees of truth and using fuzzy linguistic labels (e.g., "sometimes," "most," "few," "tall," "very").

Graph A representation of knowledge in which objects and events are shown as nodes while their properties and relations are shown as arcs (labeled edges) connecting pairs of nodes. In a digraph, the arcs denote direction.

Ground term A term that contains no free variables.

Hashing A method for speeding up searches for information in a database. In hashing, the unique key field in each record is processed by some arbitrary algorithm in order to calculate a new value (address or index), which represents the records location.

Heuristic Knowledge, experience, and expertise represented as what are sometimes called in everyday life "rules of thumb." Heuristics are commonly employed by human experts as a part of the problem-solving process. Though helpful in reducing the search space, heuristics do not guarantee that a solution will be achieved. In some problems, heuristics are the only feasible approach to dealing with inordinately large search spaces. For example, after years of research by mathematicians, no completely satisfactory algorithm exists for solving the "traveling salesman" problem, and heuristics become necessary as the number of cities to be visited increases and brute force searches consume increasing amounts of time.

Horn clause Logic clauses in which atomic formulas are connected by `or` with at most one positive proposition. In Prolog, Horn clauses take the form of rules that express the conditional relationships of a knowledge domain. The head of the Prolog rule contains a goal expressed as a single unnegated literal. The body of the rule contains a conjunction of literals representing the conditions for proving the goal.

Inductive reasoning In inductive reasoning, conclusions are typically expressed in terms of probabilities based on past experiences and what is perceived as the most likely choice among alternatives rather than on formalized rules of syllogistic reasoning.

Inference In Prolog, rules (e.g., `will_pass(Student,Subject) :- studies(Student,Subject)`), facts (`studies(john,math)`), and the backward-chaining inference procedure (based on the resolution inference rule) results in the derivation of new facts (`will_pass(john,math)`).

Inference engine The component of an expert or knowledge-based program that contains the problem-solving mechanism. The inference engine also directs searches for rules and facts in the database and determines when a solution has been achieved.

Inheritance hierarchy A feature of frames and semantic net formalisms in which knowledge is represented in a hierarchical structure and nodes lower in the hierarchy acquire attribute values of the nodes higher in the hierarchy. If it is known that mammals have hair and that a dog is a mammal, then an individual dog will inherit the attribute "hair" through the inheritance mechanism without the need to represent this information redundantly at the subordinate level.

Instantiation The process of binding variables to terms (i.e., variables, constants, and compound terms).

Iteration The repetition of a series of instructions until some criterion is met. A loop structure with a counter incremented at each pass through the loop is an iterative process.

Key A unique field within a record that is used to locate that record.

Knowledge acquisition The process of soliciting and acquiring knowledge from domain experts and other sources of information in a form that can then be represented in an expert or knowledge-based system.

Knowledge engineering A new field in which practitioners specialize in the acquisition and representation of knowledge and the design and implementation of knowledge-based software using this knowledge for solving problems usually handled by human experts.

Knowledge representation The complex process of encoding and storing knowledge in knowledge-based systems in a form that can be used for reasoning in the search for and generation of solutions to problems. Semantic nets, frames, production rules, procedures, scripts, and logic clauses are some of the conceptual structures used by knowledge engineers in designing knowledge-based systems.

Negation by failure Logic-based systems such as Prolog operate on the "closed world" assumption. This means that Prolog will respond with `no` to all queries for which there are no supporting facts and rules in the knowledge base.

Node A point of convergence in a graph or tree. Nodes can contain information about objects, events, and paths.

Nondeterminism Deterministic systems can produce but one solution. Nondeterministic systems such as Prolog can deduce as many solutions as can be found to satisfy the conditions of a query.

Nonmonotonic A monotonic system does not permit values or conclusions to change during the consultation cycle. Nonmonotonic systems do permit values and conclusions to change as information is added during a consultation cycle; however, this requires more sophisticated inferencing strategies. First-order logic and Turbo Prolog are monotonic systems.

Parallel architecture A plan for future computer systems to execute many programs, or portions of a program, simultaneously rather than sequentially as they do today. This will make possible more rapid and efficient problem solving. This concept, however, will require major changes in software as well as hardware, (multiple cooperating processors). PROLOG lends itself to this method of computing and is one reason for the Japanese selection of PROLOG as the core language of their ICOT project.

Predicate The sense of a relation that holds among entities (arguments) in a domain. The predicate name is chosen to express this relation. The fact `like`____ `each_other(john,mary)` expresses the mutual liking relation that exists between the two entities (arguments) `john` and `mary`.

Primitive A built-in predicate defined by the designers of the system.

Recursion The defining of an operation in terms of itself. A recursive procedure must execute a copy of itself as a part of the proof process.

Resolution Principle An inferencing principle first articulated by J. A. Robinson in 1965 that forms the basis for the method used by Prolog for solving queries. The method of proving that an assertion is true by showing that a contradiction is encountered whenever one resolves clauses that include the negation of the assertion.

Run-time The period of the execution of the program.

Script A knowledge representation formalism developed by R. Schank and his associates at the Yale AI laboratory. Scripts are particularly useful in representing knowledge as sequences of events and in providing missing information or contextual background for natural-language processing applications. For example, a restaurant script represents going to a restaurant as the sequence of events of entering a restaurant, sitting at a table, ordering food, eating the food, paying the bill, and leaving the restaurant.

Search space The set of all possible conditions or states generated by the interaction of elements of a problem and the operators acting on the elements. The elements of a chess space are the 64 squares and the pieces that are employed. The operations are the rules for moving the pieces in the squares.

Semantic network A formalism (graph) in which knowledge is declaratively represented as a collection of nodes. The nodes are connected by arcs, which denote the relations that obtain for the information held in the nodes.

Semantics The sense or meaning of a proposition or expression. Semantics is often contrasted with syntax, which deals with the structural aspects of propositions.

Shell A program that assists in the development of another program. An expert system shell, for example, typically has built-in mechanisms for easing the development burdens associated with implementing the user interface, knowledge acquisition, knowledge representation, inferencing, and explanation modules.

Source code The program as it is written and understood by the programmer before it is converted by a compiler or an interpreter to a form the machine understands.

Stack A portion of the computer's memory that is used to store temporary information about program functions. The inferencing method used by Prolog makes use of a stack to keep records of the program's tracking behavior.

Syntax The rules that govern the structure of a language such as English or Prolog.

Term Any Prolog data object. Prolog terms include variables, constants, and compound terms (a predicate together with its terms).

Theorem A proposition to be proved against a set of premises.

Top-down reasoning A strategy in which problem solving and analysis proceed from the whole to the component parts.

Tree A graph data structure in which there is only one path between two nodes.

Unification The process of making two atoms equal; the matching of terms in the search for substitutions for variables to provide concrete answers for queries.

Variable In Prolog, a variable is a term that can be unified with another term. Anonymous variables are used when the values of instantiated terms are not to be reported. Free variables have not yet been unified with other terms. Bound variables have unified with terms and carry the value of those terms.

Variable quantification In the predicate logic, variables may be existentially or universally quantified. That is, a variable that is universally quantified may stand for any member of the domain of interpretation ("For all X, Y is true"). An existentially quantified variable may stand for at least one member of the domain of interpretation ("There is at least one X for which Y is true").

Virtual In computer jargon something is said to be "virtual" if it appears to be exist but in fact does not. (Conversely, something is said to be "transparent" if it exists but does not appear to be so to the user.) Virtual memory employs static memory to make the computer behave as if it has more RAM. Similarly, virtual database uses static storage as if it were RAM.

Bibliography

ALLEN, J. (1987), *Natural Language Understanding*. Menlo Park, Calif.: Benjamin/Cummings.

AMSBURY, W. (1985), *Data Structures: From Arrays to Priority Queues*. Belmont, Calif.: Wadsworth.

BRATKO, I. (1986), *Programming for Artificial Intelligence*. Reading, Mass.: Addison-Wesley.

BRODIE, M. L. and MYLOPOULOS, J., EDS. (1986), *On Knowledge Base Management Systems*. New York: Springer-Verlag.

BOOLE, G. (1854), *Investigations of the laws of thought*.

BUCHANAN, B. G. and SHORTLIFFE, E. H., EDS. (1984), *Rule-Based Expert Systems: The Mycin Experiments of the Stanford Heuristic Programming Project*. Reading, Mass.: Addison-Wesley.

CAMPBELL, J. A., ED. (1984), *Implementations of Prolog*. Chichester, England: Ellis-Horwood Ltd.

CERCONE, N. and MCCALLA, G., EDS. (1987), *The Knowledge Frontier: Essays in the Representation of Knowledge*. New York: Springer-Verlag.

CHOMSKY, N. (1957), *Syntactic Structures*. The Hague: Mouton.

CLANCEY, W. J. and SHORTLIFFE, E. H., EDS. (1984), *Readings in Medical Artificial Intelligence*. Reading, Mass.: Addison-Wesley.

CLARK, K. L. and MCCABE, F. G. (1984), *micro-PROLOG: Programming in Logic*. Englewood Cliffs, N. J.: Prentice Hall.

CLARK, K. L. and TARNLUND, S. A., EDS. (1982), *Logic Programming*. London: Academic Press.

CLOCKSIN, W. F. and MELLISH, C. S., (1984), *Programming in Prolog*. Berlin: Springer-Verlag.

CODD, E. F. (1970), "A Relational Model for Large Shared Data Banks," in *Communications of the ACM,* 13, no. 6.

COHEN, J. (1985), "Describing Prolog by Its Intrepretation and Compilation," in *Communications of the ACM,* 28, no. 12.

COLMERAUER, A. (1982), "Prolog and Infinite Trees," in *Logic Programming*. K. L. Clark and S. A. Tarnlund eds. London: Academic Press.

COVINGTON, M. A. (1986), "Expressing Procedural Algorithms in Prolog," Research Report 01-0012, Athens: Advanced Computational Methods Center, University of Georgia.

COVINGTON, M. A., NUTE, D., and VELLINO, A., (1988), *Prolog Programming in Depth*. Glenview, Ill.: Scott, Foresman, & Co.

CUADRADO, J. L. and CUADRADO, L. Y. (1986), "AI in Computer Vision," in *Byte Magazine,* January.

DATE, C. J. (1983), *Database: A Primer.* Reading, Mass.: Addison-Wesley.

DREYFUS, H. L. and DREYFUS, S. E. (1986), *Mind Over Machine: The Power of Human Intuition and Expertise in the Era of the Computer.* New York: The Free Press.

DYM, C. L. and MITTAL, S. (1985), "Knowledge Acquisition from Multiple Experts," in *AI Magazine,* 7, no. 2.

ENNALS, J. R. (1983), *Beginning micro-PROLOG.* New York: Harper & Row.

——— . (1985), *Artificial Intelligence: Applications to Logical Reasoning and Historical Research.* New York: Halstead Press.

EVANSON, S. (1988), "How to Talk to an Expert," in *AI Expert,* February.

FEIGENBAUM, E. A. and MCCORDUCK, P. (1983, 1984), *The Fifth Generation: Artificial Intelligence and Japan's Computer Challenge to the World.* New York: New American Library (Signet).

FISCHLER, M. A. and FIRSCHEIN, O. (1987), *Intelligence: The Eye, the Brain, and the Computer.* Reading, Mass.: Addison-Wesley.

FLOYD, M. (1988), "Suitable for Framing," in *Turbo Technix,* 1, no. 3.

FOGELHOLM, R. (1984), "Exeter Prolog—Some Thoughts on Prolog Design." *Implementations of Prolog.* J. A. Cambell (ed.) West Sussex, England: Ellis Horwood.

FREGE, G. (1879), *Begriffschrift eine der Arithmetischen Nachgebildte Formelsprache des reinen Denken.* Halle, East Germany: Louis Nebert.

GAMMACK, J. G. and YOUNG, R. M. (1985), "Psychological Techniques for Eliciting Expert Knowledge," in *Research and Development in Expert Systems,* ed. M. A. Bramer. Cambridge, England: Cambridge University Press.

GARNHAM, A. (1985), *Psycholinguistics: Central Topics.* London: Methuen.

GEORGE, F. H. (1977), *Precision, Language, and Logic.* Oxford, England: Pergamon Press.

GIANNESINI, F., KANOUI, H., PASERO, R., and VAN CANEGHEM, M., (1986), *Prolog.* Reading, Mass.: Addison-Wesley.

GINSBERG, M. L., ED. (1987), *Readings in Nonmonotonic Reasoning.* Los Altos, Calif.: Morgan Kaufman.

HARMON, P. and KING, D. (1985), *Expert Systems: Artificial Intelligence in Business.* New York: John Wiley & Sons.

HARRIS, M. D. (1985), *Introduction to Natural Language Processing.* Reston, Va.: Reston.

HARRIS, Z. S. (1951), *Methods in Structural Linguistics.* Chicago: University of Chicago Press.

HART, A. (1986), *Knowledge Acquisition for Expert Systems.* New York: McGraw-Hill Book Company.

HAYES-ROTH, F., WATERMAN, D. A., and LENAT, D. B., EDS. (1983), *Building Expert Systems.* Reading, Mass.: Addison-Wesley.

HOFFMAN, R. R. (1987), "The Problem of Extracting the Knowledge of Experts," in *AI Magazine,* 8, no. 2.

HOGGER, C. J. (1984), *Introduction to Logic Programming.* London: Academic Press.

HOLLOWAY, C. A. (1979), *Decision Making Under Uncertainty: Models and Choices.* Englewood Cliffs, N. J.: Prentice Hall.

HUNT, V. D. (1986), *Artificial Intelligence and Expert Systems Sourcebook.* New York: Chapman and Hall.

KELLY, G. A. (1955), *The Psychology of Personal Constructs.* New York: Norton.

KERSCHBERG, L., ED. (1986), *Expert Database Systems: Proceedings from the First International Workshop.* Menlo Park, Calif.: Benjamin/Cummings.

KIDD, A. L., ED. (1987), *Knowledge Acquisition for Expert Systems.* New York: Plenum Press.

KLUZNIAK, F. and SZPAKOWICZ, S. (1985), *Prolog for Programmers.* London: Academic Press.

KOWALSKI, R. (1979), *Logic for Problem Solving.* New York: North-Holland.

———. (1981), "Logic as a Database Language," Department of Computing, London: Imperial College.

———. (1982), "Logic as a Computer Language for Children," in M. Yazdani, ED., *New Horizons in Educational Computing.* New York: Halstead Press.

———. (1985), "Logic Programming," in *Byte Magazine,* August.

———. (1988), "The Early Years of Logic Programming," in *Communications of the ACM,* 31, no. 1, January.

KRIWACZEK, F. R. (1982), "Some Applications of PROLOG to Decision Support Systems." M.Sc. thesis, Department of Computing, London: Imperial College.

LENHERT, W. G. and RINGLE, M. H. (1982), *Strategies for Natural Language Processing.* Hillsdale, N. J.: Lawrence Erlbaum Associates.

MAIER, D. and WARREN, D. S. (1988), *Computing with Logic: Logic Programming with Prolog.* Menlo Park, Calif.: Benjamin/Cummings.

MARCUS, C. (1986), *Prolog Programming: Applications for Database Systems, Expert Systems, and Natural Language Systems.* Reading, Mass.: Addison-Wesley.

MARTIN, J. (1977), *Computer Data-Base Organization.* Englewood Cliffs, N. J.: Prentice Hall.

MCCARTHY, J. (1977), "Epistemological Problems of Artificial Intelligence." in *Proc. IJCAI-77.* Cambridge, Mass. pp. 1038–44.

MCCORDUCK, P. (1979), *Machines Who Think.* San Francisco: W. H. Freeman.

MCDERMOTT, J. (1981), "R1's formative years," in *AI Magazine,* 2, no. 2.

MCGRAW, K. L. and SEALE, M. R. (1988), "Knowledge Elicitation with Multiple Experts: Considerations and Techniques," in *Artificial Intelligence Review,* Oxford: Blackwell Scientific Publications.

MILLER, G. A. (1984), "Informavores," in *The Study of Information: Interdisciplinary Messages,* ed. F. Machlup and U. Mansfield. New York: Wiley.

MINSKY, M. (1975), "A Framework for Representing Knowledge," in *The Psychology of Computer Vision,* ed. P. H. Winston, New York: McGraw-Hill Book Company.

MINSKY, M. (1987), *The Society of Minds.* New York: Simon and Schuster.

MONTEIRO, L. (1984), "A Proposal for Distributed Programming in Logic," in J. A. Cambell, ED. *Implementations of Prolog,* West Sussex, England: Ellis Horwood.

NEGOITA, C. V. (1985), *Expert Systems and Fuzzy Systems.* Menlo Park, Calif.: Benjamin/Cummings.

PAPERT, S. (1980), *Mindstorms: Children, Computers, and Powerful Ideas.* New York: Basic Books.

PEARLE, J. (1984), *Heuristics: Intelligent Search Strategies for Computer Problem Solving.* Reading, Mass.: Addison-Wesley.

PRERAU, D. S. (1987), "Knowledge Acquisition in Expert Systems," in *AI Magazine,* 8, no. 2.

QUILLIAN, M. R. (1968) "Semantic memory," in *Semantic Information Processing.* ed., M. Minsky, Cambridge, Mass.: MIT Press.

ROBINSON, J. A. (1965), "A Machine-Oriented Logic Based on the Resolution Principle," in *Journal of the ACM,* 12, pp. 23–41.

ROCKART, J. F. and BULLEN, C. V., EDS., (1986), *The Rise of Managerial Computing: The Best of the Center for Information Systems Research, Sloan School of Management, MIT.* Homewood, Ill.: Dow Jones-Irwin.

ROLANDI, W. G. (1986), "Knowledge Engineering in Practice," in *AI Expert Magazine,* December. San Francisco: Miller Freeman.

SANFORD, A. J. (1985), *Cognition and Cognitive Psychology*, New York: Basic Books.

SCHANK, R. C. and ABELSON, R. P. (1977), *Scripts, Plans, Goals and Understanding: An Inquiry into Human Knowledge Structures.* Hillsdale, N. J.: Lawrence Erlbaum Associates.

SCHANK, R. C. with CHILDERS, P. G. (1984), *On Language, Learning, and the Cognitive Computer.* Reading, Mass.: Addison-Wesley.

SCHANK, R. C. and COLBY, K. M., EDS. (1973), *Computer Models of Thought and Language.* San Francisco: W. H. Freeman.

SCHANK, R. C. and RIESBECK, C. K., EDS. (1981), *Inside Computer Understanding.* Hillsdale, N. J.: Lawrence Erlbaum Associates.

SHAFER, D. (1987), "14-Product Wrap-up: Prolog for the People," *AI Expert,* 2, no. 6.

SHAW, M. L. G. (1981), *Recent Advances in Personal Construct Technology.* New York: Academic Press.

SHNEIDERMAN, B. (1980), *Software Psychology: Human Factors in Computer and Information Systems.* Cambridge, Mass.: Winthrop.

STERLING, L. and SHAPIRO, E. (1986), *The Art of Prolog: Advanced Programming Techniques.* Cambridge, Mass.: MIT Press.

STOLFO, S. J. and MIRANKER, D. P. (1986), "DADO: A Tree- Structured Architecture for Artificial Intelligence Computation," in *Annual Review of Computer Science,* Palo Alto, Calif.: Annual Reviews.

VAN EMDEN, M. H. (1982), "Red and Green Cuts," in *Logic Programming,* Newsletter: 2.

VASTA, J. A. (1985), *Understanding Data Base Management Systems.* Belmont, Calif.: Wadsworth.

WATERMAN, D. (1986), *A Guide to Expert Systems.* Reading, Mass.: Addison-Wesley.

WHITEHEAD, A. N. and RUSSELL, B. (1910), *Principia Mathematica.* Cambridge, England: Cambridge University Press.

WINOGRAD, T. (1983), *Language as a Cognitive Process Volume 1: Syntax.* Reading, Mass.: Addison-Wesley.

WISE, M. J. (1986), *Prolog Multiprocessors.* Englewood Cliffs, N. J.: Prentice Hall.

ZADEH, L. (1975), "Fuzzy Logic and Approximate Reasoning," *Synthèse,* 30, pp. 407–28.

Index

F

G

H

I

K

L

M

N

P

R

S

T

U

V

W